South Africa

THE BRADT BUDGET TRAVEL GUIDE

The Bradt Story

The first Bradt travel guide was written by Hilary and George Bradt in 1974 on a river barge floating down a tributary of the Amazon in Bolivia. From their base in Boston, Massachusetts, they went on to write and publish four other backpacking guides to the Americas and one to Africa.

In the 1980s Hilary continued to develop the Bradt list in England, and also established herself as a travel writer and tour leader. The company's publishing emphasis evolved towards broader-based guides to new destinations – usually the first to be published on those countries – complemented by hiking, rail and wildlife guides.

Since winning *The Sunday Times* Small Publisher of the Year Award in 1997, we have continued to fill the demand for detailed, well-written guides to unusual destinations, while maintaining the company's original ethos of low-impact travel.

Travel guides are by their nature continuously evolving. If you experience anything which you would like to share with us, or if you have any amendments to make to this guide, please write; all your letters are read and passed on to the author. Most importantly, do remember to travel with an open mind and to respect the customs of your hosts – it will add immeasurably to your enjoyment.

Happy travelling!

Hilary Bradt

19 High Street, Chalfont St Peter, Bucks SL9 9QE, England
Tel: 01753 893444 Fax: 01753 892333
Email: info@bradt-travelguides.com
Web: www.bradt-travelguides.com

South Africa

THE BRADT BUDGET TRAVEL GUIDE

Paul Ash

Bradt Travel Guides, UK
The Globe Pequot Press Inc, USA

First published in 2001 by Bradt Travel Guides,
19 High Street, Chalfont St Peter, Bucks SL9 9QE, England
web: www.bradt-travelguides.com
Published in the USA by The Globe Pequot Press Inc, 246 Goose Lane,
PO Box 480, Guilford, Connecticut 06437-0480

British Library Cataloguing in Publication Data
A catalogue record for this book is available from the British Library
ISBN 1 84162 031 9

Library of Congress Cataloging-in-Publication Data
Ash, Paul
    South Africa : the Bradt budget guide / Paul Ash.
        p. cm.
    Includes bibliographical references and index.
    ISBN 1-84162-031-9
DT1717.A84 2001
916.804'65—dc21

                                                        00-051388

Cover photograph Ariadne van Zandbergen
Illustrations Annabel Milne, Hans van Well
Maps Steve Munns

Typeset from the author's disc by Wakewing
Printed and bound in Italy by Legoprint SpA, Trento

Author/Acknowledgements

AUTHOR

Paul Ash is a journalist and traveller who hopes, one day, to combine both in a financially rewarding manner. Currently working as a website editor and freelance writer in South Africa, he has realised that there is no substitute for rough and dusty travel. Living off the premise that the journey there is half the fun, imminent plans include an exploration of southern Angola and an African trans-continental crossing by WWII motorcycle and sidecar.

ACKNOWLEDGEMENTS

Many people helped me survive putting this guide together. Thanks to Fiona McIntosh, Dave Larsen, Michael 'tSas-Rolfes and Jane Wilson-Howarth for their written contributions; Hanlie Kotze at Mainline Passenger Services for help with information and cutting through the red tape; all the kind owners and managers at the many backpackers (hostels) who were quick with help, advice, enthusiasm and often a hot meal; the helpful staff in the country's various tourism offices who assisted with telephone numbers, hints and the inside track; all the friendly people by the side of the road who waved at me as I rumbled past on the bike. Most of all, thank you to Fiona Summers who, as always, took a load off my back, checked a gazillion phone numbers and other little details, looked after me and kept me sane on those days when I was about to go completely doolally.

HELP TO UPDATE THIS GUIDE

In a perfect world, we would have one travel guide (this one!) which would never, ever go out of date and would sell a million copies. But travel guides are fast-changing things. Quite often, information changes before the guide is even published. So my plea to you is this: if anything's changed, moved, gone north for winter, turned nasty or, in the case of telephone numbers, is just plain wrong, let me know.

It's also an opportunity for you to add to the information. If you discover things you think should be in the book – a new backpackers' for example, or a different way of getting around – please tell us about it.

You can reach me at wheeltapper@yahoo.com (all letters answered) or contact Bradt directly. Good luck and happy travelling. Maybe we'll meet on the road.

Contents

Introduction

If you stand on the hills at the edge of Pretoria and look north, you see, in the shimmering heat, a wide plain and low mountains beyond, coloured blue by the distance. Looking out across the plain, you feel a strong urge to head off across those mountains, compelled by the thought that out there is Africa and adventure. Locals call this urge the northward pull.

I get this feeling every time I stop long enough to absorb the South African landscape. It is a huge country with wide horizons filled by mountains, rolling bushveld plains, seas, and sweeps of semi-desert, and the desire to explore every inch of it plays havoc with my personal career advancement.

South Africa is a magical land with remarkable scenic diversity. Its 3,000km, largely unspoilt coastline, stretches from Namibian desert on the west coast of Africa, around to the lush, tropical greenery of Mozambique in the east. Often rugged and raw, the coast is littered with beautiful beaches, sand-dunes, forests, mountains and wetlands. Some of it is developed, but much of the coast is given over to conservation, and there are many nature reserves, national parks and even a world heritage site which preserve this part of South Africa's absolute beauty.

The interior of the country contains a variety of landscapes and habitats that is unequalled on the African continent. In the east and north there are sweeps of bushveld – savanna dotted with acacia or *mopani* trees. Here, the massive Kruger National Park sprawls over two million hectares of bushveld and protects more animal species than any other reserve on the continent. To the west are the red sands of the Kalahari Desert – site of Kgalagadi Transfrontier Park, the country's second largest reserve, where the last of the San Bushmen live the way they always have. The mountains, particularly the immense Drakensberg Mountains which form the country's escarpment, are crisscrossed with hiking trails and invitations to adventure. The independent traveller will find protected wildernesses, coastal wetlands, little nature reserves, country towns, empty backroads.

The people are as diverse as the landscape – Africans descended from the Bantu tribes that made a great migration from the north hundreds of years ago; Africans descended from Dutch, French, English and Indian settlers; Africans descended from the San, Khoikhoi and Hottentot peoples, or from slaves brought by Dutch settlers from Indonesia and elsewhere. There are 11 official languages, a hotch-potch of political beliefs and a new democracy which is protected by the world's most liberal constitution.

There has been a tourist boom since democracy came to South Africa, and the country is better geared for independent travel than possibly any other country on the continent. There is good internal transport, plenty of budget accommodation, banks, supermarkets – all the trappings of the West, in fact – and yet travel in South Africa often feels like an exploration into the wilderness. There are places in the Transkei where the children have never seen a white face, and tracts of vast semi-desert under a bright blue sky where hardy antelope, lions and elephants have adapted to a harsh environment.

The country's towns are generally the least of its appeal, although even here there are exceptions. Cape Town is one of the most beautiful cities on earth, protected as it is by a large, flat-topped mountain and blessed with beaches, forests, rugged coast and a deep blue sea. People who come here never want to leave. There are other towns too – pretty Karoo *dorpies* (small towns or villages) and country farming towns where Victorian houses look on to wide, quiet streets.

It is a beautiful, exciting country. I wish you well in your exploration of it.

How to use this guide

The weakness of the South African currency makes the country a reasonably cheap place to visit, but the tourism boom has seen a corresponding rise in prices. This book is about making the most of what the country has to offer while travelling on a budget. Whether or not you have the undeniable advantage of coming from a country with a strong currency, travel spending can quickly get out of hand if you aren't vigilant.

The guide is aimed at travellers wanting to unpack the country's beauty without having to shell out wads of cash. It is for people who want to see wild animals, explore the fabulous coast, amble around the cities, lie on the beaches, eat cheaply and stay in good, clean, welcoming accommodation.

People come to South Africa for its natural attractions – the wildlife, its beaches, mountains and wildernesses. They come for its culture and the chance to experience Africa. Since coming to South Africa is mostly about being out-of-doors, this guide concentrates a great deal on outdoor travel and attractions. There is advice on affordable ways to see wildlife and game reserves with bargain accommodation and activities. Hiking trails, wilderness areas and nature reserves are discussed at length. And then there is South Africa for free – the beaches, whale watching, wine tastings, self-guided tours, hiking – and all for nothing.

It is important to realise that travelling on a budget is not about making do with second-best; it's about finding new or different ways to enjoy everything the country has to offer. To this end, I welcome any feedback and advice from you. Travel guides are dynamic, which is a nice way of saying they are sometimes out of date by the time they are published. Numbers and prices change, places close, others open. Let me know, tell me your stories and give me information that can be used in future editions. You can email me at wheeltapper@yahoo.com or contact Bradt Travel Guides at info@bradt-travelguides.com.

Part One

General Information

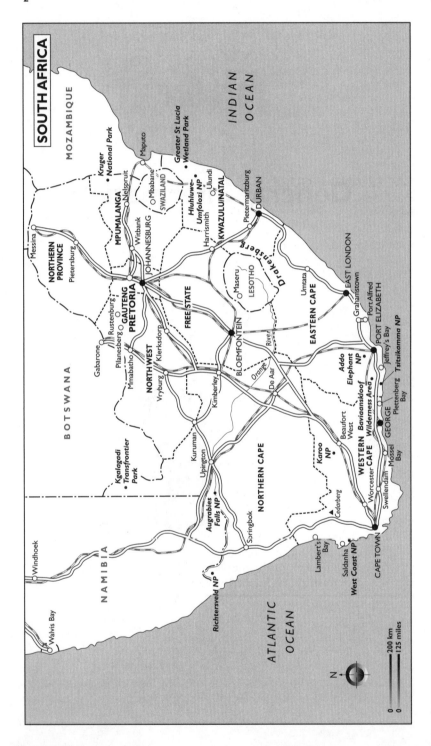

Background Information

FACTS AND FIGURES
Location
The Republic of South Africa lies at the foot of the African continent and is bordered by Namibia to the northwest, Botswana and Zimbabwe to the north and Mozambique to the northeast. Lesotho, a tiny mountainous country, and the kingdom of Swaziland both lie within South Africa's geographical borders.

Size
South Africa covers an area of 1,221,040km² (471,443 square miles), making it one of the largest countries in sub-Saharan Africa. The country is five times bigger than Britain but occupies just 4% of the land mass of the continent.

Capital
Pretoria is the capital of South Africa. Parliament sits in Cape Town, but this function is due to move to Pretoria some time in the future although no-one knows quite when that will be. Johannesburg, 50km south of Pretoria – but practically joined to it – is the economic heart of the nation and undoubtedly the richest city in Africa.

Major towns
Johannesburg is by far the largest town in South Africa. Spreading over hundreds of square kilometres, it has all but expanded into Pretoria 50km to the north, and is home to approximately 6.5 million people. This figure is inexact, as there hasn't been a census in a while and illegal immigrants flood in daily.

Cape Town and Durban, both port cities, are second and third largest respectively, followed in rough order of size by Pretoria, Bloemfontein, Port Elizabeth, Pietermaritzburg, Kimberley, East London, Nelspruit, Pietersburg and George.

People and culture
People
The population of South Africa is roughly 40 million, spread unevenly over nine provinces. Apart from the towns, the most densely populated areas are KwaZulu-Natal, the Highveld, the Orange Free State and Eastern and Western Cape. South Africa is a polyglot of different tribes, clans, splinter groups and cultures, which makes for a vibrant cultural scene. The Zulus

probably make up the single largest linguistic group but the first people to live there were the nomadic San hunter-gatherers and semi-nomadic Khoikhoi and Hottentot tribes who were around as many as 25,000 years ago. These peoples lived relatively peacefully across the country until they were caught between European expansion in the Cape and the huge migration of Bantu tribes down the east coast of Africa five hundred years ago.

By the time the first Europeans arrived in South Africa, the Bantu tribes had split into two distinct groupings – the Nguni and the Sotho. The Nguni group fragmented further, creating dozens of smaller tribes, including the Swazi, Zulu and Xhosa nations, all of which remain strong entities today. The Sotho, who occupied the huge expanse of the highveld, remained more or less homogenous in culture although the Sotho language evolved into two quite distinct forms in the north and south. There were other influences, too, from the Venda, Tsonga and Bapedi people who migrated south across the Limpopo into the northern parts of South Africa.

The first Europeans to live here were Dutch and French Huguenot settlers, the direct ancestors of the Afrikaners, the white tribe of Africa. The Dutch imported slaves from Indonesia and India and miscegenation between master and servant, as well as with the Hottentots who were living in the Cape Colony, created the Cape Coloured community.

English settlers arrived en masse in 1820 but South Africa, like America, also has significant populations of Portuguese, Greek, European and, to a lesser extent, German, immigrants.

In the late 19th century, Indians were brought over as indentured labourers to work in the Natal sugarcane plantations and many elected to stay when their contracts ended. There is a vibrant and large Indian community in KwaZulu-Natal and Johannesburg.

Languages

There are 11 official languages, all of which are supposed to enjoy equal prominence. In practice English is the language of government. Afrikaans is widely spoken, especially in the Western Cape and in the *Platteland* (countryside). isiXhosa, isiZulu and seSotho are widely spoken and tend to predominate in urban areas. The remaining languages are isiNdebele, salebowa, siSwati, Xitsonga, Setswana and Tshivenda, which are spoken mainly in their respective tribal areas.

Religion

Religious beliefs cover the spectrum of Christianity, Judaism, Hinduism, animism and ancestor worship, but it was Christian missionaries who were – and still are – most active in the subcontinent. The Zionist Christian Church, whose congregation numbers in the millions, is a strong mix of Christianity and African faiths. The faithful hold outdoor prayer meetings early on Sunday mornings and you will often see them walking home in their green, blue and white robes. ZCC men often wear khaki suits and peaked caps, with a ZCC star on green cloth pinned to their lapels. It is a fascinating but closed society.

POLITICS AND ECONOMY
Government
South Africa's political structure is based on a multi-party democracy with general elections held every five years. The ruling party is the African National Congress which, in 1994, won the country's first truly democratic elections by a sizeable majority, and followed that with a second triumph in 1999. The party has so far failed – not for want of trying – to win the two-thirds majority it needs to govern alone, but it dominates the government, not to mention the political scene. Nelson Mandela was inaugurated as the country's first black president in May 1994; his successor in 1999 was long-time ANC stalwart Thabo Mbeki.

South Africa's constitution, which took years to draw up, is regarded as one of the world's most progressive and liberal.

Economy
South Africa has the continent's most developed economy, highly diversified with modern infrastructure. Its varied resource base includes substantial reserves of strategic minerals including gold, diamonds, platinum, iron, copper and coal. The country accounts for 40% of Africa's output and around 22% of its GDP (gross domestic product).

With big business historically tying up much of the country's wealth and production, South Africa has long been a capitalist nation. Its per capita GNP (gross national product) is estimated at $2,520. There is, however, a great imbalance in the distribution of wealth and one of the government's challenges is to even out the inequalities and find work for the many jobless people. Unemployment is about 45%. Many of the jobless earn their living in the informal sector as hawkers, roadside car mechanics, sidewalk hairdressers, scrap-metal collectors and so on.

While South Africa still produces around 28% of the world's gold, unemployment rates have been exacerbated by problems in the gold mining industry which for most of the 20th century was the country's key foreign exchange earner. The metal's global decline as a store of value has hit South Africa hard: many unproductive mines have closed with the loss of thousands of jobs.

Industries such as chemical and pharmaceutical manufacture are sound, but the development of a bigger local manufacturing base, rather than the straight export of raw materials, is desperately needed if the country is to compete globally.

Transport
In keeping with its developed status, the country has Africa's best road and rail networks. The road network has been developing continually since the 1930s, and there is a network of good tarred motorways and national and secondary roads. That said, trucks in South Africa are the most heavily laden in the world and many of the main routes are quite literally under severe pressure. Local municipalities are responsible for road maintenance but, given other priorities such as housing and health care, money is not always available for repairs.

The rail network is Africa's largest with around 21,244km (13,201 miles) of track. Severe cutbacks over the past decade have seen a significant drop in passenger services but it is still possible to travel between the major centres by train and this remains one of the best methods of getting into the countryside.

South Africa's early railway development was driven mostly by greed as lines were built from the sea to the interior to exploit whatever resources lay within. On the continent, intense rivalry between competing colonial powers resulted in a spread of railways that did not connect with each other. In 1910, the South African government took control of the local private railway companies and railway building boomed as every little town and agricultural community clamoured for its own rail link. Some got one, many others didn't.

More than 50 airlines fly to South Africa's eight international airports although Johannesburg, Cape Town and Durban are the only ones of any significance for international travellers. The private aviation sector is vibrant and there are a number of domestic commuter airlines serving the smaller regional centres.

The Cape sea route is important for large crude and bulk carriers and there are six main harbours serving coastal and international sea traffic. Mail ships were in service between Durban, Cape Town and Southampton until the late 1970s, but now the only passenger ships calling at South African ports are cruise liners which visit during the summer Indian Ocean cruising season. One exception is the RMS *St Helena*, a mail ship which sails regularly between Cardiff, Cape Town and the islands of St Helena and Ascension. The ship is the only transport link that the islanders have with the outside world.

Currency
The unit of currency is the South African Rand which is divided into 100 cents. The rate of exchange in late 2000 was US$1.00 = R6.90 and UKStg1.00 = R10.60

CLIMATE AND GEOGRAPHY
Climate
South Africa enjoys a varied climate ranging from subtropical heat and humidity on the *lowveld* and east coast, through the temperate *highveld*, to hot and very dry in the semi-desert west. The humid *lowveld* and east coast regions can be unpleasant in summer, while Cape summers are very hot but dry.

Average summer temperatures range from 26°C on the *highveld*, and upwards of 30°C in the *lowveld* and western Cape. Summer temperatures in the Karoo and in the Kalahari desert are often around 40°C.

Winters – from May to August – are generally mild and dry although the *highveld* and desert regions get bitterly cold, with temperatures often falling well below zero. Snow and frost are common in the high country, and the high mountain ranges such as the Drakensbergs will be blanketed in snow. The Western Cape is unique in that it has a Mediterranean climate with hot dry summers and mild, wet winters.

South Africans take their summer holidays between December and January and prices rise accordingly. Accommodation in national parks, seaside towns and resorts is heavily booked over this period.

Geography

South Africa falls into two distinctive physical regions: a great plateau which occupies most of the interior, and a narrow coastal strip which fringes the plateau on three sides. These two regions are divided by a continuous range of mountains which forms the Escarpment. The plateau ranges in altitude from 2,000ft in the Kalahari Basin in the west to over 11,155ft in the Maluti and Drakensberg mountains which form the eastern part of the Escarpment.

Broadly speaking, South Africa is largely arid with good and regular rainfall occurring only in its eastern half and southern regions. The west-flowing Orange River is the country's main watercourse but few other perennial rivers run through the dry western region. The eastern part of the country has the bulk of the perennial rivers, including the mighty Tugela, and dozens of broad, deep rivers flow off the Escarpment tumbling eastwards to the Indian Ocean. Rudyard Kipling's famous 'great grey-green, greasy, Limpopo', which rises in the northwest, demarcates the country's northern borders with Botswana and Zimbabwe.

The country's coastline is about 3,000km long, lapped by two oceans – the Indian to the east and the Atlantic to the west. Coastal vegetation ranges from subtropical in northern KwaZulu-Natal on the east coast, to that associated with a mountainous coastal plain with a Mediterranean feel in the southern Cape, and to semi-desert on the west coast. The west coast is thinly populated, unlike the south and east coasts which, together with the country's game parks, are the prime tourist destinations.

The interior plateau is called the *highveld* and is characterised by rolling grasslands and savanna dotted with acacia trees. The *lowveld* is the hot, low-lying belt east of the Escarpment, a region dominated by thick *bushveld* – *mopani* forest and acacia trees.

NATURAL HISTORY

Thanks to sound conservation practice, South Africa has one of the largest and most stable wildlife populations in Africa. Reserves are well kept and more land is continually being returned to its natural state as the government and people realise that tourism will bring far more benefits to the country than agriculture on unsuitable ground. There are about 580 national parks and private game reserves which cover about 6% of the total land surface of the country.

The country has 6% of the world's mammals, 7% of its bird species and 8% of its higher plant species. The country is known as a destination for seeing the Big Five – lion, elephant, leopard, rhinoceros and buffalo – but the other animals – including antelope, jackals, foxes, giraffes, hyenas, and hippos – are no less fascinating.

Predators

The animal world consists of those who eat and those who are eaten, and carnivorous predators are generally at the top of the food chain. The main predators are the big cats – lion, leopard and cheetah – and members of the dog family, including jackal, brown and spotted hyenas, the bat-eared fox and the beautiful and endangered wild dog.

Of the big cats you are most likely to see **lion**. There is nothing quite like the first time you see a lion in its natural habitat – apart from anything else, the knowledge that this animal would eat you given half a chance serves to concentrate the mind. Lions are the most gregarious of the big cats and tend to move around in prides consisting of a dominant male, a group of lionesses and juveniles. The lionesses form the nucleus of the pride and do most of the hunting.

Leopards are solitary cats and their nocturnal habits make sightings rare. They are good climbers and like to sit in high vantage points in the late afternoon and early morning to watch for prey. Leopards are known for storing the unfinished remains of

Leopard

their kills in trees, out of the reach of other predators and scavengers.

Cheetahs, the fastest mammals on earth, are slimly built cats that prefer savanna habitats where their superior speed can be used to advantage. Cheetahs have a lighter build than leopards and distinguishing 'tearmark' lines under the eyes.

Cheetah

Smaller cats include **caracal** (lynx), **serval**, the rarely seen **black footed cat** and the **African wild cat** which is endangered by interbreeding with domestic cats. The caracal, a stockily built, solitary cat, is loathed by farmers and has been widely hunted, trapped and poisoned.

Black-backed jackal

Jackals are also considered a pest by farmers but these hardy carnivores are exceptionally cunning and wily. Even under extreme pressure from farming and other human activity, the jackal is one of the few of Africa's mammals that is not endangered and still occurs in most of its ancestral range. Sadly, the same cannot be said for bat-eared foxes, little carnivores with huge ears that they use to search out invertebrate prey; the bat-eared fox has often been blamed for the sins of the jackal and suffered accordingly.

Larger predators include **spotted** and **brown hyenas**, the former with a reputation for being an extremely efficient hunter, and **wild dog**. Until a few years ago, wild dogs were still shot as vermin in most countries in the subcontinent and the species has been literally saved from the edge of extinction.

Small predators include **genets**, **civets**, **badgers** and **mongooses**. Except for the mongooses, all are nocturnal hunters and rarely seen.

Herbivores

South Africa's **elephant** populations are thriving so successfully they run a risk of endangering themselves. Their habitats are too small and isolated to allow herds the necessary room to migrate and the animals often have to be culled, an unresolved issue which is causing great controversy in the conservation world. Elephants have highly developed social behaviour and mothers care for their young for up two years after birth. They have no natural enemies except ivory poachers.

There are two species of **rhinoceros** in South Africa which at first glance look exactly alike. The sociable white rhino is the more common of the two and may be seen in many of the country's game parks. The black rhino, easily identified by its prehensile upper lip, tends to be a solitary beast. Both species have been ruthlessly hunted for their horns, and the black rhino was wiped out in Zimbabwe and East Africa, even under the 24-hour protection of armed guards. Rhino horns are fashioned into highly prized dagger handles in Yemen, while in the Far East ground up horn is used for medicinal purposes. The widespread belief that rhino horn is used as an aphrodisiac is a total myth.

White rhino

Black rhino

Buffalo are gregarious but somewhat belligerent animals, with a reputation for savagery. They tend to live in large herds in habitats with plenty of water, grass and shade. The Kruger Park's buffalo are currently under severe threat from a debilitating tuberculosis epidemic and it is likely that they will have to be culled to prevent the disease spreading to other animals, including lion for whom buffalo meat is a delicacy.

African buffalo

Hippopotamus are found only where there is plenty of water. For such apparently lumbering beasts hippos have a fearsome reputation. They are semi-aquatic creatures, spending their days mostly submerged in pools or rivers, coming out at night to graze. If disturbed, their immediate reaction is to head for the safety of the water at a frighteningly rapid pace. Most people killed by hippos are run over rather than wilfully attacked. Full grown adults are massive animals and have healthy appetites – consuming 130kg of fodder in one feed is not unusual.

South Africa has three kinds of **zebra**: the Burchell's zebra is widespread, while the previously endangered Cape mountain zebra and Hartmann's mountain zebra are confined to a few parts of the country. The Cape mountain zebra population has recovered remarkably in just a few decades after being reduced by uncontrolled hunting to just a few animals hiding in impenetrable bush in the Eastern Cape.

There are also two types of **wildebeest**: the black wildebeest of western South Africa and the blue wildbeest which occurs everywhere else. Wildebeests are social animals and live in huge herds, often alongside zebra. They are a species of antelope although they look nothing like them.

Giraffe are the tallest animal in the world and one of the strangest looking. They are wonderful creatures, apparently ungainly and yet they can move at a fair clip when they have to. Giraffes can defend themselves with devastating effect using their front hooves so that even lion hunt these animals with care. While giraffe occur throughout the region, their prime habitat is acacia country.

Warthog, often confused with bushpig, occur in the drier northern and eastern parts of the country. They are distinctive animals and can often be spotted trotting through the bush with their tails sticking straight up in the air like radio antennae. Despite their fearsome tusks, warthog are not noted for their bravery or aggression.

Warthog

Antelope

Eland, the world's largest antelope, and **kudu** are found in most of the country's protected areas, being adaptable to most environments. Eland are grazers, while kudu are browsers. Although they are both big animals, they are extremely good at camouflage and both tend to be shy of humans. With its distinctive hump, the eland features widely in San rock art as these hunter-gatherers believed the animal had spiritual qualities. Kudu bulls are easily identified by their magnificent, spiralling horns.

Common eland

The beautiful **sable** and **roan** antelope are much rarer. They are often confused with each other but are easy to tell apart by the colour of their coats. Both have distinctive curving horns.

Gemsbok, a species of oryx, occur mostly in the drier parts of the country. They are unmistakeably a species of antelope, with straight horns raking back at a sharp angle, and black-and-white faces. Gemsbok are well adapted to desert life. Their coats reflect heat, they can go without water for longer than two weeks at a time and they have a unique system of blood vessels in the nose which cools their blood before it is pumped to the brain.

Other common large antelope species include **tsessebe**, **hartebeest**, **nyala**, **bontebok**, **blesbok** and **waterbuck**. The latter docile creature can be readily identified by the white ring around its rump. Waterbuck and nyala never stray far from water and prefer wet habitats.

The medium-sized antelope species include **springbok**, **bushbuck**, **reedbuck** and the ubiquitous **impala**. The latter are common to just about every piece of bushveld and game reserve except mountains, deserts and coastal areas. They have the most beautiful balletic ability and are able to jump more than nine feet up in the air and almost 30 feet horizontally.

Klipspringer

Small antelope species include **grey duiker**, **klipspringer**, **grysbok**, **oribi** and **steenbok**. The San believe that the steenbok has divine protection which apparently explains why it always stands to look at approaching danger before scampering off. The duiker is the most commonly seen of the small antelope but all species are relatively widespread.

Primates and monkeys

Chacma baboons, southern Africa's biggest primates, occur just about everywhere but the cities, but their preferred habitats are mountains, cliffs or tall trees. They live mostly in large troops and keep to themselves in the wild. However, where they have become used to humans they can be a menace, especially if they associate humans with food. Baboons will be quite happy raiding your tent or campsite if you leave food lying around.

Vervet
monkey

Samango and **vervet** monkeys are the country's only species of monkey. The latter is quite common and, although it prefers a savannah woodland habitat, it can live almost anywhere, especially along watercourses where there are trees. Samango monkeys tend to be found in mountainous hardwood forests.

CONSERVATION
Michael 'tSas-Rolfes

At the start of the 21st century, South Africa boasts one of the world's best-managed systems of nature reserves and national parks. The country is home to the world's largest population of rhinos, and provides a haven for many other rare and endangered species. But it wasn't always this way. At the start of the 20th century, South Africa had all but lost its wildlife heritage. Big-game hunters and farmers had wiped out almost all the country's large mammals. It has only been through a great deal of hard work and innovative thinking that much of its previous natural heritage has been restored.

When the first Dutch and English settlers arrived in South Africa, the country was teeming with game. Indigenous people such as the Khoisan and Bantu hunted and harvested wild species, but they did not possess modern weapons and did so mainly for subsistence purposes. The early European settlers had guns, and used them to hunt game systematically. By the early 19th century, one species of antelope – the **bloubok** – had already been hunted to extinction. The bloubok lived on the grassy coastal plains near

Cape Town, the first region in which most large mammals were exterminated.

During the 19th century the settlers increasingly moved inland, hunting indiscriminately as they went. Another species – the **quagga**, a close relative of the zebra – became extinct. By the end of that century, European settlers had claimed most of the uninhabited parts of the country as farmland, and very little wildlife remained. Large species such as elephant, buffalo and rhino, had been virtually hunted to extinction. The only survivors remained in small pockets in what were to become the Kruger National Park and the Hluhluwe–Umfolozi Park in KwaZulu-Natal.

Prior to the 20th century, the laws regulating wildlife use were limited in scope. Because wildlife was abundant, few people were concerned with conservation issues. However, once wildlife became scarce, this attitude changed. Initially, private landowners protected certain species on their property – species such as the bontebok and black wildebeest would probably have become extinct, had they had not been protected by private farmers. These initiatives were followed up, first by provincial governments, who declared certain areas as game reserves, and then finally by the national government. South Africa's first national park, the Kruger, was established in 1926.

In the first half of the 20th century, South Africa's state-run conservation agencies focused on protecting existing land areas and the game that survived there. However, in the latter part of the century, agencies started taking a far more active, hands-on approach. The most classic example of this is the Natal Parks Board's initiatives to save the southern white rhino.

At the turn of the century, the southern white rhino was almost extinct, with only a handful of animals roaming the Hluhluwe-Umfolozi district. By the 1950s, this number had increased to a few hundred. At this time, the Natal Parks Board decided to implement a bold management strategy, Operation Rhino. This involved capturing rhinos and translocating them to new areas to start new viable populations. Initially, rhinos were moved to other Natal parks, then further afield to the Kruger and parks in neighbouring countries such as Zimbabwe. Then, finally, some animals were sold to private landowners and sent overseas.

Operation Rhino was so successful that by the early 1970s, the authorities believed that it was viable to allow the trophy hunting of white rhino bulls. Some private landowners had started to run commercial private game reserves, where they profited from the sale of live game and animal products such as venison, trophy hunting and wildlife-based tourism. By selling white rhinos to private landowners, the Natal Parks Board believed they could create new incentives to breed them. At first, they were dismayed to find out that as soon as they sold white rhinos to private landowners, they would immediately be sold to trophy hunters and shot. Then the authorities realised that they were selling rhinos too cheaply.

The lack of legal recognition for private wildlife ownership, the high risk of protecting the lives of such commercially valuable animals and the high prices offered for trophies all discouraged private landowners from breeding rhinos on their property. It was easier and safer to sell them to hunters as soon as possible. Realising this, the authorities made two significant changes. First, they started auctioning rhinos to the highest bidder. Second, they passed a law that recognised the rights of private landowners to claim beneficial ownership over live wild animals under certain conditions. This combination of market pricing and secure ownership rights established a proper market, which unlocked the value of live rhinos. As a result, private landowners took a serious interest in breeding – today, rhinos on private land account for more than 20% of the total number of animals conserved, and that proportion is growing.

Although the state-run national and provincial parks provided the backbone of South Africa's conservation efforts throughout the 20th century, this is starting to change. The new South African government has many pressing priorities that take precedence over conservation. As a result, new conservation initiatives increasingly involve private commercial partners and local communities, whose cooperation and participation is essential if conservation is to survive.

Because of South Africa's history of extensive settlement and exploitation, the wildlife experience here is somewhat different from other less-developed and more sparsely populated African countries. Most of South Africa is covered with fences designed to demarcate property and to separate wildlife from farmland. The result is a landscape that appears somewhat less wild and authentic than the 'real' Africa that is often portrayed by the media. However, what the country may lack in apparent authenticity, it makes up for in other interesting ways.

South Africa today is a showcase of many highly innovative conservation projects. It is one of few countries where you can buy a live specimen of almost any wild animal at a private auction. You can also find extremely well-run, privately owned game reserves with some of the finest tourist facilities the world has to offer. You can find interesting and innovative fledgling partnerships between conservation scientists, entrepreneurs and local rural African communities which are designed to benefit everyone, but especially nature itself. And you can still find some of the world's best managed national parks, with spectacular scenery and a fascinating diversity of animals and plants, all at very affordable prices.

HISTORY
Indigenous people
The word 'turbulent' comes up frequently in any review of South Africa's history, from when the first *Australopethicus africanus* got waylaid by a sabre-tooth tiger. Fantastic anthropological discoveries have been made in the last half-century, uncovering much of the prehistory of South Africa before Iron Age people moved down from the north. There is evidence, gathered from archaeological sites in the east, of humanoid activity going back about three million years. Fossil finds at the Sterkfontein caves west of Johannesburg (see page 97) place the so-called cradle of humankind right in South Africa's front yard.

Evidence shows that *Homo sapiens* – modern man – evolved in Africa, probably about 1.5 million years ago. In Africa, two of the distinct races that developed from this spark were the San and the Negro. The former, skilled hunter-gatherers, lived in the dry savanna of eastern and southern Africa, developing an uncanny similarity in their veneration and understanding of nature and the spirit world with the aboriginal tribes in Australia. The San were probably wandering throughout the region as much as 40,000 years ago.

Over thousands of years, the Negro tribes who spread out from west Africa and one linguistic sub-group, the Bantu, began expanding southwards over time. They were pastoralists, who acquired the skills – and tools – of a developed Iron Age civilisation. Long before the birth of Christ, the Bantu-speaking tribes occupied the eastern part of the country. Two markedly different groups emerged – the Nguni, who occupied the fertile coastal plain, and Sotho, who lived in the high country.

Meanwhile, the San, reeling under the pressure from both groups had retreated westwards into the harsh semi-desert where the environment limited settlement for most peoples. They roamed freely over these huge, desolate expanses – in the Namib, east to the Kalahari and south to the Karoo in South Africa. At some point, a third people, the Khoikhoi, whose ancestors were most likely San, moved into the Western Cape and settled there about 2,000 years ago. Unlike the San, they were semi-nomadic herders who kept sheep, and they were to have the dubious pleasure of seeing the first Europeans set foot in southern Africa at the end of the 15th century.

By the 15th century, Bantu-speaking tribes had settled most of the eastern half of southern Africa, limiting themselves to areas where they could grow their crops and keep livestock. Growing populations meant that the search for new grazing lands continued. By the late 18th century, there was trouble – drought had wiped out the grazing lands and there was intense pressure to find new land. An ambitious warrior named Shaka had come to power and, through superior military ability, subjugated all the scattered tribes in the region during a series of actions called the *Mfecane*. As Shaka's empire, KwaZulu, grew, it put further pressure on the Xhosa people, forcing them further south and towards the rivers in the Ciskei where they would run into *trekboers* and the newly arrived British settlers.

Early Portuguese exploration and the arrival of the Dutch

The Portuguese are the first westerners on record at the Cape of Good Hope. For 42 years from 1418 Portugal's Henry the Navigator had equipped the expeditions sent to discover the mysteries of the sea route around Africa. The mission was to find a sea route to the East and its spices. Bartolomeu Dias de Novaes was the first explorer to round the Cape, although his three-ship flotilla had been driven so far south by a strong southeaster that the Cape was passed unseen. It fell to Vasco da Gama to make the first landing in what is today's South Africa, at St Helena Bay on November 7 1497. His was the first white face the Hottentots who watched the landings had ever seen.

The South African coast was, and is, a perilous one and the Hottentots made it clear that the Portuguese were not welcome. The Portuguese wanted settlements closer to the East anyway and, apart from erecting a few stone crosses on the coast, they mostly ignored South Africa. Table Bay was a place for refuge from storms and a place where water might be found in emergencies.

By the beginning of the 17th century, the Dutch were the rising trading force in the region, having wrested the spice trade from the Portuguese. The Dutch East India Company, the key player, needed a halfway station where supplies of fresh water and food could be taken on to their ships. The Cape of Good Hope was the logical place and in 1652 three Dutch ships under the command of Jan van Riebeek arrived in Table Bay. A fort was built, vegetable gardens planted and fresh water located. The Cape was open for business and white dominance of the subcontinent had begun.

Before long, Van Riebeek found it difficult to feed his own people let alone supply passing ships with fresh produce. He was under pressure from the company to make the settlement profitable and in desperation got authorisation to release company employees from their contracts, allowing them to start farming and trading. The company bought crops from these Free Burghers (citizens) at fixed prices and suddenly the settlement was no longer a garrison but the nucleus of a colony. Slaves were imported from the East to solve the labour shortage problem and the settlement grew rapidly. Farmers began pushing into the western and southern Cape and by the late 18th century were running into the Xhosa people who were drifting southwards in their quest for fresh grazing lands.

Many of these sturdy pioneers, the *trekboers* (trek farmers), wanted nothing to do with the mainstream of European development and had adapted to the hardship of survival in Africa, competing with the native peoples who were also roaming cattle farmers. The *trekboers'* descendants were the Afrikaners and they differed from other settlers in their individualism and Calvinist faith. They believed they were an elect of God and that the black tribes against whom they clashed had no rights either against them or to the land which they claimed as their own.

In 1779, the *trekboers* ran into the southward-migrating Xhosa along the natural border of the Great Fish River, sparking the first in a series of wars and skirmishes which were to continue for a hundred years.

By the end of the 19th century, the Netherlands had slipped dramatically in the international power rankings and the Cape Colony passed into British hands following the Anglo-French wars of 1793–1815. The British valued the Cape as a strategic asset but the vast, dispersed and somewhat unruly colony extending from the Cape was seen as little more than a nuisance.

The 1820 settlers

To strengthen the frontier area and dilute the Boer power base, Britain landed 5,000 settlers in the Eastern Cape in 1820. Many were veterans of the Napoleonic Wars who had returned home from fighting to find no jobs and many relished the chance of a new start. (See page 189.)

The settlers clashed immediately with the Xhosa people, just as the *trekboers* had first done 40 years previously. War after war was fought along the frontier. To support its embattled people, Britain established garrisons all over the Eastern Cape at places such as Grahamstown, Fort Beaufort and Queenstown. The bitter struggle for this land remains an issue to this day.

The Great Trek

The advent of British rule sparked new restlessness among the Boers who wanted nothing to do with English or any control. While it made little difference whether the masters were Dutch or English, a growing humanitarian attitude towards subject peoples worried the Boers who still believed in their right to the land, and more significantly, their right to employ native labour on their own terms. New legislation protecting some rights of natives, along with the decision to return a huge tract of annexed land along the frontier to the Xhosa, was the last straw for many of the Boers. By 1836, a few exploratory treks into the interior to find alternative settlement land had been undertaken and parties were organised to trek north across the Orange River and into the interior. The Great Trek – an event which lies close to the Afrikaner soul – was under way.

These hardy people called themselves Voortrekkers, literally meaning 'journey forward'. Whole families travelled, along with all their possessions, in sturdy wagons pulled by teams of oxen. It was a migration of a culture and something which many Afrikaners claim as part of their soul, this urge to keep moving in search of new and – most important – uninhabited land for farming and grazing. The Great Trek was also to lead them straight into the rich country which had already been settled by African peoples who, over centuries, had been moving steadily down from further north.

Some trekkers moved northwards towards the Limpopo River, clashing with the Matabele tribe and forcing them to flee, but the bulk of the groups headed for the rich grasslands of Natal which they believed had been temporarily depopulated by the growing and aggressive Zulu nation. The promise of a peaceful occupation was shattered after Dingane, the Zulu king who had succeeded Shaka, lured trek leader Piet Retief to his royal enclosure on the pretence of negotiating a land deal and murdered him and a large number of his followers. The result was a short, sharp campaign by new Boer leader Andries Pretorius, who used mounted commandos and superior firepower to annihilate a Zulu army at the battle of Blood River in 1838, ending Dingane's reign. In 1839, the Boers declared Natal an independent republic.

This move was regarded with some displeasure in England. Britain felt that the fact that the Boers had trekked beyond the boundaries of the Cape did not stop them being British subjects. Troops were sent to the British settlement at Port Natal (now Durban) and Natal was formally annexed in 1845. So the trekkers packed up again and began moving back over the Drakensberg into the highveld, preferring the peril of dragging their loaded wagons by hand up the steep slopes of the mountains to British rule.

The Boer Republics

The Boers spread out across the *highveld* and got on with their fiercely independent lives. While central government was an anathema to them, constant pressure from the Bantu tribes meant some form of mutual co-operation was necessary. The result was the formation of the republics of the Transvaal and Orange Free State, each governed by a Volksraad (People's Council) and headed by a state president who could invoke supreme authority in times of crisis.

Britain, seeing that there was little going on in them other than farming and cattle ranching, decided the republics were not a threat and formally recognised their independence in 1854. But the pressures from expanding Bantu tribes continued and the thinly populated republics were barely capable of maintaining their borders. By 1871 (when diamonds were discovered north of the Orange River in Griqualand West on the border of the Orange Free State), the Cape Colony was self-governing and colonial officials hoped that its model of government, elected on a non-racial franchise, could be applied throughout the region. Of course this would mean annexing the two recalcitrant Boer republics and, in 1877, Sir Bartle Frere tried to do just that to the Transvaal Republic, sparking the First Anglo–Boer War.

The campaign ended with the astounding defeat of the British on a mountain called Majuba in northern Natal. The Boers encamped on top of the steep-sided hill must have been amazed to see the British troops openly marching in order up the mountain, their red tunics standing out starkly against the green countryside. All the campaign achieved was to deepen the rift between Briton and Afrikaner.

Gold and war

The South African republics were muddling along as bankrupt farming nations when Australian prospector George Harrison and his friend George Walker stumbled across a particularly rich gold reef on a small mountain ridge called the Witwatersrand (ridge of white waters) in July 1886. It wasn't long before other strikes were made and the sheer size of the reef became apparent. The government declared nine farms to be public diggings in the same year and prospectors from all over the world rushed to the Transvaal.

Transvaal president Paul Kruger was very aware of the power the gold strike gave the Transvaal. So was mining magnate Cecil John Rhodes, who had a vision of a British-influenced federation in southern Africa and an extension of the British Empire all the way north to Cairo. Rhodes had made a massive fortune in the Kimberley diamond fields, buying up the claims of small prospectors and gradually assuming almost complete control of the industry. Extending his business to the Transvaal gold fields was the next logical step.

Rhodes had already helped Britain enter the territory known today as Botswana and in 1890 sent a colonising force of policemen and settlers to occupy the Shona territories north and east of Matabeleland, creating what was to become the state of Rhodesia. The idea was to encircle the Transvaal to force it to cooperate with the Cape Colony.

Kruger interpreted all this as a threat to the independence of the republic and he took further steps to isolate the Transvaal from the clutches of Empire, partly by authorising the construction of a railway from the east coast port at Delagoa Bay in Portuguese East Africa (later Mozambique) to Pretoria. The railway would give Pretoria a route to the sea, allowing it to avoid having to use the railways from Cape Town, Port Elizabeth and Durban.

Internally, Kruger had a bigger problem. The gold was being mined by an extraordinary mix of *uitlanders* (foreigners) – most of the Boers had distanced themselves from the squalor and social evils of the mining camps of Johannesburg. As the miners grew richer, they demanded more say in government but Kruger maintained that they would first have to subscribe to Afrikaner ideals.

Eager to manipulate the volatile situation, Rhodes began planning a military invasion of the republic, which would be launched in apparent support of an uprising by the *uitlanders* – Rhodes had organised the 'uprising' beforehand – and replace Kruger with a more pro-Cape government. There was plenty of division among the *uitlanders* and a few days before the uprising was due to begin, it was clear that it would be an utter disaster. Rhodes sent repeated telegrams to force commander Dr Leander Starr Jameson, waiting at Pitsani just over the border from the western Transvaal, telling him the raid had been delayed. Jameson ignored the telegrams, crossed the border with 500 mounted policemen and was swiftly and soundly beaten by a waiting Boer force at Krugersdorp, ruining Rhodes' political ambitions as a minor side effect.

The Anglo–Boer War

Direction of British foreign policy in Africa passed to Joseph Chamberlain who believed the Boers had to be conquered and anglicised. Sir Alfred Milner, the British High Commissioner in South Africa, continued to press the *uitlander* cause to the point that war broke out at the end of 1899. The conflict lasted three years, during which time it changed from a war of set piece battles and sieges to, in its closing stages, a guerrilla conflict. When hostilities began, there were just 27,000 British troops in South Africa, compared to 35,000 in the two Boer republics, the Transvaal and Orange Free State. The Boer army was a people's army, largely made up of mounted commandos raised in every farming district and backed by small, but superbly trained, state artillery regiments in each republic. The Boer cause had the blessing of Germany and the republics had for some time been receiving Mauser bolt-action rifles and artillery pieces from the Germans. The Afrikaner nationalists would remember Germany's loyalty.

When war broke out, the Boer generals were given the task of riding hell-for-leather to the coast and capturing the ports before the bulk of British reinforcements, then still at sea, could land. But on the way, the towns of Ladysmith and Harrismith in Natal, and Mafeking and Kimberley to the west, proved too tempting to the various Boer generals. Instead of bypassing them as instructed, the greater part of the Boer army tied itself up laying siege to these towns. This cost the Boers the war.

The British landed reinforcements unopposed and after a series of stunning setbacks, began to gain the upper hand through sheer military strength, eventually occupying the two republics. As the war continued the commandos took to the bush and began raiding towns, blowing up supply trains and depots, and attacking forts and garrisons in daring hit and run raids. The commandos were sustained by their countrymen on the farms. To deny them this, Lord Kitchener of Khartoum, who assumed command of the British forces in November 1900, took the war to the people. He built a line of blockhouses to defend the railway to the Cape, and established concentration camps for non-combatants, mainly women and children. Farms and houses were torched and the commandos lost their main source of food. This scorched-earth policy reduced the countryside to a wilderness and, along with the horrors of the concentration camps, created a bitter legacy which Afrikaners would be slow to forget.

Their support gone, it was a matter of time before the commandos had to give in. In 1902 they surrendered. The peace terms set out in the Treaty of Vereeniging were generous and, bizarrely, opened the way for the survival of Afrikaner ideals which would eventually culminate in the rise to power of the National Party in 1948.

The march of the Union

In 1908 and 1909, union of the two republics and the two colonies, the Cape and Natal, was debated by an all-white convention and the Union of South Africa was created in 1910. The country's black majority were not consulted on this and remained as subjugated and marginalised as ever.

South Africa remained firmly within the British sphere of interest for the next five decades. South African forces fought in both world wars. In World War I, South African forces were given the task of driving the Germans out of South West Africa and Tanganyika, tasks which were rapidly carried out under the leadership of General Jan Christiaan Smuts, a commander who had fought with great skill and cunning against the British during the Anglo–Boer War. Smuts became very pro-British, something which was to dog him when he became prime minister of the union.

In the 1920s, there was a resurgence of Afrikaner nationalism. The Afrikaner people had not forgotten what they called the 'English War' and the drive to self determination remained as strong as ever. The triumph of National Socialism in Germany had its echoes in the union. Some hardliners formed a shadowy underground group called the Ossewa Brandwag which had more than a passing resemblance to a fascist paramilitary organisation. The OB agitated for an end to British influence and when the storm clouds gathered in 1939, there were many who fervently believed that victory for Germany was inevitable and that South Africa should be unwavering in its support for the Germans. Smuts appealed to the nation and it was only by a narrow margin that parliament voted in favour of going to war on the side of the Allies. There were attacks on soldiers in dark streets, and nationalist politicians like Herzog and Daniel Malan argued that South Africa should not be involved at all.

In World War II, South Africans fought in almost every theatre of the war in Europe and North and East Africa. Protection of the Cape sea route was vital and the dockyard at Simonstown became the most important base in the southern hemisphere.

The war cost Smuts dearly. He returned home a hero to some, but his years overseas had weakened his position. As happened with Winston Churchill, he was swept aside in the next general election as the National Party stormed into power and put the country on a path it would stick to for 40 years.

The apartheid years

While the National Party came to power in 1948 on the back of fervent Afrikaner nationalism, it didn't introduce apartheid – it was already there in the race laws enacted in the four decades since Union in 1910. What the National Party did, however, was to gather up all the restrictive and discriminatory legislation and refine it into a systematic body of law.

The key piece of legislation was the Group Areas Act of 1950 which applied total segregation in cities and towns. Whereas before there had been places where people of different races lived together, now the lines were clearly drawn. Black people did most of the moving out and away. Other laws governed freedom of movement, racially based identity documents and classification according to colour and regulated workplaces. Mixed marriages were banned and under terms of the Immorality Act sex across the colour line was forbidden. The Reservation of Separate Amenities Act gave the country all those 'Whites Only' signs on park benches, beaches and station toilets. The more sinister aspect was stiff security legislation: rule by fear in a police state.

Prime Minister Hendrik Verwoerd has been widely credited as apartheid's grand architect, although the policy was in place before he took power. The government, backed by the church, academics and big business, envisaged a policy of 'separate – but equal – development'. In fact, little was equal about it. Whites benefited from a system of job reservation, the best farmland remained firmly in the hands of white farmers and whites got the best schools, services and places to live in.

In May 1961, South Africa became an independent republic.

The liberation movement

Long before the Afrikaners came to power, the black opposition was already a powerful force. Fuelled by disappointment that black aspirations had been ignored in the run-up to Union, the South African Native National Congress – today the African National Congress – was formed in 1912 to campaign for black rights by peaceful means. It kept its non-racial, liberal stance into the 1950s, despite pressure from more radical elements to use force to achieve their demands.

In 1952, the 'defiance campaign' began – black people began ignoring whites-only signs, ignoring curfews and breaking apartheid regulations. They refused to carry their *dompasse* (passes), a document that regulated movement of its bearer. They offered no resistance to arrest and pleaded guilty in court.

The government responded by strengthening the laws and imposed tougher penalties for breaking them. The turning point came at Sharpeville on March 21 1960 when nervous policemen opened fire on people protesting against the pass laws outside a police station, killing 69 demonstrators. Many of those killed were shot in the back while fleeing. International and local reaction was one of revulsion. Riots broke out in townships across the country. The government banned the ANC and the radical breakaway group, the Pan-Africanist Congress (PAC). The ANC launched its armed wing, Umkhonto we Sizwe (spear of the nation) shortly afterwards.

The Sharpeville shootings were condemned overseas and South Africa steadily became isolated as international opposition to its policies mounted. In 1976, school children in the sprawling township of Soweto took to the streets to protest about being taught in Afrikaans. The police response was brutal – a group of schoolchildren was gunned down. Among them was a 13-year-old boy named Hector Peterson whose last moments were captured by *Star* newspaper photographer Peter Magubane. His photograph of Petersen's death became a symbol of the struggle and riots broke out across the country. The townships were aflame for eight months.

Shifting deckchairs on the Titanic

The government remained unmoved, although it was clear that something had to be done. In 1978 P W Botha, former minister of defence, took over as prime minister. He started his rule as a reformer, scrapping the law forbidding mixed marriages and abolishing the pass laws and reservation of separate amenities. In 1983, following a whites-only referendum, he implemented a new constitution which gave Indians and 'coloureds' (a people of mixed race, descended mostly from miscegenation between Dutch slave owners and their Indonesian, Indian and Hottentot slaves, and now recognised as a nation in its own right) a political voice: each group would have its own legislative assembly (but the white assembly would have the power of veto of any decisions made in the Indian and coloured assemblies). Blacks, meanwhile, remained excluded as they were deemed to be citizens of the numerous Bantustans – 'independent' homelands – that the government had begun creating in the mid-1970s.

The homelands were a complete farce: each had its own seat of government, army, airport and border posts complete with petty dictators – all funded by the South African taxpayer – and presided over by one or other puppet leader chosen by Pretoria. Unsurprisingly, the rest of the world refused to recognise them as sovereign states. Tax breaks were given to South African companies to encourage them to set up shop in the homelands but there was little enthusiasm for this. The borders of each homeland were drawn to accommodate white-owned farmland and the result was a hotchpotch of fragmented areas – sometimes dozens of them. The land itself was generally too poor to support any decent farming and certainly could not cope with the sheer burden of hundreds of thousands of subsistence farmers. Within a few years, the homelands were grazed bare by goats and skinny cattle and looked like deserts. Some, like the Transkei and Bophuthatswana, supplemented their handouts from Pretoria by granting casino licences to hotel owners, in particular the Southern Sun group. This move dismayed the South African government – gambling was strictly illegal, a sin, in South Africa – and the weekends saw whites flocking to places like Sun City and the Wild Coast Sun for a bit of dice and, for some, a blue movie or two, also a no-no in South Africa.

Meanwhile, at home, the tri-cameral parliament was turning into a disaster, discredited as it was from the beginning. Botha had also enraged the conservative white communities who felt his reforms had gone too far and a number of top Nationalists, among them Andries Treurnicht, resigned and formed the Conservative Party. Meanwhile, the country was becoming steadily ungovernable as resistance continued. By the 1980s, South Africa, heavily involved in a war on the Angolan border against guerrillas fighting for the liberation of South West Africa, was also on the brink of a civil war at home. In 1985, the first of a series of emergencies was declared, giving the government and security forces terrifying powers. Newspapers were prevented, by self-censorship, from publishing stories about the struggle. Opponents of the state – political dissidents, journalists, activists, students – anyone, in fact, that the regime considered 'dangerous' – were banned (placed under house arrest and forbidden to associate with other people) detained without trial, spied upon, harassed, attacked and often murdered.

The army, already stretched to breaking point in South West Africa (now Namibia) and Angola, was deployed to police the townships. The economy was teetering as militant black labour unions called strike after strike and UN-backed sanctions began to take hold. White South Africa began to crack under the strain.

Hello, democracy

In 1989, Botha had a minor stroke and Frederick Willem de Klerk stepped into the breach. De Klerk, fully aware that he was sitting on a time bomb, took radical steps towards solving the country's political and social crises. Two of the conditions laid down by the ANC for ending the struggle were its unbanning and the unconditional release of its leader, Nelson Mandela. There were secret negotiations with the ANC and meetings between De Klerk and Mandela.

In Parliament on February 2 1990, De Klerk announced the unbanning of the ANC and other political organisations and, nine days later, ANC president Nelson Mandela, jailed in 1963 under the Terrorism Act, was set free. The first step toward black majority rule had been taken. However, the years before the first democratic elections in 1994 nearly ruined the country. The negotiations which followed were going to be tense as whites tried to hold on to their privileges. They feared that they would be swamped by black majority rule and believing that the chaos that had raged in the rest of post-independence Africa was inevitable under a black government. The task of creating the new South Africa was handed, like a time bomb, to the Council for a Democratic South Africa (CODESA), a representative group of lawyers, academics and negotiators. De Klerk wanted a federal system of government; Mandela and the ANC preferred to go to the polls and see who came out on top. The surge of violence that ripped through the townships and rural area of KwaZulu-Natal and the Eastern Cape nearly scuppered both men's plans.

The four years between Mandela's release and the 1994 elections were tense, bloody and volatile. Extremists on the left and right threatened to plunge the country into a civil war. Right-wing politicians, played heavily on the fears of nervous whites, and the Afrikaner Weerstand Beweging (Afrikaner resistance movement), whipped into a frenzy by its leader Eugene Terreblanche, prepared for war. In Natal, a civil war broke out between the ANC and the Inkatha Freedom Party (IFP), the conservative Zulu party led by Chief Mangosouthu Buthelezi, a man whom the ANC regarded as a puppet because he was the chief minister of KwaZulu, one of the homelands created by the white government.

The negotiations proceeded slowly but the fighting continued. Every time the politicians made a breakthrough, there would be a setback somewhere else. In 1992, in the last whites-only referendum, De Klerk was given a boost when two-thirds of the white population voted in favour of continued political reform. In June 1992, the friction between the ANC and the Nationalist Party (NP) worsened after 39 people were massacred in the informal settlement at Boipatong. The government blamed a mysterious 'Third Force', allegedly an unknown group which was determined to make the negotiations fail. There were more killings. In April 1993, Chris Hani, one of the ANC's key leaders was gunned down by a right-wing assassin, an act that brought the country to the brink of war. The police acted fast and Hani's killer, a Polish immigrant, was arrested within days along with his co-conspirator, Clive Derby-Lewis, a former Conservative Party MP.

No doubt feeling the pressure, CODESA fixed the date for a general election for April 1994. Shortly after this announcement, Mandela and De Klerk were jointly awarded the Nobel Peace Prize. The violence in the townships continued, however, as rivalries between the ANC and Inkatha, possibly fomented by the unknown Third Force, erupted in killings.

Buthelezi, meanwhile, was threatening to boycott the election. The ANC and NP had agreed to power-sharing in a transitional government and it looked increasingly as if the IFP would be sidelined. In response, Buthelezi joined the Freedom Alliance, a mix of conservative Volkstaaters campaigning for a white homeland and disgruntled former leaders of the old 'homelands'. Buthelezi then demanded separate ballot papers for the national and provincial elections, to which the ANC and NP agreed. But a month before the election, the Zulu leader announced that the IFP would not be running. IFP participation was crucial. Ten days before the election – after two weeks of incredible bloodshed in Boputhatswana and a massacre of Inkatha supporters during a march in downtown Johannesburg – Buthelezi agreed to stand. People sighed with relief. The weekend before the election, a bomb attributed to right-wing elements went off outside the ANC headquarters in Johannesburg, killing seven people. But the election was not delayed.

In contrast to the previous four years, April 27 1994 was almost a damp squib as the country's first ever democratic elections went off without a flicker of violence, much to the stupefaction of the cynics, both in South Africa and abroad. Most of the nation was caught up in the euphoria. People, black and white, stood side by side in endless queues, waiting to cast their vote. Some people queued all day. The result was predictable – the ANC won most of the votes but failed to get the two-thirds majority which would have allowed it to rule on its own. The National Party had managed to hold on to the Western Cape thanks to overwhelming coloured support. KwaZulu-Natal was won by the IFP. A government of national unity was formed, embracing the ANC, Pan-Africanist Congress (PAC), Inkatha and the National Party as well as a few minority groups which managed to win the odd seat in Parliament.

No easy walk

The six years since the election have not been altogether smooth for the ANC. The new government inherited a number of hot potatoes including an ailing health care system, a desperate housing shortage and a disgraceful education system. The post-election feel-good factor soon evaporated as the crime rate spiralled out of control. Numerous corruption scandals involving government and party officials have not helped.

Under the terms of its Reconstruction and Development Plan (RDP), the government stated its priorities as providing housing, health care, education and water and electricity to the large disadvantaged sectors of the population. Good progress has been made on the housing front with millions of RDP houses having been built in the past five years. Electrification of the townships has gone ahead but local municipalities face the massive problem of trying to recover payment from people used to years of rent and utility boycotts. Progress in health care and education remains patchy. State hospitals, with limited funding, have had to close their trauma units, not encouraging in a country where car accidents and violent crime account for a large proportion of hospital admissions. In education, the damage from the 1970s and 1980s, when pupils were urged to boycott schools, lingers still. Meanwhile, integration of previously whites-only schools has had mixed success. In some conservative parts of the country, the process has been undermined by violence, boycotts and bigotry on both sides.

In 1999, the country went back to the polls. Despite doubts as to whether the ANC would maintain its majority given the apparently high levels of voter dissatisfaction. The ruling party came out even stronger than before, taking 65% of the vote and this time also wresting the Western Cape from the National Party which had triumphed there in 1994.

Practical Information

TOURIST INFORMATION AND SERVICES

Every town has some kind of tourist office which can offer practical help. The overall body is the SA Tourism Board, generally known as Satour, which has offices in all the major centres. The head office is in Pretoria, tel: 012 308 8909.

International Satour offices

London Tel: 020 8944 8080; fax: 020 8944 6705; email: satour@satbuk.demon.co.uk
New York Tel: 212 730 2929; fax: 212 764 1980; email: satourny@aol.com; web: www.satour.org
Sydney Tel: 2 9261 3424; fax: 2 9261 3414; email: satbsyd@ozemail.com.au
Paris Tel: 1 45 61 01 97; fax: 1 45 61 01 96; email: OT.AF.SUD@wanadoo.fr
Frankfurt Tel: 69 92 91290; fax: 69 28 09 50; web: www.satour.de

When to visit

Being in the southern hemisphere, South Africa's seasons are the reverse of the northern hemisphere – when it's winter in Europe and the US, it's summer in South Africa. The country's climate is relatively mild and almost any time of year is suitable for visiting. Winters on the *highveld* can be bitterly cold at times but at least it's a dry winter and what little snow there is generally falls only in the mountains and in the high country around Barkly East in the Eastern Cape. Winter is the best time to visit the game parks, most of which are in the *lowveld*, as this region gets unpleasantly hot in summer; winter days here are mild with cold, crisp nights and there are fewer malarial mosquitoes around. Animals are also easier to spot in the winter months as they tend to congregate near water, and the bushveld cover stays thin until after the rainy season starts.

Durban and the subtropical east coast are also mild in winter but hot and humid in summer. Winters in the western Cape region, however, are wet and cool, with rain falling or winds blowing most days between May and September. El Nino, a cyclical weather phenomenon that occurs off the west coast of South America (but which affects global weather patterns), may change everything, but usually the best time to visit Cape Town is still from late October to early December, or between early February and mid-April when most of the South African tourists have gone back to Johannesburg and students and schoolkids are back in the classroom. The semi-desert Karoo is very hot during the day and usually cool at night in summer while winter days are usually clear and beautiful; but it often gets bitterly cold both during the day and at night in the middle of the year.

The country gets most of its rain in the long, hot summer, starting with the first thunderstorms in late October and carrying on until the autumn rains fall in April. The *highveld*'s thunderstorms are particularly famous, often marching across the country in long lines of pelting rain and hail, accompanied by incredible displays of lightning and thunder fierce enough to make you tremble.

Peak tourist season is from November (late spring) until March. South African schools enjoy a long summer holiday from early December until around mid-January. Hotel prices rise over this period and it can be difficult to find accommodation in popular places such as some of the game parks.

Public holidays
South Africa seems to have an inordinate number of public holidays and, at one stage, businesses were calling for government to scrap them as the economy is seriously affected by the constant stopping and starting they entail. Existing holidays are:

January 1	New Year's Day
Easter weekend	Good Friday and Family Day the following Monday, Human Rights Day
April 27	Freedom Day
May 1	Workers' Day
June 16	Youth Day
June 17	Public Holiday
August 9	National Women's Day
August 10	National Holiday
September 24	Heritage Day
December 16	Day of Reconciliation
December 25, 26	Christmas Day and Boxing Day

Festivals and events
Argus Cycle Tour, Cape Town takes place over the first weekend in March. This is a mammoth 140km cycle tour which starts in Cape Town's city centre and swoops down the peninsula returning to its start along the Atlantic seaboard. Some take it seriously and race to win but for many it's a social event, if a fairly strenuous one. Riders set off in groups according to their track record, previous times, etc, so if you're in one of the front groups, you'll be expected to ride like a pro. Racing bikes are the favoured vehicles but many people do it on mountain bikes, knobbly tyres and all. Riders pay R140 for the privilege of taking part; members of the Pedal Power Association get a R35 discount.

Coon Carnival is a uniquely Cape Town affair. The carnival builds for some weeks as groups of Malay and coloured street musicians take to the city's thoroughfares in fantastically bright costumes – think red blazers, white boaters and sometimes lurid make-up – and stroll around to the urgent strumming of banjos, guitars, trumpets and saxophones. It's one big competition between various groups, culminating in (literally) a playoff at the Green Point stadium some time in February,

Grahamstown Arts Festival, Eastern Cape is an excellent – and large – theatre, music and art festival held every year in this university town, normally during the first ten days of July.

Klein Karoo Arts Festival, March/April is a theatre and music festival whose aim was to nurture Afrikaans culture and talent but which has expanded into offering all sorts of things including international productions. Lots of good Afrikaner cooking: sweet pumpkin, *potjiekos*, *vetkoek*, *melktert* and *koeksisters*.

Oppikoppi music festival, held in August, started off as a gathering for Afrikaans bands and their associated followers but has mushroomed into a great annual event where the best – and worst – of local bands can be seen. It is so successful there are two venues – Northam, a few hours drive north of Johannesburg and a revolving venue near Cape Town, Western Cape. 'Oppikoppi' means 'on the hill' but it could also mean 'on the head', a vague allusion to the huge amount of partying that goes on.

Oyster Festival, Knysna, Eastern Cape is an annual food and drink festival held in July in the centre of the Garden Route. Supposedly it is only for oyster lovers; in reality, it is a collection of all sorts of diversions, even 100m abseils off the Knysna Heads.

Rustlers Valley, Free State is a four-day music festival held over Easter on a privately owned farm in a valley surrounded by sandstone cliffs. Popular among the trance community and New Age travellers, it attracts drummers, trancers, drum 'n bass lovers and other groovy people. Be prepared to camp ... or sleep under the stars.

Splashy Fen, Underberg, KwaZulu-Nata has turned into quite a major event. It's no longer just a couple of folkies with battered acoustics but a full-on music festival. I think the organisers would like it to be the local version of Glastonbury, although there's a lot less mud and no-one's going to nick your tent. The festival usually takes place on the last weekend of April and includes the Freedom Day holiday on April 27. The dates for 2001 are 26–29 April. Tickets cost R200; you can normally save about R50 or so if you book months before.

Two Oceans Marathon, Cape Town is the same idea as the Argus except it in foot and only 56km. It takes place over Easter weekend. This is one of the country's most popular marathons after the Comrades. As its name suggests, the route takes in both the Indian and Atlantic oceans, crossing from one side of the Cape peninsula to the next. To enter this ankle-smasher, visit their website, www.twooceansmarathon. org.za/raceinfo.htm and see if you qualify.

Whale migration Each winter, beginning in May, southern right, Brydes' and humpback whales make their way up from the Antarctic to breed and nurse their young in the comparatively warmer waters off the Cape coast.

There is an official whale route (for the whale watchers, not the mammals) which covers likely whale 'hotspots'. Best of these is Hermanus, a small fishing and resort town east of Cape Town. Best viewing season is around August and September when the calving is in full swing. By December, most of the stragglers have swum off south to feed in the plankton-rich seas of the Southern Ocean.

RED TAPE
Visas
Most passport holders need visas to enter the country even if they are citizens of Commonwealth countries. Check with the South African embassy or High Commission in your home country before leaving as visas are not issued on arrival. Otherwise call the Department of Home Affairs in Pretoria (012) 314 8911; fax: 314 8516. The international Satour offices can answer any red tape questions.

South African Embassies and High Commissions abroad
Australia Rhodes Place, Yarralumla, Canberra ACT 2600; tel: 06 273 2424; fax: 273 2669.
Canada 15 Sussex Drive, Ottawa K1M 1M8; tel: 613 7440330, fax: 744 8287
UK South Africa House, Trafalgar Square, London. Tel: 0171 930 4488.
USA 3051 Massachusetts Av NW, Washington DC 20008; tel: 202 232 4400, fax: 265 1607.

Foreign embassies in South Africa
Australia 292 Orient St, Arcadia, Pretoria; tel: 012 342 3740
Canada 1103 Arcadia ST, Hatfield, Pretoria; tel: 012 342 6923
New Zealand citizens' affairs are handled by the British Consulate.
UK 19th Floor, Sanlam Centre, cnr Jeppe & Von Wielligh St, Johannesburg; tel: 011 337 8940 or Cape Town; tel: 021 25 3670
USA 877 Pretorius St, Arcadia, Pretoria; tel: 012 342 1048 or Johannesburg 011 331 1681, or Cape Town; tel: 021 21 4280.

Immigration and customs
Like everywhere else, you're only allowed to bring a minimal amount of alcohol (two litres of wine and a litre of spirits) and cigarettes (400) into the country. The allowance for gifts and other goods is R500 so make sure that laptop you're carrying looks used. As always, look smart and unrumpled and you might be left alone.

Drugs
A real no-no. Following the opening of its borders post-apartheid, South Africa has become a transit point for global cocaine and heroin cartels, and the authorities are understandably eager to put a stop to this. There are stiff penalties for being caught with hard drugs. While local consumption of ecstasy and cocaine has also boomed in recent years, it's probably a good idea not to indulge.

Bribery

Stories of corruption are rampant. It probably is rife but unlikely to affect the average tourist. If an opportunity is presented to offer a bribe, please decline politely and stand up for your rights as a traveller.

Bureaucracy

Layered and treacly. Getting visa extensions and the like can be immensely time consuming and frustrating with queues lasting for days. If you need paperwork done in the major centres, try going to one of the smaller Home Affairs offices in nearby municipalities. Remember to take all your documentation with you – photocopies of passport and a stock of passport photographs. There's nothing like standing in a queue for a day only to be told by the person behind the counter that you must have photographs.

WHAT TO TAKE

Plan to travel as light possible, no matter how you travel. Travelling with minimal gear really does make life much more pleasant, especially on those occasions (and they will happen) when you have to walk with all your kit. Independent travellers should take a backpack, preferably with an internal frame as they are easier to stow in overhead luggage racks on trains and buses. Ensure that it is durable with strong zips and pockets. A day pack is very useful. Bring a tent if you plan on camping, and a lightweight sleeping bag for those cool winter nights when the train bedding runs out before the bedding steward reaches you.

Clothing should be kept to a minimum – you'll be carrying it, after all. Cotton clothing is best in Africa, especially in summer. Lightweight cotton trousers are more practical than jeans and could double as reasonably smart evening wear. Lightweight long-sleeved shirts and T-shirts are comfortable, and bring a sweater – it gets cold in the mountains and winter nights in the bushveld and the *highveld* do get bitterly cold.

Being largely westernised, there are few of the sartorial problems in South Africa that one has to deal with in many countries to the north. Shorts are completely acceptable although in African culture they are only for little boys so you may be giggled at if you wear them. Women in trousers or bikinis will not cause any riots. However, a streak of conservatism runs deep here and, certainly outside of well-trodden regions, it is worth trying to look as spruce as possible.

Odds and ends

Almost everything you need can be found here, and fairly cheaply too. Things like insect repellent, toilet paper and tampons are widely available, even in rural areas. Bring a spare pair of contact lenses and the fluids you need to go with them. Camping shops are widespread and there are a number of chains. Names to look for are: Cape Union Mart, Cymot, ME Stores, Drifters and Camp and Climb.

ELECTRICITY

Power is normally 220/230 volts AC at 50Hz, except Pretoria which is 230v and Port Elizabeth which operates at 200/250v. Plugs are either 5amp, 2 pin or

15amp with three rounded pins. Special adaptors will almost always be needed for overseas equipment.

MONEY

The South African rand, while still regarded as a hard currency and holding its value reasonably well, is not the strongest currency unit around and those travelling on US dollars, UK pounds and Deutschemarks, among many other currencies, will have a ball. The rate of exchange in late 2000 was around US$1.00 = R6.90 and UKStg1.00 = R10.60. It's not necessary to carry large amounts of foreign currency with you as everything is payable in rands.

Foreign exchange

Travellers' cheques and foreign currency notes of all major currencies can be exchanged at any commercial bank or Rennies Foreign Exchange bureaux, and most of the better hotels have exchange facilities for guests. New rates are posted daily. Enquiries may be directed to:

Thomas Cook Rennies Travel Tel: 011 407 3211; 0800 111 177 (toll free)
American Express Tel: 011 359 0200
Diners Club Tel: 011 337 3244

I have found that buying foreign exchange through a bank almost always works out cheaper than doing it through a forex bureau. Look into this before signing away precious travel money in commission fees.

Credit cards

Accepted just about everywhere on the tourist trail and many places off it. Visa and Mastercard are the standards, Diners Club and American Express less so, especially in the remoter regions. If you travel on plastic, keep an emergency cash stash for those late night arrivals in one- (and even two-) horse towns like Upington. Petrol cannot be bought on credit cards. Some banks issue garage cards which work the same way as a credit card but you can only get one if you have a local bank account.

   A useful budget tip is to pay for as much as you can on your credit card. This way you don't pay commission and you often get a better exchange rate.

VAT refunds

All foreign nationals are eligible for VAT refunds on goods purchased in South Africa. However, you must make sure the dealer fills out the necessary form at the time of purchase. You then take the form, your receipt and passport and claim the VAT back at the airport when you leave the country. If travelling overland or by sea, VAT refunds are done at the border post of exit.

Budgeting

It's not as cheap as it used to be but that's what happens when tourism booms. Budgets, unfortunately, are highly subjective and often inaccurate. At the bottom end, staying in backpackers and cooking your own food, you could get by on around R60 a day for basics, excluding transport and sightseeing. But it's not going to be much fun that way.

By European standards, train tickets, eating out and accommodation are excellent value while the bigger costs such as visiting game parks and taking part in wild adventure activities tend to inflict pain on your wallet, no matter what currency you're using. There will always be a bargain somewhere so keep a sharp eye out for the gap. State-run game parks, for example, are great value for money as prices have been kept down to make them affordable to a greater number of South Africans, not just the wealthy ones.

Travelling in South Africa on a budget is discussed in greater detail in Chapter 3.

Sports and equipment hire
Johannesburg
It's getting easier to hire bikes or camping gear here and in Pretoria. Ask at your hostel or guest house. The ever-helpful Pete Kirchoff at the Explorers' Club in Yeoville, Johannesburg argues that it can work out cheaper and is certainly safer to take organised trips. But if you do want to be independent, contact Camping Africa (tel: 011 728 4207, fax: 728 3008; email: cdt@gem.co.za; web: www.icon.co.za/~campafrica). They have a large hire division for everything from tents to waterbottles.

Cape Town
In a city where so much life is directed at outdoor activities, hiring equipment is pretty straightforward and worth considering.

Rent-a-Tent (tel: 021 557 4336) is helpful and reasonable. Two-people tents for hiking are R15 per day, large two-person tents (big enough to stand up in!) are R30 per day. They also hire out backpacks at R15 per day.

Haro Adventures (tel: 021 54 458) hire out 15-speed mountain bikes for R40 per day but owner John Peiser offers reduced rates for longer hire periods. You'll have to leave a R200 deposit. Haro also has a shop in Hermanus, the whale-watching capital (tel: 02831 76 3142).

Hunting and fishing licences
Hunters will need a licence to shoot any game. The easiest way of going about this is to join an organised party which will take care of the details. Operators include African Connection (tel: 011 468 1526), or the SA Hunters' and Game Conservation Association (tel: 012 565 4856).

You will need a fishing licence depending on whether or not you want to fish in designated reserves such as Kosi Bay National Park. Most fishing equipment suppliers or one of the national angling associations (tel: 011 824 2140) should be able to arrange this for you. You can also try the SA Deep Sea Angling Association (tel: 021 96 4454) or call the Rock and Surf Angling Association (tel: 0423 5 1140).

You can also catch your own crayfish (rock lobster) and abalone and pick mussels off the rocks (see page 116).

EATING AND DRINKING

For a country with such an incredible multicultural history, it's a surprise that overall the cooking is mostly fairly bland. There are one or two tasty exceptions – *bobotie*, a Cape Malay dish made with mince and eggs, infused with turmeric, curry and herbs, and *waterblommetjie bredie*, a mutton and spice stew whose main ingredient is water lilies.

Potjiekos, stew made in cast-iron pots over open fires, is a traditional Afrikaner dish as are *boerewors* (farmer's sausage) – never ask what goes into it – and *biltong*, salted, air-cured meat. This is a meat oriented society and the *braai* (barbecue) is at the centre of it all. The *braai* is an institution, where the women hang out in the kitchen, making salads (if there are any to be made) and the men gather around the fire, beers in hand, ostensibly to cook the meat, but often charring it instead. Fat fires are doused with beer, giving the meat a not-unpleasant ale taste. There will be *mieliepap*, savoury porridge made from maize meal, to go with the piles of meat. The staple diet of much of Africa, *mieliepap* – also known as *sadza*, *nsima* or *samp* – is found everywhere.

Drinking is taken seriously here. Beer brewing is almost a monopoly but no-one is complaining too loudly. Lager rules, since the climate is really too hot for warm ales. At least the lagers are cheap and plentiful. Look out for Castle (almost the national drink), Lion, and Black Label, as well as independents such as Old Four Legs (on the Eastern Cape coast only) Windhoek Lager and Mitchell's Draft.

The country's wine industry started in the 18th century and some of its wine is brilliant. There are almost too many estates to single any out. Hire a car in Cape Town and go cruising the Wine Route for a day or two. Take one non-drinker to handle the car.

Look out for *mampoer*, sometimes called *witblits* (white lightning), a spirit usually brewed from peaches, pears or raisins, which will bring tears to your eyes. It used to be brewed illegally in the hills of the western Transvaal and from all sorts of bases including chillies and potatoes. The hangovers are wicked, so approach with care.

SHOPPING

US-style shopping mall culture is big here, and, along with crime, is one of the reasons for inner city decay. As one would expect in a western shopping culture, there is not a lot of uniquely African shopping in the malls other than curio shops which suck in the unwary. Trading hours for most shops are from 09.00–17.00 Monday to Friday and 08.00–13.00 on Saturday. Shops in the malls are usually open all day on Saturdays and sometimes on Sunday, as well as later during the week. In the frantic weeks before Christmas, shops in malls are generally open until 21.00.

If curios are what you want, try the fleamarkets. Since the borders have opened, traders from as far away as Mali, Ghana, Republic of the Congo and Zambia, have begun heading south in a steady stream, bringing African carvings, beadwork, jewellery and drums. (You'll see them if you ride any of the trains south from the Zimbabwe border; they'll definitely see you!) Prices are much lower than in the mall curio shops and you can try to bargain further. Johannesburg's biggest fleamarket happens on Sundays on the roof of the Rosebank shopping mall (see Chapter 4); most of the curio traders line the streets outside and fill the parking lot opposite the centre. Cape Town's Greenmarket Square market is open daily in the cobbled square in the heart of the city. Those carved malachite chess sets have had to come a long way, and there are more tourists in Cape Town, so prices are higher. Bargain hard!

Outdoor gear

Not surprisingly, camping, hiking and general outdoor adventure are big news here and the country is full of outdoor outfitters. Much of the gear is imported and while it is expensive for South Africans, it is still often cheaper here than at home. Locally made items such as tents, fleeces, boots, sleeping bags and rucksacks are extremely well made and very cheap. If you plan to spend any time outdoors, it may make sense to buy your equipment here rather than at home. In Johannesburg, shops to look out for are:

Outdoor Warehouse Tel: (011) 792 8331, (021) 948 6221 or (031) 263 0851
Drifters Tel: (011) 783 9200
Cape Union Mart Tel: (011) 325 5038
ME Stores 70 Juta St, Braamfontein, tel: (011) 403 1354

Tipping

It is standard practice in South Africa. Minimum is 10% although I'm sure no-one will object if you feel the service is worth more. At garages, it is usual to tip petrol attendants a few rand, for they which they will be very grateful.

MEDIA AND COMMUNICATIONS

The local media industry is strong and vibrant and, these days, often controversial. There are plenty of newspapers, magazines and radio stations. The South African Broadcasting Corporation, which is responsible for disseminating the party line, controls the bulk of TV and radio services and programming is multi-lingual. There is also M-Net, a subscription entertainment television service and Summit TV, an independent business programme broadcast on satellite. Satellite TV is a fairly new concept in South Africa but entertainment-hungry locals – or at least those who can afford it – have taken to it with a vengeance.

Post

Fairly reliable, although many South Africans may warn you not to send anything valuable by mail. The Post Office has cleaned up its act and scenes such as the postal worker caught on closed circuit TV as he opened registered mail and pocketed cash, postal orders or cheques, are hopefully a thing of the past. Airmail to the UK takes around one week, a little longer to the US. Rates are low. There are 24-hour, door-to-door speed services. For postal information, call 0800 02 31 33.

A private upstart operation called PostNet (tel: 011 805 0395) offers a relatively cheap courier postal service as well as Internet facilities, faxing and copying services. PostNet has been a huge success and there are branches everywhere.

Phone calls

The telecommunications network is quite sophisticated. International calls are simple to make and are half-price between 20.00 and 06.00 weekdays and from 20.00 on Friday to 08.00 on Monday.

If you have a US long-distance calling card such as those offered by Sprint, AT&T and MCI, you should be able to use it here from an ordinary pay phone. Hotels may be reluctant to connect you to an international operator; if so, call the operator direct on 0903#. If you have problems, ask for the Home Direct service which allows you to call an operator at home free of charge so that you can arrange a reversed-charge or credit card call.

The country code for South Africa is 27. Callers dialling from abroad should drop the first zero from the local area codes. Dialling overseas, the following codes apply: UK – 09; US – 091; Canada – 091; Australia – 0961; New Zealand – 0964. International codes, area codes and time zones are found at the front of local telephone directories.

Phone cards for public phones are widely available and cellular phones can be rented at major airports. If you have a GSM phone, you should be able to use it here as long as you have arranged in advance to do so with your service provider back home. Pay-as-you-go phones compatible with the local frequency should work here but you will naturally need to buy a local SIM card. The two local cellular network operators are MTN (tel: (011) 301 6000) and Vodacom (tel: 086008 2600).

Internet

Internet cafés, once on every corner, seem to have dwindled as more people get PCs at home. PostNet (see Post above) offers Internet services as do most of the backpackers.

PHOTOGRAPHY

South Africa has gorgeous light; there is something about its quality that has photographers in ecstasy. Winter days (except in Cape Town) generally have deep blue skies and clean, cold air, particularly away from the towns. If that were not enough, there are incredible landscapes, beautiful and interesting people, wildlife and the vibrant colours of traditional clothes.

The country is geared towards looking after photographers. All kinds of films are available and a full range of processing services from one-hour labs to fully professional outfits. Film, especially slide film, is a lot cheaper than in the UK – expect to pay around R70 for a 36 exposure roll of Fuji Provia, for example – and slide film processing is an absolute bargain at around R25 per roll in a professional lab. It might even be cheaper to do all your developing here before going home. X-ray machines at all airports are film-safe.

Most of the better-known brands of cameras, lenses and accessories are readily available but import duties are high so photographic equipment is quite expensive. However, there are some incredible bargains to be had if you buy second-hand. Try Kameraz (Rosebank Mews, Rosebank, Johannesburg; tel: 011 880 2885), a brilliant place to snuffle around in.

That said, sometimes I would rather not travel with a camera because I often find myself thinking more about the pictures I want to take rather than just enjoying the moment. Give it some thought – often the best pictures are in your head.

LOCAL TIME

South African Standard Time is two hours ahead of GMT, one hour ahead of Central European Winter Time and seven hours ahead of the USA's Eastern Standard Winter Time. Australia is 6–9 hours ahead and New Zealand 11 hours ahead. There are no time zone changes between South Africa and its neighbours.

HEALTH

Dr Jane Wilson-Howarth and Dr Felicity Nicholson

A number of tropical diseases are present in South Africa but, although most travellers who spend a while in the region will become ill at some point, the chances are that it will be nothing more dangerous than diarrhoea or a cold. Provided that you have had the necessary immunisations before you travel, the biggest dangers are accidents, then malaria, a risk that can be minimised, though not eliminated, by using prophylactic drugs and taking precautions against mosquito bites.

Preparations

In addition to considering the points made directly below, do read this entire section before you leave, since subjects such as malaria prevention are discussed under a separate heading.

Immunisations

Preparations to ensure a healthy trip to Africa require checks on your immunisation status: it is wise to be up to date on tetanus (ten-yearly), polio (ten-yearly), diphtheria (ten-yearly), hepatitis A and typhoid.

The majority of travellers are advised to have immunisation against hepatitis A with hepatitis A vaccine (eg: Havrix monodose, Avaxim). One dose of vaccine lasts for one year and can be boosted to give protection for up to ten years.

The course of two injections costs about £100. The vaccine can be used even close to the time of departure. It is always preferable to gamma globulin which gives immediate but short-term partial protection since there is a theoretical risk of CJD (human form of mad cow disease) with this blood-derived product.

The newer typhoid vaccines last for three years and are about 75% effective. They should be encouraged unless the traveller is leaving within a few days for a trip of a week or less, when the vaccine would not be effective in time.

Vaccinations for rabies are advised for travellers visiting more remote areas for longer periods of time. Ideally three injections should be taken over a period of four weeks at 0, 7 and 28 days. The timing of these doses does not have to be exact and a schedule can be arranged to suit you. (See *Rabies*.)

A BCG vaccination against tuberculosis (TB) is also advised for trips of two months or more. This should be taken at least six weeks before travel.

Ideally then you should visit your own doctor to discuss your requirements about eight weeks before you plan to travel.

Travel clinics
UK

British Airways Travel Clinic and Immunisation Service 156 Regent St, London W1, tel: 020 7439 9584. This place also sells travellers' supplies and has a branch of Stanford's travel book and map shop. There are now BA clinics all around Britain and three in South Africa. To find your nearest one, phone 01276 685040.
MASTA (Medical Advisory Service for Travellers Abroad) Keppel St, London WC1 7HT; tel: 09068 224100. This is a premium-line number, charged at 50p per minute.
NHS travel website, www.fitfortravel.scot.nhs.uk, provides country-by-country advice on immunisation and malaria, plus details of recent developments, and a list of relevant health organisations.
Nomad Travel Pharmacy and Vaccination Centre 3–4 Wellington Terrace, Turnpike Lane, London N8 0PX; tel: 020 8889 7014.
Thames Medical 157 Waterloo Rd, London SE1 8US; tel: 020 7902 9000. Competitively priced, one-stop travel health service. All profits go to their affiliated company InterHealth which provides health care for overseas workers on Christian projects.
Trailfinders Immunisation Centre 194 Kensington High St, London W8 7RG; tel: 020 7938 3999. Also 254–284 Sauchiehall St, Glasgow G2 3EH; tel: 0141 353 0066.

USA

Centers for Disease Control 1600 Clifton Road, Atlanta, GA 30333; tel: 877 FYI TRIP; 800 311 3435; web: www.cdc.gov/travel. This organisation is the central source of travel information in the USA. Each summer they publish the invaluable *Health Information for International Travel* which is available from the Division of Quarantine at the above address.
Connaught Laboratories PO Box 187, Swiftwater, PA 18370; tel: 800 822 2463. They will send a free list of specialist tropical-medicine physicians in your state.
IAMAT (International Association for Medical Assistance to Travelers) 736 Center St, Lewiston, NY 14092. A non-profit organisation which provides lists of English-speaking doctors abroad.

Australia

TMVC tel: 1300 65 88 44; website: www.tmvc.com.au. TMVC has 20 clinics in Australia, New Zealand and Thailand, including:
Brisbane Dr Deborah Mills, Qantas Domestic Building, 6th floor, 247 Adelaide St, Brisbane, QLD 4000; tel: 7 3221 9066; fax: 7 3321 7076

Melbourne Dr Sonny Lau, 393 Little Bourke St, 2nd floor, Melbourne, VIC 3000; tel: 3 9602 5788; fax: 3 9670 8394.

Sydney Dr Mandy Hu, Dymocks Building, 7th floor, 428 George St, Sydney, NSW 2000; tel: 2 221 7133; fax: 2 221 8401.

South Africa

There are six **British Airways travel clinics** in South Africa: *Johannesburg*, tel: (011) 807 3132; *Cape Town*, tel: (021) 419 3172; *Durban*, tel: (031) 303 2423; *Knysna*, tel: (044) 382 6366; *East London*, tel: (043) 743 7471; *Port Elizabeth*, tel: (041) 374 7471.

Medical kit

Take a small medical kit. This should contain malaria prophylactics, soluble aspirin or paracetamol (good for gargling when you have a sore throat and for reducing fever and pains), plasters (Band-aids), potassium permanganate crystals or another favoured antiseptic, iodine for sterilising water and cleaning wounds, sunblock, and condoms or femidoms.

Travellers' diarrhoea

Most travellers to the tropics suffer a bout of travellers' diarrhoea during their trip. The newer you are to tropical travel, the more likely you are to suffer. Travellers' diarrhoea comes from getting other people's faeces in your mouth, which most often happens from cooks not washing their hands after a trip to the toilet, but even if the restaurant cook does not understand basic hygiene you will be safe if your food has been properly cooked and arrives piping hot. As for what food is safe to eat, any fruit or vegetable that you've washed and peeled yourself should be fine, as should hot cooked food. Raw food and salads are risky, as is cooked food that has gone cold or been kept lukewarm in a hotel buffet. Avoid ice-cream, which is often not kept adequately frozen due to power cuts. Ice may have been made with unboiled water or deposited by the road on its journey from the ice factory.

It is less common to get sick from drinking contaminated water, but it can happen, so try to drink from safe sources. Tap water in South Africa is normally OK. Any dodgy water should be brought to the boil (even at altitude this is all that's needed), passed through a good bacteriological filter or purified with iodine. Chlorine tablets (eg: Puritabs) are less effective and taste nastier.

Treatment

Dehydration is the reason you feel awful during a bout of diarrhoea, so the most important part of treatment is to imbibe lots of clear fluids. Sachets of oral rehydration salts give the perfect biochemical mix, but any dilute mixture of sugar and salt in water will do you good. Try a solution of a four-finger scoop of sugar with a three-finger pinch of salt in a glass of water, with a squeeze of lemon or orange juice to improve the taste and provide necessary potassium which is lost in diarrhoea and vomiting. If no safe drinking water is available, then Coke or similar with a three-finger pinch of salt added to each glass will do the trick. Drink two large glasses after every bowel action, more if you are thirsty – if you are not eating you need to drink three litres a day plus the equivalent of whatever is pouring into the toilet.

With most diarrhoea attacks, medication will be less effective than simply resting up and forsaking greasy foods and alcohol. If you are hungry stick to dry biscuits, boiled potatoes or rice. The bacteria responsible for diarrhoea and related symptoms normally die after 36 hours. Avoid the use of blockers such as Imodium, Lomotil and codeine phosphate unless you have no access to sanitation, for instance if you have to travel by bus, since these blockers keep the poisons in your system and make you feel bad for longer. It is dangerous to take blockers with dysentery (evidenced by blood, slime or fever with the diarrhoea). Should diarrhoea or related symptoms persist beyond 36 hours, or you are passing blood or slime or have a fever, then consult a doctor or pharmacist. Chances are you have nothing serious but you may have something treatable, for instance giardia (indicated by severe flatulence, abdominal distension, stomach cramps and sulphurous belching), which is cured by taking 2g of Tinidazole as a single dose (repeated seven days later if symptoms persist) and avoiding alcohol. If you can't get to a doctor, a three-day course of an antibiotic such as ciprofloxacin (500mg twice daily) or norfloxacin is effective against dysentery and severe diarrhoea.

Malaria

Malaria kills a million Africans annually, and (after accidents) it poses the single biggest serious threat to the health of travellers to tropical Africa. There is no malaria transmission above 3,000m; at intermediate altitudes (1,800–3,000m) there is a low but finite risk. Much of South Africa is free from the disease, although it is a risk in some parks including the Kruger and the Transvaal in the north. It is unwise to travel in malarious parts of South Africa whilst pregnant or with children.

Prophylactic drugs

Because resistance patterns are changing rapidly in malarial areas, it is crucial to seek advice on prophylaxis from a travel clinic. There is no vaccine against malaria, but using prophylactic drugs and preventing mosquito bites will considerably reduce the risk of contracting it. Seek professional advice for the best anti malarial drugs to take. All prophylactic agents should be taken with or after the evening meal, washed down with plenty of fluid and continued for four weeks after leaving the malarial area.

Once in a while, I meet travellers who refuse to take prophylactics, either because they want to acquire resistance to malaria or else because they believe there is a homeopathic cure for this killer disease. Unfortunately, they think they're being very clever. For the record, travellers to Africa can't acquire effective resistance to malaria, and the medical profession would leap on any viable homeopathic cure for the disease. Travellers who don't use prophylactic drugs risk their life in a manner that is both foolish and unnecessary. Equally important as taking malaria pills is making every reasonable effort not to be bitten by mosquitoes between dusk and dawn – see *Insects*.

Diagnosis and cures

Even those who take their malaria tablets meticulously and do everything possible to avoid being bitten may contract a strain of malaria that is resistant to prophylactic drugs. Untreated malaria is likely to be fatal, but even strains resistant to prophylaxis respond well to prompt treatment. You should visit a doctor or hospital as soon as you experience malarial symptoms: any combination of a headache, flu-like aches and pains, a rapid rise in temperature, a general sense of disorientation, and possibly nausea and diarrhoea.

It is preferable not to attempt self-diagnosis. Local doctors regularly deal with malaria and any laboratory or hospital will be able to give you a quick malaria test. Nevertheless, you may be some distance from a doctor and could go from feeling healthy to having a high fever in the space of hours, in which case the risk associated with not treating malaria promptly should outweigh that of taking an unnecessary cure. Expert opinion is that the most safe and effective cure at present is to take two quinine tablets every eight hours until the fever subsides for a maximum of three days, then a single dose of three Fansidar tablets. Provided you follow this procedure before the symptoms have become chronic, it is practically 100% effective. Be warned that you must drink a lot of water after you take Fansidar, and that you should carry Fansidar, quinine and a thermometer with you since these are not always available locally. It could be that a better cure emerges during the lifespan of this edition, so seek advice from a travel clinic or another reliable source before you leave for Africa. And be warned that another popular cure called Halfan has been banned as dangerous and is not recommended for anyone any more, particularly if you are using lariam as a prophylactic. Finally, if you have a fever and the malaria test is negative (which does not completely exclude malaria), you may have typhoid, which should also receive immediate treatment. Where typhoid-testing is unavailable, a routine blood test can give a strong indication of this disease.

Dengue fever

This mosquito-borne disease resembles malaria but there is no prophylactic available to deal with it. The mosquitoes which carry this virus bite during the day time, so it worth applying repellent if you see them around. Symptoms include strong headaches, rashes and excruciating joint and muscle pains and high fever. Dengue fever only lasts for a week or so and is not usually fatal. Complete rest and paracetomol are the usual treatment. Plenty of fluids also help. Some patients are given an intravenous drip to keep them from dehydrating.

Bilharzia

With thanks to Dr Vaughan Southgate of the Natural History Museum, London
Bilharzia or schistosomiasis is a common debilitating disease afflicting perhaps 200 million people worldwide. It is rare in South Africa, but avoid swimming in stagnant water. Those most affected are the rural poor of the tropics who repeatedly acquire more and more of these nasty little worm-lodgers. Infected travellers and expatriates generally suffer fewer problems because symptoms

will encourage them to seek prompt treatment and they are also exposed to fewer parasites. But it is still an unpleasant problem, and worth avoiding. When someone with bilharzia excretes into freshwater, the eggs hatch and swim off to find a pond snail to infest. They develop inside the snail to emerge as torpedo-shaped cercariae, barely visible to the naked eye but able to digest their way through human or animal skin. This is the stage that attacks people as they wade, bathe or shower in infested water. In 1995, 75% of a group of people scuba diving off Cape Maclear for only about a week acquired the disease. The snails which harbour bilharzia are a centimetre or more long and live in still or slow-moving fresh water which is well oxygenated and has edible vegetation (water-weed, reeds). The risk is greatest where local people use the water in any way, bearing in mind that wind can disperse cercariae up to 100m from where they entered the water. Scuba diving off a boat into deep offshore water should thus be a low-risk activity. Showering in lake water or paddling along a reedy lake shore near a village carries a high risk of acquiring bilharzia.

Water which has been filtered or stored snail-free for two days is safe, as is water which has been boiled or treated with Cresol or Dettol. Some protection is afforded by applying an oily insect repellent like DEET to your skin before swimming or paddling.

Cercariae live for up to 30 hours after they have been shed by snails, but the older they are, the less vigorous they are and the less capable of penetrating skin. Cercariae are shed in the greatest numbers between 11.00 and 15.00. If water to be used for bathing is pumped early in the morning from deep in the lake (cercariae are sun-loving) or from a site far from where people excrete there will be less risk of infestation. Swimming in the afternoon is riskier than in the early morning. Since cercariae take perhaps 10–15 minutes to penetrate, a quick shower, or a splash across a river, followed by thorough drying with a towel should be safe. Even if you are in risky water longer, towelling off vigorously after bathing will kill any cercariae in the process of penetrating your skin. Only a proportion of those cercariae which penetrate the skin survive to cause disease. The absence of early symptoms does not necessarily mean there is no infection, but symptoms are normal about two or more weeks after penetration: typically a fever and wheezy cough. A blood test, which should be taken six weeks or more after likely exposure, will determine whether or not parasites are going to cause problems. Treatment is generally effective, but failures occur and retreatment is often necessary for reasons that aren't fully understood but which may imply some drug resistance. Since bilharzia can be a nasty illness, avoidance is better than waiting to be cured and it is wise to avoid bathing in high-risk areas.

Other diseases
AIDS and venereal disease
HIV and other sexually transmitted infections are widespread in the region to a degree that is unimaginable in Western countries, and AIDS-related deaths in many of the countries covered in this guide have reached epidemic proportions. The risk attached to having unprotected sex with anybody but a

regular partner is prohibitively high. Condoms and femidoms offer a high level of protection against HIV and other sexually transmitted infections. Ideally purchase them before you leave your own country to ensure they are of a high standard. The additional use of spermicides and pessaries further reduces the risk of transmission. If you notice any genital ulcers or discharge, seek prompt treatment.

Hospital workers in South Africa deal with AIDS victims on a regular basis. Contrary to Western prejudices, health professionals do realise the danger involved in using unsterilised needles, and you are unlikely to be confronted with one in a town hospital or clinic. If you need treatment in a really remote area where supplies are a problem, you might be glad to be carrying a few needles and hypodermic syringes in your medical kit.

Rabies

Rabies is carried by all mammals (beware the village dogs and small monkeys that are used to being fed in the parks) and is passed on to man through a bite or a lick of an open wound. You must always assume any animal is rabid (unless personally known to you). The closer the bite is to the face the shorter the incubation time of the disease. But it is always wise to get to medical help as soon as possible. Remember though it is never too late to bother.

In the interim, scrub the wound with soap and bottled/boiled water then pour on a strong iodine or alcohol solution. This helps stop the rabies virus entering the body and will guard against wound infections including tetanus. If you intend to have contact with animals and/or are likely to be more than 24 hours away from medical help, then pre-exposure vaccination is advised. Ideally three doses should be taken over four weeks. Contrary to popular belief these vaccinations are relatively painless!

If you are exposed as described, then treatment should be given as soon as possible, but it is never too late to seek help as the incubation period for rabies can be very long.

Those who have not been immunised will need a full course of injections together with rabies immunoglobulin (RIG), but this product is expensive (around 800 US dollars) and may be hard to come by. Another reason why pre-exposure vaccination should be encouraged in travellers who are planning to visit more remote areas!

Tell the doctor if you have had pre-exposure vaccine as this will change the treatment you receive. Remember if you contract rabies, mortality is 100% and death from rabies is probably one of the worst ways to go!

Tetanus

Tetanus is caught through deep, dirty wounds, including animal bites, so ensure that such wounds are thoroughly cleaned. Immunisation gives good protection for ten years, provided you do not have an overwhelming number of tetanus bacteria on board. If you haven't had a tetanus shot in ten years or you are unsure, get a tetanus toxoid injection and a tetanus booster as quickly as possible. Keep immunised and be sensible about first aid.

Insects and ticks

Even if you take malaria tablets, do all you can to avoid mosquito bites. The imperative reason for this is the increasing level of resistance to preventative drugs, while of lesser concern are several other mosquito-borne viral fevers which could be present in low and medium-altitude parts of the region. The Anopheles mosquito which spreads malaria emerges at dusk, as do most other disease-carrying mosquitoes, so you will greatly reduce your chances of being bitten by wearing long trousers and socks after dark and covering exposed parts of your body with insect repellent, preferably a DEET-based preparation such as Jungle Jell or Repel. The Anopheles mosquito hunts mostly at ground level, so it is worth putting repellent on your ankles, even if you wear socks. When walking in scrub and forest areas by day, you should also cover and spray yourself, since the Aedes mosquito which spreads dengue and yellow fever is a day-biter (solid shoes, socks and trousers will in any case protect you against snakes, sharp thorns and harmless but irritating biters like midges).

Like many insects, mosquitoes are drawn to direct light. If you are camping never put a lamp near the opening of your tent, or you will have a swarm of mosquitoes and other insects waiting to join you when you retire.

In hotel rooms, be aware that the longer you leave on your light, the greater the number of insects with which you are likely to share your accommodation.

Once you are in bed, the best form of protection is a net. Mosquito coils, which are widely available, will also reduce the biting rate, and even though strains of mosquito have evolved that are skilled at flying in turbulent air, so will a fan. Far better, though, is to carry your own permethrin-impregnated net, which will protect you against everything. Nets and impregnation kits are available from MASTA at the London School of Tropical Medicine and Hygiene, Trailfinders Immunisation Clinic and from British Airways Travel Clinics (see page 36).

Tumbu flies or putsi occur in hot, humid climates, where they often lay eggs on drying laundry. When a person puts on clean clothes or sleeps on a fresh sheet, the eggs hatch and bury themselves under the skin to form a crop of 'boils', each of which hatches a grub after about eight days before the inflammation settles down. In putsi areas, you should dry clothes and sheets in a screened house, or in direct sunshine until they are crisp, or iron them.

Jiggers or sandfleas latch on if you walk barefoot in contaminated places; these parasites set up home under the skin of the foot, usually at the side of a toenail where they cause a painful, boil-like swelling. They need picking out by a local expert and, if the flea bursts during eviction then douse the wound in spirit, alcohol or kerosene – otherwise more jiggers will infest you.

There are several unpleasant illnesses which can follow a tick bite in South Africa, including Lyme Disease, but the good news is that, even if a tick is carrying disease organisms, it will not inevitably infect you. You are less likely to be infected if you get the tick off promptly and do not damage it. Remove any tick as soon as you notice it on you - it will most likely be firmly attached to somewhere you would rather it was not – by grasping the tick as close to your body as possible and pulling steadily and firmly away at right angles to your skin. The tick will then come away complete as long as you do not jerk or twist. If possible douse the wound with alcohol (any spirit will do) or iodine. Spreading redness around the bite and/or fever and/or aching joints after a tick bite imply that you have an infection which requires antibiotic treatment, so seek advice. To balance the warnings, it should be stressed that the overwhelming majority of insects don't bite people and, of those that do, the vast majority are entirely harmless. Mattresses quite often contain bedbugs and fleas, both of which are essentially harmless.

Skin infections

Any insect bite or small nick gives an opportunity for bacteria to foil the body's defences. It will surprise many travellers how quickly skin infections start in warm, humid climates, and it is essential to clean and cover the slightest wound. Creams are not as effective as a good drying antiseptic such as dilute iodine, potassium permanganate (a few crystals in half a cup of water) or crystal (or gentian) violet. One of these should be available in most towns. If the wound starts to throb, or becomes red and the redness starts to spread or the wound oozes, antibiotics will probably be needed: flucloxacillin (250mg four times a day) or cloxacillin (500mg four times a day) or, for those allergic to penicillin, erythromycin (500mg twice a day) for five days should help. See a doctor if it does not start to improve in 48 hours.

Fungal infections also get a hold easily in hot moist climates so wear 100% cotton socks and underwear and shower frequently. An itchy (often flaking) rash in the groin or between the toes is likely to be a fungal infection which will need treatment with an antifungal cream such as Canesten (clotrimazole) or if this is not available try Whitfield's ointment (compound benzoic acid ointment) or crystal violet (although this will turn you purple!).

Marine dangers

Don't swim or walk barefoot on the beach, or you risk getting coral or urchin spines in your soles or venomous fish spines in your feet. If you tread on a venomous fish soak the foot in hot (but not scalding) water until some time after the pain subsides; this may be for 20–30 minutes in all. Take the foot out of the water to top up otherwise you may scald it. If the pain returns, re-immerse the foot. Once the venom has been heat inactivated, get a doctor to check and remove any bits of fish spine in the wound.

Sharks are common in the Indian Ocean and attacks, although extremely rare, do occur from time to time. There is not much you can do about this, except to stick to beaches that are protected by coral reefs or shark nets.

Sun and heat

Although it is impossible to avoid some exposure to the sun, it would be foolish to incur it needlessly. Tanning ages your skin and it can cause skin cancer. If you are coming to South Africa from a less harsh climate, let your body get used to the sunlight gradually or you will end up with sunburn. Take things too far and sunstroke – a potentially fatal condition – may be the result. Wear sunscreen and build up your exposure gradually, starting with no more than 20 minutes a day. Avoid exposing yourself for more than two hours in any day, and stay out of the sun between 12.00 and 15.00.

Be particularly careful of sunburn when swimming or snorkelling. A shirt will protect your shoulders and a pair of shorts will protect the back of your thighs.

In hot areas, you may sweat more than normal. To counter the resultant loss of water and salt, you should drink more than normal and eat extra salt if you develop a taste for it (salt tablets are useless). Prickly heat, a fine pimply rash caused by sweat trapped under the skin, is a harmless but highly uncomfortable and common problem when people first experience a humid tropical climate, such as on the coast. It helps to wear 100% cotton clothing, splash regularly with water (avoiding excessive use of soap), dab (don't rub) the area with talc powder and sleep naked under a fan. If it's really bad, check into an air-conditioned hotel room or head for a higher, cooler place.

Mountain health and safety

South Africa boasts no peaks of the loftiness of Kilimanjaro, but there are many montane hiking areas in the region, in particular the Drakensberg.

Several climatic factors should be taken into consideration when you prepare to hike on a mountain. An increase in altitude is typically accompanied by a drop in temperature and, on clear days, by an increased ferocity in the sun's rays. Even in the tropics, many mountains are seasonally prone to fog, snow and blizzards, conditions which may descend with little warning.

Before you hike in any mountainous area, it is inadvisable to ask locally about potential weather conditions and to ensure that you are equipped for the worst. At the minimum, this means plenty of warm clothes, a windproof rain jacket, a warm sleeping bag, an insulation mat, a pair of thick socks, and solid shoes or preferably boots. Where sub-zero conditions are a possibility, you ideally want a pair of gloves and a balaclava as well. Less obviously you should bring sunglasses to counter glare, sunscreen, water bottles and an adequate first-aid kit.

If you notice foggy conditions building up as you climb a mountain, you should consider turning back, depending on where you are in relation to overnight huts or shelters. If you are unfortunate enough to be trapped in foggy or blizzard conditions, you will have to decide whether visibility is such that you can safely attempt to descend. If in any doubt, stay put. In such conditions, you will be glad of a generous food supply, even more pleased if you've made the effort to find out what rescue services exist, and delighted if you registered your name and intended route.

Hypothermia is a lowering of body temperature usually caused by a combination of cold and wet. Mild cases generally manifest themselves as uncontrollable shivering. Put on warm dry clothes and get into a sleeping bag; this will normally raise your body temperature sufficiently. Severe hypothermia is potentially fatal: symptoms include disorientation, lethargy, mental confusion (including an inappropriate feeling of well being and warmth) and coma. In severe cases, a rescue team should be summoned if possible.

Depending to some degree on speed of ascent and individual susceptibility, most people who climb to an altitude of 3,500m to 4,000m will start to feel symptoms of altitude sickness: headaches, nausea, fatigue, sleeplessness and swelling of the hands and feet. The best way to limit these symptoms is to give yourself time to acclimatise by taking the ascent slowly, eating and drinking properly, and trying not to push yourself – it's worth noting that very fit people are more prone to altitude sickness because they tend to ascend too quickly. While a certain level of discomfort is normal at high altitudes, severe symptoms require an immediate descent – even going down 300m is enough to start recovery.

Pulmonary and cerebral forms of mountain sickness can be rapidly fatal if you do not descend. Symptoms of the former include shortness of breath when at rest, coughing up blood, and gurgling sounds in the chest. Symptoms of the latter are headaches, a general lack of co-ordination, disorientation, stumbling, poor judgement and even hallucinations. The danger is that the sufferer often doesn't realise how sick he/she is and may argue against descending. Once again, you are far less likely to have such problems if you ascend slowly.

Snakebite

Poisonous snakes are widespread but rarely encountered since they generally slither away when they sense the seismic vibrations made by a walking person. You should be most alert to snakes on rocky slopes and cliffs, particularly where you risk putting your hand on a ledge that you can't see. Rocky areas are the favoured habitat of the puff adder, potentially lethal and unusual in that it won't always move off in response to human foot treads. Wearing good boots when walking in the bush will protect against the 50% of snakebites that occur below the ankle, and long trousers will help deflect bites higher up on the leg, reducing the quantity of venom injected. Snakes rarely attack people unless provoked and most snakes are harmless; even venomous species will only dispense venom in about half of their bites. In South Africa, where venomous snakes are widespread, fewer than ten snakebite fatalities are recorded annually - more people die from being struck by lightning!

In the event of a snakebite, be aware that most first-aid techniques do more harm than good. Cutting into the wound is harmful, tourniquets are dangerous, and suction and electrical inactivation devices do not work. The victim must be taken to a hospital which has antivenin. While being transported, remember that the venom will spread more slowly if the victim stays calm, and if the bitten limb is splinted and kept below the height of the heart. If you have a crepe bandage, bind up as much of the bitten limb as you can, but release the bandage every half hour.

NEVER give aspirin; you may offer paracetamol which is safe.
NEVER cut or suck the wound.
DO NOT apply ice packs.
DO NOT apply potassium permanganate.

If the offending snake can be captured without risk of someone else being bitten, take it to show the doctor, but be aware that a severed head can dispense venom in a reflex bite.

Medical care

There is no national health service, so it's best to buy comprehensive medical insurance before leaving home. Private care is excellent – as good as the best in Europe or the US – but state hospitals are generally not where you want to go in an emergency. Private doctors and treatment are expensive; in emergencies, the cost can be horrendous. Without medical insurance, private hospitals demand that you pay before being admitted. If you only do one thing before leaving home, make sure you take out a decent insurance package, preferably one that includes medical air evacuation. I learned about this the hard way. Do it!

Further reading

Self-prescribing has its hazards, so if you are going anywhere very remote consider taking a health book. For adults there is *Bugs Bites & Bowels, the Cadogan guide to healthy travel*, by Jane Wilson-Howarth. If travelling with children look at *Your Child's Health Abroad: A manual for travelling parents* by Jane Wilson-Howarth and Matthew Ellis, published by Bradt.

SAFETY

The recent and rapid changes in South Africa have caused some problems. While the police state mentality has blessedly faded, there is a severe unemployment problem; poverty is rampant in places and crime has risen sharply in many areas. Daylight muggings are frequent in downtown Johannesburg but generally, violent crime against tourists is rare.

Basic precautions apply in South Africa's cities as they would anywhere. There are a number of places you should avoid such as deserted areas and streets, and poorer areas, especially at night. Women, especially, should not walk alone in any of these places.

* Busy streets and well-used parks are safe enough but do not walk around in either the city or suburbs at night – take a taxi.
* Do not carry large amounts of cash around with you.
* Leave your valuables in a safety deposit box, not in your hotel room.
* Don't wear moneybelts. They make obvious bulges and can be cut off with electrifying ease. The front pockets of a pair of jeans are about the most effective deterrents to pickpockets I have ever experienced. You try and get your hand in there in a hurry. You are also likely to notice anyone else trying to do so.
* Blending in and not looking too much like a tourist helps. I have found that walking like I know exactly where I am going, even if I don't, generally deters trouble.

The political violence which tore the country apart in the 1980s and 1990s has all but disappeared. However, the townships are still dangerous places and you should not venture there alone or without someone you can trust to show you around.

Safety for women travellers

African women generally get a raw deal. African societies are blatantly sexist. Women do the hard work – fetching water and firewood, working in the fields, rearing children, taking care of their husbands. Polygamy is still common in rural areas. A recurring issue for Aids workers trying to educate people about the disease is that while the women generally understand the absolute necessity of using condoms, they are more often than not overruled by the men. The new constitution attempts to remove some of these inequalities, but in practice it is going to take some time to change attitudes and women travellers should be aware of these cultural considerations.

Blatant propositioning for sexual favours does happen although much depends on the time and place. Unless you have a chaperone, who is preferably a local himself, you should stay away from places like shebeens (beerhalls), certain nightclubs, townships and the less salubrious parts of the major cities (Hillbrow and Berea in Johannesburg, the Durban beachfront at night, Cape Town's inner city and the Sea Point and Bo Kaap districts at night). Naturally, minibus taxi ranks, railway and bus stations have their fair share of unsavoury characters hanging around, especially after dark, and you should take particular care in such places.

As always, common sense is your best protection. Get advice from people you can trust. You don't want to be paranoid but you must be aware of the risks.

GIVING SOMETHING BACK

South African tourism minister Valli Moosa has pinned the country's hopes on tourism as the one sector that can save its economy. South Africa's immense natural beauty, its wildlife and its culture are the main attractions, aside from the fact that the weak rand makes it a relatively cheap place to travel in. Moosa's optimism has had a great effect on many people traditionally excluded from the tourism industry as he encourages communities to invest their resources in eco-tourism. It is fair to say that the results have been mixed. But it is quite moving to see people who before had a pretty bleak future ahead of them making a go of community-based or cultural tourism.

This is the one area where travellers can make a difference. If the people on the ground see the benefits of tourism – and benefits here means jobs – then the industry has a good chance. This section deals with a few of the projects that are either community-run or indirectly contribute tourism income to where it's needed. There are many community tourism projects dotted around the country and you will more than likely stumble across some of them on your travels. The following list merely scratches the surface.

Wild Coast Horse trail

This Non-governmental organisation (NGO)-funded project is operated by the Pondoland people in an effort to let local communities benefit directly from tourism. Clever planning ensures a wide spread of revenue and benefit – everything, from horses to pillows is owned by a member of the community, which employs around 80 people. There is heavy emphasis on sustainable resource use and the empowerment of local communities and guides get training in horsemanship, river safety and catering.

Kgalagadi Transfrontier Park – the threat facing the San

A couple of San Bushmen groups are permitted to live and hunt in this huge park, just as their ancestors have done for 30,000 years, in order that their way of life is preserved for future generations, especially their own children. In an effort to generate funds for the Khomani clan, park visitors are able to join the fleet-of-foot hunters on a tracking trail through the park. The hunter-gathers have an encyclopaedic knowledge of ecosystems and possess brilliant tracking skills. The idea behind the project is that getting tourists interested in experiencing the art of tracking first hand will help preserve a vast store of indigenous knowledge that is under threat as the last of the San lose touch with their ancient way of life.

Cape Town's District Six Museum

Tour guides who are descendants of the original inhabitants of the multiracial suburb, which was bulldozed during the Apartheid era, take visitors around the old site. There are no set fees but they do ask for a donation.

Township tours

Every little town in the country has grasped the potential of taking foreigners out to the black townships to see how the other 90% live. Some tours are excellent; on others it will feel a bit like a zoo experience, especially if you are just sitting in a bus watching the dusty streets zip by. The best tours are those where you interact with real people, maybe have a drink in a proper shebeen (speakeasy). The smaller tours are often better (and cheaper.) An example is Sempiwe's Choice in Jeffrey's Bay in the Eastern Cape. Sempiwe will take you to his grandmother's house where you sit down and have a cup of tea with her.

A number of the backpackers also run tours. Ask others who've been on one what it was like before committing.

Missions

A lot of the old missions still survive, making a little extra cash on the side through the sale of farm products or craft-making. One such is Elim, near Hermanus in the Western Cape. A town of thatched cottages, founded in 1824, the mission is home to a small community of Moravian adherents. They survive on cottage industries, such as making sausages and salamis. This is cultural tourism at its least developed end and it could use a boost.

Street traders

Hawkers and traders are a significant part of the informal economy which consists largely of unemployed people who have found other ways to earn the rent. I should draw a distinction between vegetable hawkers and traders selling curios in the markets. This is one of the few places where individual craftspeople – rather than a mall-bound shopkeeper – benefit directly from tourist dollars. Many of the traders, such as the 'Doily Mamas' from Zimbabwe, spend most of the year making their wares before travelling south to earn a bit of cash. Some of them do very well, others scrape by. This is really one place where you can put something back.

Community tourism

A good example of this is at Amalienstein and Zoar, 14 miles from Ladismith in the Little Karoo. A steady decline in agriculture in recent years has meant rising poverty in the district but the locals have been proactive in preserving their heritage and luring travellers off the road. There is great accommodation in the form of the six-bed, self-catering Aunt Carolina's Guest House, Amalienstein (tel: 028 561 1000). They could use some encouragement.

Pony trekking in Lesotho

Malealea Lodge (tel: 051 447 3200; email: malealea@mweb.co.za; web: www.malealea.co.za) is very much a community development, albeit aided by the efforts of owners, Di and Mick Jones. Revenue from the treks goes directly to the horse owners and accommodation providers, into essential saddlery and equipment and to projects such as building schools and irrigation,

Around About Cars

Around About Cars in Cape Town encourage their hirees to add R1 to each day's car hire; they will match it and send all the money raised to the Ebony Orphan Fund, a Cape Town-based charity which provides underprivileged children with a chance of a decent education.

Mission work

Over the Top (tel: 083 527 7097) is a Christian adventure and tour organisation which runs trips to visit missions and can organise volunteer workers in disadvantaged communities in KwaZulu-Natal and Mozambique.

Many of the backpackers adopt or help set up community tourism projects. For example, Durban's Tekweni Lodge (tel: 031 303 1199; email: tekwenihostel@global.co.za) have their own tour company/community project offering trips to Valley of 1,000 Hills outside the city.

Budget Travel in South Africa

In the last year of the old century, the South African rand fell to an all-time low. Twenty years ago, two rands bought one pound sterling and the dollar was sitting at US$1.35 to the rand. Those were heady days for the budget traveller and they will never be seen again. But while South Africa's currency is weak, the country is not the world's cheapest place to travel in. It is true that the exchange rate will always be joyously in your favour if you are travelling with dollars, pounds, or just about any of the more valuable European currencies, but budget travellers are budget travellers.

It is easy to spend too much money. This section looks at ways of stretching your funds, travelling cheaply so that you can go longer or maybe break the budget every now and again if something special should come up. That said, budget travel isn't about skimping and making do with second best. It's about finding fresh ways to enjoy the adventure and getting something out of the experience that perhaps others, for all their luxuries, never quite grasp.

GETTING THERE

The air ticket to and from South Africa will be the single largest chunk of cash you will part with. Fortunately, South Africa, and Johannesburg in particular, is well-served by airlines. At last count, there were about 35 foreign carriers flying into Johannesburg. All this means more competition which is a good thing. The UK–Johannesburg route is one of the most competitive routes in the world, with Virgin, British Airways and South African Airways flying direct from London. The best deals, however, are usually indirect flights on other carriers. Flying London–Johannesburg on EgyptAir, for example, involves two legs, one from London to Cairo and then another to Johannesburg. Doing it this way can get you deals that can save £100 or more off the price of a direct flight. It all depends on whether you mind the stopovers. These can be anything from an hour or so to an entire night. On average, you should expect to pay between £280–550 for a Europe–South Africa ticket, depending on season and availability.

London's bucket shops are a good place to go hunting for deals. Shop around and don't say yes to anything until you are certain that they have what you want – too many unscrupulous bucket shop operators bully people into buying tickets they do not want. Even if you have made a booking with an operator, you are not obliged to take up the offer. Bucket shops advertise in the back of London's weekly *Time Out* but there is a huge bargain travel section in

TNT, the Australian/New Zealand/South Africa weekly which is distributed free outside all major tube stations. The main hassle with the bucket shops is that you are enticed with deals that they are unlikely to have. For example, an ad may quote a fantastic high-season fare of £327 London–Johannesburg return but often they only have one seat at that price (which is sold long before you phone) or the restrictions attached are unrealistic for you. Invariably you will end up paying £50 and upwards on top of any deal you see in the papers.

The explosion of e-commerce has given you another bargain hunting tool as agents, and more importantly, individuals sell tickets on-line. At the time of writing, lastminute.com was one of the best sites for cheap deals all over the world. Sample fares generated from a couple of sessions of surfing were: London Heathrow–Johannesburg return £266, Manchester–Johannesburg return £282, Glasgow–Johannesburg return £327, and London–Johannesburg direct return flight £340. All prices included taxes. The premium on the direct flight from London was a hefty £74. That's a couple of weeks worth of accommodation in the average South African backpackers' hostel.

When you fly is probably more important than how you fly. South Africa's high season is from November to February and the aircraft flying south around this time are often crammed with homesick South African immigrants going to get a dose of family love and Christmas cheer. It pays to book well in advance if you plan to head to South Africa during this time. My most expensive ticket cost me £390 one way from London to Johannesburg – with a ten-hour stopover in Dubai and a stop in the Comores – because I dallied until September before booking.

Travellers coming from the US or Australia do not have the benefit of cheap fares as there is hardly any competition on these routes. No US carriers fly to South Africa, and South African Airways monopolises the Johannesburg–Miami and New York routes, with predictable consequences. The cheapest economy fare from New York or Miami to South Africa costs US$1,400–1,700, while with an open jaws ticket via another African capital such as Windhoek or Harare will add at least another US$500 to the straight return fare. It sometimes works out cheaper for US travellers to fly via the UK, as long as you can get a decent deal across the Atlantic. Flying from direct from Australia and New Zealand is expensive, with a high season, one-way youth fare from Sydney, via Perth, to Johannesburg currently at about A$1,700. You can use a ISIC student card to get a marginal discount. Flights from Singapore, Hong Kong and India are much cheaper. Bangkok still has a reputation for being the cheapest hub in the eastern hemisphere and Khao San Road is littered with bucket shops.

GETTING AROUND

Now that you are here, you can really start saving. The main daily budget concerns are transport, accommodation and food. Cheap transport centres on train and bus travel, and cycling. You can also get very good car hire deals in some of the major centres. At some stage you may need a car, depending on where you want to go, and it makes sense to keep some money in the kitty for this.

Air

Once you've arrived in South Africa, forget about flying. SAA, the local carrier has a virtual monopoly on all domestic routes (there are other carriers but they are too small and cannot hope to match SAA's frequency). As an example, the standard economy class airfare from Johannesburg to Cape Town is R2,500 which is more expensive than the cheapest Johannesburg–London return flight. Having said that, there are some fantastic deals to be had on www.bidorbuy.com, a locally run auction website where you can pick up anything from a luxury cruise to bargain domestic air tickets. It works on a simple bidding process – check out what tickets are being offered and post your bid. You then wait to see if anyone bids above you. The site is designed so you can see exactly how high the previous bids are. I have seen one-way tickets from Johannesburg to Cape Town being offered at R50 and once an open return ticket to Paris for R950.

Train

Train travel is one of the cheapest ways to cover the long distances between the main centres. While many South Africans – invariably white – raise their hands in horror when I tell them I'm travelling by train, all the major centres are linked by reliable overnight passenger trains and with a bit of judicious planning, one can cover the country's main points by train without too much hassle. For what you get – a clean compartment, the chance to get a good night's sleep and the chance to save on a night's accommodation while looking at amazing scenery – train travel is a bargain.

There are three classes of travel – 1st, 2nd and 3rd (Economy) – but in terms of accommodation there is almost no difference between 1st and 2nd in both fare and accommodation. The only advantage of going in 1st is that you are assigned a compartment of your own whereas you will have to share in 2nd class. When the trains get full, even 1st class passengers are expected to share. Travelling in Economy is not much fun as you travel in seater coaches on hard plastic benches. Fine during the day, but miserable when you want to sleep at night.

If you do travel in Economy – and by the way, doing so will give you the opportunity to interact with real South Africans – be extra vigilant. Keep an eye on your stuff and be wary of accepting food or drink from strangers until you can trust them. It would be useful to make friends with a family group because they are likely to keep an eye on you. Women travelling alone should stay away from Economy.

The fare for the 26-hour journey between Johannesburg and Cape Town – one of the longer train rides in the country – is R390 in 1st, R264 in 2nd and about R160 in Economy. Fares for the Cape Town–Durban run, the longest ride in the country, cost R510 in 1st, R340 in 2nd and R214 in Economy. This is good value, considering that you get two nights accommodation in a decent bunk bed, unless you're travelling in Economy.

Bedding costs an extra R18 and meals in the fast-food style dining cars start at around R7.90 for *pap* (maize meal porridge) and gravy, rising to R22.95 for fish and chips. As appealing as the idea of a dining car is, it is a bit low on the style ratings and I prefer to take my own food with me. I also use my own sleeping bag instead of the bedding.

Travelling by train and bicycle will give an enormous amount of flexibility and open up parts of the country that would otherwise be difficult to reach. Bikes travel free in the guard's van.

Broadly speaking, the main hubs for South African passenger train traffic are Johannesburg/Pretoria (the 'Reef'), Cape Town and Durban. Port Elizabeth, East London, Bloemfontein and Kimberley are served by fewer trains but are useful cities to build itineraries around. Most of the trains run between the coast and inland and start or terminate in Johannesburg or Pretoria. The exceptions are the trains between Durban and Cape Town, Durban–Mozambique, Cape Town–Oudtshoorn and East London–Cape Town.

Three trains head west from Cape Town – the weekly *Southern Cross* to Oudtshoorn, the weekly *Trans Oranje* to Durban and the twice-weekly 3rd class service to East London. There are just three passenger trains from Durban – the daily *Trans Natal* to Johannesburg, the weekly eastbound *Trans Oranje* to Cape Town and a twice-weekly service to Maputo in Mozambique, via Swaziland.

Four passenger trains (two north–south, two east–west) start in or pass through Bloemfontein, and three go through Kimberley. If you end up in Port Elizabeth or East London, you have a choice of one train from Port Elizabeth and two out of East London.

For train information, tel: 011 773 2944.

List of main services

Trans Natal Overnight between Johannesburg and Durban; daily

Trans Karoo Overnight linking Pretoria and Johannesburg with Cape Town; daily

Trans Oranje Weekly service between Durban and Cape Town; takes two nights/one day

Southern Cross Weekly train between Cape Town and Oudtshoorn at the start of the Garden Route; leaves Cape Town on Friday, returns from Oudtshoorn on Sundays

Bosvelder and **Doily** Overnight trains between Johannesburg and Messina on the Zimbabwe border; daily

Diamond Express Overnight service linking Pretoria and Johannesburg with Bloemfontein, via Kimberley; daily except Saturday

Komati Overnight between Johannesburg, Pretoria and Komatipoort on the Mozambique border; connection with shuttle to/from Maputo; daily

Trans Lubombo Twice-weekly sleeper service between Maputo, Mozambique, and Durban, via Swaziland

Amatola Overnight service between Johannesburg and East London, via Bloemfontein; daily

Algoa Overnight sleeper between Johannesburg and Port Elizabeth, at the eastern end of the Garden Route; daily

Grahamstown–Alicedale Daytime service from Alicedale to Grahamstown in Eastern Cape; connects with daily Algoa.

East London–Cape Town Weekly all classes overnight service

Taxi Daytime service between Mafikeng and Kimberley

Johannesburg–Bloemfontein–Zastron Monthly overnight train, with 2nd and 3rd class accommodation only; usually runs on the Friday nearest the end of the month

Pretoria–Nelspruit–Kaapmuiden–Hoedspruit Weekly train, leaving Pretoria on Fridays, returning Sundays; on weekdays, the Kaapmuiden–Hoedspruit return service connects with the daily Komati trains

Johannesburg–Kimberley via Mafikeng Weekly overnight train leaving Johannesburg on Friday, returning on Sunday

Bus

Long-distance bus services proliferate, covering almost all the major routes. Bus companies mushroomed after the government deregulated road transport in the 1980s and long-distance luxury services became so popular that South African Railways was forced to start its own luxury coach line to compete with the other bus lines (going into competition with its own trains as a result). The major companies are **Greyhound**, **Intercape Mainliner**, **Elwierda Tours** and **Translux**, the railways own bus line.

For bus information, contact Translux (tel: 012 315 2333 or 011 774 3333), Greyhound (tel: 012 828 4040 or 011 333 3671) or Intercape Mainliner (tel: 011 654 4114).

The long-distance buses run mostly at night and are naturally more cramped than the trains (no getting up and walking around here), although they are quicker. The journey from Johannesburg to Cape Town takes about 18 hours. Sample fares are R375–390 Pretoria/Johannesburg–Cape Town, depending on which company you use, R380 Cape Town–Durban, R175 Cape Town–Port Elizabeth and R175 Johannesburg–Maputo.

Translux has the most extensive network and covers areas that otherwise would have no public transport at all, such as the back roads from George to Worcester. All three companies have joined the information age with decent websites where you can check timetabling, fares and routes. Greyhound has a frequent busser's club which works exactly like an air miles scheme (but you do have to do a lot of riding, and they also have decent low season special offers. Check out www.greyhound.co.za.

Baz Bus

The **Baz Bus** is the one service likely to be of most interest to budget travellers. Aimed firmly at the backpackers market, the Baz Bus line runs all the way along the coast between Cape Town and Durban and then either via northern KwaZulu-Natal, up into Swaziland, Mpumalanga and Johannesburg, or direct up the main N3 national road between Durban and Johannesburg. It calls at many backpackers hostels on route.

The Baz Bus runs daily in each direction between Cape Town and Port Elizabeth and four to five times a week on the other routes. You buy a single ticket but are allowed to break your journey at any point for as long as you want. Basically you buy your ticket for the whole journey and get on. Cape Town–Durban costs R900 one way, R1,300 return; Cape Town–Johannesburg via the Drakensberg costs R1,005/R1,850; and Cape Town–Johannesburg via Swaziland costs R1,250/R1,850. The quoted prices are based on a rand/sterling exchange rate of 10:1, so they may fluctuate. Visit the website: www.bazbus.com for up to date information (tel: 021 439 2323, fax: 021 439 2343, email: mailto:info@bazbus.com).

Local services
All the major cities have their own municipal bus services but efficiency and usability vary. Durban and Pretoria have the best, followed by Cape Town and then Johannesburg which has an extensive network but on a hub and spoke system which is basically useless for getting around the greater conurbation. It would literally be quicker to walk if you were going across the city. Fares are cheap – about R4 for any journey. The biggest drawback is that the buses stop running in the early evening in all the cities.

Taxi
There are two kinds of taxi – the normal passenger cars one sees worldwide and minibuses. The former are confined to the bigger cities and are expensive to use.

The minibus taxi industry is something else altogether. The result of abysmal public transport from the cities to the townships, the sector has grown at a staggering rate since deregulation into a multimillion rand business. It has brought transport to people who otherwise would have spent hours commuting to and from work by municipal bus. It is a fiercely competitive business and fares are low. White South Africans will say you are mad for using them but as long as you keep thinking, you will be fine. Your fellow passengers will probably talk about you but they will also more than likely be utterly helpful. Enjoy the thronging humanity.

Minibuses tend to work set routes in the cities and fares for short hops should be no more than R4–6, depending on distance. They can be hailed, using what seems to be a complicated variety of hand signals which indicate to the driver where you want to go – ask someone to help you. Taxis are supposed to pull over in lay-bys or in the emergency lane; in practice they stop wherever passengers want to get off, to the eternal annoyance of car drivers travelling behind them. Sometimes empty taxis will shoot right on by, no matter how frantically you gesticulate. These are generally buses from rival companies who, according to the tentative agreements thrashed out by the various associations, are not allowed to stop and pick you up.

Long-distance minibus taxis
These run between the major centres and to and from the border towns. While fares tend to be competitive, I cannot recommend using them. A good deal of the carnage on South Africa's roads is caused by overloaded or

unroadworthy minibuses or just plain atrocious driving. While taxis are supposed to be administered by one of the various taxi associations, many operators are fly-by-nighters, using unroadworthy vehicles and sometimes unlicensed drivers. A police probe into the industry discovered that unscrupulous taxi operators were importing condemned, time-expired vehicles from the Far East as scrap and then immediately putting them to use. Turf wars are also fought between taxi operators and too often, it is the innocent passengers who are quite literally caught in the crossfire.

The government has attempted to bring the lawless industry to heel by making the frequently seen minibuses illegal and forcing taxi owners to buy bigger 20-seat vehicles. While government intervention is welcome, the results have been predictable – no one is listening and the associations are carrying on as before. If you plan to use any minibuses, use your common sense first – if either vehicle or driver look dodgy, go and find other transport.

Car hire

Cheap car hire firms are thin on the ground although the growing influx of backpackers has sparked a cheap car hire boom in Cape Town. You could get to most of the country by train or bus but there are some occasions when a car would be a boon, such as when visiting some of the game reserves. In the Kruger National Park, for example, you must be in a vehicle and unless you are charming and brilliant at cadging lifts, you'll be spending a lot of time outside the park gates.

Nationally, the cheapest car agency is **Tempest Car Hire** (tel: 021 934 3845), who have branches in all the main centres. Expect to pay R120 per day including insurance, plus R0.77 per kilometre. They do have special deals for seven days or more.

You can find car hire bargains in Cape Town and the city's yellow pages are full of hire agencies. As a benchmark, **Around About Cars** (tel: 021 419 2728), an agency aimed at the backpacker market, were in mid-2000 renting out vehicles at R99 per day including insurance and unlimited kilometres.

Global Car Rental (tel: 021 423 5211) also had good deals with daily rates for the cheapest model starting at R65 per day plus R0.80 per kilometre. Naturally, the longer you rent a car, the better the deal gets.

Buying a vehicle
Cheap cars

For travellers who intend spending a few months or more in the country, it might make sense to by an old heap and run it into the ground. New car prices are high, so late-model second-hand cars hold their value. At the lower end of the scale you can get real bargains especially if you are not fussed about appearance. What you need to achieve is finding a vehicle that has been around the block but isn't about to conk out on you. The best places to search for a second-hand car are either in the national weekly *Auto Trader* or the free ads newspapers: *JunkMail* in Johannesburg, Pretoria and Durban, *CapeAds* in Cape Town.

I would investigate two price ranges: R10,000–15,000, and below R10,000. For R10,000 or more you can expect to get something like a ten-year-old Volkswagen Citi Golf with significant mileage – 150,000km and more. Cars in the price range are in average to good condition and if it has been regularly serviced you should have no problems. Do ask the driver if the car has a full service history and check it carefully if it does. Check for the services where a lot of work has been done as this could indicate the car's potential weak spots.

Below R10,000 – the place where us bargain hunters like to sniff around – the process becomes tricky. This is the world of high mileages and worn out engines, dented bodies and bent chassis. I bought a 1984 Renault 9 for R7,800 and drove it 1,000 miles from Johannesburg to Cape Town the next day. It did give me a few minor problems which, had I known anything about cars, could have been solved without relying on two half-witted mechanics as I did. Only after a year of hard driving did the car start to give me serious problems. If you go this route, it would help to know something about cars. If you don't, have a mechanic look at it or send it to the **Automobile Association** (tel: 011 799 1000), where mechanics will spend a couple of hours crawling all over the car and give an objective report on its condition. The AA test costs about R200 which the potential buyer must cover. If the owner refuses to let the AA look at the car, you have your answer – smile and walk away quickly.

The AA also publishes a free guide on what to look for when buying a second-hand car. Read this before going car hunting as spotting the obvious problem areas like oil-encrusted exhausts and hearing odd rumblings when the engine is running will save you a lot of time and anguish. The AA's technical centre (tel: 011 799 1963) may answer questions over the phone.

The car buying process is somewhat easier than in the UK and Europe but there are some pitfalls. The owner will sign the car over to you on a change of ownership form and it is then up to you to register the vehicle in your name and pay the licence fees. It helps greatly if the car comes with a roadworthy certificate (RWC); if it doesn't, you will have to put it through a roadworthy test at one of the traffic departments. If it's an old car, it will more than likely fail the test. Alternatively, take the car to a mechanic and ask him to roadworthy it for you. You will have to pay the cost of the test plus his time but it will work out a lot cheaper than trying to do it yourself.

Take the roadworthy certificate, the change of ownership forms, your passport, drivers licence and go and stand in the queues at the traffic department. You will have to pay a licensing fee which also automatically covers your third party insurance. The clerk will give you a disc which is then affixed to the windscreen. It is a bureaucratic but necessary process. The last thing to do is insure the car for fire and theft – the minimum insurance you need to take out – or comprehensively to cover your costs in case of an accident that you cause. Comprehensive insurance is not compulsory, but it is worth thinking about doing. Basic fire and theft insurance for a Citi Golf costs around R130 per month.

Land Rovers and Kombis

Many budget travellers come to South Africa hoping to pick up a cheap Land Rover or VW Kombi and live in it as they tour the country. This is viable but you should know something about these vehicles first.

Old Series III Land Rovers in good condition can be bought for R20,000–30,000 and there are loads of them about which makes finding spares easy. You should definitely have it checked out by a professional before buying as Land Rovers tend to work long, hard days in Africa. Especially check the chassis of coastal vehicles thoroughly for rust. It is worth remembering that while a second-hand Landie might be cheap to buy, it won't be cheap to run, having a prodigious thirst, and you will probably end up spending all the money you saved on bus fares and car hire on petrol instead.

VW Kombis, the classic hippie wagon, are getting thin on the ground, but you can still find a decent example for around R15,000. As with Land Rovers, it will help if you know something about them or have it checked out by a pro before buying. As touring vehicles Kombis cannot be beaten. There is loads of space to set up an entire home in the back and you will have a roof over your head whenever you need it. And that big picture window in front does a great job of letting in the view.

Motorcycles

For those who can, biking is a fab way to get around South Africa. The weather is fine more often than not and the roads, especially in the back country, tend to be empty and in excellent condition. You will also save significantly on petrol. After losing my patience with cheap cars I bought an old scrambler, and have used it extensively on my travels ever since. If you don't plan to go anywhere in a great hurry, think about getting an off-road bike as it will allow you the freedom to get to places that road bikes cannot. Whatever bike you choose should be simple, reliable, strong and have minimum electrics. Most older single-cylinder bikes – the Yamaha XT500 and Honda XL or XR500 – fit this description. Expect to pay around R6,000–7,000 for a 500 in good condition. Newer models such as the Yamaha XT600 Ténéré, the Honda XR600R and the Suzuki DR650 are faster but not necessarily much stronger. The average price for a good one will be around R12,000.

Bicycles

Probably one of the best ways of seeing Africa would be on a combined bike/train tour (the bus companies are a bit iffy about carrying bicycles). The freedom of having your bike to pedal away from the station on is priceless, not to mention the opportunity you will have of meeting local people. South Africa really is bike country, especially in the remote rural areas where public transport is patchy. It is a brilliant way of exploring those parts of the country that trains don't reach. In between cycling, you can just bung the bike in the guard's van and let someone else do the driving for a change. Mountain biking has also really taken off here and there are all sorts of trails and self-guided mountain bike adventures to be had.

Bike travel is slow and gives time for both you and the people you will be meeting to adjust to each other. As always, you should find out as much as you can about the area you intend cycling in beforehand. This will prevent you from cycling into embarrassing situations like a Transkei peasant's marijuana field.

Bike-wise, the best machine for the job is a sturdy, preferably broken-in, mountain bike with which you are familiar and, more to the point, know how to fix when things do break. Although mountain biking is really taking off, specialist spares are likely to be scarce in rural areas – bring the important ones with you. Learn how to mend your own punctures before you have to give yourself a crash course out in the bush. For further inspiration, read Dervla Murphy's *South of the Limpopo*, the story of her long ride from Zimbabwe through South Africa.

A note of concern Deciding when to go can be tricky. If you are planning a cycle tour, it is better to travel through dry, hot places like the Karoo, northern Cape and Little Karoo in winter when the days are perfect for cycling. However, winter generally – although not always in these strange, El Nino days – means persistent rain in the Western Cape, which will be utterly miserable for cyclists.

Hitchhiking

Hitching, when it works, is brilliant. It is unplanned travel in its truest sense, putting you at the mercy of other people. If I am honest, I have mixed feelings about hitchhiking, probably because I've had only mixed success with it. Certainly it has become a much more difficult way of getting around as South Africans – frightened by crime statistics and horror stories – become wary of picking up strangers. Off the main routes and without your own transport, however, hitching might be the only way of getting around. Your success will largely be determined by your physical appearance, what part of the country you are in and a good dose of luck.

South Africans throw up their hands in dismay when you tell them you are hitchhiking (they do the same about local train travel as well) and you should take some basic precautions. Incidents involving the rape and/or murder of hitchhikers have increased in the last few years. It has also happened to car drivers as well with the result that South Africans are lot more choosy about who they pick up. It is difficult to gauge the problem as people have a joyous predilection for latching on to horror stories, even when they are quite obviously the stuff of urban legend. Overall, I doubt whether it is any more dangerous to hitch in South Africa than it is in the US.

The basic rules
- Be selective about whom you accept a lift from and do not ever hike after dark.
- Women should not hitchhike, either alone or even with a girlfriend. In my experience, mixed-sex couples have a much better chance of getting a lift than a single man.

- If you can, try to hitchhike from somewhere like a busy petrol station in a town – this way you have the advantage of being able to suss out your ride before getting in the car.
- Where public transport – buses, trains or minibuses – exists, use it: save your hitching luck for when you need it.
- There is also a lot more to hitching than standing glumly by the side of the road. Stand where drivers can see you from a long way off – standing on a curve not only hides you but also raises the chances of you being hit by a car.
- Make sure there is enough room for a car to pull safely off the road to pick you up.
- Try and hitch where the traffic is moving slowly, either at an on-ramp or traffic lights.
- Look like a traveller and not a bum. Keep your backpack visible (of course, if it's a huge, horse-sized pack, no-one's going to stop anyway).
- In big cities use public transport to get to the city limits – no-one picks up hikers in cities.
- Plan your journey with a map and have a back-up plan for when things do not pan out as anticipated.
- Start early, finish early. I once set from Durban at five in the afternoon, foolishly expecting I would get one lift all the way to Jo'burg. My sixth lift of the evening dumped me 200 miles away at a remote turnoff in the middle of the Free State at three the following morning. I had no tent and no back-up plan. My mother said it was the stupidest thing she'd ever heard anyone do.

At the end of the day, hitchhiking is the ultimate expression of freedom and without a doubt one of the cheapest ways to get around. Hilary Bradt, the publisher of this excellent guide once said in a magazine interview that hitching was her favourite mode of travel. 'What could beat the generosity of strangers – or as is so often the case, their astonishing kindness? Hitching, you see, exposes us to those gestures that unite the human race. But you're also exposed to the words that push us apart. And you're forced to master the knack of communicating when there is no common language. Isn't that how travel should be.'

Riding the rods

In an ideal world, freight trains would run to every part of South Africa and I would use them as my primary mode of transport. In reality, freight hopping or hoboing – the art of illegally stowing away on a freight train – has never had the same following in South Africa as it does in America, possibly because of the presence of over-attentive railway officials. The recent decline of the network means fewer trains and the hassle of finding one going your way usually means taking a bus instead.

However, if and when the opportunity arises of riding Jack Kerouac-style, 'free means you don't have to pay', you should take it. There is nothing quite like the feeling of riding across a vast land on your own personal hot freight. It stirs the buried hobo in all of us. The best way of cadging rides on freight trains is to ask. Although it's not allowed, if there are no bosses around, you might be invited to ride up front on the locomotive. I have managed to bum lifts on two freight trains this way and both times I was treated like an ordinary, albeit freeloading, passenger.

In case you feel compelled to ride in empty freight cars, remember that being exposed to the elements at 50 miles an hour could be fatal, especially in the Karoo on a winter's night. Another absolute no-no is to jump on or off a moving train. Jumping off at any speed greater than 10 miles per hour is going to hurt and at worst you could end up under the wheels. Information is the key to successful hoboing, which means finding out where the train is going before trying to get a ride on it. If the crew says no, walk away.

ACCOMMODATION
Backpackers

The growth in budget accommodation, specifically backpackers, has been phenomenal. From almost none ten years ago, bar a few government youth hostels, there are now hundreds, even in some of the smallest towns in the Great Karoo. Some have come and gone quite quickly, others have seen out the initial flash and are thriving as backpacker tourism continues to grow.

Aside from camping, backpackers offer the best value-for-money accommodation in the country. Dorm beds usually cost R30–50 per night; the average price seems to be about R40 at the time of writing. Most establishments have begun creating or building extra double rooms following increased demand from travellers for privacy. Many travellers apparently regard the average cost of a double room at R110–130 as within their daily budget. You have to weigh up whether it's worth spending an extra R60–80 for the privilege of having your own space. If money is tight then treat yourself from time to time and save the bucks for something else.

Another welcome trend is the willingness of backpackers to accommodate older travellers and families. Many places have either family rooms or bungalows, and in some cases where the hostel spreads over two separate houses, one of them is tacitly reserved for people wanting more private accommodation.

You should make use of all the extras that the various backpackers offer. In some places, your third, fourth or fifth night will be free; other places offer free vegetarian meals once a day, or free pick-ups at the airports or railway stations. Whatever you do, do not become over concerned about your funds. You are on holiday, after all, and money worries can blow the good feeling out of a trip in an instant. If you are in a spot, ask if you can trade labour for food and lodging. Many of the places do this, and if they like you, you may even be hired, with pay.

Since everyone is thinking along similar lines, the backpackers are the best source of information and gossip on where to go next. Word of mouth from other travellers is usually the best way of finding out about deals and bargains in other places. Good places will also have a wall covered in flyers from other backpackers, tour operators, cheap car hire companies and adventure outfitters.

As budget travel booms in South Africa, it has become inevitable that some organisation needed to be applied to the sector, and the Backpacker Tourism Association of South Africa (tel: 021 424 4016) serves as a governing and standards-setting body of sorts. If you have questions about anything to do with budget travel, give them a call. Otherwise contact Lisa at Ashanti Lodge, email: Ashanti@iafrica.com, as the lodge is really the organisation's home.

A note on prices The prices given in the guide are per person for a dorm bed and per room in the case of a double or single, unless otherwise stated.

Camping

One of the best ways of saving money while travelling is to camp as often as possible. South Africans love camping and there are sites everywhere, although you'll often have to share with the caravanning fraternity. Most backpackers have campsites and prices range from R20–35, allowing you use of the kitchen and bathrooms. It's the budget way to sleep. Prices vary according to the facilities on offer as well as location. Generally, public sites will have some kind of ablution block with either flush or long-drop toilets and showers, sometimes hot ones. Prices vary enormously, from over R60 in some places down to absolutely free in others.

An advantage of lugging a tent around with you is that it gives you a degree of flexibility. In places like the Baviaanskloof or Wolkberg wilderness areas, accommodation options are invariably limited to camping. It is also special to arrive on some deserted beach in the late afternoon and be able to pitch your tent and stay there.

Game and nature reserves

One of the main reason for visiting South Africa is to see wild animals in their natural habitat and conservation is one of the country's great strengths, not least of all because its fruits are available to more than just those who can afford to stump up US$600 a night for a luxury game lodge.

The state-owned and managed reserves generally offer a high-quality but cheap game viewing experience. In the Hluhluwe-Umfolozi Park in KwaZulu-Natal, for example, self-catering hutted accommodation in the rest camps costs between R130–200 for 2- or 4-bed chalets. And this is an exquisite Big Five reserve. Accommodation in game reserves is generally in huts, chalets or bungalows and while facilities are basic, they are usually spotless. Ablution facilities may be en suite but often there will be communal shower and washing blocks. There may be a restaurant but the emphasis tends to be on self-catering.

B&Bs

Also a relatively new trend, the B&B idea has spread rapidly across the country, especially in the tourist regions. The B&B phenomenon is almost out of control, actually, with just about anyone with a spare room or two putting up a sign and opening their house for business. While backpacker rates tend to be more or less the same around the country, B&B prices fluctuate enormously, depending on the style of accommodation, the facilities on offer, proximity to notable locations or even if the owner reckons the view is worth an extra R50. In short, check it out first. You will always pay more than at a backpacker but sometimes the difference may be only R20. They are generally highly visible but Satour or a travel agent will be able to recommend some.

On recent travels, I have noticed that some backpackers are almost indistinguishable from B&Bs in terms of the accommodation and extras on offer. A lot of backpackers have superb double rooms in beautiful houses, for example, or self-catering cabins tucked away in the trees. If you have the time and the inclination, it makes sense to check out as many options as you can.

Farm stays

Farmers have started getting involved in tourism and the number of farm stay operations is growing fast. There is often little difference between a farm stay and a normal B&B except that the former are generally away from towns and villages and there is an opportunity to see a unique part of South Africa's culture. For more information on farm stays, contact Farm and Country Holiday, 8 Erin Rd, Rondebosch, Cape Town; tel: 021 689 8400.

Self-catering

There is a huge range of options in this inexpensive way of enjoying your trip. If you want a seaside flat or a cottage in the hills, get hold of Satour, the country's tourism organisation, or speak to a travel agent. Remember, prices will rocket in season, especially around December–January, and flats overlooking Cape Town's Clifton beach on the Atlantic seaboard, for example, will *always* be let out at extortionate rates.

FOOD

Food is probably the greatest budget breaker of all. You've been on the road all day, you're cold and the last thing you feel like is scrounging around in your pack for another lousy mix of tomato paste and pasta. So you hit the nearest restaurant and the next thing you know you're blinking at a R150 bill. In fact there's not much wrong with this scenario – a hard day deserves a treat but trouble starts when every day is a hard day.

By UK and European standards, food in South African restaurants is absurdly cheap, and the bill in a medium-priced restaurant will rarely be more than R100–150 per person unless some serious drinking has been going on. For South Africans, though, that's pretty steep and after a spell of travelling on a budget, you will feel it so too.

The best way to eat on a budget is to cook your own food much of the time and make use of those places that throw in free breakfasts or fish dinners. Ingredients, especially vegetables, are cheap to buy and every little town will have a supermarket of some kind. Supermarkets are generally the cheapest place to shop but you can also buy vegetables and fruit from the hawkers that seem to occupy every pavement. They need the money a lot more than the supermarket chains do.

There will be times when you can gather your own food, like collecting mussels off the rocks, fishing, or diving for crayfish, which are similar to Maine lobster but without claws. If you happen to be near a fishing village, try to buy fresh fish straight off the boats when they come in.

Diving for crayfish and abalone is a South African passion. Too much of a passion it seems – you need to apply for a permit which limits you to taking no more than four crayfish per day. Each crayfish must be measured with a special gauge, which is available from local diving and boat shops, and returned to the sea if too small. Females in berry may also not be taken. The season kicks off in November and runs through until late April. There are two ways of catching crayfish: diving for them and netting. Nets are easier but you need a boat. Diving requires only a mask, snorkel and fins, which limits your underwater time and levels the fishing field a bit. You need to clean them before cooking. This involves leaving them in a bucket of fresh water, the effect of which is to stun them and flush out their systems. Then peel the intestinal tract out of the abdomen. Boil them in lightly salted water until the carapace (shell) turns an orange red. Serve with mayonnaise dressing and white wine, on the beach at sunset and you'll make a LOT of friends.

Black mussels, for which no permit is needed, can be picked off the rocks at low tide and cooked in a pot of boiling sea water right there on the beach. Beware of red tides – upswellings of planktonic organisms which colour the sea brown, orange red or purple – which poison shellfish such as mussels, and make them fatal eating.

ACTIVITIES

South Africa's main drawcard is its natural attractions – wild animals, fine beaches, stunning scenery, adventure and outdoor pursuits and pockets of community-led eco-tourism. Inside every backpacker is a rack crammed with flyers and leaflets advertising the most amazing stuff, from shark cage diving to beach walking to flying. Most of these activities don't come cheap, which raises all sorts of dilemmas for the budget traveller. Yet many can be experienced for free or at least for relatively little money.

There are two ways of looking at this. Either you treat these things as a once in a lifetime opportunity and indulge to the full extent, or you find other ways of extracting the juice out of the South African experience.

Many travellers would rather skimp on their sleeping and eating arrangements to afford some great adventures, a trend which various backpackers' owners and managers have noticed. Others live well, eat properly and sleep in nice double rooms with sea views. And some, of course, do it all. As one traveller put it to me, 'The worst thing in the world is to come back from a trip and kick yourself for turning down unique experiences because you were too busy counting pennies.' The trick is not to waste money, nor get ripped off.

Wildlife

Thanks to a well-supported conservation department, the country boasts the best-managed wildlife reserves on the continent, with mostly stable animal populations. Driven by the promise of tourism, the process continues as more and more land is bought back from farmers and returned to its natural state.

Happily, some of the best parks and reserves are easily affordable for budget travellers. The state-owned reserves, for example the Kruger National Park, Pilanesberg Game Reserve and Hluhluwe-Umfolozi National Park, always have cheap accommodation, ranging from large resorts with chalets to small tented camps.

The country's smaller reserves, such as the Cape Mountain Zebra National Park and the Karoo National Park, are often much better value for money, especially if they do not offer the Big Five – lion, elephant, leopard, rhino and buffalo. It is often possible to have more soulful bush experiences in the smaller parks, looking at mountain zebras in the Eastern Cape or listening to jackals yip at night in the Karoo, for example.

Beaches

With more sun than rain, the beaches get a lot of attention from both locals and travellers. The whole coast is lined with beach after beach, great endless sweeps of sand, and all of it free. Boulders Beach near Cape Town is the only beach in the country where there is a nominal entry fee, which goes to pay the guard who looks after the penguins. The beaches are basically one big playground and people use them like a resource. No wonder the poor city dwellers in Johannesburg are so riven with envy.

Outdoor adventure

This one of the country's fastest growing attractions. Rafting, climbing, mountain biking, hiking, horse trails, diving, surfing, and paragliding are offered at various levels and budgets. Much of the growth in this sector has come from the backpacker market, so it tends to be competitively priced. Hiking especially is excellent value – one wilderness area charges 60p per person per day for access to a vast mountainous hiking area. These are the sorts of activities and places I will focus on.

Hiking

One of the country's greatest attractions, hiking is open even to budget travellers with the leanest wallets. In keeping with the country's reputation as an outdoor nation, South Africa is well served by hiking trails, nature reserves and mountains with footpaths and big game trails. Not much of the hiking is free (although Table Mountain is a notable exception with excellent and accessible free rambling) but the daily fees average R30 per person which is an almost nominal amount. The funds go towards the upkeep of trails and huts. The only exceptions are the big game wilderness trails which tend to be quite pricey (see below). There are also plenty of free trails, often lying within the boundaries of a park or reserve.

Hiking is a brilliant way of getting to grips with South Africa's landscapes, plants and creatures. In many areas, it is the only way of seeing the land. The Otter Trail traverses some of the southern Cape coast's most dramatic scenery and less than 1% of the visitors to this country actually get to see it. The Baviaanskloof is another example – an awesome mountain wilderness that most travellers do not even know is there. Yet all you have to do is get there, pay your R6 camping fee and hike until you drop.

It is also a phenomenally cheap way to travel. Paying R30 a day on a trail guarantees you – in most cases – a roof over your head each night and somewhere to cook food. Shelter is normally in hiking huts with bunks and mattresses, with fully equipped kitchens, and even showers on some trails. There is drinking water (often from a mountain stream and not a tap). In some wilderness areas, you pay a one-off entry fee for a permit and then a nominal amount, say R10 a night, to camp. That's your accommodation taken care of.

Hiking is a popular in South Africa and trails are often booked months in advance. It makes sense to plan the hiking side of your trip before you set off. One advantage travellers will have over locals is that they are usually able to do trails during the week which is when they tend to be emptier, although the Otter Trail proves that this isn't always the case (see below).

Trails are the gift of various government departments and agencies. Some are owned and operated by the various provincial nature conservation organisations, others run through forests and are controlled by forestry companies, and others might run across private land with access handled by farmers. This may seem confusing, but if you want to do a trail that isn't mentioned in the book, contact the Hiking Federation of South Africa (tel: 011 316 1242). As the country's wildernesses and nature reserves keep expanding, many trails now run across national parks and access is controlled by South African National Parks Office (tel: 012 343 1991; email: reservations@parks-sa.co.za). In the case of wilderness areas like the Baviaanskloof, there is no formal point-to-point trail but rather a network of hiking paths on which you set your own itinerary.

The local hiking scene has been exceptionally well managed by the various departments. Paths are maintained and huts are in good shape. A key strategy has been to limit the number of hikers on all trails. On some this might be no more than 30 people per hut or section a day; on other treks like the fabulous Otter Trail, it is a mere 12 people per day. While this does mean that you will have some privacy, the downside is that it can be impossible to get a spot on your chosen date. The Otter Trail (see page 160), for example, has a one-year waiting list. That said, some people book a year ahead and are unable to take up their booking or even just don't bother to pitch up at the trailhead. If you are in the area it is worth arriving early in the morning and asking if there is room. I have heard of people pulling this one off.

The unfortunate exceptions to the cheap hiking scene are the big game trails in game reserves such as the Kruger National Park or Umfolozi Game Reserve. These very popular but specialised trails can be anything from 1 to 6 days long, trekking through raw bush country with all the real excitement of having to stay out of the way of often cantankerous wild animals, including buffalo, elephant, rhino and just about all the predators. This means having an armed guard as well as a full support set-up. You stay in a fully equipped camp and your meals are taken care of. Prices start at about R1,000, putting them out of the scope of this guide. Of course, to track wild animals on foot in real Africa might just be worth blowing a hundred quid.

Adventure travel

Adventure activities are one aspect of the South African experience that will not be cheap, certainly not as cheap as going on an overnight hike. Yet the growth in activities such as whitewater rafting, sea-kayaking, scuba-diving, canyoning, climbing and mountain biking, among others, has been extraordinary. It really comes down to what the average budget traveller is prepared to pay. A six-day canoe trip down the Orange River in the Northern Cape will cost around R900, about a quarter of the price of an air ticket from London.

The budget traveller scores when he or she can do these things on his or her own. If you are an experienced river runner, say, there's nothing to stop you hiring boats and gear and organising your own trip down the Orange River. Just get advice first. A less extreme example is that of whale watching. You have the choice of forking out R200–300 to go out and approach them by boat, or you can stand on the shore at Hermanus with a pair of binoculars and often get a better view than you would have from the water.

If you do choose to go on some of the adventures on offer, cost factors should not be an issue when choosing an operator. Most of these activities are described as 'adventure' because they entail some sort of risk to the participant. If you are inexperienced you are putting your life in someone else's hands. This is not to say that cheap operators are more dangerous than expensive operators, but rather that you should do some research and go with the company that has the best reputation, regardless of what kind of tight budget you may be travelling on.

BUDGET ITINERARIES

The fact that there are great distances between some of the country's prime tourist attractions poses a problem for some travellers, especially if time and money are tight. The Cape and the Garden Route are a long way from the bushveld where the wild animals are to be seen, good news for any Capetonians who are afraid of creatures of the night, but not very helpful for budget travellers who want to soak up the Cape's incredible beauty and see some wildlife.

Given the size of the country, you really need to plan your time here carefully. Two weeks is about the minimum length of stay I would recommend; a month (or two) would be better. While you could cover a lot of ground in a two-week visit, if you're using public transport, a lot of your holiday is going to be spent in transit. If you do visit for a shorter time, I would suggest hiring a car for the most efficient travelling.

You could also make your life a lot easier by getting an open-jaws air ticket which would allow you to enter the country via one city and leave by another.

However, these are always more expensive than straight returns because of the imbalances they cause. The best open-jaws deal would be to fly into Johannesburg and out of Cape Town. Durban's proximity to the national parks at St Lucia, Hluhluwe-Umfolozi and the Drakensberg makes it a useful start or end point, but it is served by fewer flights than Jo'burg or Cape Town.

Overall, the best advice is not to get too hung-up on an itinerary. Aside from catching your flight at the end of the trip, you really have nothing to worry about except having fun. Go with your instincts: if some particular place appeals then spend more time there. Remember too that travel in Africa – especially away from the urban centres – often makes a mockery of schedules. If that happens, kick back, watch the scene unfold and have fun.

Some suggested ways of getting the most out of little money in South Africa:

Using public transport
Itinerary 1: Two weeks
Broadly, try to spend a week each in Cape Town and one of the game reserves.

Fly into Johannesburg. Overnight train to Nelspruit for guided visit to Kruger National Park (2 nights). Train to Cape Town (via Johannesburg). Exploring Cape Town and environs (3 nights). Baz Bus up Garden Route – stopping at Wilderness, Knysna and Plettenberg Bay en route (3–4 nights) – to Port Elizabeth. Overnight train to Johannesburg.

If you fly into Cape Town instead, keep the same route but end the trip with four or five days in Cape Town – there is no finer place to rest before flying on elsewhere.

Itinerary 2: Three weeks
One extra week could make all the difference, allowing you divide your time more or less equally between Cape Town and surrounds, the Garden Route and one of the national parks. You're still going to be pretty rushed on public transport, but it is doable, especially if you use buses along the coast.

a) Fly into Johannesburg, catch overnight train to Cape Town. Explore region – Cape Town (4–5 nights) winelands, Hermanus in whale season (3 nights). Overnight train to George/Oudtshoorn (1 night). Baz Bus up Garden Route, stopping at Wilderness, Knysna, Plettenberg Bay, Storms River (4–5 nights), to Port Elizabeth (1 night). Overnight trip to Addo Elephant Park (1 night). Overnight train to Johannesburg (1 night) then train to Nelspruit for Kruger National Park (3 nights).

b) Same route as above until Storms River but then Baz Bus up Wild Coast, stopping at Cintsa (2 nights), Port St Johns (1 night) and on to Durban (1 night). Baz Bus to Hluhluwe-Umofolozi National Park (2 nights) and St Lucia Wetland Park (1–2 nights). Return to Durban and take the overnight train to Johannesburg.

Itinerary 3: One month
Same basic route as above but allows you to spend more time in various places and not be rushed. Alternatively, head north from Durban, via Hluhluwe-

Umfolozi, to Swaziland (the Baz Bus runs all the way) and make your way northwards to Nelspruit and continue the Kruger Park itinerary from there.

Using a hire car

With a car the routes stay pretty much the same except that you obviously have much more flexibility regarding journey times and distances. A car also gives you the luxury of getting to places that other forms of transport – buses, trains and taxis – do not reach.

A good way of maximising your travel efficiency would be to travel on public transport where you can and hire a car from a budget rental operation to get to those otherwise out-of-the-way places. This option works especially well in Cape Town which has plenty of cheap car hire agencies and a lot of surrounding country that is poorly served by public transport. It usually works out cheaper to hire a car only for short forays (eg: from Port Elizabeth to the Baviaanskloof) but this is not always so. Do some shopping around, too, especially out of season, when many companies have special offers, or may be willing to strike a deal.

Note that car hire companies – especially the budget ones – might not allow you to pick up the car in one city and drop it off in another, and those that do often whack on a hefty surcharge. Factor a circular route into your travel plans.

The following itineraries are suggested as add-ons to the basic routes described above and thus will demand a little more time:

Itinerary 1: Cape West Coast and Overberg

From Cape Town, drive north up the West Coast to Paternoster and Tietie se Baai and then east into the Cedarberg. In flower season (August–September) keep heading north into Namaqualand for awesome flower displays. From there you can head east over the mountains to Calvinia (best done in winter) for spectacular desert scenery, or take southeast loop through Ceres, Prince Alfred's Hamlet, and down into the Overberg. Take a circular route from Swellendam, via Arniston and Cape Agulhas to Hermanus and back to Cape Town on the coastal road. Time: 1 week

Itinerary 2: Cape Town via Little Karoo to Garden Route

Head east from Cape Town, through the winelands and mountains to Montagu. Take the R62 to Barrydale, Ladismith and into the Little Karoo. Turn south at Oudtshoorn and head for George, or keep heading east along the R62, down the Langkloof, to Port Elizabeth. Continue with one of the above itineraries. This route works best if your car hire company allows you to drop off the car in George or Port Elizabeth, but it is also a superb circular route, returning to Cape Town along the coast. Time: 4–7 days.

Itinerary 3: Drakensberg and KwaZulu-Natal battlefields

Public transport to Durban. Then by hire car, via Pietermaritzburg and Midlands, to Drakensberg. Spend time working along the base of the mountains, staying in backpackers or camping, and doing day hikes into the 'Berg. Head northeast, via Ladysmith and Dundee, into Zululand. Take guided tour of battlefields at Rorke's Drift and Isandlwana. Head east to national parks at Hluhluwe-Umfolozi and St Lucia, returning south to Durban. Time: 7–10 days

The ultimate itinerary

Time, not money, is usually the main obstacle to budget travel. Given time – 2–3 months – this is how I would see South Africa, using the cheapest transport available, camping as much as possible and cooking my own food.

Fly into Cape Town. Head north up the West Coast, camping at Paternoster and Tietie se Baai. With luck I would catch my own fish off the beach; otherwise, there are always fishermen around to buy fresh fish from. Bus north to Upington to visit the Augrabies Falls National Park, and break the budget a bit on a multi-day rafting trip down the Orange River where it runs through the desert.

Bus to Johannesburg or Pretoria for a few days in Africa's most booming urban conurbation. Use local transport to get into the Magaliesberg for hiking. Train to Nelspruit. Spend a few days in the Kruger National Park, using independent operator for transport.

Bus south to Swaziland for a different taste of Africa and then Baz Bus to national parks at Hluhluwe-Umfolozi and St Lucia, returning south to Durban by bus. Side trip from Durban to Drakensberg, using buses and local taxis. Baz Bus south from Durban to Wild Coast for horse trail and hiking. Time permitting, hike the Wild Coast from Port St Johns to Coffee Bay – a nice break from vehicles.

Bus to Cintsa and then on to Port Elizabeth. Side trips from PE to Baviaanskloof, Addo Elephant Park, and Mountain Zebra National Park. Bus down Garden Route, visiting Tsitsikamma National Park, Storms River, Nature's Valley, Plettenberg Bay, Harkerville and Knysna.

Steam train from Knysna to George, stopping in Wilderness. Side trip from George over Outeniqua Mountains to Oudtshoorn. If possible, arrange lift over Swartberg Mountains to Prince Albert in the Karoo. Return to Oudtshoorn, take overnight train or Baz Bus to Swellendam.

Bus from Swellendam to Cape Town. Explore Cape Town and surrounds by bicycle, minibus taxi and on foot. Side trips to Hermanus (excellent whale watching July–November) and winelands around Stellenbosch/Paarl. Spend time on Cape Town's fine beaches and winding down from trip before flying out.

SOUTH AFRICA FOR FREE
Activities

- Walk on Table Mountain. All routes are free and there are enough paths to keep you busy for years. All you need is a map (available from Cape Town Tourism, tel: 021 426 4260) and a good pair of hiking shoes or boots

- Catch your own fish or crayfish and cook it on the beach
- Take a free tour of Parliament
- Watch the whales frolic in Walker Bay, August–October
- Cycle along the Cape Peninsula
- Lie on a beach. You have 2,500km of coastline to choose from
- Check out an African sunset
- Feed the squirrels in the Company Gardens
- Visit the country's craft and fleamarkets

Free museums
- Dias Museum complex, Mossel Bay
- The Holocaust Museum in Hatfield Street, Gardens, Cape Town
- District Six Museum in Buitenkant Street (by donation)
- The Archives in Roeland Street, Cape Town
- Cape Medical Museum (by donation)
- Michaelis Old Townhouse, Greenmarket Square, Cape Town
- Rust-en-Vreugd Museum, Cape Town
- SA Air Force Museum

Free festivals
Festivals by their nature are free spectacles but you'll have to pay as soon as you want to eat or drink something. Looking costs nothing, though.

- Knysna Oyster Festival; July
- The Cape Minstrels Carnival; December–January
- University of Cape Town Rag Show
- Cape Women's Festival; August
- One City Festival; September
- Observatory Festival; December

Part Two

The Guide

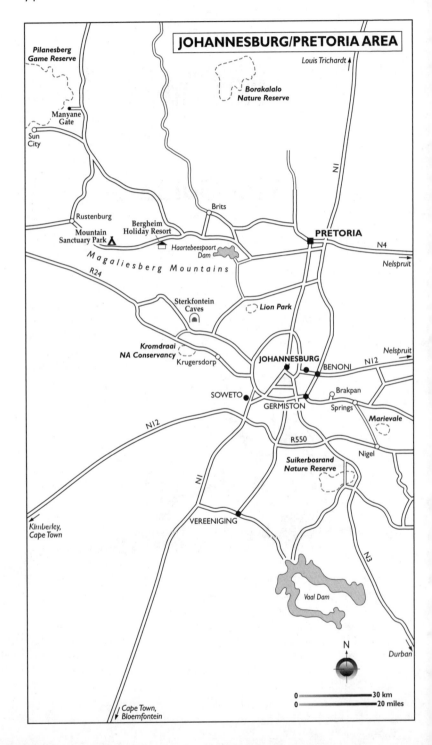

The Capital Cities

South Africa really has two capitals – Pretoria, the seat of government, and Johannesburg, which is the economic heart of the country and the most frenzied city in Africa. They are, officially, 35 miles (50km) apart and on different planets as far as the state of mind in each is concerned, but because Johannesburg has been sprawling northwards for decades, the two cities have become one vast conurbation.

Both are in Gauteng province, the smallest province in the republic but home to over 10 million of its people and accounting for about 65% of its GDP. It's likely that many travellers coming to South Africa will pass through one or both cities at some stage of the journey (most international flights arrive and depart from Johannesburg) and both places have some charm, although you may have to dig for it. But they are certainly not holiday centres, very definitely not so in parts of Johannesburg.

PRETORIA

The official seat of government, Pretoria was the first of the two cities to be founded. It was named in 1854 as the *kerkplaas* (church place) for the central Transvaal and became the capital of the new independent Voortrekker republic in 1860. The settlement was named after Voortrekker leader Andries Pretorius who had prevailed over the Zulu army at the gory battle of Blood River in 1838 (see page 16).

The city lies in the valley of the Apies River, somewhat lower and warmer than Johannesburg. The warm climate was ideal for exotic plants and people were crazy about roses here in the early days. The arrival of jacaranda trees from South America in 1888 altered the city forever and when the trees blossom in late spring, the city looks as if it's lying under a purple blanket created by the flowers of an estimated 70,000 trees.

Pretoria was never much more than a sleepy farming town, until the Anglo–Boer War when it became the focus of nationalist fervour. Even today it has that feel of a town which became capital almost by accident – there doesn't seem to be much urgency about the place. It might be the heat, which can be dreadful in summer, or perhaps it's part of the general lack of excitement that plagues seats of government everywhere, except perhaps London. It's a place of wide, tree-lined avenues and a collection of government

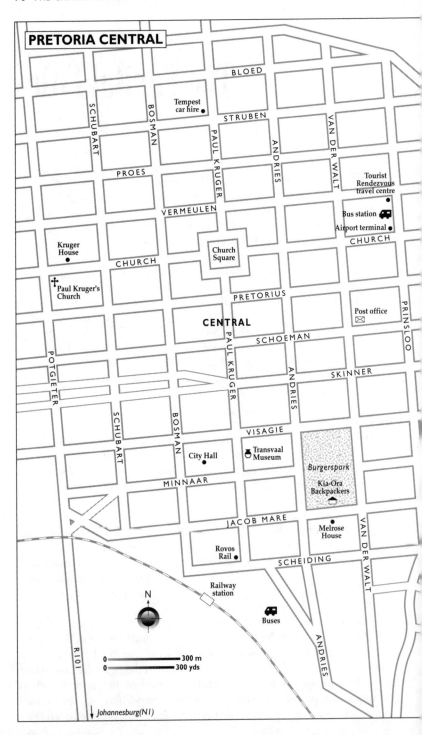

PRETORIA CENTRAL

BLOED

Tempest car hire

STRUBEN

SCHUBART

BOSMAN

PAUL KRUGER

ANDRIES

VAN DER WALT

PROES

VERMEULEN

Tourist Rendezvous travel centre

Bus station

Airport terminal

CHURCH

Kruger House

CHURCH

Church Square

Paul Kruger's Church

PRETORIUS

Post office

PRINSLOO

CENTRAL

POTGIETER

PAUL KRUGER

SCHOEMAN

ANDRIES

SKINNER

SCHUBART

BOSMAN

VISAGIE

City Hall

Transvaal Museum

Burgerspark

Kia-Ora Backpackers

MINNAAR

JACOB MARE

Melrose House

VAN DER WALT

Rovos Rail

SCHEIDING

N

Railway station

Buses

R101

0 ———— 300 m
0 ———— 300 yds

ANDRIES

↓ Johannesburg(N1)

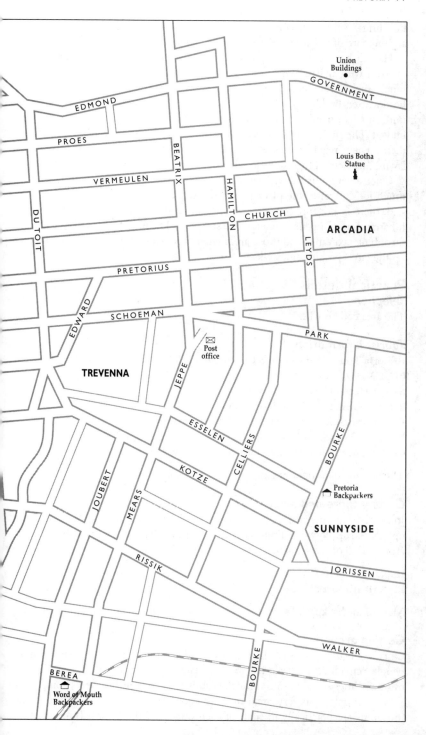

buildings, some of which are beautiful colonial structures, while the architecture of the remainder is ghastly 1960s government-style.

Having been the seat of government more or less since 1854, Pretoria is overrun with civil servants, soldiers and diplomats. In the 1980s, the streets at lunch times were packed with military personnel as the city was full of headquarters buildings, military depots and bases, but the steady stream of brown uniforms has, thankfully, all but disappeared along with the country's defence budget. The civil servants are still there, though, and the city would sink without them. The foreign embassies, usually lovely residences in acres of manicured lawns, lurk behind high walls in quiet tree-lined streets east of the city centre.

Once a very white city, Pretoria is slowly adapting to Africa and there is a much looser feel to the place than there was even just a few years ago. That said, there is a deeply conservative aura about the place and it is nothing like Johannesburg for general energy and streetlife. The most vibrant places are the throbbing taxi ranks and those areas where the hawkers have edged their way up the city's pristine sidewalks.

Practical details
Telephone
The area code is 012.

Tourist information
Pretoria Tourist Information Centre Sammy Marks Centre, Vermeulen St; tel: 012 333 4337
Satour Head Office Tel: 012 347 0600
Train information Tel: 012 315 2436
Bus information Translux; tel: 012 334 8000 or Greyhound; tel: 012 323 1154
National Parks Board 643 Leyds St, Muckleneuk; tel: 012 343 1991; fax: 012 343 0905. For reservations for all national parks and some hiking trails.

The various **backpackers** are also excellent sources of information.

Getting there and away
Johannesburg International Airport serves both cities and a couple of bus operators run between Pretoria and the airport. The fare should be around around R50 one way, depending on who you go with.

Impala Tel: 012 323 1429
Pretoria Airport Shuttle Tel: 012 346 3175

Most of the backpackers run their own airport shuttles so give them a call first.

Getting around
Once again the echoes of the old apartheid economy ring clear. Most white people remain firmly wedded to their cars, one person per car, while the municipalities scratch around for the funds to keep their bus fleets going.

The central area is very small and easily done on foot or bicycle. Most of the museums are practically in sight of each other and the Union Building, the beautiful seat of government, is no more than a 25-minute walk northeast of the central Church Square. As cities go, Pretoria with its slower pace, wide streets and reduced traffic levels is one of the safer South African cities to cycle in, but take care. Generally South Africa's urban drivers don't win any prizes for being nice to cyclists, or to each other, for that matter.

Most of the backpackers are based in eastern suburb of Sunnyside or in Hatfield but Pretoria's municipal bus service is a lot better than its Johannesburg counterpart. Buses run on a hub-and-spoke system from the main terminus at the southeast corner of Church Square in the centre of the city. Fares are quite low (about R3) but the services are not as frequent as one would like. However, the bus to Sunnyside, east of the city, runs until 22.30, which is a miracle in South African municipal bussing. Getting to the Voortrekker Monument and SA Air Force Museum will require a taxi, hitchhiking or a bit of creative thinking.

Normal meter taxis can be taken from designated taxi ranks or booked over the phone but, unlike many other cities, meter cabs cannot be hailed in the street. The no-hailing rule is an odd hang-over from the days when the country's public transport was heavily regulated and one that seems grotesquely out of place given the near-chaos that exists in the now unregulated minibus industry. These taxis are expensive but if it's after dark and you're lost, do not hesitate to use one.

Pretoria is a major rail centre, with lines radiating in all directions, including the main lines to the northeastern part of the country and Mozambique, and north to Messina and Zimbabwe. Some of the country's state-run passenger trains start their journeys here and three others pass through daily. There is a regular commuter train service with trains running from Pretoria to the outlying townships and to Johannesburg, a one-and-a-half hour journey which costs about R10 in 1st class (there is no 2nd). Don't go to the townships, nor on the commuter trains, unless you are with someone you trust and who can show you around. Trains to Johannesburg run every half-hour early in the morning and then hourly until 22.00 during the week and one-and-a-half hourly on weekends.

Safety

Pretoria seems largely to have escaped the crime wave which hit Johannesburg and other parts of the country in the early 1990s, possibly because this is after all a military city. Many refugees from Johannesburg have set up home here, preferring the daily purgatory of commuting to fearful living in the Golden City. However, criminals have followed the money (diplomats' luxury saloons seem to be a favourite target) and standard precautions apply. Try not to walk around after dark in the city centre or around the railway station and do not carry valuables openly. If you arrive at night, take a taxi from the station or airport.

Accommodation

Word of Mouth 430 Reitz St, Sunnyside; tel: 012 343 7499; email: wom@mweb.co.za. Double R120, single R80, dorm R40. WOM also has 2-person loveshacks for R100. Famous, centrally located backpackers with excellent internet café with equipment such as scanners and fax services. It has a reputation for being a budget travel centre.

North South Backpackers 355 Glyn St, Hatfield; tel: 012 362 0989; fax: 362 0960; email: northsouth@mweb.co.za. Double from R120, dorm oom R25, camping R25. Situated in the popular Hatfield district, close to restaurants, bars, clubs and shops. The house is set in a big garden with a pool. An airport shuttle is available. The Baz Bus stops here as well.

Kia Ora 257 Jacob Mare St; tel: 012 322 4803; fax: 322 4816; email: kia-ora@iafrica.com. Double R130 per person, dorm R40. One of the country's oldest backpackers. Meals are available but there is a big kitchen for self-catering. Near station but offers free lifts. Baz Bus stops here. Also agents for Greyhound and Intercape buses.

Pretoria Backpackers 34 Bourke St, Sunnyside; tel: 012 343 9754; fax: 343 2524; email: ptaback@netactive.co.za. Centrally located hostel which is spread out over two adjoining properties so there is plenty of space. It has a pool, free bike hire and free soup every night during the winter. Pick-ups in Pretoria are free, the hourly airport shuttle costs R55 per person. Producing an ISIC student card will earn you a 15% discount on long-distance bus tickets.

Things to see and do
Buildings and monuments
Some of Pretoria's colonial buildings survive, most notably president **Paul Kruger's house**, a modest single-storey building which is now a museum, where he would sit on the *stoep* (verandah) and hold court, ruling the country from his rocking chair. On the whole, the dominant architectural theme seems to be 1960s government-inspired blandness. Apart from Kruger's house, other buildings worth looking at are **Melrose House** (275 Jacob Mare Street), a neo-Baroque mansion where the treaty ending the Anglo–Boer War was signed, and the impressive **Union Buildings**, east of the city centre on Church Street. The red sandstone Union Buildings were designed and built by Sir Herbert Baker (the man behind many of South Africa's better looking constructions) and are utterly perfect for a seat of government, with a commanding view across a huge expanse of well-trimmed lawn and gardens and into Pretoria. Stand on the expansive lawns below the buildings and imagine nearly a million people cheering the crowning of their new president, Nelson Mandela, just as it happened one bright May day in 1994.

The skyline just south of the city is dominated by two incredible structures. To the east is the ugly University of South Africa administration block, to the west, a towering slab of granite called the **Voortrekker Monument**. The monument, 6km south of the city centre, is the one to visit. Built in 1938 in lasting memory of the Voortrekkers (see page 16), it reflects a time when Afrikaner nationalism was surging. Over 250,000 people came to the opening ceremony and it is an intense symbol for the Afrikaner people. The inside walls are a detailed bas-relief history of the Great Trek. There are depictions of wagon trains rumbling over the vast wastes of the interior, epic struggles of mountain crossings and plenty of battle scenes including the battle of Blood River when in 1838 200 Boers inside a laager (encampment) of wagons annihilated a Zulu force of over 6,000 warriors without the loss of single man. On December 16, the anniversary of Blood River, a shaft of sunlight falls through the roof and lights up the inscription *Ons Vir Jou Suid Afrika* (we for you, South Africa) on a cenotaph in the basement of the monument. The views from the dome and the roof are awesome.

Museums

The **Museum of Natural History** in Paul Kruger Street is worth a look, not least for the massive whale skeleton excellently mounted outside. The **Transvaal Museum**, also on Paul Kruger Street, has an excellent fossil collection. *Open Mon–Sat 09.00–17.00, Sun 11.00–17.00. Admission R6 (R3 for children).*

Two superb art museums are the **Pierneef Museum** (Vermeulen Street), a tribute to a distinctive landscape painter, and the **Pretoria Art Museum** (Schoeman Street) which contains the works of South Africa's finest – or at least best-known – artists. *Open Mon–Fri 08.30–16.00. Admission free.*

The **South African Air Force Museum** is one of the best aviation museums in the world, sprawling over a large corner of Air Force Base Swartkops, 10km south of the city. The collection includes a large number of airworthy planes which are flown at airshows and museum open days, and covers the country's entire aviation history, not just military flying. *Open Mon–Sat 10.00–16.00. Admission free.*

The **National Zoological Gardens** (tel: 012 328 3265) are regarded as the country's best. If you like zoos then go as you will not be disappointed. However, since you are in Africa, it makes better sense to see wild animals in their natural environment instead. *Open daily 08.00–17.30. Admission R18 (children R12).*

Outside Pretoria
The Magaliesberg

The Magaliesberg mountain range is one of South Africa's best-loved places. Approaching from the south, it rises up in a great 120km-long wall of quartzite and red sediments – its highest point is 1,852m above sea level – with a more gentle slope to the north. Countless streams have carved great, deep kloofs (gorges) into the northern slopes, and even in the dry mid-winter the rivers run clear and clean from sources at top of the range. Natural forest grows thickly in the cool, dark *kloofs* and in summer the deep pools are a beautiful relief from the thick heat.

The range is crisscrossed with hiking paths, most of which start at the foot of the northern slopes. Much of the land, unfortunately, is privately owned and access is restricted, with many of the land owners adopting a preservationist approach to their stewardship of it.

However, there are still some excellent public walks and campsites. One of the best camping spots is **Mountain Sanctuary Park** (tel: 014 534 0114), a spacious campsite on the north side of the range about 45 minutes' drive from

Pretoria. Staying in the park allows you access to a wonderland of wind-eroded sandstone outcrops, deep *kloofs* and lovely swimming holes in two of the mountain streams. A couple of paths head up the slopes and a two hour walk brings you to the edge of the range and a superb view of Hartbeespoort Dam far below. Wildlife includes grey duikers and klipspringers (both small antelope), baboons, vervet monkeys and there are resident leopards although you will be extremely fortunate to see one. The sites to go for are under the trees on the western side of the camp. You can make barbecue fires at the designated spots. Firewood is supplied and costs very little. Camping costs R30 per adult, R25 per child plus R10 for a vehicle. You must book ahead. It will be tough to get here without your own transport but there should be minibus taxis from Pretoria to the settlement of Maanhaarand. Get off at the Utopia turnoff and hike about 4km up to the park. Better still, arrange a lift through the backpacker or guesthouse.

Tonquani Kloof is a beautiful and deep gorge right next to Mountain Sanctuary Park. Tonquani is better known in some circles as one of the country's best rock climbing areas, offering dozens of routes of all grades on sun-baked sandstone. Traditional rather than sport climbing on bolted routes is the dominant form here, so if you are a climber, you will need a full climbing rack. Tonquani is owned by the Mountain Club of South Africa (tel: 011 807 1310), from which you will have to get a hiking or climbing permit. You will also need a tent if you plan to stay overnight. Although getting the permit is an extra hassle, it does mean that numbers are restricted, with the result that you can camp more or less anywhere among the sculpted boulders above the *kloof* and you are unlikely to run into hordes of other campers, even at weekends.

Also on the northern slopes and a tiny bit closer to Pretoria is **Bergheim Holiday Resort** (tel: 014 537 2363), which offers access to a number of *kloofs*. The area is thick with hiking and scrambling opportunities. One of the best hikes involves quite a bit of swimming in icy cold pools but it is terrific adventure. There are also a couple of bolted routes for sport climbers. Bergheim's accommodation ranges from six-bed *rondawels* (round huts) for R330 down to R130 per night for a two-bed hut. Camping costs R15 per person per day, while day visitors pay R6 per car and R6 each for a permit.

If you want to see cheetah, wild dogs and maybe a couple of the smaller cats, head for **De Wildt Cheetah Sanctuary** (tel: 012 504 1921), near Brits, about 30 minutes' drive from Pretoria. The centre is a research and breeding centre for cheetah and has a few healthy king cheetah specimens, so-called for their rare and distinctive markings. The centre also looks after a large pack of wild dogs along with a couple of brown hyenas, caracals (similar to the North American lynx) and servals. Although the animals live in large, separate enclosures, giving the place a bit of a zoo-like feel (albeit a very spacious one) it is a breeding centre rather than a game reserve. At least a cheetah-sighting is guaranteed. Entrance costs R90 per person including a game drive in an open game viewing vehicle.

JOHANNESBURG

People who live here might tell you it's Africa's most vibrant city and the continent's second-most populated after Cairo. They might also fill your head with horror stories of crime and violence. The broad picture of Jo'burg (also known in tsotsi-slang as *Jozi* or *Egoli* – the City of Gold, a somewhat tarnished moniker since the decline of its gold-mining fortunes) is a vast conurbation of very rich and very poor, a city without a centre. The former downtown business district has almost ceased to exist as companies flee the city for the perceived safety of the suburbs; shopping malls and office parks now dominate the suburbs which themselves keep on spreading away from the centre. The amount of petty crime in the city centre is the main reason behind this exodus. It is an unfortunate trend because as big companies move out so do the coffee shops, lunch-time delis, bookshops and the like. There are plans to revitalise the city centre, in much the same way as some of America's inner cities have been revived, but this depends on the will of businesses to move back to the centre.

The city is built on the Witwatersrand (the ridge of white waters), a low range of rocky hills where George Harrison – no relation to the Liverpool one – discovered a gold outcrop in 1886. The area is known locally as the Reef, after the line of rich, gold-bearing ore which runs east–west, from Springs to Randfontein and beyond. The city owes its existence to gold and greed, something which has tainted its soul. Two things stand out about Johannesburg: it is one of the world's only major cities not built on or near a body of water, and it apparently has more trees (mostly exotics, planted to provide shade on the otherwise bare expanses of veld) than any other city on earth. It is also the country's undisputed crime centre and a good number of tourists have found themselves at the wrong end of a gun or knife. However, although you are likely to pass through Jo'burg at some stage on your travels (the city is still the region's airline hub), with a little bit of commonsense you can make an interesting time of it (see *Safety*, pages 87–8).

The city started out as a shabby mining camp, a lawless, rough place like mining towns everywhere. It feels pretty lawless these days too, or at least that's what people will take perverse delight in telling you. Its redeeming features are its incredible climate, energy and money. Jo'burgers work hard and relax hard and testosterone and adrenalin levels are high. It can be a fascinating place to visit, even if just see how people live. It's not a place to relax in.

The city is about money and this has been its lure since the beginning. When rural communities falter or little country towns go bust, their inhabitants invariably end up migrating to Johannesburg. The result is a constantly swelling population and a massive growth in what are known in polite circles as 'informal settlements', squatter camps or ragged collections of shacks made from wood, iron and bits of plastic (townships to you and me).

The downtown district bustles with a different energy as it transforms itself into an African city. Hawkers selling everything from vegetables to *muthi* (traditional medicine) line the pavements and the air is thick with the

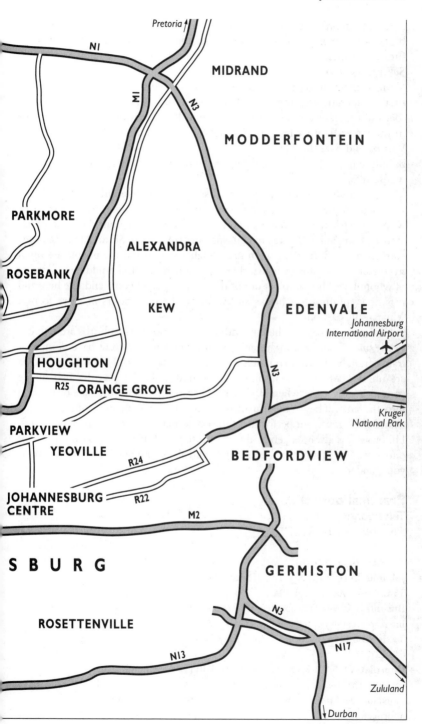

smell of onions and *boerewors* (thick, farmer's sausage) being cooked on braziers. It's messy but alive and you should go and see it because it is the future Johannesburg. Just take very good care if you do go downtown (see *Safety*, page 87).

Since the country's borders opened to the rest of Africa following the first democratic elections in 1994, Johannesburg has become the intense focus of much of the rest of the continent. If you go downtown, the babble in the streets is now French, Portuguese and the unfamiliar lilt of Wolof, Yoruba and Swahili. Home to about 10 million people, Johannesburg is a bubbling pot although it might not be cooking the way many white people would like.

North of downtown are the suburbs which look like affluent suburbs do anywhere in the world, except for the often obscenely high walls with razor wire or electric fences on top and the signs put up by 24-hour armed response security companies. There are fantastic opportunities in South Africa but they come at a price: the dogs seem more highly-strung and the people are often hyper-tense. The upside is that there is an emerging black middle class, many of whom have chosen to get out of the townships and come and live here and it is now common for blacks and whites to be neighbours in these former whites-only bastions.

Choose your base in the city with care. The northern suburbs are safe but sterile and it can be a nightmare to get around if you don't have your own transport. The downtown hotels and high-rise flatland of Hillbrow and Berea are unsafe, both to stay in and walk around. Hillbrow was the first of the country's 'grey areas' when black people began challenging the state by moving into the area. They rented apartments from slumlords who often charged extortionate rents but performed little or no maintenance on their buildings. Hillbrow was always a centre for prostitution and drugs and is even more of one now. The life on the streets is wild and absorbing but take extreme care if you wander around here.

Practical details
Telephone
The area code is 011.

Tourist information
Johannesburg Publicity Tel: 011 883 4033
Train information Tel: 011 773 2944
Bus information Translux, tel: 011 774 3333; Greyhound, tel: 011 333 3671; Intercape Mainliner, tel: 012 654 4114
Taxis Rose Taxis, tel: 011 725 3333; City Taxis, tel: 011 336 5213; Maxi Taxi, tel: 011 648 1212
Consulates USA: 1 River St, Killarney, tel: 011 646 6900; most other embassies and consulates are based in Pretoria.
Individual **backpackers** and **guesthouses** are probably the best sources of information.

Getting there and away

Most of the backpackers should have a shuttle service to and from the airport so your best bet is to phone the place of your choice as soon as you arrive. Alternatively, shuttle buses run between Johannesburg International Airport and various hotels in the city's northern suburbs, Johannesburg railway station and the adjacent Rotunda coach terminal. The area around the Rotunda is unsafe and you should phone from here to organise a lift. The station has recently been refurbished and has a few bars and restaurants where you can wait for your train or bus. For shuttle or taxi information, ask at the Info Africa desk on the ground floor of the airport's international arrivals hall.

Getting around

Transport-wise, Johannesburg is a pain unless you have your own wheels. The city's inhabitants are besotted with their cars and public transport spending has been neglected as a result. Municipal buses run on a hub-and-spoke system from the centre of town into most of the suburbs but the service is often sparse with no buses after early evening. Johannesburg's size also means that many areas are just not adequately covered. On some routes buses run only infrequently and you can expect to wait an hour or more at off-peak times.

People without their own transport can use, at their own discretion, minibus taxis which run on all the major routes in and out of Johannesburg. The system can be highly confusing: it's a fully private industry and there is lots of competition between the various operators and taxi associations. This rivalry often becomes violent and many of the vehicles are of dubious integrity (see page 45). Minibuses are supposed to stop only at designated pick-up/drop-off points but in practice they stop anywhere. Hailing one is pretty straightforward. If a bus is going your way, the driver will pull over in rapid fashion and pick you up. Or he may just ignore you – welcome to South Africa's *other* lottery.

Conventional meter cabs can be found only at designated taxi ranks, usually outside hotels, the airport or main railway stations, and cannot be hailed in the street.

There are commuter train services to the West and East Rand, to Pretoria and south to Vereeniging. The trains are unlikely to be of much use to most travellers as they only serve dormitory towns and industrial locations and don't go anywhere else. Now that armed guards patrol the railway lines on horseback, the trains are generally pretty safe although you should ride in 1st class – muggings and assaults are rife in 3rd and unfortunately not unheard of in 1st either. Don't travel at night.

Safety

Johannesburg is the crime capital of the country. While not wishing to make prospective travellers completely nervous, one should be aware that it can be a dangerous place. Unlike other places where the danger can be mostly defined in terms of safe versus no-go areas, the crime in Johannesburg is widespread and indiscriminate. Last year, however, there were two serious robberies and

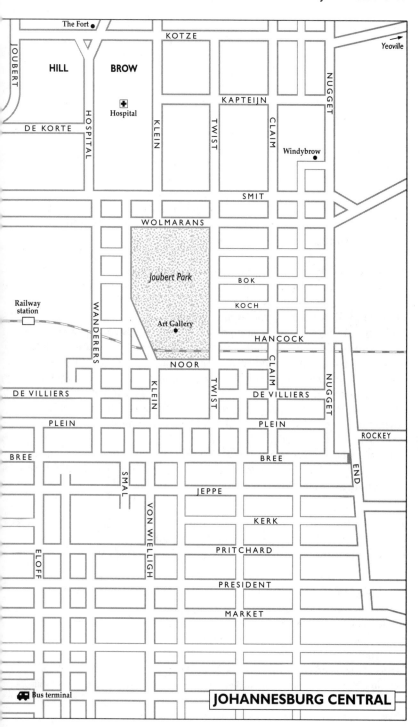

JOHANNESBURG CENTRAL

asssaults aimed specifically at tourists. Both took place in backpackers in Yeoville which unfortunately is close to the mean streets of Hillbrow and Berea, a definite no-go zone of high-rise slums, big-time drug trafficking, prostitution and a haven for criminals.

Since well over half the international flights fly through Jo'burg, the chances are you will have a stopover here. As this chapter shows, there are a lot of diversions in Jo'burg – it remains the country's largest city and its economic heart. But, unless you are really keen to see it, you might save the money and head off somewhere much nicer.

If you do decide to visit, choose your base with some care. Last year's attacks have shattered the complacent, relaxed attitude that permeated most of the hostels. Ensure that your hostel is secure – both inside and out – and that the managers are serious about looking after you properly. If the doors and gates are left open at all times for strangers to drift in and out, that's a problem. Save the relaxed stuff for when you get out into the country.

The hostels away from the city are likely to have fewer unsavoury people hanging around them since the surrounding areas are better policed and less run-down. Do not be paranoid but be circumspect and use your good judgement.

As with any big city, the usual precautions apply. Unsafe areas include most of downtown, the area around the railway and bus station (Rotunda), Hillbrow and Berea, Yeoville at night, and all townships and squatter camps. Walk with confidence, and on the street side of the sidewalk. Always be aware of what's going on around you. Daylight muggings in Hillbrow and downtown are rampant. Looking like a tourist will attract unwelcome attention – do not display cameras, money belts and such like openly. Leave money, air tickets and passports in your hotel/hostel safe and don't carry anything with you that can't be easily replaced. If you must take your camera, carry, and use it, discreetly.

If you arrive in the city after dark, take a meter taxi or arrange for someone to pick you up. Walking around with all your gear late at night is silly. If you do get mugged, do not resist but be unthreatening and fully cooperative.

Accommodation

Johannesburg is happily blessed with a good collection of backpackers; the following list is my choice but there are undoubtedly others which are as good or even better.

Zoo Lodge Jan Smuts Av, Dunkeld; tel: 011 788 5182. Double and single R70–90 per person, dorm R30–40.
Explorers Club Lodge and Safaris 9 Innes St, Observatory; tel: 011 648 7138; fax: 648 4673. Double R120, en-suite R140, dorm R45, camping R30. Lovely, friendly backpacker in the once cutting edge suburb of Yeoville. In keeping with the progressive history of the suburb, owner Pete Kirchoff, travel guru and explorer, takes nightlife tours into Yeoville and Hillbrow, the belly of the monster. If you want to meet locals, this is the only way to do it. Explorers is also a ticket and booking agent for Spoornet trains, the Baz Bus and long-distance coaches. Free pick-ups from station.

Airport Backpackers 3 Mohawk Rd, Kempton Park; tel: 011 394 0485; email: airportbackpack@hotmail.com. Double R120, dorm R50, camping R30. Just 2km from the airport and set in a large garden with a pool and bar, this is a good place to arrive, especially if it's late at night. They offer a free pick-up from the airport.

Eating, drinking and nightlife
Downtown
There are hardly any restaurants left in the city as most have fled to the suburbs. One outstanding exception is **Kapitan's**, a famous Indian restaurant on Kort Street where Nelson Mandela is alleged to have dined regularly before being imprisoned in 1964. It is a place for extending your budget a little.

Yeoville
Yeoville is a bohemian suburb a few blocks east of high-density flatland of Hillbrow, is a much mellower place although there is a significant underworld vibe. Like Hillbrow, it was another early multiracial suburb and retains a lot of its anti-establishment feel. There are quite a few backpackers around here and the place still buzzes at night, a rare thing in South African towns and cities. Most of the action happens along Rockey Street with its line of bars and restaurants. Take a slow walk down and look for something that appeals. Be careful at night. Recommended are **House of Tandoor** (sit on the roof terrace in summer, drink Black Label and play pool) which has great, cheap Indian food and sometimes live bands, and **Ba Pita** at 5B Rockey Street, a long-standing bar of mixed repute but which still manages to conjure up great, cheap food, mostly of the pita kind.

Yeoville has the not-undeserved reputation of being the easiest place in Johannesburg to score marijuana and a stroll down Rockey Street will be punctuated with mutterings of '*Swazi, Swazi*' (a reference to the place of origin of the most commonly available brand). If you indulge, remember that despite the apparent free-and-easy attitude of the dealers, marijuana use is illegal, and penalties for possession can be severe. Some dealers moonlight as police informers and perhaps some police as dealers.

Melville
On the other side of the city from Yeoville is Melville, a much trendier suburb with a vibrant and safe nightlife at its heart. The houses and shops have tin roofs and jacaranda trees line the streets. It's probably the most happening place in the city as far as after-hours goes and is overrun with restaurants, coffee shops and bars. Some places have live music. Most of the action happens on the L formed by 4th Street and 7th Avenue; good places to eat on the former include **Nuno's** for excellent Portuguese food, **The Ant Café**, **Buzz 9**, **Nino's** and **The Full Stop**, a place in which I have spent a great deal of time. Drinking centres around Ratz, a loud and vibrant trendy bar, **The Foundation Café** where glamorous young things like to party. Live, local music is available at **The Bassline** three or four nights a week; much of the line-up is Afro-jazz but the owner will give any worthy band a chance and it is the best place in town

for listening to South African bands. On 7th Avenue, there is good food at **The Question Mark** (formerly owned by the proprietor of The Full Stop), **Sahib** for cheap curries and the **Hard Times Café** two blocks along.

Walking three blocks west along 7th brings you to Main Road, Melville, more of a drinking and late-night partying place than 4th Street. If you're hungry, try **Roma's** for excellent and reasonable Italian food. Up the road is **The Ocean Basket**, part of a national chain of cheap seafood places. On 7th Avenue, next to Roma's, is **Cool Runnings**, a rambling outdoor bar but which does serve pub food. For drinking and partying, try **Catz Pyjamas** which is open more or less all night as a service to clubbers and the legendary **Roxy Rhythm Bar** which has live local bands most nights playing to their loyal student followings. The idea in Melville is to walk around until you find something that appeals. The area is busy until late and safe – stay on the main thoroughfares, though.

Westdene
There are a couple of places in Westdene, another trendy suburb about 1km west of Melville. For wonderful cocktails and cheap food, try **The Jamaican Coffee Bar** (tel: 011 726 6921), which serves main courses from R24. On Thornton Avenue, the suburb's centre, try **Luchi's Place** (tel: 011 477 4813) for exceptionally well-priced Italian food (Luchi is famous for his Monday Specials like a heaped plate of vegetarian pasta for R15). **Gujarat**, a good, cheap Indian vegetarian restaurant is nearby.

Henri Street
Some of Jo'burg's best bars and clubs are in Henri Street, Braamfontein, the city's thriving gay district. The vibe is mellow and friendly and there is less of the aggro that plagues some of the other nightspots. **Fly** is a cheerful, happening place; **Akwa** next door is a lot more trendy. **Therapy**, just around the corner is probably Jo'burg's best dance club; straights are welcome on Friday nights but not on Saturday.

Rosebank
Rosebank is about 10km north of the city centre, in the grip of a mad boom as its growth as one of the city's business centres continues. It's clean, safe and generally expensive, food-wise. However, **Mimmos**, om Cradock Avenue, serves great, cheap pizza. On Sunday, when the great flea market on the roof of nearby Rosebank Mall kicks off, there are plenty of food stalls. The newly built Zone @ Rosebank promises even more wallet-lightening adventures but save this for the end of your trip.

Parkhurst
This is a richer version of Melville. The main street is lined with antique shops or restaurants and on the whole, eating out here costs more. It is close to Rosebank and fairly accessible but doesn't quite have the pulse of some of the other places.

HOW MUCH FOR THE TEN-FOOT GIRAFFE?

Buying curios is a fine art: you need to bargain hard without being bolshie about it. Keep smiling but be firm. Keep in mind what a fair price would be and aim to end up there. If you do not want anything, be polite but firm from the start. At the same time, do not pretend to be interested as this will only leave a sour taste in the mouth.

What's important to note is that this is one of the few places where individual craftspeople – rather than a mall-bound shopkeeper – benefit directly from tourist dollars. Many of the traders, such as the 'Doily Mamas' from Zimbabwe, spend most of the year making their wares before travelling south to the promised land to earn a bit of cash. Some of them do very well, others scrape by. This is really one place where you can put something back.

I spoke to various traders to try and get fair, average prices for different things; they, naturally, would have none of it. Either I was a buyer trying to sneak in the back door, or I'd give the secrets away. So what follows is merely a rough guide of what you should pay.

Wooden giraffes 6ft, R400; 3ft, R150
Carved masks R55 for a tiny one to R350 for a traditional mask
Painted, wooden colonial figures R100
Mozambican drums R60–250
Genuine **Senegalese** or **Mali djmembe drums** start at R400, but a decent one with excellent sound will cost about R700
Ndebele beadwork little dolls, R40; R600 for a 3ft-high beauty

Shopping

As US-style shopping malls are the norm, there is not a lot of uniquely African shopping to be had here. South Africa eats, sleeps and dreams America. However, since 1994, traders from far afield have begun heading south in a steady stream, bringing real Africana that was not available here before. Not much of it is truly South African work although there are some fine exceptions such as the bright and intricate Ndebele beadwork and hand-carved wooden bowls. The best place to buy this sort if thing is at the various flea markets, not in the mall curio shops where everything is overpriced for the benefit of khaki-clad, dollar-bearing German and American tourists.

If you're looking for bargains, stay away from the malls. One exception is Johannesburg's **Oriental Plaza** at the top (west end) of Bree Street in Fordsburg. As its name implies, the Oriental Plaza is a rambling complex of Indian-owned shops where you can buy anything from spices to really sharp suits (I bought one for my wedding and the crowd loved it!). Prices are generally lower than in the suburban shopping malls and the buzz of people and smell of cooking spices and samosas generates something more of an experience than the average sterile, suburban mall.

South Africa is blessed with precious minerals and stones. Gold jewellery is generally cheaper to buy here than overseas – after all, the country has a little less than half the world's known gold reserves. For jewellery, the Oriental Plaza is not a bad place to start, but your best bet might be to approach jewellery sellers at the flea markets. If they can't actually make whatever your heart desires, they'll know someone who can or at least be able to recommend jewellery shops off the beaten path.

For a genuine African experience, try the city's original flea market which is open on Saturdays in the parking lot of the Market Theatre Complex, Bree Street. This is the where the traders from the north first started appearing back in the early 1990s, and some of them are still here. It's an apt place too, as the Market Theatre is built around the Johannesburg's first fruit and vegetable market. Prices here are likely to be lower (depending on how good a negotiator you are) than the curio market at Rosebank where there are loads more affluent white people to sell to. Once you've bargained up a thirst, there is a bar opposite the theatre, formerly the preserve of hacks from the various newspapers whose offices were nearby.

The inner city crime wave and competition from other markets really hammered the original market, but on a recent visit it was happily beggar-free and there was no sign of any trouble. If you do visit it, use your commonsense – the market area and theatre complex itself are safe during the day; the surrounding area much less so.

Johannesburg's biggest fleamarket happens on Sundays on the roof of the Rosebank shopping mall. While some curio sellers hang about on the fringes of this market, most of the traders set up shop in Cradock Avenue which runs along the east side of the mall and it is down here where you'll be able to find the best deals. The curio market continues during the week at the upper end of Cradock Avenue, just past the entrance to the mall.

If you miss the fleamarkets, the **Giraffe Centre** (2nd Avenue, Melville) is worth visiting. Here, in a typical tin-roofed Melville house, are room after room of artwork, carvings, drums, spears, masks, bowls. The centre supports a group of local craftspeople and you can often watch them doing their work behind the house.

Things to see and do

Unlike most of the world's big cities, Johannesburg's social and cultural life is patchy. With the decline of the city centre itself, the focus has split. Restaurants, museums, galleries, cinemas and theatres are now spread out in the suburbs. Restaurants are often located inside antiseptic shopping malls, although you can often sit 'outside' under an umbrella.

Worthwhile diversions include the **Market Theatre complex** at the bottom of Bree St in downtown Johannesburg, a collection of bars and restaurants, a theatre, drama and music workshops, the Museum Africa, a jazz bar called Kippies, and the city's original flea market in the parking lot on Saturdays.

Just up the road in the complex of old Indian shops and modern high rises around Diagonal Street, a few metres away from the doors of the

Johannesburg Stock Exchange, are a couple of *muthi* shops where traditional medicine is sold. One, the **Museum of Man and Science**, is legendary. It most definitely is not a museum but it is one of the wildest things you will see in Africa. The proprietor will answer any questions as long as he thinks you're not merely rubbernecking. People take traditional medicine seriously so a deferential attitude will help.

Museums

Museum Africa (121 Breet St; tel: 011 833 5624), at the Market Theatre complex, has excellent exhibits on the contribution made by black people to the development of Johannesburg – life in the gold mines; township life and Sophiatown, a legendary multi-racial Johannesburg suburb which was bulldozed in the 1960s as the Group Areas Act came into force; and the political struggle. The Bensusan Museum upstairs has a fantastic display exhibit of cameras and photographic technology. *Open Tue–Sun 09.00–17.00. Admission R5 (children R2.50).*

The **South African National Museum of Military History** (20 Erlswold Way, Forest Town) is the best such collection in the country. It covers all of the conflicts that shaped South Africa's history, although some historians feel the military struggle against apartheid is not as fairly represented as it should be. *Open daily 09.00–16.30. Admission R10.*

The **James Hall Museum of Transport** (Turf Road, La Rochelle – next to Wemmer Pan; tel: 011 435 9718) has a collection of old cars, buses, animal-drawn vehicles and locomotives. Located south of the city, it often gets neglected which is a pity because it is a good museum. *Open Tue–Sun 09.00–17.00. Admission free.*

If you want to see how South African farmers of all cultures have battled to tame this harsh land over the centuries, head for the **Diepkloof Farm Museum** (tel: 011 904 3964) inside the Suikerbosrand Nature Reserve south of Johannesburg. Getting here might require a bit of creative thinking unless you have a car. *Open Mon–Tue 08.00–16.00, Sat–Sun 10.00–15.00 Admission R6 (children R3).*

Galleries

The **Johannesburg Art Gallery** (Klein Street, Joubert Park) is still the country's most famous gallery. It is open Tuesday–Sunday, 10.00–17.00 and admission is free. The area around the gallery is not safe so take a taxi or have someone drop you off there. *Open Tue–Sun 10.00–17.00. Admission free.*

The **Standard Bank Gallery** (corner of Simmonds and Frederick Street, downtown; tel: 011 636 4231; web: www.sbgallery.co.za) has three exhibition spaces showing contemporary South African art as well as the annual World Press Photo entries and selections from international and local collections.

The **University of the Witwatersrand** in Braamfontein (tel: 011 717 1390) has the Gertrude Posel art gallery, the city's **Planetarium** and one of the friendliest travel agents in the universe. Non-student courses and programmes are also offered. *Shows Fri 20.00, Sat 15.00, Sun 16.00. Admission R20 (R10 for children, students and senior citizens, R50 for a family of four).*

Townships

If you want to see what the townships look like, take a tour rather than wander off there on your own. You will definitely need someone to show you around and make sure you stay out of trouble. There are various tours on offer but try and find one offered by a local resident – not only will it be more genuine but it will also be cheaper. Unfortunately it is hard to shake off the feeling of being a voyeur. It all depends on how badly you want to see how the other 90% live. The best way of doing this is to go with someone you know and trust, should you be fortunate enough to meet such a person. There is nothing like the genuine experience of being invited into someone's home to get a feel for life in the townships and squatter camps.

Otherwise, do not stray into the townships or squatter camps on your own at all. Life there is hard and you will be putting yourself in considerable danger.

Outside Johannesburg

The skyline used to be dominated by the mine dumps, the tailings from the mining process. Some still remain but many are being removed thanks to a new refining process which allows the remaining traces of gold to be extracted from them – much cheaper than drilling 4km into bedrock. A gold mine tour is a good way to get a sense of what built Johannesburg and South Africa. The Chamber of Mines (tel: 011 498 7204) arranges tours down working gold mines for around R200. The trips last all day, largely because there are no longer any working gold mines in the city itself; instead visitors are taken to one of the huge mines west of the city.

Gold Reef City is a working museum based around an old mine just south of the city. You go down a couple of metres in a typical miner's cage (lift) and tour an old underground working. On the surface is a typical restored mine village complete with working shops and saloons. It is a bit contrived with its paved streets and is more popular with school groups than travellers.

If you've run out of time and still have not seen any wildlife, the **Rhino and Lion Nature Reserve** (tel: 011 957 0034 or 957 0109), 30 minutes' drive west of the city, might help satisfy that craving. There are no thorn trees and rolling plains and the lions roam around in a large enclosure inside the reserve but these are real lions with real pride, scary yellow eyes and healthy appetites. As wildlife parks go, this is a good one, despite its small size. To see a rhino and her calf ambling down a green hillside is a worthwhile experience no matter where you are. Among the 20 or more species of game in the reserve are cheetah, hippo, buffalo and a decent population of endangered wild dog. You explore the reserve in your own car. Adult day visitors pay R28, children under 12 pay R15.

The reserve also has an excellent rest camp with three chalets, each sleeping four people, although mattresses will be provided for an extra two people on request. Rates start at R400 per chalet per night, including the entrance fee for the first four people; the extra mattresses cost R30 per person. Given that three of the Big Five animals roam the reserve, this is pretty good value.

A nice way of game viewing is from horseback. Local operator Danielsrust Horse Trails offers rides lasting from one hour to half a day on well-trained horses. Prices start at R75 for one hour; the half-day trail costs R285. Book through the reserve office.

The **Kromdraai Conservancy**, of which the Rhino and Lion Reserve is a small part, is near **Sterkfontein Caves** (tel: 011 956 6342), where in 1947 anthropologist Dr Robert Broome discovered the first adult remains of one of our early ancestors, *Australopethicus africanus*. In fact, it was prospectors looking for limestone deposits under the dolomite hills who discovered Mrs Ples' jawbone but Dr Broome recognised the real significance of the fossil. The discovery of 'Mrs Ples' rocked the anthropological world, placing the cradle of humankind, quite literally, in Johannesburg's back yard. Subsequent exploration of the cave system uncovered one of the world's richest hominid fossil sites. The caves are open Tuesday–Sunday, 09.00–17.00, and guided tours start every half-hour from 09.00.

Sterkfontein is one of tens – perhaps even hundreds – of cave systems in the area. Some, like the nearby Wonder Cave, are single, hollow chambers full of gorgeous stalactite and stalagmite formations; others like **Bat Cave** are lengthy, rambling systems. If squeezing down tight, dark tunnels appeals, the three-hour, 4.2km Bat Cave trip is a bargain at R50. If nothing else, the trip may teach you a few things about yourself. Bookings must be made at the Conserv office (tel: 011 957 0034).

Johannesburg's natural attractions are often ignored but there is a fair number of day hikes in the nearby Magaliesberg (see page 80 for details), mountain biking, horse riding and even whitewater rafting. The whitewater rafting is confined to the Crocodile and Juskei Rivers, both of which start on the Witwatersrand, join just north of the city and then flow north to join the mighty Limpopo in the northwest of the country. The Crocodile is a gentle river (no more than Grade 2 with the odd Grade 3 rapid at high water levels) and is easily accessible to beginner river runners. Dave and Rowan at Paddle Power (tel: 011 794 3098) offer a highly satisfying full-day trip for R235 (R195 each for a group of eight or more) including lunch and guides' fees. The company also manages a couple of excellent peri-urban mountain bike trails, horse trails and hiking routes and can combine these activities on request. It costs R65 to hire a bike for a day; taking a guide along will cost another R65. Their campsites on the banks of the Crocodile River are some of the nicest in Africa.

Another bargain hiking trail is run by Jacana Trails (tel: 012 346 3550) in the Hennops River area, about 25km north of the city. The two-day trail (R20 per person per day) traverses typical *highveld* grassland but there is wildlife such as zebras and blesbok to add interest, and a stunning viewpoint over the large Hartbeespoort Dam.

If you are looking for a real African bushveld experience, head for the **Pilanesberg National Park**, a one-and-a-half-hour drive from

Johannesburg. The 150,000 acre park sprawls over the floor of an extinct 100 million-year-old volcano. It is a beautiful reserve, home to the Big Five which wander freely across its central plain and on the slopes of the surrounding mountains. Game numbers are not nearly as high as, say, the Kruger National Park or Umfolozi Game Reserve, but the advantage is that you have a pretty good chance of seeing just about everything there. The reserve is best-known for its healthy population of white rhino, an animal that South African conservationists rescued from the very brink of extinction back in the 1960s. I have never been to Pilanesberg without seeing rhino, which is not something I can say for any other game park in the country. You will need a vehicle, both to get there and to tour the park on its network of tar and gravel roads, although accommodation at Metswedi Camp includes one game drive a day. Accommodation tends towards the luxurious since the reserve is right next door to Sun City, a massive, ritzy gambling and entertainment hotel complex carved out of the bush in the late 1970s in what was then the 'independent' homeland of Boputhatswana (see page 22). However, there are some cheaper options:

Manyane Tel: 01465 55 351; reservations 011 014 555 6135, fax: 011 465 1228. Chalets: 2-bed R425 per chalet, 4-bed R635 per chalet, 6-bed R840 per chalet. This is the park's main rest camp, aimed at local travellers who cannot afford the luxury lodges elsewhere. Rooms with thatch roofs, all with kitchen and bathroom. The restaurant is open daily for all meals but you will save money by self-catering. The camp has large walk-in aviaries where you can get really close to many of the bird species that live in the park.

Metswedi Tel: 011 014 555 6135; fax: 011 465 1228. Two-bed tents R520 per person including three meals and daily game drive. A tented camp overlooking a waterhole right in the middle of the park. The tents are large, safari-style walk-in tents, sleeping two each. There is a central kitchen and shower block. Self-catering only. Watch out at the waterhole viewsite – a fall off here is a legbreaker; I know.

The reserve is also easily visited on a day trip from Pretoria or Johannesburg.

Cape Town

A writer named Lawrence Green said the only cure for the melancholy and nostalgia – 'homesickness as a disease' – that ruled his life while in exile during the two World Wars, was the promise of a swift return to Cape Town.

> I fell under the spell of Cape Town soon after I became conscious of this world. Most of this century I have lived within sight of Table Mountain. For me it would be an evil turn of life's wheel if I were forced to end my days elsewhere.
>
> *Tavern Of the Seas*, 1947

Cape Town is South Africa's fabulous playground. It is one of the world's most beautiful cities, cradled at the foot of Table Mountain, at the northern end of a slender 75km-long peninsula, with the Atlantic Ocean lapping its blinding-white beaches. The Cape of Good Hope marks the southern end of the peninsula, which is made up largely of a mountainous plateau. Forests grow on the flanks of the mountains but the most striking vegetation is the heath-like Cape *fynbos*, distinctive enough to ensure the Cape has been classified as one of the earth's six discrete floral kingdoms.

The Cape has a Mediterranean climate – a cool, wet winter and hot, dry summer, a little out of sync with the rest of the country. Summer days can be violently hot but the icy Atlantic waters provide some balance. The weather is governed by two prevailing winds – the rain-bearing, boat-wrecking northwester which blows mostly in the winter, and the summer southeaster, a wind that can blow with some fury. Locals call it the 'Cape Doctor' because it used to blow all the dust off the streets and into the sea; it can also blow for days, driving people to despair with its incessant howling and whining. The southeaster is usually followed by hot, still days and the calm, blue sea shimmers in the 30°C heat, until a cold front drifts in from the ocean to cool everything down.

Winds or no, the weather and its incredible setting are the reason for Cape Town's rocketing tourism figures, and it is no secret that the city has been getting the lion's share of new tourism arrivals since 1994. A number of airlines fly directly to Cape Town from Europe, which means you can skip Johannesburg and Pretoria entirely, if you want to.

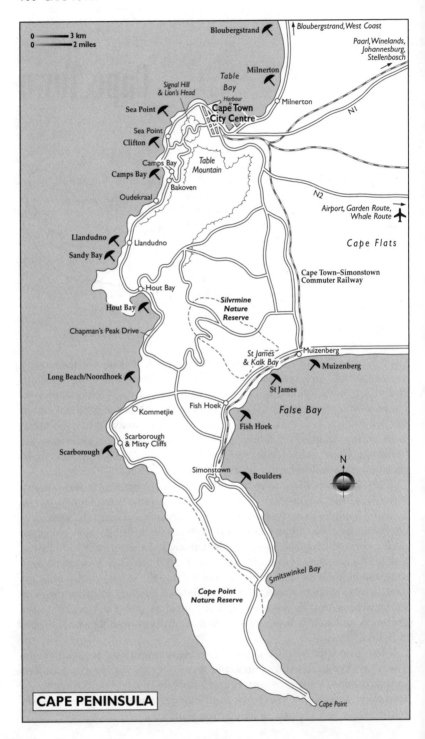

CAPE PENINSULA

People have lived at the Cape for around 40,000 years. For thousands of years, the Khoikhoi and San people roamed the rich game country stretching north from the foot of Table Mountain into the interior. The San were gradually displaced by the pastoralist Khoikhoi who were to have the debatable privilege of welcoming the first white men to the Cape when, in 1487, the Portuguese navigator Bartolomeu Dias became the first recorded European to make landfall in Table Bay. He named it Cabo da Boa Esperança (the Cape of Good Hope). Although the place had abundant fresh water and plenty of fresh meat roaming the countryside, the Portuguese were evidently little impressed and sailed on round the coast. They wanted a victualling station to supply ships bound for the Far East and settled on Delagoa Bay, today's Maputo. It was another 150 years before any Europeans settled permanently at the foot of Table Mountain, when three Dutch ships, commanded by Jan van Riebeek arrived in the bay in 1652. The settlement was to serve as a supply point for ships of the Dutch East India Company on their long journey to Asia and back. Vegetables were grown in the company gardens and a hospital and fort were built and animal bartering with the Khoikhoi flourished. Table Bay became a stopover point for ships from all over the world, a role which has diminished somewhat this century. The harbour remains an important centre for fruit and grain exports, and its ship repair facilities are impressive. It has mostly been eclipsed as a bulk cargo port by Richards Bay and Durban, both on the KwaZulu-Natal coast.

Cape Town is worth a whole book on its own so what follows is brief. Impossibly laid back, the city is unlikely to ever replace Johannesburg as the country's key economic centre, despite the mass emigration of skilled people away from the latter. It is the perfect place for a complete holiday. There are exquisite beaches to bake on, mountains to climb, forests to hike in, hundreds of restaurants, bars and coffee shops and dozens of vineyards just beyond the city limits. Tourism has become its key industry and yet Cape Town has so far avoided the tackiness that usually comes with such a boom.

It is the parliamentary capital of the South Africa, although this function is expected to move to Pretoria, much to the disgust of the MPs who have got used to having large second homes by the sea and the undeniable pleasure of spending six months a year 'working' in one of the most beautiful cities in the world.

Cape Town can do funny things to your head. It is a mixture of African and European but not really one or the other – too western to be African and too African to be European. It is a fully cosmopolitan city and during apartheid was often regarded as the most liberal of South Africa's cities, even though Nelson Mandela, and almost the entire imprisoned leadership of the African National Congress, were languishing on bleak Robben Island five miles across the bay from the harbour entrance. However, the gulf between white and black is disturbingly pronounced here. The city's affluent suburbs spread up into the trees at the foot of the mountains but just a few miles away lie the densely-packed, wind- and sand-swept townships of the Cape Flats, quite visible if you get up on to the west facing slopes of the mountain.

That said, it is a wonderful city to spend time in. A week would be barely adequate – most people need a lifetime. The city is defined by the 1,068m-high flat-topped bulk of Table Mountain. The mountain is a massive location indicator. Locals might say 'keep the mountain on your right...' when telling you how to get somewhere. The sheer Africa Face towers over the City Bowl and harbour; to its right, the bulk of Lion's Head dominates Sea Point, Clifton and the western edge of the City Bowl; to the east, Devil's Peak rears up over the eastern side of the City Bowl and looks down on the southern suburbs. In the afternoons and evenings, cloud seems to pour over the mountain in a cotton-wool waterfall that people call the 'tablecloth' which adds a sense of unreality to an already impossibly beautiful place.

ORIENTATION

As if all that beauty wasn't enough, the mountain is also Cape Town's best map. If you look down from the edge of the mountain, the city spreads out before you. The quiet City Bowl suburbs cling to the lower slopes and the few skyscrapers of the city stand at the edge of the foreshore, with the harbour and Table Bay beyond. To the left is Lion's Head and Signal Hill, its rump, from where a cannon is fired every weekday exactly at noon. The boom, if you can hear it above the traffic, is a reminder to Capetonians to set their watches, although as writer Lawrence Green observes, you will be a *little* out:

> The report reaches the Observatory eighteen and a half seconds after
> the flash, and even in the main streets of the city the sound is received
> nearly five seconds late.

Maybe this is why locals have a nationwide reputation for being tardy.

On the lower slopes of Signal Hill are Tamboerskloof and Bo Kaap (above Cape), the latter a jumble of old houses and wide streets, and traditionally home to a strong Cape Malay community whose ancestors were brought here from Indonesia, Madagascar and India as slaves. The area, known as the Malay Quarter, has some of the city's oldest and nicest architecture – flat-roofed houses, cobbled lanes and mosques, many dating back before the mid-18th century.

Across the bay, spread out along the fine white beaches are Milnerton and Bloubergstrand, newer and somewhat characterless suburbs but with a fantastic view across the sea to *the* mountain. Far beyond Milnerton is a line of hills which mark the edge of the Boland, which literally means 'high country' (although it's not very high). Looking east, you will see a fantastic towering range called the Hottentot's Holland which marks the end of the flat coastal plain and is where Stellenbosch, the university town, huddles.

Behind the impassive granite face where you stand, a chain of mountains stretches for 75km down the peninsula to end in tumbling, rocky finality at Cape Point, seemingly at the end of the earth. The rocky shoreline is interspersed with exquisite beaches and greater Cape Town seems to occur in fits and starts in the form of scattered towns and villages along the coast.

The Atlantic coast is washed by the cold water that comes all the way up from the Antarctic. It is rugged and beautiful with mountains tumbling steeply into the sea, broken only by a couple of long fine-sanded beaches. This ruggedness has limited human settlement and, four centuries after the first landfall, most of it is still raw and wild. One of the world's most spectacular drives traces the coast, clinging to the mountainside. The section from Hout Bay, over Chapman's Peak, to Noordhoek is awesome with the road perched hundreds of feet above the sea. It is not a place for bad or nervous drivers.

Not surprisingly, Capetonians are generally in love with their city. They live in a vast playground – the mountain is laced with superb hiking paths over its slopes, rock climbers can gorge themselves on hundreds of routes, paragliders launch off Lion's Head and drift down the Atlantic coast where the blue sea rolls up on to the beaches.

In summer, when the sun sets only after eight, people head for the Atlantic side to have sundowners on the rocks, chuck a frisbee around, walk their dogs on the beaches or stroll on the Sea Point promenade. When night comes, the city throbs with life in its restaurants and bars. The live music scene is vibrant and there is always something happening at the theatre or on at the movies. In winter, on the other hand, it can get a bit quiet as people go into hibernation and wait out the monotonous wind and drizzle.

For many of the people who live here, this is Eden and it sometimes shows in their condescending attitude, especially towards people from 'up country', which is anyone who lives beyond the first range of mountains that hold the peninsula in its embrace. In retort, those who have the misfortune of being from 'up country' are quick to point out that it's their sweat and toil up in Gauteng that keeps the economy ticking over and allows Capetonians to continue living their mellow lives behind the Grape Curtain.

PRACTICAL DETAILS
When to go
Unlike the rest of the country, Cape Town's winter (May to September) is usually wet and windy. That said, I have been in Cape Town in winter with day after day of brilliant sunshine and not even a whisper of an air current. Summers, on the other hand, are supposed to be very hot and dry, although the southeast wind, when it gets going, can blow for days.

You will get a much better deal on prices for accommodation, tours, activities and some transport during the winter months. Discounts of 10–20% are standard. The region is also beautifully green during these months when the rest of the country will be throat-tighteningly dry. Remember that the sea on the Atlantic coast is *always* cold, regardless of season.

Although the whole summer (October–April) is regarded as high season, prices really rocket in December–January when the country takes its summer holidays. This is a time to avoid Cape Town unless you enjoy mixing *really* closely with strangers.

Telephone
The area code is 021.

Tourist information

Cape Town really does pull out the stops when it comes to tourism marketing and information with one organisation handling metropolitan tourism and another looking after the city itself. I'm not quite sure what the difference is; suffice to say, the information provided is superb.

Cape Town Tourism Tel: 021 426 4260; email: captour@iafrica.com. They have a truly excellent tourist information centre and Internet café, corner Burg St and Castle St, tel: 021 426 4260. The bureau is absolutely chock-full with free pamphlets and maps, arranged by region throughout the country.
Cape Metropolitan Tourism Tel: 021 487 2718; fax: 487 2977; email: cmt@cmc.gov.za; web: www.gocapetown.co.za
Train information Tel: 021 449 3871
Bus information: Translux, tel: 021 405 3333; Intercape Mainliner, tel: 021 386 4400; tel: Greyhound 021 418 4312
Car hire Around About Cars, tel: 021 419 2728 or 082 419 2727, email: info@aroundaboutcars.com; web: www.aroundaboutcars.com
South Africa National Parks Board Tel: 012 343 1991; fax: 012 343 0905; email: reservations@parks-sa.co.za. For reservations for all national parks and some hiking trails. *Note that this is a Pretoria – 012 – telephone number.*
The various **backpackers** are also excellent sources of information.

GETTING THERE AND AWAY

The **Intercape Shuttle** bus (tel: 021 386 4444) runs every half-hour from the airport to the city centre, fare R40. Buy tickets at the desk in the arrivals terminal. There is also a **taxi** rank here and drivers will tout vigorously for your business; fares are around R90 but ask first. The usual car hire companies have desks in the arrivals hall but if you want **cheap car hire**, you will have to go to the city first.

The **Backpackers' Bus** (tel: 082 809 9185 or 021 788 5440 after hours), runs between the airport and backpackers in the City Bowl, Sea Point and Observatory but you should call from the airport to find out when the next one will be heading your way. The bus is supposed to pick up at hostels and run *to* the airport on the hour from 08.00 to 18.00. The fare is R60 for one person (R80 at night) rising to R200 (R220 at night) for seven people so try and hook up with some other travellers at the airport. Some of the backpackers run their own airport shuttles so give them a call as well.

GETTING AROUND

Cape Town has probably the best public transport in the country, with a substantial commuter train service radiating out of the city into the suburbs and beyond, a reasonable bus network and ubiquitous mini-bus taxis which reach places other forms of transport don't. It also has the cheapest car hire in the country and a couple of companies compete for budget business.

Commuter trains

Metrorail (tel: 021 449 2443) operate an extensive commuter rail service with lines radiating out of the city to the suburbs, False Bay coast, Stellenbosch and the Cape Flats. The trains are a good way of getting to Stellenbosch, Strand, a seaside town on the eastern end of False Bay, Simonstown, the naval base and resort town on the Cape Peninsula, and Malmesbury and **Wolseley**, both small agricultural towns. There is not a lot to do in either of these little farm towns but the ride out there is beautiful in winter when snow-covered mountains look down on the Western Cape's green wheat fields.

The ride to Strand is less interesting as the line runs through Cape Town's industrial district and then over the blandness of the Cape Flats. However, the beach at Strand is pretty and the swimming is safer and warmer than in many other parts of the region. My advice would be to head for the next door village of **Gordon's Bay** which huddles in a crook of False Bay under the Hottentot's Holland mountains. It is an attractive place with a fine stretch of beach with luxury holiday houses clinging onto the mountainside and overlooking a pretty small-craft harbour. The residents have one of the finest views in the Cape, all the way across the heaving blue of False Bay to the distant mountains of the Cape Peninsula. It is a long, long walk from Strand, though – get a bike in Cape Town and take it with you on the train.

There are no trains to the Atlantic seaboard (Green Point, Mouille Point, Clifton, Camps Bay, Llandudno) but the minibus taxis are common and there is always the odd municipal bus.

Minibus taxis

Cape Town is one South African city where travellers do make use of the minibus taxis but the safety issues raised in Chapter 3 still apply. They are one of the best ways of getting out to the otherwise transport-starved Atlantic seaboard (Green Point, Sea Point, Clifton and Camps Bay). The main minibus rank is on the Grand Parade, one block south of Cape Town station. To hail one, put a finger in the air; the driver will stop right next you, and probably provoke a bit of road rage in motorists behind him. They are often packed to the gills but you will get to experience a bit of local flavour. If they're talking loudly in Afrikaans, using words like *laarnie* (see Glossary) and giggling then they're probably talking about you. The average fare is about R3.50.

You can also use **Rikkis** (tel: 021 424 3888), which are like semi-open lightweight vans. Sample fares are City Bowl – R7, Sea Point – R12, Clifton – R15, and Camps Bay – R15. Rikkis cover parts of town that the usual minibuses might not reach, such as the Cable Car – R10, Signal Hill – R10 and Devil's Peak – R12. They also do excursions for up to four people to the Kirstenbosch Gardens, the massive theme park at Ratanga Junction and Hout Bay. Prices start at R50, which is a bargain. You can also ask Rikkis to send a van to pick you up.

Buses

Cape Town has a **municipal bus service** which has muddled along for years as it battles for funding from government. The most useful bus is the shuttle to the Victoria and Albert Waterfront which runs every ten minutes from the tourist information office in front of the railway station on Adderley Street.

Golden Arrow, a private bus company, has a large fleet serving the City Bowl and the suburbs, running from the main terminus on the Grand Parade. Fares are low since it is a service aimed at ordinary people. However, Golden Arrow have had unfortunate publicity of late, with the fatal shooting of a number of its drivers as the vicious war for market share continues between rival taxi associations. Golden Arrow has a good safety record and so is well supported. It seems the taxi companies do not appreciate this and are attempting to persuade commuters to throw themselves at their mercy instead. Although no passengers have been hurt, check the current situation before climbing aboard.

Car hire

Cape Town has the best car hire deals in the land with a couple of firms competing for budget traveller dollars.

Around About Cars, Coen Steytler Garage, 2nd floor, Foreshore; tel: 021 419 2728 or 082 419 2727; email: info@aroundaboutcars.com is the cheapest and the one I found most willing to help. In mid-2000, it was possible to rent a late-model car for R99 per day including insurance and unlimited kilometres, which has to be the ultimate bargain in car rental. They also offer free delivery and pick-up all over southern Africa and chuck in a 10% discount on accommodation at selected places in the country. Add R1 to each day's car hire – they will match it and send all the money raised to the Ebony Orphan Fund, a Cape Town-based charity which provides underprivileged children with a chance for a decent education.

Global Car Rental corner Loop St and Castle St; tel: 021 423 5211; fax: 423 5280, also have good deals. Daily rates for the cheapest models start at R65 per day plus R0.80 per kilometre, and they also offer long distance rates with free unlimited kilometres, starting at R199 a day for 2–3 days, falling to R109 per day for 11 days or more.

Tempest Car Hire Tel: 021 934 3845. A national firm with branches in all the main centres which is the cheapest of all the large hire agencies. They have a branch at the airport. Expect to pay R120 per day including insurance, plus R0.77 per kilometre. They have special deals for seven days or more.

Motorcycles

Cape Town is great biking country. Those twisting coastal roads with the wind in your face and the sun on your back will make you scream in delight. A couple of places rent out bikes but you will need a full motorcycle licence to hire one. Cheapest of the lot is Mitaka Cruiser Rentals (345 Main Rd, Sea Point; tel: 021 439 6036, web: www.mitaka.co.za) who have a range of cruiser-style offerings. Scooter hire costs R160 per day, cruisers are R300–450 per day, including 350 free kilometres.

Bicycle

Another great way to see the city, although some of the hills can be quite terrifying, both slogging up and going down. The advantage of having a bike is that it opens all sorts of other excitement on the many mountain bike trails which wind all over the peninsula's slopes and forests. If you have not brought your own bike with you, wander down to **Extreme Sports Shack** (220 Long Streeet; tel: 021 426 0294 or 083 265 6661; email: extremesports@ worldonline.co.za) which hires out mountain bikes (and a bunch of other stuff such as surfboards, snorkelling gear, camping equipment and golf clubs).

The cycling gets better the further one gets from the city and the roads along the False Bay and Atlantic coasts are magnificent. It's much nicer cycling along at sea level as it's mostly flat, although there are one or two notable and curseworthy exceptions. The problems begin when you want to head over to the other side of the peninsula from the side you are on, or up into the City Bowl and the lower slopes of Table Mountain. This is mountain country and it is no wonder that South Africa's most famous cycle race, the annual Argus, is held here.

Foot power

Cape Town people are beautiful, healthy people and you will see plenty of roller bladers, skateboarders, joggers and walkers, mostly down along the sea front. These are all excellent ways to get around and you will be in good company. Those little collapsible push-scooters that have caused so much carnage on London's pavements have, not surprisingly, appeared all over Cape Town.

SAFETY

Cape Town is a lot safer than Johannesburg but crime has increased over the last few years. You won't see the high walls and electric fences that that infest Johannesburg nor sense the same paranoia. That said, you need to take some precautions. The city centre is safe during the day although you should steer well clear of the dingy area east of Roeland St. Further east, Salt River is quite insalubrious and Woodstock is not somewhere to be lost in at night.

To the east of the city lie the desolate Cape Flats, site of some of the country's worst squatter camps and bleakest townships. The Flats are a wind-blown wasteland of shifting sands and scant vegetation. Much of the area is overrun by gangs who are locked in a permanent battle over the lucrative drugs trade, and the crime rate in these areas is appalling. But unless you do a specific tour, you are unlikely to see the townships although you will skirt a massive shackland which sprawls up to the edge of the airport motorway. Do not head there unless you are escorted by someone you can trust and who preferably lives there. Instead take a tour – some of them are not as zoo-like as you might expect (see *Things to see and do* below).

There have been reports of muggings on the commuter trains at night. At all times try and ride in a carriage with other passengers and you'll be fine. The lines to avoid, unless you have a friend escorting you, are *any* of the lines to the townships on the Cape Flats. Criminal activity is rampant on these trains.

If you are using the minibus taxis, make sure you are dropped at the correct place. You do not want to be dropped at night at the edge of a township. If in doubt, ask your fellow commuters for directions or help.

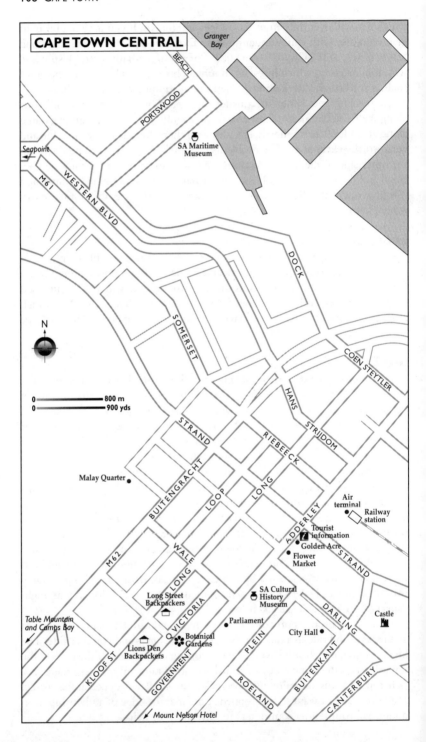

CAPE TOWN CENTRAL

Granger Bay

BEACH

PORTSWOOD

Seapoint

SA Maritime Museum

M61

WESTERN BLVD

DOCK

SOMERSET

N

COEN STEYTLER

0 ——— 800 m
0 ——— 900 yds

STRAND

RIEBEECK

HANS

STRIJDOM

Malay Quarter

BUITENGRACHT

LOOP

LONG

Air terminal

Railway station

ADDERLEY

Tourist information

M62

WALE

LONG

Golden Acre

Flower Market

STRAND

Table Mountain and Camps Bay

Long Street Backpackers

VICTORIA

SA Cultural History Museum

Parliament

DARLING

Castle

Lions Den Backpackers

KLOOF ST

GOVERNMENT

Botanical Gardens

PLEIN

City Hall

BUITENKANT

ROELAND

CANTERBURY

↙ Mount Nelson Hotel

ACCOMMODATION

In keeping with its status as the country's most popular destination, Cape Town is awash with places to stay. There are around 70 backpackers alone although in season this number probably tops 100 or more. Many of them are excellent, clean and well-run places; others, especially those that just suddenly appear in season, are often holes in the ground.

The various places are spread out across the city and this may be a determining factor. Places in the City Bowl are generally quiet, close to town and the Waterfront and offer immediate – if very steep – access to the mountain. Sea Point and Green Point hostels tend to be larger – some are converted hotels – and are convenient for the Atlantic coast beaches, restaurants and nightspots. Observatory and Woodstock, on the east side of the mountain are funkier suburbs – think of narrow streets with lots of old houses with tin roofs and you've got the picture. 'Obs', where a lot of university students have digs, has quite a leftie feel to it, a hangover from the days when The Struggle was in full swing and the University of Cape Town was a bubbling pot of subversive political activity.

There are also superb places in Simonstown, Hout Bay, Claremont in the southern suburbs and, my personal favourite, Scarborough. One factor you may want to consider before heading straight out this way is that these places, Claremont excepted, are way out of town and even if you have a car, missioning to and fro becomes, well, a mission. A better idea is to stay in town for a while and then when you feel like a bit of space and some really fresh sea air, head off down the peninsula to one of the smaller places.

The following list is not the last word. Backpackers come and go. Some of these are my favourites but the nice thing about Cape Town is that there is always something new happening.

City Bowl

Ashanti Lodge & Travel Centre 11 Hof St, Gardens; tel: 021 423 8721; fax: 423 8790; email: ashanti@iafrica.com; web: www.ashanti.co.za. Double R150 per room, single R110, dorm R55, camping R35. A huge, vibey place in a gorgeous, old Gardens house with wooden floors, a couple of pressed-steel ceilings and wrought-iron balconies with a fine view of Table Bay. Some of the dorms are a bit pokey but the double rooms which open out onto the large swimming pool are lovely. There are also a couple of en-suite flatlets at the side of the house, offering the kind of privacy one would not expect in a place this big. The travel centre could sort out your entire trip right there in the office and certainly you should make use of their willingness to impart information. It is a good place to start your journey.

Oak Lodge 21 Breda St; tel: 021 465 6182; fax: 465 6308; email: oaklodge@intekom.co.za; web: www.intekom.co.za/~oaklodge/. Double R140–200, dorm R55. Rates change with the season and you can make a deal if you want to stay for longer than a week or a month. Travellers rave about this old house with its beautifully carved oak panelling. It is a big place but there are 18 double rooms, decorated with antique furniture, in the flats next door if you want a bit of privacy. They can organise amazing trips too. There is a free *braai* on Sunday nights and meals are available throughout the week.

Cloudbreak Backpackers Lodge 219 Upper Buitenkant St; tel: 021 461 6892; fax: 461 1458; email: cloudbrk@gem.co.za. Double R130, dorm R45. ISIC card holders get a 10% discount. Long-lived hostel at the lower slopes of the mountain but still within walking distance of town.

Train Lodge Monument Station, Old Marine Dr; tel: 021 418 4890; fax: 418 5848; email: train@trainlodge.co.za. Double R90, quads R70. The lodge is made up of an entire train of refurbished passenger coaches, parked in an old railway station. The rooms, being compartments, are all doubles or quads and they are spotless. It's small but different. There is a bar, a restaurant coach, and a swimming pool.

Overseas Visitors Club OVC House, 230 Long St; tel: 021 424 6800; fax: 423 4870; email: hross@ovc.co.za; web: www.ovc.co.za. Dorm R50. ISIC members get 10% off. OVC used to have an unwelcoming feel about it and its telephone could use some sharpening up. It is a nice place though, situated right in the middle of Long St and it picks up the vibe of the area. They are eager to please: new arrivals get a free Waterfront cruise and all guests get a 20% discount on OVC's trips which basically cover the whole region.

Sea Point and Atlantic coast

Aardvark Backpackers 319 Main Rd, Sea Point; tel: 021 434 4172; fax: 439 3813, email: aardbp@mweb.co.za; web: www.lions-head-lodge.co.za/aardvark.htm. Double R101 per person, single R202 per person, dorm R55. What I like about this place are the comfortable self-catering flats which all have their own bathrooms. It's more of a hotel than a standard backpacker. Some rooms have TVs and phones, and there is a pool, a laundry service and free baggage storage. If you don't feel like cooking, eat in the restaurant.

The Carnaby 219 Main Rd, Three Anchor Bay; tel: 021 439 7410; fax: 439 1222; email: carnaby@netactive.co.za. Double R140–195 per room, single R95–125, dorm R50–60. Definitely a bargain. Another former hotel (although at a slightly calmer address), The Carnaby offers budget en-suite rooms which are serviced daily. It is a rare budget gem. It is blessed with the usual hotel facilities – a pool, bars and a restaurant as well as a good travel information centre.

Fawlty Towers Upper Portswood Rd, Green Point; tel: 021 439 7671/ 1075; email: fawlty@mweb.co.za. Double R150, studio flat (sleeps 3–4) R200, dorm R50. Nothing like the original, thankfully. This is another good budget option for travellers who don't want to slum it in some busy backpacker. The rooms are actually flats sleeping 2–4 people, all with kitchens and bathrooms. There is a bar downstairs where you can get pub meals, and there is a pool.

Woodstock, Observatory and Claremont

Africa Calling 12 and 16 Erica St, Woodstock; tel: 021 447 5158; fax: 448 8835; email: africa.calling@treffers.co.za. Double R150 per room. Small, quiet place with just three double rooms. You feel like someone has taken you into their home, so it is special. Full travel information and booking service.

Green Elephant 57 Milton Rd, Observatory; tel: 0800 222 722 (toll free); fax: 021 448 0510; email: greenelephant@iafrica.com. Double R150, dorm R50. Large backpacker split over two houses. It is a busy, vibrant place with a pool, jacuzzi and a bar or two. One house is dorm rooms, the other doubles. They have a great travel service and good Internet facilities.

SA's The Alternative Place 64 St Michaels Rd, Claremont; tel: 021 674 2396. Double from R150, dorm R55. An excellent homely place that really is someone's home; not a backpacker but cheaper than a B&B. Of all the places in South Africa, this comes closest to the homestay concept but since the owners are travellers, you will relate to them. No aloof and grumpy B&B owners, these. Rooms are quiet and spotless and meals are provided.

Other places
A Sunflower Stop 179 Main Rd, Green Point; tel: 021 434 6535; fax: 021 434 6501; email: devine@sunflowerstop.co.za. Double R145, dorm R50. Free airport pick-up
The Hip Hop 11 Vesperdene Rd, Green Point; tel: 021 439 2104; fax: 439 8688; email: hiphop@cis.co.za. Double R130, dorm R45, camping R30. Free pick-up.

EATING AND DRINKING
Where do you start? Or rather, how much time and money do you have? The whole attitude of the city is reflected in the number of restaurants, bars, delis, fast food joints and cafés that fill its suburbs. The first thing to do when you arrive is pick up a copy of *Cape Review*, Cape Town's version of *Time Out*, which tries to list every possible thing going on.

Local prices have unfortunately been climbing steadily higher in recent years, along with house prices, rentals and the cost of vegetables. Some people blame this on the constant one-way traffic of refugees from Gauteng but it is more likely caused by locals cashing in on the tourism boom. Make no mistake – eating out is still cheap by European standards, especially when you do the conversion from hard currency.

There are a couple of well-defined zones: the Waterfront and Camps Bay, which are generally overpriced as you are paying for the great view and surroundings rather than the quality of the food, Kloof Street, which you would be forgiven for thinking had tried to turn itself into one long restaurant, and Long Street and its surrounds.

Coffee shops and second-hand bookshops go well together and Long Street has both. It tends to be more active during the day than at night although a couple of good bars really do hum late at night. Take a walk along here and see what appeals. For some reason Kloof Street, which runs directly up the slopes of the mountain from the edge of town, seems to have a disproportionate number of cheap places to eat. There is a nice, busy vibe here which is enhanced by the sense of rebellion against the Waterfront.

The Waterfront is a piece of so-called marketing genius. The developers took the concept of San Francisco's Mariner's Wharf and applied it to a run-down part of Cape Town's harbour. Old warehouses were demolished and a glittering mall and a covy of restaurants, bars and shops rose from the dust. The mall would be almost as bland as any other except for its position, and by the saving grace of plenty of ironwork and glass the overall impression is one of light and space. The real bonus is that there are bars and places to eat tucked away all over on different quays, sometimes linked by bridges or, in one case, by the Penny Ferry, an old rowing boat which creaks across the Cut, the entrance to the Alfred Basin: fare R1 which as some wits will tell you is worth about as much as a penny.

Camps Bay, down on the Atlantic seaboard, also has many restaurants and bars lining the beachfront road. It is a spectacular setting but prices are generally not inclined to suit budget travellers.

The following list is a collaboration of mine and that of my down-and-out friends who live here.

Eating

You will be able to eat just about anything you want here, as long as it's from some other country. South African cooking tends to reflect its distant origins and Malay and Afrikaner cooking aside, there is not much that can be considered uniquely South African. Unless you count charred, beer-infused meat on a *braai* as unique. One bonus is the ready supply of fresh fish straight off the fishing boats but the best place for this is usually at the little fish-and-chip shops in the harbours. At least in Cape Town you will readily find Malay food and I urge you to track down a *roti*, a curried meat or vegetable filling in rolled *nan* bread. Try any of the cafés (corner shops) on the upper side of Long St.

Malay
Noon Gun 273 Longmarket St. Curries, *dhal, bobotie* and *bredie* in an old tearoom with awesome views.

Fish and seafood
Ocean Basket Kloof St. Part of a national chain serving good, cheap seafood.
Seaforth Rondebosch A legendary place with the best battered fish and chips in town. Not open at night.
Fisherman's Wharf Hout Bay harbour. Fish straight off the boat and the setting is pretty spectacular. Crowded in season and over weekends.

Italian
Peasants Kloof St. Great Italian cooking in a friendly place.
Café Paradiso Kloof St. Known everywhere for its warm loaves of olive bread.

Noodles, Asian cooking
Long Life Noodle Bar Long St. The noodle bar came to Cape Town and stayed.
The Happy Wok Kloof St. More cheap Asian cooking.
Yum Deli Highland Rd, Vredehoek.

Faster food and pizza
Naked Kloof St, Tamboerskloof. Excellent wraps in a diner-ish setting.
Mimmos For the best, cheap pizza and pasta around. Couple of branches.
The Waterfront also has loads of good fast food places.

Healthy
Kauai Juice Company Loop St.
New York Bagel Deli, Sea Point. More of a breakfast place (and serving classic fry-ups, naturally), where you basically wander around choosing your food and have it cooked in front of you. It is healthy.

Drinking
Cape Town's nightlife is thriving with dozens of bars, coffee shops, clubs, and other places opening and closing all the time. Names to look out for include The Shack, The Jam and 206, all in the same complex near Gradens; Café Dharma, the trendy Sand Bar on the beachfront in Camps Bay, La Med which heaves on Friday and Saturdays but has probably the best view of any bar in Cape Town. The trick is to sniff around until you find something that appeals. Make use of any free lifts that the backpackers offer as this will allow you to spread your wings a little.

THINGS TO SEE AND DO
Visitors could be forgiven for thinking that life in Cape Town is totally focused on being outside, in summer, at least. With all the beaches, hiking paths and trails no more than 30 minutes away, it's no wonder that Capetonians really do go outside to relax (even one of the theatres, Maynardville, is outside (its summer Shakespeare productions are usually superb). One gets the feeling sometimes that the whole city is doing something *healthy*. It would be a sin to ignore such gifts although one can get complacent when too much of a good thing is right on the doorstep.

The inhabitants are also quite aware that Cape Town was the first European settlement in South Africa and regard themselves as the guardians of the country's culture and a good hunk of its history. The arts certainly do thrive here, more so than in Johannesburg. There are a couple of theatres, a rash of cinemas and the Cape Town Philharmonic Orchestra (the National Philharmonic had its funding cut in 2000: numbers were down and it was regarded in some circles as elitist) and some fine museums.

Cape Town's city centre seems to have escaped the rush for the suburbs which happened in Johannesburg and it remains a lively place. **Long Street**, with its line of coffee shops, bars, backpackers' hostels, second-hand book shops, antique dealers, pawn-and-junk brokers and cafes, is worth exploring. With its balconied Victorian and Georgian buildings, it looks like the main street of some colonial backwater and still has a slightly shabby feel to it.

Greenmarket Square, one block down, between Shortmarket and Longmarket Streets, has an almost permanent flea-market set up, a purpose the square has served four two centuries although you won't find fresh fish here now. Carry on through the square down the side streets into **St George's Street**, a pedestrianised mall which runs parallel to Long Street – if you want overpriced curios, this is where to find them. The buskers are pretty good, though.

Robben Island, recently proclaimed a World Heritage Site, is where Nelson Mandela and the dozens of other African National Congress activists endured their prison terms. It is worth the effort to get to, not necessarily because it's politically correct to do so but to see what a forbidding place it is. As bleak prisons go, it surpasses even Alcatraz. When the north west gales blow, they howl over the outcrop and hiss over the sea to the Cape. For the prisoners it must have been awful; there, just seven miles away, is Cape Town but it is seven miles of icy water and vicious currents away. There were no successful escapes. The *1952 Year Book & Guide to Southern Africa* says:

> From very early times Robben Island was used as a prison, and the
> old records contain frequent references to sentences passed on
> persons condemned to labour there in chains. Important native chiefs
> have been detained there from time to time and one of them,
> Linchwe, was drowned on Blaauwberg beach in attempting to escape.

A prescient piece of writing, given that Nelson Mandela was sent to the island 12 years later. Naturally, the only way to get there is by boat. Call the Robben Island Museum (tel: 021 419 1300) for details. Tickets cost R100 which includes a tour of the island; the guides are former political prisoners.

Going from the Island to the **Houses of Parliament** (Parliament Street, tel: 021 403 2460) would make an interesting journey now that many of the inmates on the former are serving in the latter. The houses are open when parliament is in recess over Easter or during winter but attending a debate is so much more real. You must bring your passport and reserve a seat in the gallery by phoning ahead. Free tours run every day on the hour from 09.00–13.00.

Afterwards, cool off with a stroll in the adjacent **Company Gardens**, the remainder of the huge vegetable patch laid out by Van Riebeek's people (see page 15); it has, however, grown into a place of oak-lined avenues, paths and trimmed lawns. Squirrels will compete fiercely for any food you might have handy.

Nearby is the **Groote Kerk** (big church) (43 Adderley Street; tel: 021 461 7044) which is unique for its enclosed pews, massive pulpit carved from stinkwood and Burmese teak, and a 6,000-pipe organ. Open daily 10.00–14.00. Tours are free.

The **Castle** on Buitenkant Street (tel: 021 469 1249) was completed in 1679 as a replacement for the original mud fort built by Van Riebeek and it is worth the R15 entrance which includes a tour. The defence force uses it as a base but it is more or less unchanged, right down to the gloomy subterranean dungeons.

The **Victoria & Alfred Waterfront** seems to have become the main tourist attraction. Set in a working part of the harbour, it's a collection of shops, restaurants, cinemas and bars. Its location among the quays of Cape Town's fishing fleet is the only thing that saves the Waterfront from being just another Mariner's Wharf. A number of boat operators work from here, offering tours *around*, but not *to*, Robben Island as well as sundowner cruises, scuba diving, sailing and seal-watching trips.

If you do only one thing at the Waterfront, go to the **Two Oceans**

Aquarium (Dock Road; tel: 021 418 3823). Marine life in all its forms from both the cold Atlantic and warm Indian oceans, is the motif in massive displays and vivid colours. Getting in costs not much less than a dorm bed in most backpackers but then this is why you're cooking the odd meal in your hostel, right? *Open daily 09.30–18.00. Admission Adults R40, students and pensioners R30 (with ID) and R20 for children up to 17.*

Museums

South African Cultural Museum (Adderley and Wale Street; tel: 021 461 8280) displays the full history of the country's early settlers in fine detail. *Open Mon–Sat 09.3–16.30. Admission R5.*

The **South African Museum** (25 Victoria Street; tel: 021 424 3330) concentrates on natural history, focused mainly on the sea. Also has exhibits on the San Bushmen, Khoikhoi, Xhosa and Sotho people. *Open daily 10.00–17.00. Admission R5.*

District Six Museum (25a Buitenkant Street; tel: 021 461 8745) demonstrates what apartheid was about. The fate of District Six is one of apartheid's many disgusting legacies. It was a busy, multiracial neighbourhood just east of the city on the lower slopes of the mountain. In 1966 the Nationalist government proclaimed the area 'for whites only' and evicted the suburbs' residents, mostly Indians and coloureds, and dumped them on the Cape Flats. District Six was flattened to make way for new houses; only the mosques and churches were left standing. The action created such a stench that new development was abandoned and the site remains bleak and windswept. The museum is a collection of photographs and stories, street signs, drawings – fragments of an otherwise physically obliterated piece of the country's history. *Open Mon–Sat 10.00–16.30. Admission R3, but you can donate more if you want. In this case, it really does go to a worthy cause.*

Bo Kaap Museum (71 Wale Street; tel: 021 424 3846) is a restoration of a typical 19th century Malay household. On the route of guided tours around the quarter but you may visit independently. *Open Tues–Sat, 09.30–16.30. Admission R3.*

The **Holocaust Museum** (84 Hatfield Street; tel: 021 462 5553) is a good museum on the history of Jews in South Africa, based on articles, photographs and artefacts. *Open Tue and Thur 13.30–17.00; Sun 10.30–12.00. Admission free.*

The **South African Maritime Museum** (Dock Road, Victoria & Alfred Waterfront; tel: 021 419 2505) displays South Africa's shipping history in full colour. Admission includes entrance to SAS *Somerset*, the preserved boom defence vessel moored nearby. *Open daily 10.00–17.0. Admission adults R10, children R3.*

OUTSIDE CAPE TOWN

The city's best features are its outdoor attractions. What's more, most of them are free! Beaches line both sides of the peninsula so if the wind is blowing, head to the other coast. The mountain is crisscrossed by walking trails, some severe, some gentle. When the sea is calm – which is often – there is sea kayaking on both coasts. Mountain bikers will be in rapture over routes that lead through forests, winelands and down mountains.

The **Peninsula National Park** was recently proclaimed a reserve over its entire 29,165ha and is full of mammals, birds and 2,500 species of flowering plant. The Cape Fynbos, with its 8,500 plant species, is the smallest of the world's six floral kingdoms, all of it limited to a coastal stretch running from Clanwilliam on the West Coast to Grahamstown in the east. It is this unique vegetation that you will see on the peninsula, along with mammals such as baboons and small antelope. For a quick and easy introduction to the world of fynbos – pronounced 'fain-boss' – go to the **Kirstenbosch National Botanic Gardens** on Rhodes Avenue in the southern suburbs (tel: 021 762 1166). Open daily 08.00–18.00 (19.00 in summer). Admission R5.

Mountain walks

You could spend years hiking the peninsula's trails and still not do the same walk twice. For walks on Table Mountain itself, the first thing to do is get a map of the approved paths, available from the **Mountain Club of South Africa** (tel: 021 465 3412), which shows every route in excellent detail. Contours are shown so you can get an idea of the topography as well. If a route looks like it might be beyond your capabilities then it probably is. Get advice from the Mountain Club.

On Table Mountain's flat top there are walks of around 30–40 minutes which take you all over the area around the cable station and down to the city's reservoirs at the back of the mountain. But it is much more rewarding, and cheaper, to tackle the mountain from the bottom. People normally hike up and then take the cable car down (tel: 021 424 8181), one-way fare R30. This saves both time and significant wear and tear on your knees. The cable car runs from a station high over the city to the western tip of the massif itself. At R50 for a round trip, it is not a cheap ride, but people still flock to it in droves anyway.

There are too many walks on the peninsula to describe here. The Mountain Club publishes a walking guide but if you plan to spend time here and mountain walking is your thing, get a copy of Mike Lundy's *Best Walks in the Cape Peninsula*, published by Struik, and available at just about any Cape Town bookshop. The following routes are my favourites.

A few routes

The hike up **Lion's Head** is one of the best. Two hours of fairly stiff walking will give you a truly fantastic view of the city, the Atlantic coast and north across the dunes to the Boland. Try it at full moon for added effect, but see page 103. There are two sets of chains on the way to aid scramblers over tricky sections but you can avoid them by taking the alternative, longer route.

The **Pipe Track** is a three-hour amble on the west side of the mountain, starting at Kloof Nek and following a level path to Slangolie Ravine. You return the same way. The view of the Atlantic coast is excellent.

The **Arrow Face Traverse** is a remarkable hike that starts at the lower cable station, soars up a steep gully and then traverses the Right or Arrow Face

MOUNTAIN MADNESS

Every year, hundreds of people have to be rescued from Table Mountain. It may have something to do with the fact that just because the mountain overlooks the city, people think hiking on it is like having a picnic on the beach. So they wander off up the slopes, wearing shorts and flip-flops, the mist comes down or it starts raining and they get lost. But instead of sitting tight and waiting for better conditions, they start blundering around, looking for the way home, because hey, the city's just down there after all. In 1993, eight people in one party fell to their deaths while walking on Devil's Peak. The rules of mountain walking apply:

- Never hike alone. Three is the minimum size of a party, four is ideal. That way, at least one person can go for help if there is an accident.
- Never split up the party. Move at the pace of the slowest walker.
- Tell someone where you are going and when you expect to be back. Don't deviate from your route because if there is an accident, at least the search and rescue people will be looking in the right place. It might help to note that in the event of an accident caused by your own stupidity – such as deviating from your chosen route on a whim – you will be charged for the cost of the rescue. Given that this invariably involves fuel-guzzling helicopters and the services of highly-specialised personnel, this is likely to be expensive, even with a beneficial exchange rate.
- Use a map or a guide book or go with someone who know where they are going.
- Take warm clothing. Even though it may be 35°C in the city, the weather on the mountain can change terrifyingly quickly. A lightweight, breathable waterproof jacket should be part of your travelling gear anyway. Take a hat as well. If it's sunny, you have sun protection; if it's misty, raining or cold, a hat will help retain body heat.
- If the mist comes down, stop walking. It is very easy to walk off the edge of a precipice in these conditions, even if you are following a path.
- If you get lost, stop. Do not blunder on but retrace your steps until you get your bearings again.
- Drink plenty of water. Water is not always available on some routes so take a full waterbottle and fill it whenever you get a chance.
- Do not set off too late in the day. Hiking on mountains in the dark is pointless as well as dangerous.
- Keep an eye on the weather. If it looks threatening, go down.

of the mountain about two-thirds of the way up the steep, flat part that dominates the city. While still a walk – as opposed to a full-on rock climb — it has some extremely exposed sections where the ground is hundreds of feet below. If you are not an experienced mountain walker or have a fear of heights, find another walk.

The hike up the back of the mountain from Constantia Nek to the upper cable station via the **Waterworks Museum** is fairly long (four hours) but not too arduous, depending on how you handle it. Most people start by taking the cableway up and ambling downhill to Constantia but unless you have a car at both ends, this will result in transport hassles. I prefer to tackle it as a round trip from Constantia Nek. The museum houses artefacts left over from the construction of the reservoirs including a narrow gauge steam locomotive that was left up there when building was finished.

Abseiling

One way of getting a different experience of the mountain is to abseil off it. There are a couple of sites but the 100m abseil down the front of the mountain is the one to test your nerves on as you lean back into 1,000m of air. It is completely safe. There are a couple of operators: Cape Town School of Mountaineering (tel: 021 671 9604; email: simon@orc-industries.co.za) or Abseil Africa (tel: 021 424 4760; email: abseil@iafrica.com).

Rock climbing

Rock climbers are blessed with some of the country's finest routes; the intense exposure more than makes up for the low grades on some routes. For information and maps, contact the Mountain Club of South Africa, (tel: 021 465 3412; email: mcsacc@iafrica.com). If you can, bring your own gear because there is plenty of good climbing elsewhere in the country.

Mountain biking

There are various routes for all levels of experience. Locals rate highly the **Tokai Forest** and the routes around **Silvermine**, both near Constantia, south of the city and the **Table Mountain Double Descent**, just below the cliffs at the lower cable station. You can hire bikes through Rent 'n Ride (tel: 021 434 1122), R60 for a day; you must leave a credit card as a deposit. If you want a guided tour, contact Downhill Adventures (tel: 021 422 0388; email: downhill@mweb.co.za).

THE BEACHES
Atlantic coast

There's something for everyone here. Locals tend to pick a beach and make it their spot. If the sun is shining, people will be on the beach, even on weekdays, which does make you wonder who's doing the work. Even if the wind is blowing, some beaches will be protected from it. There's really too much choice. Starting in the far north:

Blouberg, 15 miles from town, and **Milnerton** Long, fine stretches of sand and the place to get *the* view of the mountain. The wind often pumps here and the water is cold. No surprise that this is windsurfing/kite flyers' heaven. Take a bus from the terminus in Adderley Street.

Sea Point Not a lot of sand on this part of the coast but there are some nifty little hideaways like **Rocklands**, just over the rocks from Beach Rd, and **Graaff's Pool**, a men-only nudist – and mostly gay – tidal pool.

Clifton A gorgeous beach divided by granite boulders into four separate beaches, all signposted, and each with its own trendy crowd. A glamorous place, lots of hot bodies on show and icy water to cool off in. Good for sundowners and sheltered from all but the north gales. Minibuses, Rikkis and buses serve this route. The beach is at the foot of a steep set of steps leading down from the road.

Camps Bay Long beach with great surfing. It has a great view of the Twelve Apostles, a geological feature which runs in a great sandstone chain down the Atlantic coast. With its palm trees and the line of restaurants and bars lining the road just behind, it has quite a Miami feel to it and can get fearsomely crowded too. Buses, Rikkis and minibuses run here.

Bakoven Small and exclusive, and a long way from any shops and cafés. Models – the most beautiful of the city's beautiful people – used to hang out here. Take a bus or minibus from Adderley Street.

Oudekraal A group of tiny beaches separated by rocks. Lots of rock pools and even the remains of a tanker which is visible at low water. Good diving spot. It is halfway between Camps Bay and Llandudno, so harder to get to than most. Take a bus or minibus.

Llandudno Superb beach on a lovely bay dotted with granite boulders. A long way from town so it is generally less crowded than others (although this theory goes out the window in December). Llandudno is one of Cape Town's affluent suburbs as its massive houses attest.

Sandy Bay Beautiful, utterly secluded and relaxed nudist beach (although stripping off is optional) 20–30 minutes' walk along the coast from Llandudno. The effort of access means that there are fewer scaly, voyeur types hanging about but lone women should take care. There is a very obvious gay section. You can take a bus from town but you'll have to do the extra walk from the main road turn-off down into Llandudno first.

Hout Bay Long, south facing beach which is popular with Hobie Cat sailors. The view is lovely but the nearby fishing harbour and its attendant reeks might ruin things a little. Take a bus or minibus from town.

Noordhoek and Kommetjie Two villages separated by 8km **Long Beach**, one of the finest in Africa. The water is cold but the walking is excellent. It is a place where dogs can go crazy with excitement. The wreck of the steamship *Kakapo* is buried in the sand half-way along. Be wary of walking alone as there have been some muggings. Unless you have your own transport, it is difficult to get to. The best way is to take a train to Fish Hoek and then a taxi to Kommetjie. Women should not hitchhike on this road.

Scarborough and Misty Cliffs These are the wildest beaches in the Cape with few people hanging about, even though here are quite a few holiday homes on the mountain behind. The surfing and fishing are excellent and Scarborough's rock pools are great for picking fresh mussels (check with the Sea Fisheries Institute on 402 3911 to make sure there is no poisonous red tide first). To get here, follow the instructions for Kommetjie and then think creatively.

Accommodation
Scarborough Fair 79 Hilltop Rd, Scarborough; tel: 021 780 1775 or 082 955 9152. Double R300 (it's the view, you see), dorm R50. As positions go, this place is hard to beat. The house looks down onto the beautiful curves of Scarborough Beach, a million dollar view if ever there was one. There are dorm rooms on the top floor or doubles with own bathrooms below.

Stormy Sea Cottage Scarborough; tel: 021 419 2727 or 780 1384 after hours; fax: 419 2729; email: stormysca@aroundaboutcars.com. Cottage R150. This is a self-catering cottage, sleeping 2–3 people, set in the most magnificent surroundings. The owners – of Around About Cars fame – offer a great accommodation and car deal for R225 per day. Your fourth day here is free.

Brightwater Lodge 9 Brighton St, Hout Bay; tel: 021 790 2031; fax: 790 2025; email: briwater@mweb.co.za. B&B R210 per person sharing (R150 May–Sep low season), Apartment R500 per night (R400 low season). Lovely, spotless double-storey cottage and a self-catering apartment which sleeps four, one block back from the beach.

The False Bay coast
False Bay is the huge sweeping expanse of water that lies in the embrace of Cape Point to the west and Cape Hangklip, 33km to the east. It was named by the Portuguese who at first thought that Cape Point was the tip of Africa and that the bay was the Indian Ocean. The water here is generally about 5°C warmer than on the Atlantic seaboard but the beaches are less spectacular. As the wind often gets up in the afternoons, this side is best saved for morning jaunts.

One of the best ways to get to, and explore, this side of the peninsula is by commuter train on the **Simonstown railway**, Metrorail (tel: 021 449 2443); it's even better if you take a bike along too.

The Simonstown line follows a dramatically beautiful route, at least for the second half of the journey. From Cape Town, the line runs through the leafy southern suburbs before swinging west at Muizenberg and picking its way over the rocks along the seashore to Simonstown.

Trains run on the Simonstown line around every 30 minutes, from 05.00–20.00 There are more trains at peak times. Not all the trains run through to Simonstown, some services terminating in Fish Hoek. Try and ride in a coach with fully opening windows – many of the newer coaches have sealed, tinted windows of which only the top third opens. Be careful riding the trains at night (see *Safety*, page 47). Fares for the full distance are R9.50 single (double return) in 1st and R5.50 in 3rd.

If you're hungry or needing a beer to fight the heat, look out for Biggsy's Restaurant Carriage, the country's only restaurant car on a commuter train. It is attached to one of the sets running between the city and Simonstown and makes five return trips a day, starting at 06.15, while the last departure is from Simonstown at 19.00. The full English breakfast is an outstanding way to start the day if you're heading for the city. You can also book in advance (tel: 021 449 3870).

The railway line is jammed between the sea and the shore and sea spray floats through the train windows on blustery days. Open the window, sit back and it feels like you're at sea. The line skirts the pretty fishing village of Kalk Bay and the seaside villages of Muizenberg, St James, Fish Hoek and Clovelly. It's worth taking a slow trip along the line and getting off to explore these little places. Muizenberg sits at the western end of a fine, endless white beach. Vaguely reminiscent of an English seaside town (it always makes me think of Eastbourne), it has faded in recent years although the locals are pushing hard to restore its amenities. Years back, the local council built a tasteless entertainment centre called the Pavilion which has not been a major success.

If you like bears and trains and things, it is worth stopping off at the **Muizenberg Toy Museum**, 8 Beach Road (tel: 021 788 1569), two blocks down from the railway station. *Open Tue–Sun, 10.00–16.00. Admission R3.* Most people come for Muizenberg's exceptional beach. Its warm water and predictable, even sets of waves make it a great place to surf, especially for beginners. Excellent beaches can also be found a few miles along the coast towards Simonstown at St James and Fish Hoek. St James is famous for its brightly painted Victorian bathing huts which line the sea shore.

You can buy fish and chips wrapped in newspaper at the little quayside chippie in Kalk Bay harbour and sit and watch the boats come and go. Kalk Bay also has the **Brass Bell**, one of the world's best situated pubs, perched on the edge of a tidal pool, between the railway line and the ocean. The pub has an open air courtyard where you can sit and be overwhelmed by the sweeping view of False Bay. The front door of the upstairs restaurant opens right onto the station platform which is useful for those days when you have spent too long in the sun with a cold beer in your hand. There is also the **Olympia Café and Deli** (tel: 021 788 6396), a lovely café across the road from the harbour where you can watch the boat action over the rim of your cappuccino cup.

If you want to do some *real* **fishing** then Kalk Bay is the place. Every day the 30-foot trawler *Violet Glen* sets sail from Kalk Bay carrying a bunch of trippers, brave people who want a day's Cape-style fishing using handlines. You spend the day on the water and then the boat returns to harbour where the catch is generally sold on the quayside. The boat is owned by – wait for it – Robert Fish (tel: 021 785 1657); trips cost R60 per person.

Simonstown, home port of the South African navy, is the terminus of the 90-minute train ride from the city. It is very much a naval town, albeit with many fine Victorian buildings lining its main street. The naval dockyard is the dominant feature, but it is also a calm anchorage for privately owned sailing boats. The British Atlantic Squadron founded the town as a naval base in 1814, building workshops and a drydock and some of the early buildings remain, including South Africa's only intact Martello Tower. It is not open to the public but you can ask at the gates to be allowed to look around the outside. Simonstown remained a British naval base until it was handed over to South Africa in 1957. Don't ask where the navy is – it is a sore point and one that will likely only be soothed when the first of four corvettes ordered from Spain and a submarine from Germany arrive. Meanwhile, the country urgently needs to beef-up its sea-going capability to be able to end the illegal fishing and poaching that goes on in its territorial waters on a horrific scale.

A brass statue of a great dane in the parking lot off the main street is in honour of Able Seaman Just Nuisance, a dog of no fixed address who, among other things, used to escort drunken sailors off the train and to their ships during World War II. AB Just Nuisance was a formal member of the Royal Navy and received full pay to the end.

The town's two museums, the **Simonstown Museum**, Court Road (tel: 021 786 3046) and the **South Africa Naval Museum**, St George's Road (tel: 021 787 4686) are right next door to each other. The former tells the story of the town as well as the history of the San and Khoikhoi people who were first here. The naval museum is noteworthy for its mock-up of a submarine control room. Both museums occupy historic buildings built in 1777 and 1815 respectively.

Incredible views and a reasonably sheltered position have pushed real estate prices through the roof but many well-off pensioners have made this their last anchorage. Near Boulders Beach, named for the distinctive rounded rocks which surround it, is a **penguin sanctuary**, home to a large colony of jackass penguins. There is a R5 fee to get onto the beach; the money is partly used to pay the penguin watchman who is there to make sure people don't abuse them. The beach is sheltered and the water quite warm and you can swim among the penguins if they don't swim away first.

This part of the coast is excellent for **sea kayaking**, especially in winter when the bay is sheltered from the north west winds. **Coastal Kayak Trails** (tel: 021 439 1134, web: www.kayak.co.za) runs trips in very stable two-seat kayaks along the coast. Travelling by kayak is fantastic. It puts you *into* the marine environment along with seals, dolphins and penguins and the absence of noisy engines means these creatures are much more relaxed. Trips cost R150 for a half-day.

Heading south from the town takes you towards **Cape Point**. This part of the coast remains almost totally undeveloped. Its remoteness means fewer people, at least down in the coves and little beaches. Capetonians have their secret spots down here. Places to explore are Smitswinkel Bay and Buffels Bay with its tidal pool, both a few miles south of Simonstown. There are plenty of fine coves and bays and it is a beautiful road to cycle on. Watch out for the baboons, though: they have been spoiled by tourists who feed them out of their cars and have become aggressive as a result.

The **Cape of Good Hope Nature Reserve** (tel: 021 762 9620; email: LeanneV@parks-sa.co.za) is part of the Cape Peninsula National Park, covering most of the southern portion of the peninsula. It is a mountain fynbos habitat with lots of birds and a number of mammals including springbok, Cape mountain zebra, bontebok and eland, Africa's largest antelope species. You can get about the reserve on foot or by mountain bike, although guides are required for the latter. There is an overnight hiking trail (bookings, tel: 021 780 9100) which can take no more than six people per night. R60 per person per day if you stay overnight and R20 for a day permit.

At Cape Point itself, a long path with steps leads up from the car park (or you can ride up on the funicular, which hardly seems worth the money) to a stunning lookout over the sea. The land tumbles away below you and you feel as if you're at the end of the world. *Everyone* should make this pilgrimage.

Accommodation

Topsail House St George's St, Simonstown; tel: 021 786 5537 or 082 677 7277. Double R130, dorm R55. Free pick-up from the station (Simonstown, not Cape Town). Set in the grounds of a restored convent school right in the heart of the quiet town. Beaches and restaurants are nearby. If you are going sea kayaking at dawn, this is the place to stay the night before.

African Lizard Rock Sunnycove (near Fish Hoek); tel: 021 782 3807; fax: 782 7646; email: lizroc@iafrica.com; web: http://users.iafrica.com/l/li/lizroc. Cabin R120 (low season), R280 (high season). A family of four could quite easily stay here. Hideaway on the mountain slopes overlooking False Bay. Mountain walks lead out of the back door.

Tom's Cabin 30 Camilla St, Glencairn (near Simonstown); tel: 021 782 7329; fax: 021 787 7329. 2-bed cabin R120 (low season), R180 (high season). Self-catering cabin with a view of the bay.

Sunbird Lodge 66 Clovelly Rd, Clovelly (near Fish Hoek); tel: 021 782 2778; email: crida@mweb.co.za. R60 per person (low season – minimum of 2 people), R330 per night for the whole cabin in high season. Self-catering holiday apartment set back on the mountainside. Sleeps four people and has a sea view.

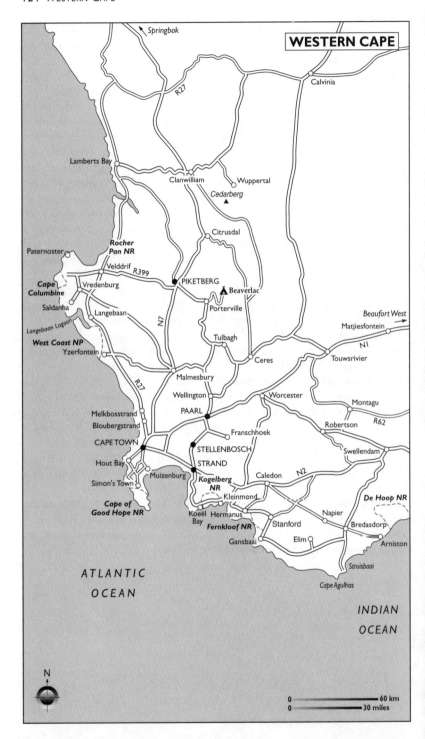

WESTERN CAPE

Springbok

Calvinia

R27

Lamberts Bay

Clanwilliam   Wuppertal

Cedarberg ▲

Citrusdal

Paternoster

Rocher Pan NR

Velddrif   R399

Cape Columbine   Vredenburg   ● PIKETBERG

Saldanha   ▲ Beaverlac

Langebaan   Porterville

Langebaan Lagoon   N7

Beaufort West →

Matjiesfontein

West Coast NP   Tulbagh
Yzerfontein   N1

Ceres   Touwsrivier

Malmesbury

R27   Wellington   Worcester   Montagu

Melkbosstrand   ● PAARL   R62
Bloubergstrand   Robertson

Franschhoek

CAPE TOWN   ● STELLENBOSCH   Swellendam

Hout Bay   ● STRAND

Simon's Town   Muizenburg   *Kogelberg NR*   Caledon   N2

De Hoop NR

Cape of Good Hope NR   Kleinmond   Napier   Bredasdorp

Koeël Bay   Hermanus   Stanford   Arniston
Fernkloof NR

Gansbaai   Elim   *Struisbaai*

Cape Agulhas

ATLANTIC
OCEAN

INDIAN
OCEAN

N

0   60 km
0   30 miles

Western Cape

Wine making is one of the country's oldest industries. The first vineyard was planted in 1655. On February 2 1659, Commander Van Riebeek (see page 15) wrote in his journal: 'To-day, glory be to God, wine was pressed for the first time and the new must fresh from the tub was tasted.' Things really got going, however, after governor Simon van der Stel arrived in 1679 when by his order the winelands in Stellenbosch and Constantia were established. He also encouraged French Huguenot settlers fleeing religious persecution back home to come to the Cape and these knowledgeable people brought further expertise to a new industry.

The wineries are on some of the most exquisite real estate in the country. Imagine white-washed Cape Dutch homesteads set in green meadows with oak-lined avenues, all presided over by the towering mountains of the Western Cape, and you have a pretty good idea of the setting (for some of the wineries anyway). Most of the estates welcome visitors and wine tasting is either free or for a nominal fee.

To get around them requires careful planning though; in the western Cape alone, there are enough vineyards spread over three distinct areas, with three different wine routes, to keep you busy for weeks. Trying to rush around to all of them would be a great injustice, not least of all to your pocket. I am no wine expert and thankfully the vineyards don't expect you to be either. I also have not been to all the estates so in some cases you will be going in without any preconceived ideas.

Maps and brochures are available from the Stellenbosch Tourist Bureau (36 Market Street; tel: 021 851 4022) or from the excellent Cape Town Tourism office (corner Burg Street and Castle Street, Cape Town; tel: 021 426 4260). Pick a few estates that sound good and then plan how to get there. Even if you are carless, you could cycle around or do a vineyard trail on foot.

PRACTICAL DETAILS

Stellenbosch Tourist Bureau 36 Market St; tel: 021 883 9633; fax: 883 8017; email: eikestad@iafrica.com

Metrorail Tel: 021 449 2443. The station is about ten minutes' walk from the centre of the town.

GETTING THERE AND AROUND
Train
A fairly sparse commuter train service runs from Cape Town to Stellenbosch, the ride taking little over one hour. The route passes through industria for a few miles out of Cape Town but then later through rolling hills and vineyards for the rest of the trip. Bear in mind that there may be a long wait between trains and plan your day accordingly. Metrorail can tell you what trains are running when. Do not ride after dark and try to stick with other people as muggings have been reported on these trains. The station is about ten minutes' walk from the centre of the town.

Car
Take the N1 north from Cape Town and follow the signs to Stellenbosch. This route will also take you to the Franschhoek and Paarl wine routes; for Paarl, stay on the N1 until you see signs for the town. All the wine routes are clearly signed for motorists.

Bicycle
Stellenbosch and its immediate surrounds are great for cycling and it is possible to do a self-guided tour of some vineyards by bike. You will need to be realistic about how much ground you can cover and also how much you will feel cycling under a hot African sun if you you've spent more time than you should have sampling the wares at any of the estates. You can take your bike on the trains but check with Metrorail first in case peak restrictions apply on some trains.

In Paarl, you can hire bikes at Bike Point (1 Kaapse Draai, tel: 021 683 3901) for R40 for a full day or R200 per week. If you take a guide, they'll lop 20% off the cost. In Stellenbosch, there are bikes for hire at Stumble Inn (see *Accommodation* below).

On foot
One of the best ways to get around, although not into the actual wineries themselves, is on foot, following the **Vineyard Hiking Trail** which rambles across a couple of estates. The trail starts at Stellenbosch Farmers' Winery and climbs up through forests and vineyards to Kuils River. There are two routes, one 16 miles and the other four miles. You have to buy one permit (R10) and then pay R4 per hiker. Phone 021 883 3584; email: eikestad@iafrica.com for permits.

The **Boland Trail**, a far tougher walk, runs along the top of the mountains that dominate the horizon east of Stellenbosch. The three-day 30 mile trail runs north over the Hottentots' Holland mountains, starting either at Sir Lowry's Pass or down in the valley at Grabouw forest station and finishing high above Franschhoek. It is a magnificent, lonely hike and you should be prepared for some hard walking. I had the misfortune of being conscripted into the South African army and the bosses sent a group us on the trail, in army boots and with full kit. Among other things, it was an early lesson in the importance of hiking in the right footwear. Book through the Western Cape Department of Forestry (tel: 021 582 5466).

ACCOMMODATION
Stellenbosch
Backpackers Inn De Wet Centre, Church St; tel: 021 887 2020; fax: 887 2010. Double R160, dorm R50. Simple, clean hostel. The manager runs tours on foot to Lwandle township, a good opportunity to see how other South Africans live.
Stumble Inn 12 Market St; tel: 021 887 4049; email: stumble@iafrica.com. Double R140, dorm R45. Two houses, one hostel. Since the overland trucks call here for a bit of fun, you have a choice – go crazy or go quiet. They offer horse and bike tours of the region.

Stellenbosch is awash with B&Bs of varying quality. Prices range from R65 for a bed in a self-catering flatlet to R500 per person and upwards in a top B&B in an old town house. The best source of information is the tourist bureau who have a comprehensive list of just about every place in town.

Franschhoek
Backpacker establishments have yet to surface in this quiet place so you are limited to B&Bs or self-catering lodges. It tends to be more expensive here too. A few options, based on low season rates in 2000.

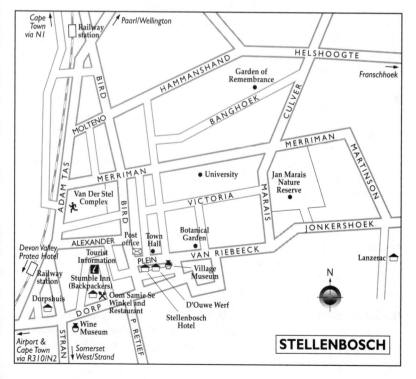

Belle Fleur Happy Valley Rd; tel: 021 876 2280. B&B R135 per person, self-catering R110.
Klein Oliphants Hoek 14 Akademie St, tel: 021 876 2566. B&B R225 per person
Bordeaux House Huguenot Rd; tel: 021 876 3190. Self-catering R200 per room
Erica Guesthouse Erica St; tel: 021 876 2425. B&B R125 per person

THINGS TO SEE AND DO

The three main wine routes around Cape Town are based on the towns of Stellenbosch, Franschhoek and Paarl. A fourth area, Constantia, just south of Cape Town itself, is beautifully located on the back slopes of Table Mountain.

Franschhoek

Of the three main regions, Franschhoek, named for the French settlers who made their home at the foot of the Franschhoek Mountains, is easily the most spectacular. The village is one of the prettiest in the land but is a relatively expensive place to spend time in. The valley is home to the exquisitely beautiful **Boschendal** estate (Pniel Road, Groot Drakenstein; tel: 021 870 4210), 300 years old and one of the best wine tasting experiences in the area. Afterwards, you can sit under the oak trees, have a light lunch and gorge yourself on the surroundings. Tough to get to without a car but worth the effort. *Open Mon–Sat 08.30–16.30, Sun 08.30–12.30 (Dec–Jan); Mon–Fri 08.30–16.30, Sat 8.30–12.30 (Feb–Nov). Tasting R5.*

Another superb Franschhoek estate is **L'Ormarins** (Franschhoek Road; tel: 021 874 1026), a classic example of Cape Dutch architecture which you approach down an avenue of oaks. *Open Mon–Fri 09.00–16.30, Sat 09.00–12.30. Tasting R5.*

Paarl

Paarl might not have the spectacular scenery but it does have excellent estates, including my own favourite. The town itself is dominated by Paarl Mountain, a looming granite outcrop, but, this feature aside, it is a pretty unremarkable farming town. On Main St you will find some beautiful Cape Dutch, Georgian and Victorian buildings, one of which, the Old Pastorie (Parsonage) is now the home of the **Paarl Museum** (303 Main Street; tel: 021 872 2651).

The wine estates include:

Nederburg Meaker Road, Huguenot; tel: 021 862 3104. Probably the country's most successful vineyard; it's certainly the best-known and you will find their wines on every wine list. *Open Mon–Fri 08.30–17.00; Sat 09.00–13.00. Tasting free.*

Backsberg Simondium Road; tel: 021 875 5141. Backsberg has a self-guided cellar tour which explains the whole wine-making process which is great for wine virgins like me. But this is no lightweight vineyard – their wines have won acclaim. *Tastings R5.*

Fairview Suid-Agter-Paarl Road; tel: 021 863 2450. My favourite, with its goat tower and roaming animals (and I am a sucker for animals). The goats are there to provide raw material for the estate's own fine range of cheeses which can be bought from the deli, along with plenty of other goodies. You can take your picnic on to the rolling lawns while the goats watch approvingly from their tower. *Open Mon–Fri 08.30–17.00; Sat 08.30–13.00. Tasting R10, but cheese is included.*

Stellenbosch

Stellenbosch, the country's second-oldest town, is situated in the shadow of the Helshoogte mountains. It is a wonderful place with long oak-lined avenues fronted with Cape Dutch, Georgian and Victorian buildings. Sloots (irrigation furrows) with running water line some of the shaded streets and give an impression of coolness on blinding summer days. It is an important place for Afrikaners who regard it as the centre of their language and culture. There are a number of good museums and galleries and plenty of restaurants. The surrounding mountains are laced with superb hiking and mountain biking trails. The university is the town's other pervasive influence. The fact that the town owes its prosperity to wine and the University of Stellenbosch proves that you can mix students and lots of wine without carnage being the only possible outcome.

It is a great town to amble around and you will find yourself wishing you lived here. A walking tour (get a map from the tourist information bureau on Market St) takes you to just about all the historic buildings including the **Rembrandt van Rijn Art Museum**, the **Stellenryk Wine Museum**, the **Stellenbosch Village Museum** and **Oom Samie se Winkel** – a re-creation of a general store which actually does sell carnage in the forms of bottles of mampoer (moonshine).

Stellenbosch has the lion's share of the vineyards dotted about on the surrounding hills and too many to do any real justice to here. Those I have been to include Spier, Simonsig, Thelema and the exquisite Vergelegen.

Spier R310; tel: 0800 220 282 or 021 881 3096. A wine-making and restaurant experience, not just a vineyard, it is popular and its wines have won awards. Spier is pretty easy to get to if you don't have a car. Take the commuter train from Cape Town to Stellenbosch and get off at Lynedoch. It's a ten minute walk from the station to the estate. Just watch out for the traffic! 1st class return fare costs R19. *Open daily 09.00–17.00. Guided tastings every hour (R12); for R6 you can do it yourself.*

Simonsig Kromme Rhee Road; tel: 021 882 2044. Yet another beautiful estate and one that welcomes people and their picnic hampers. *Open Mon–Fri 08.30–17.00; Sat 08.30–16.00. Price of tastings starts at R4 but varies according to the number of wines you try.*

Thelema Helshoogte Pass, on the Franschhoek road; tel: 021 885 1924. A brand-new name in wine making which has been responsible for a flood of good wine. (I trust my dad on this score – he holds up bottles of Thelema's finest while giving voice to great chortles of satisfaction.) The estate has such a grand view, you'll ask yourself why you didn't think of going into wine-making. *Open Mon–Fri 09.00–17.00, Sat 09.00–13.00. Tastings free.*

Vergelegen Lourensford Road, Somerset West; tel: 021 847 1334. One of the oldest and most beautiful estates of the lot. The old – try 1700 – Cape Dutch homestead (now a museum) sits against a backdrop of towering blue Cape mountains on an estate that once had 250,000 vines growing on it, thanks to the overwrought enthusiasm of Willem Adriaan van der Stel, son of the Cape governor. The estate now gets most of its grapes from other vineyards although it does have flourishing vines of its own. *Open 09.30–16.00. Tastings R5 (none on Sunday); entrance to the estate R10.00.*

WORCESTER AND THE HEX RIVER PASS
The winelands of the Boland are almost completely encircled by towering mountains which, for hundreds of years, limited expansion into the hinterland. There were passes from the fertile valleys into the hot, dry Karoo, known firstly to San hunters, and later used by trekboers, explorers and missionaries.

The Valley of the Hex
Heading north from the wine and farming towns of Wellington and Paarl, the countryside begins to be squashed between encroaching mountains. Worcester, the last town of any size before one leaves the Western Cape for the Karoo, huddles beneath the Hex River Mountains. The main route to the Karoo is through the valley of the Hex River, starting where the national road and the railway squeeze between a sheer rockface and the river, and into a beautiful, narrow valley lined with vineyards. The first Europeans settled here in the early 1700s and the valley has been a notable grape producing centre ever since. The railway line and road closely follow the course of the twisting river until De Doorns where the road begins to claw its way up the mountainside and the railway plunges into the lengthy gloom of the Hex River tunnels.

The Hex River Pass
The range of high, granite mountains was the biggest single obstacle facing railway and road builders. From De Doorns in the heart of the Hex River valley, the railway climbs to 959m above sea level, an altitude gain of 482m in just 25km. The railway pass itself is now closed, replaced by a series of long, dark tunnels. The ruling grade is an easier 1-in-66 and the route 7km shorter. The longest tunnel is 12km long. It is quicker and smoother but the magic of the ride over a mountain pass has been lost. The road sweeps up the mountainside, leaving the fertile country with its vineyards behind and, in a somewhat shocking transition, plunging into the arid plains of the Karoo on the other side.

THE OVERBERG

The Overberg region is to South Africa what the South Downs are to England. It is farming country, a region of rolling hills bounded by the ocean to the south and the Langeberg mountain range to the north. It is sheep and wheat country (although I am told they do grow other things) and huge apple and pear farms lie in the embrace of the Hottentot's Holland mountains.

The coastline from False Bay around Cape Hangklip and past Hermanus, Danger Point and Cape Agulhas is *beautiful*. Where the mountains fall straight into the sea, the coast is rugged and wild, but it opens up into sweeping bays with long, curving beaches, and fynbos and farmland as you head further east. Its tip is at Cape Agulhas, the southernmost point of Africa, where the Indian and Atlantic Oceans meet. The coast is littered with shipwrecks, including the legendary *Birkenhead*, which sank off Danger Point in 1852 and, when you get away from the seaside villages and farming towns, there is a sense of almost overwhelming loneliness. It is certainly a relatively sparsely populated area – the coastal plain with its dune scrub was once regarded as too poor for agriculture and most of the development happened inland. It was also cut off from the Cape by the steep Hottentots Holland and remained so until engineers built a pass over the mountains in the late 19th century.

Here, in the shelter of the Langeberg mountains, settlers were busy farming as long ago as the late 17th century. They farmed sheep, grew wheat and tried to cut the apron strings that tied them to Cape Town. Not much has changed except that you are as likely to see huge fields of rapeseed as wheat, and the locals are relatively tolerant of their government. Well, sometimes.

Practical details

One of the best places to get up-to-date tourism information is from the Overberg Tourism Office (18 High Street, Napier; tel: 028 423 3169 or 214 1466; fax: 423 3325).

Getting there and away

There are two routes from Cape Town into the Overberg – over the Hottentot's Holland mountains via Sir Lowry's Pass on the busy N2 national road, or along the coast road which picks its way over the steep mountain slopes from Gordon's Bay, at the east corner of False Bay, to the seaside town of Kleinmond. This route covers the southern part of the coast from Gordon's Bay, through Hermanus, Cape Agulhas, Bredasdorp and then up to Swellendam.

The coast road rivals Cape Town's Chapman's Peak Drive for the title of most beautiful road in the world. As soon as you leave Gordon's Bay, it climbs sharply, clinging to the side of the mountain with the sea pounding the rocks hundreds of feet below an almost vertical drop. The road swoops and turns along the coast, sometimes dropping to sea level. There are lay-bys every few kilometres so that people can pull over and marvel – or gather their shattered nerves when the wind is blasting off the sea. For cyclists and bikers, a spin down this route on a calm day is nothing less than the perfect two-wheeled adventure; on a windy, rainy day, it is evil and dangerous.

It is worth dawdling on the drive. There are good viewpoints where you can pull off the road safely and have a picnic. In some places, it is easy to scramble down to the sea but vicious rip currents make swimming dangerous on this part of the coast. If you are cycling, it makes sense to break the journey overnight at the municipal campsite at **Koeël Bay** (20km from Gordon's Bay) – which must be one of the world's best-placed campgrounds – and carry on the next day. Since the coast road is a much longer way round than the main N2 route from Cape Town, there is a lot less traffic on it as well.

The mountainous terrain has defied development in all but a few places. Most of these are sleepy collections of holiday houses (some of which are disgustingly ugly) or weekend retreats for lucky Capetonians and there is little in the way of diversion for the passing traveller. If, on the other hand, you know someone with a holiday cottage on this part of the coast, you are recommended to try and wangle a few days holiday in it.

Betty's Bay, 33km from Gordon's Bay, is unremarkable except for the Harold Porter Botanic Reserve, a wildflower reserve with paths leading up the slopes to Disa Kloof and its lovely waterfall (in which you can swim). The flowers and trees are tagged which makes the fynbos kingdom accessible to everyone, not just flower spotters.

The eastern end of the coast road is marked by **Kleinmond**, a small holiday village built at the mouth of a small lagoon. While it has little to recommend it as a beauty spot, thanks to the ruinous effects of ugly face-brick architecture that proliferates in South Africa's seaside towns, there is a superb nature reserve with trails leading into the Palmiet Mountains behind the resort.

Things to see and do

The **Kogelberg Nature Reserve** (tel: 021 945 4570) is centred on the Palmiet River which tumbles down into the sea not far from Kleinmond. The reserve, which remains largely unknown, even to locals, has a 40km overnight trail into these fantastic mountains; you overnight in a mountain hut which sleeps ten. There are also plenty of short day hikes and there is also the 25km Kogelberg trail. Day permits (R11) can be collected at the Oudebosch office which is just off the coast road between Betty's Bay and Kleinmond. Permits for the overnight trail are R18 per person; phone 028 271 4010 to book.

Kleinmond also has the only backpacker on the whole road. Roots Rock (Harbour Road; tel: 028 271 5139) is a quiet place with great views of both sea and mountain. With 16 beds, it is also one of the smaller backpackers around. They go the extra mile by picking up guests at the Baz Bus stop in Bot River, a town on the other route from Cape Town. Double R120–140, dorm R45, camping R30.

Whale country

Springtime along the southern Cape coast means whales. Southern right whales migrate from the cold waters of the Southern Ocean to calve and nurse their young in the warm, protected waters of the coast. By December, most have returned to their feeding grounds in the south.

The whale-watching centre of the country is **Hermanus**, one of the nicest towns in the country with its fishing village atmosphere and laid-back feel. Its setting on the gentle curve of Walker Bay is hard to beat. From the east edge of the town, the beach runs in an unbroken white line to the fishing village of Gansbaai. Behind the town are the fynbos-covered Kleinriviersberge (little rivers) mountains where locals walk their dogs in the wild nature reserve and gulp crisp sea air into their lungs.

Hermanus has been through a bit of a boom in recent years, helped along no doubt by its whale capital status. Twenty years ago, it was a sleepy secret, populated by retirees and fishermen, and it only boomed when absent landlords arrived during the holiday season. But now there are restaurants on every corner, dozens of B&Bs and even a daily minibus to the airport and Cape Town. Ten years ago, there was not one single backpacker in Hermanus; now there are at least three (see *Accommodation* below).

All this means that Hermanus has a couple of busy times during the year: the December and April holiday periods as well as whale season from July to November. As a budget traveller this is unlikely to affect you other than that the place can get unpleasantly crowded. Plan accordingly.

Whale watching
From July until November whales can be seen all along the Cape coast but the holiday and fishing town of Hermanus has arguably the best viewing and has been called the whale capital as a result. It is good marketing on the part of the local tourism bureau, but I have had my best whale sightings right there on the promontory above the Old Harbour at the end of Main Rd. The creatures are not shy and they drift close inshore. On calm nights you can hear them grunting and splashing as they frolic 30m off the rocks.

The town has a lovely cliff path which runs along most of its shoreline and it is from the various rocky outcrops that jut into the bay that you will have the best sightings. Take a pair of binoculars and be patient. Every day during whale season, the 'whale crier' wanders around the village, blowing a horn and telling people where the best sightings are.

There are operators who offer whale watching trips on boats. I have mixed feelings about these. While you can get close to the creatures, I believe the boats are an intrusion. Some of the boat trips are run by competent operators while other operators have been warned repeatedly for getting too close and disturbing the whales. At the end of the day, it is infinitely cheaper to stand on the rocks for free and be closer than you can get in a boat.

On rainy days or when there aren't any whales around, visit the **Old Harbour Museum** which depicts the town's fishing and whaling history. The Old Harbour also has a whale buoy which picks up whale sounds and transmits them through a loudspeaker on shore.

Walking
The air and the setting make this one of the finest walking places in the world. There are paths along the cliffs, mile after mile of beach and a network of trails

leading into the mountains. I rate all of them highly especially the amble along Grotto Beach to where the lagoon opens into the sea.

The **Fernkloof Nature Reserve**, which encompasses much of the mountainside behind the town, is crisscrossed with trails; some are short, circular walks, others climb to the summit ridge where the views are superb. You can get a map from the Hermanus Publicity Association (tel: 028 312 2629). Entrance to the reserve is free.

Beaches

Hermanus has some of the best beaches on the whole coast. Nearest the village is Langbaai, a long narrow beach protected by rocky headlands on both sides. A few minutes walk away is Voîlklip, which is divided into swimming and surfing sections in order to minimise the number of people being carted off the hospital with bits of surfboard in their heads. Another short walk along the cliff path brings you to Grotto beach which continues, almost unbroken, all the way to Danger Point on the other side of the bay. Swimming is generally safe and both Grotto and Voëlklip have lifeguards during the holiday season. The water can be cold, though, and watch out for stinging bluebottles if a southeaster has been blowing for a few days.

Accommodation

Zoete Inval Traveller's Lodge 23 Main Rd; tel: 028 312 1242; email: zoetein@hermanus.co.za; web: www.zoeteinval.co.za. Double R120, dorm R40. The name means 'sweet place to fall in to' and it is. One of the nicest backpackers anywhere. If you want to know about anything in the region, ask the owners. The lodge is on the edge of the village as you approach from the Cape Town side.

Moby's Backpackers 8 Main Rd; tel: 028 313 2361; fax: 313 3519; email: moby@hermanus.co.za. Double R100–170, single R75–100, dorm R40–45, camping R35. A backpacker where double rooms outnumber dorm beds. Free breakfast included. They can organise tours such as shark-cage diving, whale and dolphin watching trips, fishing and crayfishing.

Hermanus Backpackers 26 Flower St, Hermanus; tel: 028 312 4293; fax: 313 2727; email: moobag@mweb.co.za. Double R130, dorm R45. Bright, lively backpacker in a quiet part of town but still with a view of both mountains and sea. They throw in free breakfasts and shuttles to the beach. They will pick up travellers from the Baz Bus at Bot River.

Danger Point

The road from Hermanus to Gansbaai and Danger Point loosely follows the curve of the bay, although well inland. There has been almost no development along the coast, which is remarkable in this region where every piece of beachfront land seems to have a price tag on it, and is characterised by thick swathes of dune-loving scrub.

The tiny farming village of **Stanford**, 23km from Hermanus, is worth stopping in. It is a pretty place and although it is well back from the coast, it makes a nice change from the bustle of Hermanus. New here is **The Green**

THE LOSS OF THE BIRKENHEAD

Shortly after two in the morning on a cold, clear night on February 26 1852, the troopship SS *Birkenhead*, carrying reinforcements to serve in the Eighth Frontier War raging in Eastern Cape, tore its hull open on a submerged rock half a mile off Danger Point. This ripped the bottom out of the ship and many men were drowned as they lay in their hammocks. As the ship began sinking, the surviving soldiers – some 500 – were drawn up in good order on the deck.

With just two lifeboats and a gig, there was clearly not enough room for everyone, so the seven women and 13 children on board were ordered into the boats first, starting a tradition which persists today. Then, with as many men as could safely join them, the lifeboats, along with the gig carrying nine men, stood off from the rapidly sinking ship. The soldiers remained at their posts as the *Birkenhead* sank from under them. In twenty minutes she was gone and the survivors, among whom were panicking cavalry horses, struck out for the shore through pounding surf. Some survivors were left clinging to the mainmast and the remaining part of the hull which was still on the rock but 368 officers and men and 89 sailors drowned or were taken by sharks. Sixty-eight men and eight horses made it safely to shore and another 50 were later rescued from the hull and mainmast.

On February 9 1917, there was an eerie echo of the *Birkenhead* disaster when another troopship, the *Tyndareus*, struck a mine near the same spot and started going down. A gale was blowing and it looked as if the ship would sink. Men of the Middlesex Regiment were drawn up on deck to await their fate but fortunately the ship did not sink and made it to Simonstown.

The last survivor of the *Birkenhead* died in 1937. Meanwhile, a legend persisted for decades that wild horses, apparently descendants of those cavalry chargers who survived the long swim to the beach, were living in the dunes near Gansbaai.

Roof Lodge (26 Shortmarket Street; tel: 028 341 0331; email: helre@netactive.co.za) which has doubles for R170 and dorm beds at the usual R45 and meals are cooked on request. There is not a whole lot to do in Stanford except relax for a couple of days, and maybe do some hiking or paddling on the Klein River.

The nearby **Salmonsdam Nature Reserve** (tel: 028 341 0789) is one of those little gems that almost get forgotten because they do not have big mammals. It's a small but pretty mountain fynbos reserve with some small mammals but fantastic birdlife. There is a campsite with a couple of fully equipped four-bed huts in the middle of the reserve. A couple of day trails radiate from here into the forests and mountain fynbos. The reserve is on the R316 between Stanford and Bredasdorp.

Gansbaai

Gansbaai is a fishing village but there are some fine caves at De Kelders ('the cellars') on the Hermanus side of town. It also has a great beach which, out of season, you will have to yourself. The village huddles on the leeward side of Danger Point, a thin finger of land that reaches far out into Walker Bay. The waters here are a breeding ground for great white sharks and most of the shark-cage dive boats operate from Gansbaai.

I find Danger Point a much more compelling attraction than shark-cage diving, not least of all because it's free. A rough track leads down the peninsula toward the tall lighthouse. It is a rough, often windswept place but the Walker Bay side of the coast is dotted with little sheltered coves and inlets where you can spend sun-baked days in splendid solitude. The area is protected and you will need to get permission to get into the lighthouse itself. A plaque set into the base of the lighthouse commemorates the heroism of the officers and men who went down with the troopship *Birkenhead*.

The coast beyond Danger Point remains wild and undeveloped. There are a few campsites at Uilenkraalsmond, Pearly Beach and Die Dam, which are good, if somewhat lonely places to camp. (During holiday season it is exactly the opposite when it looks as if every man, his caravan and dog has descended on the place.) Another 25km inland on a gravel road from Pearly Beach is Elim, an old Moravian mission station which used to be a bustling little place where the inhabitants made salamis and sausages for export to Germany, but which seems to have lost some of its spark.

The tip of Africa

Wait until the weather turns bad before going to **Cape Agulhas**. This, the southernmost point of the African continent, should be much more spectacular than it is. It is a pity really because you feel as you stand at the point, marked by a brass plaque set into a rock, where the Indian and Atlantic Oceans meet that there should be some sort of thunderous finality to Africa, not just a bland expanse of flat rock and some low hills behind. But if you get sentimental about this sort of thing, you should make the pilgrimage. The 12-million candlepower lighthouse, built in 1848, is a national monument and houses the **Agulhas Lighthouse Museum**, *open Tues–Sat 09.30–16.45, Sun 10.00–13.15. Admission R5.*

If anything, sailors probably feel more strongly about Agulhas; with over 250 wrecks recorded off the coast since 1673, its name, meaning 'place of needles', is particularly apt. The best time to visit Agulhas is not when the sun is shining and the sea looks like a pond, but rather when a gale is ripping in from the sea and surf is pounding the coast. Then a sense of dread hangs in the air, enough to make the hair stand on the back of your neck.

There is one more thing: the best fish and chips I have ever had was at Agulhas Sea Foods, right on the main street just before the lighthouse (R12.50 for a massive portion of both).

Arniston

This small and quaint fishing village is about 38km east of Agulhas, lying on a stunning bay with a sand dune wilderness dominating its eastern outlook. It is one of the last places on the coast where you can see genuine *kapstyl* fishing cottages: the people who live in them still work on the sea. Arniston used to be a lot quieter before it was discovered by holiday home owners but the town has escaped the ugly ravages of suburban brick houses that have ruined other places.

The town is named after the British transport ship *Arniston* that went aground here in a storm one night in 1815. No boats were got away from the ship and only six of the 378 people on board survived. Artefacts from the wreck are on display in the **Shipwreck Museum** in nearby Bredasdorp.

Unlike most of the coast, the water here is relatively warm and safe for swimming and there is some great snorkelling in the clear sea. You can also walk over the rocks at low tide to the massive Waenhuiskrans (wagon house cave), named because it is big enough to turn a wagon and a full span of oxen around inside. The beach east of the town runs unbroken for many kilometres and there used to be isolated fishing settlements further up the coast at Ryspunt and Skipskop. In the 1980s, however, the government built a missile test range nearby and fenced off a few thousand hectares of land and closed off the beach. The fishing communities were packed up and sent to Arniston while the holiday makers moaned that they could no longer drive their Land Rovers up the beach. The forced removal of the Skipskop community was immortalised in a song by South African comedy/protest singer David Kramer. On the upbeat side, at least the land has been protected, albeit in the strangest way. The military facility is still here and it's still top secret. If you try and walk up the beach, it won't be long before a soldier pops up over a dune and asks you to leave.

Accommodation

South of Africa Backpackers Die Herberg, Arniston; tel: 028 445 9240; fax: 445 9254; email: info@southofafrica.co.za. . All the rooms are triples; rates are per person. R95 single, R75 sharing double, R60 sharing triple. The missile range has had another odd spin-off in the form of a smart hotel and convention centre, attached to which is probably the cleanest backpacker I have ever stayed in, occupying one wing of the centre. Accommodation is in huge double/triple rooms complete with TV. The restaurant is open all day and there are extras like mountain bike hire, a sauna, gym and satellite TV. It has a vaguely university residence feel about it and the dining room is nice in a commuter-belt golf club kind of way. The complex is on the left about two miles before Arniston. Breakfast is included.

De Hoop Nature Reserve

De Hoop (tel: 028 542 1126) is one of the region's best-kept secrets. Stretching 42km along the coast and about 10km inland, it is a coastal fynbos refuge boasting 1,500 plant species of which 50 are unique to the reserve. Mammals include eland, bontebok, Cape mountain zebra and, since the park extends 5km out to sea, southern right whales.

There are a couple of hiking and mountain bike trails and you can wander at will through the reserve. Accommodation is in four-bed huts (R322 fully equipped or R207 for a basic hut) or you can camp. Bring all your own food. Entry to the reserve is R12.

At some stage in your travels you will pass through **Bredasdorp**, the region's main town. While its main focus is farming and not tourism, it does have the excellent **Bredasdorp Museum** (Independent Street; tel: 02841 41240) which devotes much of its space to shipwrecks. Since 1673 over 120 ships have been wrecked in the the coast around Agulhas – the graveyard of ships – and the museum is thus well supplied with material such as figureheads, cannons and the most extraordinary stuff that washes up on the local beaches. Exhibits include artefacts from the transport ships *Arniston* and *Birkenhead*. *Open Mon–Thu 09.00–16.45, Fri 09.00–15–45, Sat 09.00–12.45, Sun 11.00–12.30. Admission R5. The museum is only open from September to April.*

A classic example of a real Overberg farming town is **Napier**, worth stopping in to have a look around. Some buildings date back to 1838 and the place retains much of its old character. It is calm and quiet but its tourism office, one of the most enthusiastic in the country, can help with information on anything in the Overberg region. The office is at 18 High Street, Napier; tel: 028 423 3169 or 214 1466; fax: 423 3325.

Swellendam

It's a bored person who doesn't like Swellendam. This little town, South Africa's third oldest, huddles at the foot of the Langeberg in a tree-shaded jumble of quiet streets and lush gardens. It was founded by the Dutch East India Company as a farming centre and was destined to drift along in quiet, agricultural contemplation until it had its 15 seconds of fame in 1795: for three heady months, Swellendam was a capital city after its townspeople fired the company's magistrate and declared the town an independent republic. It didn't last: the British occupation of the Cape was under way and the town's expansionist ambitions were swiftly crushed.

Getting there and away
Bus
The Baz Bus calls here twice daily (once in each direction) and Intercape Mainliner have a drop-off in town.

Train
The *Southern Cross* express runs once a week each way between Cape Town and Oudtshoorn. The eastbound service stops here briefly at 00.34 on Saturdays, the westbound at 02.10 on Mondays. The train is a good way to travel if you're heading for the Garden Route from Cape Town as it means a full night's sleep (well, a good chunk of it anyway) on a proper bunk and you arrive at your destination at the beginning of the day.

Accommodation

The town is overrun with B&Bs but not backpackers, of which there is only one (another having closed). Rates for B&Bs vary widely and if you intend to go this route, ask the tourism office to recommend one in your price range.

Swellendam Backpackers Lodge 5 Lichtenstein St; tel: 028 514 2648; fax 514 1249; email: backpack@dorea.co.za. Double R150, cabin R130, dorm R45, camping R30 per person. This is a nicely placed backpacker with a stream running through the bottom of its huge garden. There are double-bedded cabins in the garden and a few doubles in the main house. It is also one of the quietest backpackers in the country. The Baz Bus stops here and the lodge's managers will pick up at the railway station. The vibe is extremely relaxed – a group of us had a wild dinner party here and moved the table out into the road; no-one minded. All sorts of tours and activities can be arranged.

Things to see and do

Swellendam is an agricultural town but a good place either to relax in for a few days or walk in the mountains. Diversions in town include the fine **Drostdy Museum** complex, housed in the magistrate's old residence, which contains period furniture and other intriguing bits and pieces. There are plenty of historic buildings such as the **Dutch Reformed Church** with its mixture of gothic, renaissance, baroque and Cape architecture, and it's worth taking a walk around the town. The tourist information office (tel: 028 514 2770) on Voortrek Street is open Mon–Fri 09.00–12.30 and 14.00–16.00, Sat 09.00–12.30.

Hikers should head for the 74km **Swellendam hiking trail** – a real tough one which starts at the forest station just outside town, climbs over to the other side of the mountain range and runs along the far side before circling back to the start. The trail can be shortened by crossing the range on one of the traverses including the terrifying and aptly-named Vensterbank (window ledge) – not a route even to *think* about on rainy, windy or misty days or if you have a fear of heights. Book through Marloth Nature Reserve (tel: 028 514 1410). Hikers pay R10 entry plus R35 per day each.

The **Grootvadersbos Conservancy** (tel: 02934 22044) is a magnificent mountain reserve about 33km east of Swellendam. The conservancy has excellent day trails radiating out of a single campsite (the only accommodation, so you will need a tent). A R10 permit gives you access to a network of paths, mountain bike trails, deep kloofs with icy cold mountain streams, mountain scenery and the country's only surviving stand of Californian redwoods, seriously impressive 50m-high trees that have been here for a century.

The nearby **Bontebok National Park** (tel: 028 514 2735) was created 40 years ago to save the bontebok from extinction. It is also a sanctuary for Cape mountain zebra, another species that has been saved just in time. The lovely Breede River forms the park's western border and there are camping and picnic sites on the river banks.

The **Breede River** is the focus of a lot of adventure with a couple of operators offering trails lasting between one and two days. It is a much more mellow river than, say, the Orange River, and the emphasis here is on drifting through a beautiful landscape. Some trips include tours of riverside vineyards. Some operators: River Tours and Safaris (tel: 011 803 9775; email: rivtours@global.co.za), Wildthing Adventures (tel: 021 461 9693; email: wildthing@icon.co.za), Felix Unite (tel: 021 683 6433; email: bookings@felix.com).

Unless you have the gear and experience, it is a hassle to do a self-guided trip on the Breede. That said, if you are determined, speak to one of the operators about hiring canoes and other gear. Also contact the South African Rivers Association (tel: 012 667 1838; email: sara@intekom.co.za) for advice and information.

The West Coast, Namaqualand and the Kalahari Desert

North of Cape Town, in a harsh arid land lying between high mountains in the east and the icy waters of the Atlantic Ocean to the west, is a place that everyone forgot, with lonely fishing villages on its coast and little *dorpies* huddling under the dry, rocky mountains. The West Coast is more than just a place: on my trips up there, I've felt a subtle change in the air. Things feel different I think it's the locals – a hardened bunch of farmers, fishermen and diamond seekers, people who, when I first went there in 1994, did not seem to realise that there would be black majority rule within just a few months. It was like stepping back 40 years. But it is also an area that is like nothing else in this country. It is strange to stand in a pea-soup fog so thick that car headlights are useless, feel moisture on your skin and surrounded by a landscape, when you can see it, that looks like the surface of the moon.

It is actually a rich land. The southern part of the region, known as the Swartland on account of its rich, black soils, is the Western Cape's wheat belt. A little north is potato country; and north of that still, in Namaqualand where the land looks driest, every spring a miracle occurs when the desert blooms with a carpet of bright wildflowers and turns the dry expanses of rocky and sandy soil into a miracle of colour. Moisture from the thick fogs, spawned by hot air off the land meeting the sea air cooled by the Benguela Current, gives life to tiny plants and insects. The sea, a rich fishing ground, is famous for its crayfish, abalone and mussels.

If you like deserts, you will like Namaqualand. The coast is outrageously beautiful and the mountains, especially the Cedarberg range, are jumbles of rock where wind-sculpted arches and other formations add another dimension to the weirdness of the region. To the south are the wetlands, two of which of are registered under the 1975 Ramsar Convention as being of vital importance to birds; the lagoon at Langebaan, with its thousands of flamingos, is also a protected area.

WEST COAST
Tourist information
Jolene Rabe Tel: 022 433 2380

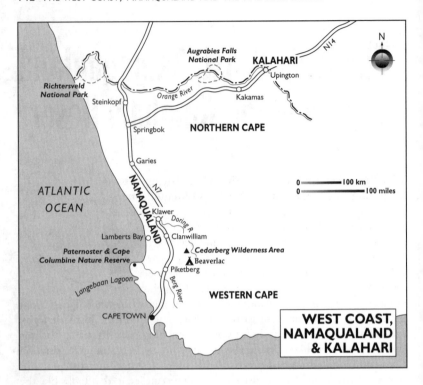

WEST COAST,
NAMAQUALAND
& KALAHARI

Getting there and away

Bus or car are really the only ways of getting into Namaqualand. Driving yourself is best: it will allow you to explore at will as public transport is sparse. Once there was a train called the *Namaqualand Mail* which used to run overnight from Cape Town to the copper mining towns in the north. In later years, the schedule was reduced to one journey a week and only as far as Klawer. The service was withdrawn in 1999 and now only long distance buses head up this way.

Car

For cheap car hire, see *Getting around* in Chapter 3.

Bus

Intercape Mainliner buses (tel: 021 386 4400) run daily each way between Cape Town, Clanwilliam, Springbok, Upington and Windhoek in Namibia, stopping at all the major towns en route. This is your best option if, for example, you want to reach the Richtersveld National Park but don't have a car. Cape Town–Windhoek costs around R290.

Elwierda (tel: 021 418 4673) run daily buses from Cape Town to Saldanha (R24). Journey time is around 2¹/₂ hours

Bicycle

This is beautiful, open country and with a bit of resourcefulness you could embark on fantastic bike journey. But distances between towns are huge – it is

560km between Cape Town and Springbok, Namaqualand's capital. If you are planning a summer trip, you will also need to carry plenty of water as daytime temperatures in the region often exceed 35–38°C.

Hitchhiking

There is a better chance of getting a free ride in this part of the country than in many others. As always, looking neat rather than dishevelled will be to your advantage – people are conservative here. Equally, the rules of hitching apply here too (see *Getting around* in Chapter 3).

THINGS TO SEE AND DO
Langebaan Lagoon and the West Coast National Park

As you head north from Cape Town, the first place of real interest is Langebaan Lagoon which is part of the **West Coast National Park**. The park is a mix of wetlands, lagoons and beaches and there is some wildlife, including zebra and bat-eared fox. The park was also the site of the discovery of two fossil human footprints – the footprints of Eve – dating back 117,000 years, putting them among the oldest known fossilised traces of anatomically modern humans. (The original footprints have been removed to Cape Town for safekeeping and plastercasts left in their place, which is not quite the same thing.) The nearby **West Coast Fossil Park** (tel: 083 694 1755) has fossils dating back 4–5 million years including the remains of the *Agriotherium africanum*, the first bear found in Africa south of the Sahara, and sivathere, a giraffe-like creature that roamed the sub-continent until about 500,000 years ago.

The R27 skirts the edge of the park but there is a sandy track to the lovely village of **Churchhaven** which is on a peninsula that separates the lagoon from the Atlantic Ocean. The lagoon is excellent for windsurfing and sea kayaking although the water is barely warmer than the Atlantic.

Accommodation

The region is a bit behind the rest of the country but the camping is superb so I live in my tent. You don't have to rough it – there are some brick buildings here.

Windstone Backpackers 10km from Vredenburg (on R45 to Hopefield); tel: 022766 1645; fax: 766 1038. Bunk room R50, camping R30. Five big en-suite bunk rooms and one family double. They have horses for you to ride.

Langebaan Beach House 44 Beach Rd, Langebaan; tel: 022 772 2625; fax: 772 1432; email: ibh@intekom.co.za. Beach-facing suite R200 per person, back room R150 per person. This B&B is right on the beach which couldn't be better.

Paternoster and Cape Columbine

North of Langebaan the coastline forms a distinctive bulge. At the southern edge is Saldanha, site of the South African Navy's main training base, fish factories and an ore loading terminal so it is not a place for a holiday. However, north of here is **Paternoster**, a traditional West Coast fishing village with whitewashed cottages dotted on a hillside and overlooking the most fantastic beach. There is nothing *ersatz* about this place; hardy fishing people live in the cottages and the place has a defiant character about it. The nearby Paternoster Hotel is a typical *platteland* watering hole with a bar that is famous throughout the region, a good place to cut the road dust and eavesdrop on the locals (which may sometimes be disturbing but is always interesting).

Accommodation

The Cottage Paternoster (next to the hotel); tel: 022 715 3034. R200–400 per day, depending on the number of people. It's a bargain. A two-bedroom cottage overlooking the bay and 200m up from the beach. There are seven beds plus a further two beds for children.

Heading south for a few kilometres along the coast from Paternoster brings you to **Cape Columbine Nature Reserve** and one of my favourite campsites anywhere. **Tietie se Baai** (Tietie's Bay, named for a fisherman who drowned nearby) is a real gem, with a curved, white beach embracing a typical little West Coast bay. Large granite boulders provide excellent shelter for tents and there are basic facilities with toilets and running water. (It's a moot point as to whether the sea is warmer than the showers). You need to bring your own firewood (available at the general store in Paternoster) and camping gear, of course. The campsite is spread over a mile or two of coast so unless it's high season (December–January) finding somewhere private to pitch your tent is easy.

Then kick off your shoes and relax. There isn't much to do here except explore rock pools, swim in the very sheltered bay (if you can handle the cold), take a walk through the nature reserve and look at the wildflowers, lie in the sun, listen to the waves, have sundowners and watch the beam from Cape Columbine's lighthouse compete with the glow of a gazillion stars at night. Camping costs R30 per person per night; pay at reception as you enter the reserve.

Along the coast

A good but lonely dirt road hugs the coast all the way from St Helena Bay to Strandfontein before turning inland. The villages and towns along the coast are mostly fishing towns and none of them have the character of Paternoster or other fishing villages elsewhere in the Cape. It is an interesting drive though, with a sea of deep blue on your left at odds with the harsh dry hills and plains on your right. This aridity is relieved by two towns of note. The first, **Elands Bay**, sits at the edge of a lagoon inhabited by flamingos and other waterbirds and its beach stretches off into the sea mist. Velorenvlei, the lagoon, actually stretches nearly 33km back inland, providing refuge for birds and some measure of relief in an otherwise dry place. Elands is really known for its incredible left-hand surf break, a predictable and lengthy ride that, when it's cooking, draws surfers from all over the province, much to the disgust of the local surfers.

The next town along the coast is **Lamberts Bay**, also a fishing port but home to a vast colony of seabirds, most of which seem to be Cape cormorants and gannets. You can get really close to the colony which inhabits a fair spread of rock called Bird Island at the edge of the harbour. The noise and smell are indescribable but it is a stunning sight. Thankfully, the city fathers have built a shelter with a roof from which visitors can watch the birds – you'd be dodging guano bullets otherwise.

There is little in the way of decent budget accommodation in either place but the seafront campground in Lamberts Bay is really nice, with low hedges marking off the sites. Camping costs R30 per person; no bookings, just arrive and pay.

From Lamberts Bay, you can either stick to the coast road or head back inland to **Clanwilliam**, a pretty farming town at the foot of the Cedarberg mountains. It is a nice enough place to spend a day in and if you've grown fond of *rooibos* tea, well Clanwilliam is to *rooibos* what Lourdes is to holy water. The town is best used as a jumping-off point to get into the Cedarberg but it is also one of the best places to catch the wildflower explosion in late August.

The Cedarberg

It is hard for people who know it to be objective about the Cedarberg mountain range. They use words like 'magic', 'pristine', 'wonderland' and 'surreal' in their descriptions. The range is named for the Clanwilliam cedar trees (*Widdringtonia cedarbergensis*) that used to grow thickly on its slopes. Its attractions are a combination of high mountains, bizarre sandstone rock formations, desolate plains, the odd sparkling, tumbling mountain stream, hidden rock pools and fynbos everywhere.

The 71,000ha wilderness area is accessible to hikers and mountain bikers and there are naturally many routes for climbers and scramblers. Various hiking trails crisscross the park and hikers are allowed to explore the area at will. The San and Khoikhoi people lived here from early times and San rock art, some it as much as 6,000 years old, is common in the hundreds of caves and overhangs.

Mammals you are likely to encounter include baboons, dassies and antelope such as duikers, grey rhebok and klipspringers. Porcupines, honeybadgers and otters are also resident but seldom see. Resident predators include leopard, which are fairly common but very shy, African wild cats, caracals (lynx), bat eared foxes and Cape foxes.

The main access point is at the **Algeria forest station** which has 46 campsites (R35 per site) but some other sites have bungalows as well. Of the latter, Kromrivier Farm (tel: 027 482 2807) has the most atmosphere. This site is close to the spectacular Apollo Peak, which you can scramble up.

It is worth making the trek from Algeria to Wolfberg Arch, an astounding feature that wind has scoured out of the sandstone. You can camp nearby but get a permit from Cape Nature Conservation (tel: 027 482 2812), R15 per day as well as a one-off R15 entrance fee. The hike starts from Sandrif (tel: 027 482 2825), which is a pretty campsite next to rock pools. Campsites cost R50 per site for four people, and they also have 4-bed cottages for R175–220 per night.

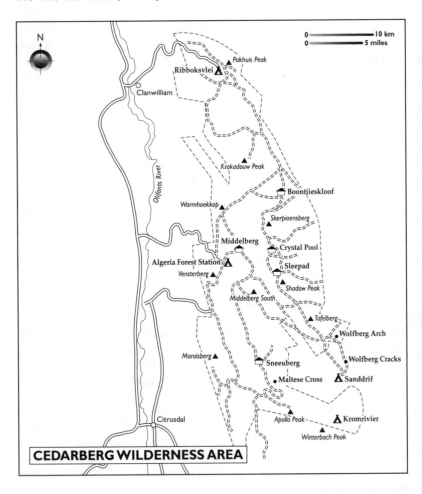

CEDARBERG WILDERNESS AREA

Winters in the Cedarberg are cold and wet, with snow in the high parts while summers are warm and dry: summer temperatures often reach 40°C. Its popularity means it's also difficult to get in during high season (December–January) since there's a strict limit on numbers, so book early. It's a fabulous place and you could spend weeks exploring the wilderness and still not get bored.

Olifant River mountains

South of the Cedarbergs, where the range meets the Olifants River mountains, is another wilderness area offering great hiking, swimming and a bit of mountain biking. **Beaverlac** (tel: 02293 12945), kept as something of a secret by people who have discovered it, huddles on a farm in the bottom of a deep valley at the end of an appalling road. If you are driving, go slowly. To get there, take the R44 from Paarl to Porterville and take the first right outside the town and follow the road up the side of the mountain.

But once down there you will understand why it is such a special place. The campsite rolls over different meadows, some of it under trees, other parts in open grassland. There are also a few huts dotted around. Paths lead off from the camp down to secluded pools on the Olifants River (the swimming is superb) or up into the craggy hills overlooking the valley. Mountain bikers can tackle a long trail, mostly on very rough jeep track, around the boundaries of the farm.

There is a little shop where you can buy basics but it's best to bring your own food and drink. Camping costs R25 per person, huts (sleep up to four people) are R100–150. Bring your own sleeping bags.

NAMAQUALAND
The flower season

In spring, the desert goes beserk as it erupts in a blanket of brightly coloured wildflowers. The sight of it never fails to surprise people, especially if they have seen how harsh the land looks the rests of the year. The phenomenon has much to do with the ancient geology of the area. Namaqualand was not always arid but was once a much more lushly vegetated area. About 50 million years ago, the sea currents shifted and cold water pushed up the West Coast, sparking off a change in climate as the cold water resisted evaporation and the lush countryside turned into desert. The few surviving plants included succulents and members of the daisy family that were able to adapt to the harsh conditions. Their seeds can lie dormant for years so that when the rains come briefly in the spring, there is an opportunistic explosion of life as *vygies* and Namaqualand daisies enjoy their brief flowering.

It can be tricky to plan a trip to coincide with the flower season. Everything depends on the rains, wind and sun, while flowers bloom in different areas at different times. The best thing to do is be nearby – in Cape Town perhaps – and check with the local tourist information service every day. For many of the local towns, the flower season is also their equally brief tourist season and they are more than eager to keep the world updated on the progress of their daisies, where the best displays are and even which roads to take. Start by phoning Jolene Rabe (tel: 022 433 2380) and ask where the action is. Remember that Capetonians also come up to see the flowers as well so there could be a bit of a scrum for accommodation. If you are camping, no problem; if you want a little more comfort, plan ahead.

Up to the copper country

There is little to tempt travellers to journey this far north unless you are heading for the exquisite **Richtersveld National Park**, the country's only true mountain desert; a place, it has to be said, that is staggeringly beautiful.

The main towns of the region, Springbok and Port Nolloth, both exist to serve mining operations, the former the copper mines and the latter alluvial diamond dredging off the coast. Copper was discovered by the Nama Hottentot tribe who used the metal to make weapons and ornaments which they bartered with other tribes. The first European on the scene was Simon van der Stel, the governor of the Cape himself (the man seems to have gone everywhere). In 1685, van der Stel led an expedition to the north and found enough copper in the shadow of Koperberg (copper mountain) to impress his masters in the Dutch East India Company. But the distance to the Cape made exploitation impossible and it was only in the 19th century that copper mining began there in earnest.

When proper mining began in the middle of the century, copper ore was dragged by ox-wagon to the Orange River and then floated down to the Atlantic on barges. A harbour was established at Port Nolloth, high on the West Coast. On January 1 1876, the privately built, two-feet-six-inch gauge line, laid from Port Nolloth to Okiep in the heart of the copper area, was opened and ore moved over this line until well into the 20th century. When copper production began tailing off in the 1940s, the railway gradually fell into disrepair and by the 1950s, copper was being transported by road instead. The last remnant of the line was an 8km stretch from the port to Five Mile Halt which was kept open so trains could bring water down for the town's reservoirs.

South African writer and traveller Lawrence Greene remembered the railway and the people connected so closely with it.

> Port Nolloth and the copper mines were outposts of Cornwall for many years, and they left many Cornish names along the line. Sailing ships from Swansea came up to the jetty at Port Nolloth and discharged coal which was railed to O'kiep. The trains brought the copper ore to the port, and that went back to Swansea. Most of the work was done by Cornish miners, St Helena craftsmen and Hottentot labourers. To this day (1960-ish), old Hottentots still speak English with Cornish phrases and accent.

Springbok has a brief flutter every year when the flowers bloom; the rest of the time it is desperately quiet. It does have a good nature park 6km from town: the **Goegap Nature Reserve** (tel: 0251 21880). The **Hester Malan Botanical Garden** inside the reserve has a fascinating collection of northern Cape flora including the very odd *halfmens boom* (half person tree) which looks like it sounds. The rugged scenery is home to many antelope including springbok, eland, the very rare Hartmann's mountain zebra and the majestic gemsbok (oryx) which has adapted to desert life in the most fascinating way. There are walking trails and bike trails (bikes can be hired for R30 per day).

The Richtersveld National Park

For independent travellers who don't mind a bit of hardship, the park is the best reason to make the journey this far north. As austere and frightening beauty goes, the Richtersveld cannot be beaten. It is the harshest land in the country – sun-baked mountains rearing up over desert valleys, a vast and punishing landscape that has defied exploitation by mass tourism. Its northern border is the mighty Orange River which provides an easier, if more expensive way of seeing the park (see *Upington* below).

The park is unique in that it is inhabited, if very sparsely, by Nama pastoralists who roam at will over the area, grazing their goats, a life that must surely rank among the world's toughest. There are not many animals to be seen here either, although some species of antelope are common along with predators such as leopard and bat-eared fox. Rather it is a place to appreciate the immense solitude of real wilderness.

Getting there and away

Access to the 160,000ha park is difficult; the roads are really only suitable for 4x4 vehicles so if you have one, excellent; if not, your options are limited. The area is however, becoming known among the mountain biking elite as something quite extraordinary. A hiking trail is also being developed although it has been in progress for years. There are two ways of getting in – through Sendelingsdrif, about 108km from Alexander Bay, or from the Namibian side which is a bit of a mission since it involves leaving South Africa at Vioolsdrif, west of Port Nolloth, and trekking around the top of the park. Alexander Bay is about 125km from Port Nolloth. If you don't have a car, you will have to hitchhike, which may be problematic if you are lugging a bike with you. Whatever you do, do not try to ride there because you will expend all your good humour and enthusiasm long before you get to the nice bits.

Once there, you can base yourself at De Hoop, one of the camps, and do day rides or walks from there. You should be active from dawn and back in camp by 11.00 – daytime temperatures can easily top 52°C and you do not want to be away from shelter and liquid under these conditions. It won't be easy, but you will have the pleasure of enjoying a unique experience that few other travellers will be tempted to try.

There are a few basic rules.

- Do not photograph the local people or visit their camps without asking permission first.
- Do not hike alone, ever – a minor accident like a broken ankle can be fatal here.
- Some demarcated areas are not open to the public – in this environment, where tyre tracks never disappear, going off the path destroys fragile life forms.

Park entry fees are R30 per person and camping costs R40 per person per night for two people, and R30 per night if there are more than two people. Book through the National Parks Board well in advance (tel: 027 831 1506). You will need to be self-sufficient – the nearest shop is 100km away.

Back of beyond
Getting there and away

From Springbok, a lonely national road, the N14, stretches east across the desolate wastes of the northern Cape, to Kakamas and ultimately Upington. There is almost nothing in the way of civilisation out here apart, that is, from the town of Pofadder. The town, named after a local Hottentot chief who in turn was named after a thick, sluggish adder, is famous among South Africans (even though almost none of them will be able to tell you where it is) for being the source of hick, redneck jokes, or as a measure of remoteness from planet earth; here, Pofadder is a synonym for limbo. It is a small town and there is probably no reason to dally here unless this kind of thing intrigues you.

Things to see and do

Kakamas is not much bigger but it is the jumping-off point for the **Augrabies Falls National Park** (tel: 054 451 0050). The park is based around the powerful spectacle of the Augrabies waterfall which has been described by an early visitor as 'the most desolate and malign'. At this point in its 2,800km meander to the sea, the Orange River forces itself through a narrow gap and thunders hundreds of metres into a deep canyon. The name comes from the Hottentot word *loukurubes* (the noisemaking place). When the river is in flood, the falls can be heard from miles away. Stand outside on a quiet, desert night and you will hear the roar. It is quite sobering.

It is an awesome place as the river plunges 190m in a series of cascades and roars into a 215m-deep canyon in a single 43m torrent. The river rushes down the narrow canyon for another 20km before the cliffs open up a little. Only around Sendelingsdrif does the river leave mountain country and enter the coastal plains. At peak levels, 400 million litres of water per minute drop into the boiling pool at the base of the falls.

The park covers 5,403ha and is very much centred on the river and its islands. Causeways and suspension bridges provide access and you can scare yourself by standing right on the edge of the main cataract.

Accommodation

Accommodation in the park is chalets (R420 for four people) or camping, R40 per site.

The three-day, 40km **Klipspringer Hiking Trail** starts just south of the gorge; if you are feeling strong, it is an excellent way to get a feel for the area. It gets punishingly hot in the afternoons and you are urged to start hiking at dawn and call it quits by midday. Take – and drink – plenty of water. Accommodation on the trail is in overnight huts. The trail costs R60 per person which includes your hiking permit and use of all facilities. You need to book well in advance since the trail is closed during the hot summer months. National Parks (tel: 012 343 1991; fax: 343 0905; email: reservations@parks-sa.co.za).

The parks board also manage **Riemvasmaak**, a 70,000ha wilderness area north of the river. The area is remote and protected so getting about under your own steam is tough, unless you have your own vehicle. The best way to get in is with an organised tour. Ask the parks board for information or speak to the people at the Kalahari Adventure Centre (see *Accommodation* below).

Accommodation

Surprisingly good as travellers start venturing this way.

Kalahari Adventure Centre Augrabies; tel: 054 451 0177; fax: 451 0218; email: Kalahari@augrabies.co.za. Double R120, dorm R50, camping R20. An oasis, no less, and a very welcome sight when you've been gathering road dust in your throat. They offer, among other things, rafting and canoe trips on the Orange River as well as overland safaris into the Kalahari and Riemvasmaak.

Upington

The nearest town of any size is Upington, a relatively sprawling, affluent farming town on the banks of the Orange River. Large-scale irrigation has pushed back the desert and turned the town into a thriving agricultural settlement. There are even vineyards here and the place has a vaguely satisfied air about it. Its airport also boasts the world's longest runway; why that is, no-one knows, and I don't think it is a major drawcard. If you are in the area, you will likely spend a night here. It is a biggish centre so things like banking and telephoning are no hassle.

Getting there
Bus
Intercape Mainliner buses (tel: 021 386 4400) run through Upington a few days a week in each direction between Cape Town and Johannesburg. Check the timetable in advance. The meeting point is outside Palm Springs Hotel.

Minibus taxi
These run from right outside the railway station to Kimberley, De Aar and Johannesburg. Use at your discretion: if the taxi is overloaded or looks unsafe, find another one. The day I took one to Kimberley, there were 19 people and all their voluminous bags crammed inside – six people were jammed in the front seat. Fares to Kimberley are R60.

Train
The only passenger train that calls at Upington is the twice-weekly TransNamib service from Namibia. This is one of the best ways of getting Namibia (see *On to Namibia* below)

Hitchhiking
There are not many places to go, so hitching lifts should be easy. If you are planning to go a long way, set off early before the sun starts to bake the earth, and take plenty of water. Note also that Upington is a conservative town so a neat appearance will go a long way to improving your chances of a ride. If you are offered one by anyone who looks like the greatcoat-wearing psychopath in *The Hitcher*, decline the offer.

Accommodation

I am happy to say the backpacker situation in Upington has improved dramatically since my first visit and there is even a bit of competition!

Mafanie Lodge Left off River St, on banks of the river; tel: 054 332 1442 or 082 492 9939. R75 per person. Your last chance to enjoy air conditioning, icy beer and a swimming pool. En-suite rooms throughout.

Yebo Backpackers and Guesthouse 21 Morant St; tel: 054 331 2496; fax: 332 1336; email: teuns@intekom.co.za. Double R85, en suite R100, dorm R50, camping R35. Very relaxed place with good traditional Afrikaner cooking to make you stay longer.

INTO THE KALAHARI

Upington is the jumping-off point for the Kalahari Desert and Namibia. The Kalahari Desert is one of the world's great wilderness areas, a massive expanse of aeolian sand covered in shrubs, and dotted with acacia trees. The two rivers, the Nossob and the Auob, are almost permanently dry, although the heavy rain that soaked southern Africa early in 2000 saw the Nossob run for the first time in many years. What little rainfall there is collects in shallow pans. Despite the aridity, there is plenty of wildlife and the area is one of the last hunting grounds of a few wandering groups of San Bushmen.

Getting there and away

The feeling of solitude has a lot to do with the park's remoteness – it is 1,080km from both Cape Town and Johannesburg and you should set aside a week if you plan to visit. Without a car, you will have to work hard to get here. Hiring a car in Cape Town or Johannesburg (or from Avis in Upington) is your best bet, especially if you can share the cost among four of you. To put it in perspective, the car hire is likely to be the most expensive part of the expedition. This is a national park, rather than a private, dollar-oriented swanky game reserve and prices for accommodation are accordingly low.

When to visit

Winter is probably the best time if only because daytime temperatures will be somewhat more bearable and because, other than in July, you will see few other people. It will get fearsomely cold at night though, so take a good sleeping bag and a warm jacket.

Accommodation

There are three rest camps – **Mata-Mata**, **Nossob** and **Twee Rivieren**, which is the biggest. All three camps have a range of cottages (R400 for a 6-bed), 2-bed bungalows (R290) and huts (R105 for three people), as well as campsites (R40 for 2 people and R11 for each additional person). Booking is not usually necessary if you are camping, but you should book in advance if you want a roof over your head. Bookings are through either the National Parks Cape Town offices (tel: 021 22 2810; fax: 021 22 2816) or Pretoria (tel: 012 343 1991; fax: 012 343 0905; email: reservations@parks-sa.co.za).

Things to see and do
Kgalagadi Transfrontier Park
Formerly known as the Kalahari Gemsbok Park, this park sprawls for a million hectares across the red sands. As its name suggests, it extends across the national boundaries of South Africa, Botswana and Namibia, tacit recognition of the fact that the movement of animals is, or should be, governed by physical boundaries, not political ones. The park is the first of a number of 'Peace Parks' planned for southern Africa, where political boundaries in the form of fences will be dropped so that wildlife can move freely according to nature's boundaries instead of man's.

It is a sanctuary for herds of endemic antelope species such as gemsbok (oryx), springbok, eland and wildebeest, cheetah, brown hyena, the black-maned Kalahari lion and smaller species like honeybadgers, jackals and bat-eared foxes. About 58 species of mammal, 55 reptile and 260 species of bird live in the park. The attraction for visitors is that even a short trip to the park will turn up sightings of plenty of game, especially predators. You won't see the Big Five here since elephant, rhino and buffalo are absent but as wilderness experiences go, the park is one of the best.

Tracking with the San
A couple of San groups are permitted to live and hunt in the park, just as their ancestors have done for 30,000 years. In an effort to generate funds for the Khomani clan, park visitors are able to join the fleet-of-foot hunters on a tracking trail through the park. The hunter-gathers have an encyclopaedic knowledge of ecosystems and brilliant tracking skills. The idea behind the project is that getting tourists interested in experiencing the art of tracking first hand will help preserve a vast store of indigenous knowledge that is under threat, as the last of the San lose touch with their ancient way of life.

Adrift on the Orange River
The Orange River, South Africa's longest and mightiest watercourse, rises at the top of the high Escarpment that divides South Africa down its eastern side. From its headwaters, you can, on a clear day at least, almost see the Indian Ocean 190km away. But by nothing more than a slope, the Orange is sentenced to undergo a 3,300km meander to spill out into the Atlantic Ocean on the west coast of the country.

The river is a highway through the country and it's one of the nicest ways to see it. There are sections where you can float along at 5km per hour and there are also sections where the river plunges furiously down cataracts or squeezes through narrow gaps that it has carved out of the rock. For experienced kayakers and rafters, the Orange River is a 3,300km adventure. With a bit of careful planning, most of the river is runnable from source to sea, with a few obvious exceptions such as the Augrabies waterfall.

The Northern Cape region offers probably the best access to the river for travellers and a number of companies run trips down this section. There are a few scary rapids on the Richtersveld part of the river but these adventure trips are more about drifting down a wide, mellow river during the day and sleeping under a desert sky at night. The scenery is spectacular – high cliffs, expanses of desert and sun-baked mountains. But if whitewater action is what you want, the Orange River Gorge and Augrabies Gorge sections have plenty of that.

Trips can last from one to ten days, depending on the section and the operator, of whom there are many. On the lower section through the Richtersveld, you will paddle stable Indian-style open canoes. On whitewater trips, you will be in an unsinkable, inflatable raft instead. Prices vary according to length of the trip and it makes sense to shop around among the various operators and ask them for their best deal. Expect to pay around R845–1,100 all inclusive for a 4–5 day canoe trail.

The cheapest way of getting some river thrills is to spend a day running the whitewater above the falls for around R145, or hiring canoes and doing the lower section on your own. The latter option is only possible if you have good river experience and you know what you are doing.

Operators include:

Wildthing Adventures Tel: 021 461 9693; email: wildthing@icon.co.za
Felix Unite Tel: 021 683 6433; email: bookings@felix.com
Gravity River Tours Tel: 021 683 3698
Kalahari Adventure Centre Tel: 054 451 0177; email: Kalahari@augrabies.co.za
Orange River Adventures Tel: 021 426 5430; email: bundi@mweb.co.za; web: www.bundi.co.za
The River Rafters Tel: 021 712 5094; email: rafters@mweb.co.za; web: www.riverrafters.co.za

Although you are travelling on a budget, when it comes to river tripping, cost factors should be set aside when choosing an operator. For more information or a full list of operators, contact SARA, the South African Rivers Association (tel: 012 667 1838; email: sara@intekom.co.za).

If you are a kayaker or rafter planning an independent trip, get advice and information from SARA before setting off. The river is full of surprises for the unwary, some of them deeply unpleasant.

ON TO NAMIBIA
Getting there and away
Upington is a natural jumping-off point to Namibia. Happily, there is a regular train service between South Africa and Namibia although at the time of writing, this was limited to two through trains a week between Windhoek, Namibia's capital, and Upington. It took the Namibian rail operator TransNamib two years to persuade the South Africans to let the train run as far as Upington. Before that, the service had stopped at the border, at a horrendous little town called Ariamsvlei, from where passengers had to make their own way by taxi.

Until the mid-1990s, there was a daily train between Upington and De Aar, a junction on the Cape Town–Johannesburg main line. TransNamib hopes to restore this service which, if it does happen, will be an incredibly useful service for budget travellers. At the moment, passengers coming from Namibia have to overnight in Upington and then catch a bus or minibus taxi to Johannesburg and Kimberley the following day. A through rail service to and from De Aar will at least allow passengers the relative opulence of rail travel and the choice of northbound and southbound rail connections.

One advantage of taking the train across the border is that customs and immigration formalities are completed on the train. The southbound train invariably arrives after dark but it's not too far to walk. Just stay on the main street and you can't miss the glare of the orange sodium lights. There may be taxis waiting at the station when the train arrives.

As both northbound and southbound trains do much the journey during the day, you will get a real feeling for Namibia's vastness as it slips past at an ambling gait. The country seems to stretch forever and there is not much to alter the horizon except for rock formations near Grünau and when the line twists and turns through a canyon near Ariamsvlei.

The northbound train leaves Upington at 05.15 on Sundays and Wednesdays; southbound trains arrive in Upington at 21.19 on Tuesdays and Saturdays. If you have missed the through train, a TransNamib train still runs daily as far as the border. For rail enquiries phone TransNamib in Windhoek (tel: +264 61 298 2032; fax: +264 298 2495).

The fare for the 24-hour journey is around R110. Don't be surprised when you arrive at the station to find what looks like a freight train standing at the platform. TransNamib passenger trains consist of a single air-conditioned passenger coach with aircraft-style seating, attached to an express freight train. At least it's unique.

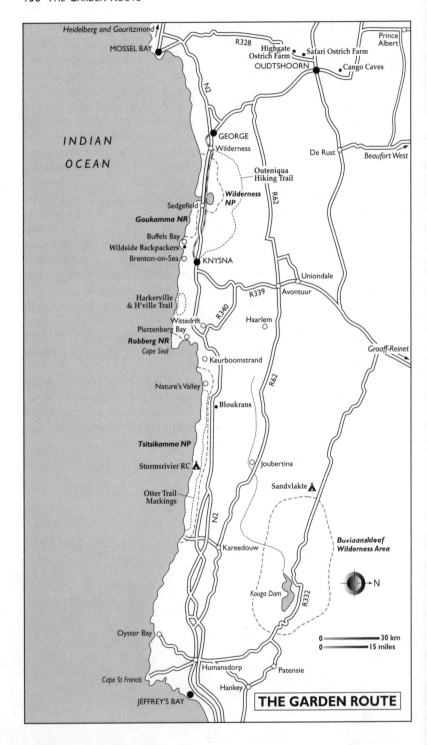

INDIAN
OCEAN

Heidelberg and Gouritzmond

MOSSEL BAY

R328

Highgate
Ostrich Farm

Safari Ostrich Farm

OUDTSHOORN

Prince
Albert

Cango Caves

N2

GEORGE

Wilderness

De Rust

Beaufort West

Outeniqua
Hiking Trail

Wilderness
NP

R62

Sedgefield

Goukamma NR

Buffels Bay

Wildside Backpackers

Brenton-on-Sea

KNYSNA

Uniondale

Harkerville
& H'ville Trail

R339

Avontuur

R340

Haarlem

Wittedrift

Plettenberg Bay

Robberg NR

Cape Seal

Keurboomstrand

R62

Graaff-Reinet

Nature's Valley

Bloukrans

Tsitsikamma NP

Stormsrivier RC

Joubertina

Otter Trail
Markings

Sandvlakte

Baviaanskloof
Wilderness Area

N2

Kareedouw

Kouga Dam

R332

N

Oyster Bay

0   30 km

0   15 miles

Cape St Francis

Humansdorp

Patensie

Hankey

JEFFREY'S BAY

THE GARDEN ROUTE

The Garden Route

Adventure sections compiled by Fiona McIntosh

The Garden Route is an exquisite piece of the country, stretching from Heidelberg in the west to Tsitsikamma in the east. It's a narrow strip of land, squeezed between the sea and a range of high mountains that loom over the coastal plain. It is less harsh and rugged country than the Western Cape and one of the lushest parts of South Africa, embracing wide, placid freshwater lagoons, stretches of wild coastline broken by fine beaches, mountains and hills covered with flowering plants and huge tracts of thick indigenous forest. The warm currents of Indian Ocean ensure that the coastal belt enjoys a mild climate with fynbos giving way to a dense rainforest that cloaks the wetter mountain slopes. This corner of the southwest Cape is the centre of the Cape floral kingdom, the smallest and richest in the world, with over 8,600 different plant species, part of the reason that the region is recognised as the country's natural garden.

The Outeniqua and Tsitsikamma mountains are the region's life source – 2,500mm of rain fall annually on their peaks, supplying the coastal strip and abundant forests with plenty of water and feeding the tannin-coloured streams and rivers that tumble down into the sea. Some of the country's largest tracts of indigenous forest survive here on the mountain slopes between Knysna and George and in the Tsitsikamma National Park. While much of the area is an undeveloped wilderness, some parts – especially the little towns along the main N2 national road – have been ruined by thoughtless development as people cash in on the tourism boom. You will find it rewarding to head off the beaten trail and use the backroads as much as possible.

The Garden Route is known as an adventure playground, hence the separate sections on adventure in this chapter. Hiking trails in the mountains and along the coast include the Otter Trail, the country's most sought-after hike, as well as inland trails through the forests. There are plenty of free day hikes, especially around the Knysna-Plettenberg Bay region, and plenty of adventure activity opportunities, including mountain bike trails, sea kayaking, whale watching, bungee jumping off terrifyingly high bridges, abseiling and surfing to name a few. The coast is exceptionally rugged in places but there are a number of superb beaches, especially at Plettenberg Bay and Buffels Bay near Knysna.

The emphasis on tourism and adventure means that backpackers are well looked after. The area probably boasts the greatest number of establishments after Cape Town, including, it must be said, some of the country's best. Transport links between Cape Town and Port Elizabeth are excellent and the main N2 national road is one of the easier roads to hitchhike on.

HISTORY

The first people to live in the area were the Strandlopers – beachwalkers – a primitive, nomadic race of beach dwellers whose diet consisted mainly of mussels. The San and Khoikhoi followed and it must have been good living in such a fertile, well-watered place.

The first Europeans were the Portuguese explorers, Bartolomeu Dias and then Vasco da Gama nearly ten years later. Dias landed at Mossel Bay then sailed along the coast, having had a not very friendly welcome from the Khoikhoi herders he met. Da Gama was more successful and managed to establish friendly relations with the herdsmen. For years, Portuguese ships called at Mossel Bay for fresh water and to leave messages in the branches of an old milkwood tree to be picked up by ships going in the opposite direction.

By the mid-18th century, *trekboers*, hunters and explorers from the Dutch outpost at the Cape of Good Hope had drifted into the area and settled there semi-permanently. It was wild country, full of wildlife and covered in thick forests. Animals and timber were in abundance and the unchecked slaughter of both followed, to the extent that the wildlife, especially the large herds of elephant that lived in the forests, was wiped out. When it was realised, almost too late, that the area was being turned into a desert, conservators were appointed to save what was left. It was too late for the elephants but at least great chunks of the magnificent forests survived and are among the Garden Route's best attractions.

Orientation

Officially, the Garden Route begins on the Cape Town side of the harbour town of Mossel Bay, running 280km from Heidelberg in the west to beyond the Storms River, near Port Elizabeth. The main towns are Mossel Bay, George and Knysna, while the seaside town of Plettenberg Bay booms in the holiday season.

When to go

The Garden Route is blessed by the warm Mozambique current and its climate is mild all year round. The area is best in spring and late summer but almost any time of year is good for visiting. Mid-summer is the region's prime season as the country goes on holiday. Winters here tend to be cool and wet but you may still experience day after day of baking sunshine in mid-July. Thanks to the warm current, the sea is almost always warm (warmer than Cape Town anyway).

GETTING THERE AND AWAY
Bus

Not surprisingly the Garden Route is well served by bus companies, with no less than three operators running daily between Cape Town and Port Elizabeth: Baz Bus (tel: 021 439 2323), Translux (tel: 021 405 3333) and Intercape Mainliner (tel: 021 386 4400).

Train

The *Southern Cross* runs weekly between Cape Town and Oudtshoorn, via George, leaving Cape Town on Friday evenings and returning from Oudtshoorn on Sunday evenings. It's a pity that some of the country's best scenery passes by during the night – it's mountainous country, and the swaying of the coach, the squealing wheels and the string of fairy lights winding through the darkness will leave you in no doubt about what kind of terrain you're in. Eastbound trains reach George, at the western edge of the Garden Route, early on Saturday morning, before climbing the terrific Montagu Pass over the formidable barrier of the Outeniqua Mountains to Oudtshoorn, the main town of the Little Karoo. The train's early morning arrival is convenient if you want to continue ambling along the Garden Route, some of which can be done on the country's only regularly scheduled steam-hauled train.

Hitchhiking

The N2 is the main route along the coast and traffic is heavy. There are also enough places en route to break your journey and hitching between the centres should be quite easy. As always, start early.

HEIDELBERG TO GOURITZMOND
Things to see and do
Adventure

The Garden Route starts at Heidelberg, a little farming town at the foot of the Langeberg mountains and somewhat inland from the sea. On the coast, San Sebastian Bay (Witsand), the eastern gateway to the Garden Route, is the breeding ground for southern right whales and whale watching is naturally a major attraction. Mobile phone network operator MTN's highly acclaimed Cape Whale Route was awarded a British Airways' Tourism for Tomorrow Award. August is the peak calving season and the mothers and calves are best seen from Suzy's whale-watching tower. You can also phone the MTN Hotline (tel: 083 212 1074 or 021 418 3705; email: cwr_master@mtn.co.za) for likely sitings then head along the coast through picturesque villages such as Vermaaklikheid, with its unique Kapstyl cottages, and spot the whales from special vantage points.

Breede River

The Breede River mouth is a paradise for fishermen, birdwatchers and nature lovers; for a closer inspection of the marine life contact Still Bay Divers (tel: 028 754 3843) to check out the diving or fishing sites at the 'Bay of Sleeping Beauty' where ancient fish traps are still visible at low tide. Learn to waterski or take whale- or dolphin-spotting trips with Still Bay Watersports (tel: 028 754 2352). Moonlit boat trips are laid on for the romantics. The annual **Strandloper Festival**, at Lapskuit, in late September, includes a beerfest, arts and craftmarkets, watersports and, for the masochistic, a half-marathon and cycle tour.

Hiking, mountain biking and horseriding

Opportunities for these activities abound along the coast and inland, particularly in the majestic Langeberg mountains. Contact the tourist offices for details or contact the local tourism organisation (tel: 044 873 6355), and ask for the excellent hiking pamphlet which outlines the major trails throughout the Garden Route.

The undoubted highlight for adrenalin junkies is bungee jumping and bridge-swinging off the bridges in the Gouritz River gorge. Three high bridges (two road, one rail) cross the 100m-deep gorge very close to one another and the old road bridge is used as a bungee and bridge-swinging platform.

Face Adrenalin (tel: 021 97 7161; email extreme@iafrica.com) operate the bungee jumping and **Wildthing Adventures** (tel: 021 461 1653; email wildthing@icon.co.za) the terrifying bridge-swing where you swing in a 30m pendulum from the old bridge and under the new. Check out the excellent café by the registration office while you are waiting – or recovering – or wander off on the trail into the forest for a pleasant hike.

Tourist information
Regional Tourism Organisation Tel: 044 874-4040.
Still Bay Tourism Tel: (028) 754-2602.

Accommodation
Skeiding Guesthouse 12km west of Heidelberg on N2 (look for the brown sign); tel: 028 722 1891. Double, single R150 B&B. A working ostrich farm off the regular backpacking circuit, but offering a range of adventure activities. Meals available.
Mont Blanc Adventure Farm 13km north of Riversdale; tel: 028 713 3214. R100 per person. Bush camp: R150 per person for the whole weekend. Basic farm cottage, lit by candles and hurricane lanterns.

MOSSEL BAY
Mossel Bay lies in the embrace of a protecting bay, built on or below the cliffs which dominate the town. It is one of the country's smaller harbours which owes its apparent revival to tourism and drilling in the offshore natural gas fields.

On February 3 1488, Portuguese navigator, Bartolomeu Dias, became the first known European to set foot on the eastern coast of South Africa when he landed at Mossel Bay. He called it the Bay of Cowherds after the Khoikhoi herdsmen he encountered on the beach. When Dias tried to talk to them, the herdsmen threw stones at him so he sailed on.

Tourist information
Mossel Bay Tourism Tel: 044 691 2202.

Accommodation
Santos Express Backpackers Munro Rd, Santos Beach; tel/fax: 044 691 1995; email: trein@mb.lia.net. Double compartment R120, single R85, dorm R45. A

backpacker in a couple of restored train coaches on a siding near the beachfront. The rooms are small but the view is outstanding.

Park House Backpackers 121 High St; tel: 044 691 1937; fax: 044 691 3815; email: meyer@law.co.za. Double R130, dorm R45, camping R30. A fine 130-year-old stone house with wooden floors with a wide veranda. It's an *Out of Africa* kind of house. Great ambience.

Barnacles Econo-lodge 112 High St; tel: 044 690 4584; fax: 044 691 3435; email: shivas@mweb.co.za. Double R130, dorm R45, camping R30. Clean, centrally located backpacker with great views of sea and mountains. Tours such as shark diving, surfing, are offered.

Things to see and do

Many of the monuments and activities of the region reflect the rich heritage of the ancient trading town. Attractions include the **Bartolomeu Dias Museum Complex**, the **Mossel Bay Cultural Route** (you can take a guide) or the country's first post office, an ancient milkwood tree from where you can send a specially hand-franked letter. The story is that a letter tied to the tree by Petro de Ataide, a Portuguese sailor, warned fellow seamen of conflict in Calcutta. The finder, grateful for the warning, left another letter, starting a centuries-long tradition of attaching letters to the tree for passing ships to carry home.

The **Dias Museum** (Church Street and Market Street; tel: 044 691 1067) includes a full-scale replica of a Portuguese caravel which was sailed from Portugal in a re-enactment of Dias' journey. It is sobering to see the small size of the ships the Portuguese sailed in while building their fabulous empire. Included in the complex are a shell museum with its massive display, and the local history museum. *Open Mon–Fri 09.00–17.00, Sat 10.00–16.00, Sun 14.00–17.00 (history museum closed). Admission free.*

Sea life

The south coast of South Africa is regarded as the best place in the world to see great white sharks. Yes, they *are* there, living in the bay, but shark attacks are rare in this part of the world. Mossel Bay's thrills include shark-cage diving – not the sole preserve of qualified divers since you can do it with just a mask and snorkel – so you can shudder as the kings of the sea come and have a close look at you. You don't have to leave the relative safety of the boat as viewing is just as good from the deck. Phone Shark Africa (tel: 044 691 3796; email: sharkafrica@mweb.co.za).

Those preferring less intimate marine encounters can view whales, dolphins and seals from the shore or boats. It is cheaper and less stressful for the creatures if you watch them from the shore, but boats do offer the chance to get closer. Take a good pair of binoculars. Check out the operation's reputation first. Two that have been recommended are Ramonza (tel: 082 455 2438; email ramonza@mweb.co.za) and Orpa (tel: 044 691 3371), who offer fishing and seal island trips. You can also dive the shipwrecks with Mossel Bay Divers (tel: 044 691 1441; email: marij@mweb.co.za). If you'd rather not get wet, visit the shipwreck diving exhibition at the Maritime Museum (tel: 044 691 1067).

Golden beaches

At Mossel Bay some of the country's best waves add to the coast's allure. Don't worry about the sharks as human/shark interaction is mercifully almost unheard of. The St Blaize trail is a 13km hike that starts below the lighthouse at Cape St Blaize and follows the coast as far as Dana Bay. It is a lovely, five hour walk along the cliffs and down to bays and coves. Best of all, it's free.

Sky diving

The adventure is not limited to sea or land. Mossel Bay is one of the cheapest and most scenic places to go skydiving. The weather is invariably excellent which means no hanging about at a rain-soaked airfield, and the view of the southern Cape coast from 3,000m is unbeatable. Phone Outeniqua Skydiving (tel: 082 705 2761; email: henk.vanwyk@sbs.siemens.co.za).

Trails

Inland, in the foothills of the Outeniqua Mountains and along the Great and Little Brak Rivers, hiking, mountain bike and 4x4 trails wind through the fynbos. Take a bike from or hire a trike from Bonnidale Adventure Farm (tel: 044 695 3175) and take off and explore. This is king country for horseriding (Bonnidale offers trails for up to eight days) and the farm has piqued the interest of the paragliding fraternity with the promise of outstanding thermals.

GEORGE

A pretty town on the wide, green plain at the foot of the Outeniquas, George feels like the centre of the Garden Route, although the fun hasn't even begun if you're approaching from the west. It does have a relatively busy airport (think two or three airliners per day) so it's a logical jumping-off point if you're flying in.

Lying at the foot of the towering Outeniquas, George is now a bustling town. The first town to be proclaimed after the British occupation in 1806, it was named after King George III, who donated a bible to the local church. The town is a fairly important economic centre and boasts a large timber industry. The region was covered with indigenous hardwood trees, Outeniqua yellowwood and white stinkwood trees especially, but rampant logging almost wiped them out. In 1936, the government banned harvesting of indigenous hardwood trees for 200 years, allowing some of the species to grow back. The town streets are lined with trees and the place has a pleasant feel about it.

Tourist information

George Tourist Information Centre Tel: 044 801 9295; fax: 044 873 5228; email: info@georgetourism.co.za; web: www.georgetourism.co.za
Garden Route Tourist Information Centre Tel: 044 873 6355

Getting there and away

It was quite a conservative town but the tourist boom has done a lot to change attitudes. Eight kilometres from the beach, it's less of a seaside town than somewhere to cash travellers' cheques. The airport is served by domestic flights

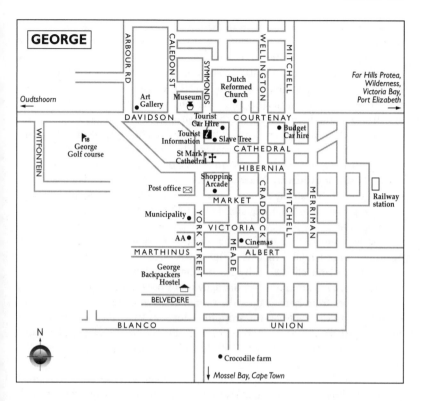

from Cape Town, Johannesburg and Port Elizabeth. The airport is about 15km out of town, but there are usually cabs hanging about to meet the flights.

Accommodation

Sunshine Backpackers 103 Merriman St; tel/fax: 044 873 0424; email: gribl@pixie.co.za. Double R120, dorm R45, camping R25. Big, quiet suburban house with a pool. It's close to the railway station which is useful for those early morning departures/late afternoon arrivals.

Eating and drinking

George is not known for its nightlife and even in the days when the Army Women's College was here, there was not much going on. There are a couple of pubs and hotel bars and there is a small cinema showing reasonably up to date films. Restaurants are mostly of the steakhouse-chain variety although the Oakus Hotel (tel: 044 874 7130) serves great pub lunches.

Things to see and do

George is not the most cultured town in the world, it has to be said, but there are some worthy diversions for otherwise slothful, wet-weather days. The **George Museum** (tel: 044 801 8223) reveals every bit of trivia on the town's growth since it was a mere timber trading post for the Dutch East India

Company, but its most fascinating exhibits revolve around the life of P W Botha, the *Groot Krokodil* (big crocodile) who was South Africa's second-last white president and still lives in nearby Wilderness. Included in the exhibits is a replica of an AK47 assault rifle carved out of ivory which was presented to Botha by Jonas Savimbi, leader of UNITA, the anti-communist anti-government rebel army in Angola. In the long years before UNITA captured the diamond fields, the group received strong backing from Pretoria and funded much of its military activity from the slaughter of Angola's elephant herds. The museum is an uncomfortable echo of the Apartheid era and worth visiting for it. *Open Mon–Fri 09.00–16.30, Sat 09.00–12.30. Admission R5.*

The **National Railway Museum** recently opened at the end of a siding at the east end of the railway station. This wonderful place is the result of nearly 20 years of planning, scheming and drama while officialdom tried to make its mind up. The entire history of the railways is covered, the main shed is full of locomotives and rolling stock, much of it in working order, and there are paintings, photographs, models, displays of gleaming SAR silverware and china, signals and all the oddly fascinating paraphernalia needed to run a railway. Special steam trains (*not* the daily trains between George and Knysna) usually depart from here as does the Outeniqua Power Van, a motorised rail trolley that takes people up the stunning Montagu Pass. The local classic car club has put most of its members' cars on display on one of the platforms. *Open Mon–Fri 09.00–16.30, Sat 09.00–12.30. Admission was free when I visited in mid-2000 although the fee is expected to be R10.*

The nearby beach villages of Herolds Bay and Victoria Bay have great swimming but unless you like camping, accommodation is a bit limited. Victoria Bay is on the branch railway to Knysna and has its own railway station perched high on the hill overlooking the village; check with the conductor first if you want to alight here.

The steam-driven Garden Route

If you're heading east, the best way into the Lake District and Knysna is on the slow steam-hauled train which woofles along the coast, through forests and over the wide, still lakes. The train ride is the best way of easing into the Outeniqua frame of mind – relaxed, somnambulant and in no great hurry to do anything.

Getting there and away

Three trains run daily from George to Knysna and back; however the first and last trains are freight only. Bizarrely, for what is a major tourist attraction, there are no trains on Sundays, mainly because of a persistent and outdated civil service mentality at various levels of the railway administration. For train information and bookings, contact the Outeniqua Choo-Tjoe (tel: 044 801 8288; fax: 044 801 8286; email: debbiex@transnet.co.za) or Knysna station (tel: 044 382 1361; fax: 044 382 3465).

The branch railway which runs from George to Knysna is the official museum railway but is run by Transnet Heritage Foundation as a genuine, working railway, complete with steam-hauled freight and passenger trains.

The 46km line was an inspired choice for a working museum. The area is thriving in South Africa's tourist boom. The countryside is exquisite. The railway drops down from George through thick forest to the coast, hugs the seaside briefly and then gallops over bridges and causeways in what locals call the Lake District. The train hugs the hillside before rolling across the stunning curved viaduct over the Kaaimans River, said to be the most photographed bridge in South Africa. Lean out of the window and you look straight down into the sea which can be a sobering view when the blowing wind shakes the carriage. The railway drops down to sea level at **Wilderness**, a seaside town, and then heads into the Lake District proper, skirting lagoons and forest-covered hills, passing the Fairy Knowe halt just 2km past Wilderness.

Wilderness used to be a popular honeymoon destination, with a sprawl of beach houses and a couple of hotels. Aside from being a breathtaking piece of coast, it's also famous for being the home of P W Botha, who occasionally breaks his silence to lambaste the new order. The area falls within the **Wilderness National Park** (tel: 044 877 1197; web: www.george.co.za/parks) which includes five rivers, four lakes, two estuaries and 28km of coastline in its boundaries. There are four hiking trails in the park and canoes are available to paddle up the Touw River and the Serpentine.

From Wilderness, the railway line passes a number of lakeside settlements and resorts at Swartvlei, Bleshoender and Sedgefield, crosses the Goukamma River, and then doubles back violently as it climbs over the hills which overlook the Knysna and the lagoon. After coasting down through forests, past a little stone church at Belvidere, the train rolls across the long bridge over the lagoon into Knysna.

Accommodation

Fairy Knowe Backpackers Dumbleton Rd; tel: 044 877 1285; email: fairybp@mewb.co.za. Double R130, dorm R45, camping R30. One of the world's greatest such places, it is hidden in a clump of trees two minutes' walk from the station. The train is supposed to stop here, now that the owners and railway have come to an agreement. And, since it is a public railway, you should stand up for your rights as a passenger. The backpackers itself is in an old colonial house with a view over the lakes and mountains. The double rooms are terrific. Watching the sun rise from the front veranda is an event that may make you want to stay longer, which is no hardship. Fairy Knowe's owners Chris and Monica can arrange canoeing, cycling, abseiling, paragliding, hiking, horseriding, fishing – the place is a mini Outward Bound centre, without the instructors. They also get discounted tickets for the steam train and they can organise cheap car rentals so you can explore the area. Excellent meals available.

Adventure

Take a drive or ride up the Outeniqua and Montagu passes. The latter is a little-used, savagely twisting route which closely follows the railway pass over the mountains. If you're not up to the ascent, there's the Outeniqua Power Van (tel: 044 801 8239), a motorised rail trolley which drops cyclists and hikers off at the summit to swoop (or hobble) down Montagu Pass; ask the operators about bikes if you don't have your own. Conquering the Seven Passes road to Knysna is a worthy victory for mountain bikers – if your legs are up to it try the seven-day mountain bike tour over these historic passes, through the forests and coastal fynbos and along the rocky shores.

Ask locally about trails to the secret places in this forest-cloaked mountain wilderness, or go on one of Cherie's horses (tel: 082 962 3223, email: rnw@george.lia.net), or take a guide to see Khoi rock paintings and other places of interest.

Herold's Bay and **Victoria Bay** are popular whale viewing locations; the latter is also a promised land for surfers and body boarders. Diving, yachting and deep-sea fishing, horseriding and scenic flights are all within easy reach.

Wilderness is a true adventure playground, an ecologically unique and sensitive region of lakes and vleis (deserted beaches), high dunes and sculpted gorges set against the spectacular backdrop of the towering Outeniqua mountains. The mountains are a fine source of adventure. The **Outeniqua hiking trail** runs from Beervlei to Harkerville Forest Station: book through the forestry office (tel: 044 382 5466). It's seven days of hard hiking but it can be broken up in to shorter sections. Accommodation is in fully equipped overnight huts with bunks and mattresses, and costs R30 per person per day.

The **Wilderness National Park** (tel: 044 877 1197) has hiking, birding and an imaginatively designed, incredibly cheap, self-catered, three-day canoe and hiking trail from the Touw to the Serpentine River, up to hidden waterfalls deep in the forest and through a series of lakes to Sedgefield. The reserve's well-sited chalets and campsites make it easy to linger.

If this sounds too leisurely, the **Kaaimans Gorge** is the setting for a spectacular abseil next to a waterfall – an escape canoe waits to pick you up at the bottom. Abseiling can be combined with the Kaaimans Canyon tour which includes walking, swimming, flat-water tubing and optional cliff jumping. Wetsuits are provided. The operators, Eden Adventures (tel: 044 877 0179; email: edenadventures@mweb.co.za) also run guided canoe and mountain bike trips and the latter perfect for riders of all levels. Hard-core bikers can sweat up the passes and swoop down the long, exhilarating descents while less active companions can make use of the back-up vehicle. Hillbillies Mtb Club (tel: 044 873 2982) have a fun ride every Saturday which visitors are welcome to join.

Rock climbers and river runners should contact Chris Leggatt, of Eden Adventures for information and updates on conditions. The steep slopes mean that the most of the rivers are steep and fast mountain creeks. However, if you happen to be around when it has been raining for a couple of days, see if the Gouritz, Keur (at the bottom of the Montagu Pass) or Kaaimans Rivers are running, as these have stretches of excellent paddling.

Oudtshoorn, just over the Swartberg pass, renowned for the Cango Caves and ostriches, is also the main climbing area, with predominantly bolted sport climbing routes. Joy Rides (tel: 044 279 1163) and Eden Adventures run mountain biking tours and you can get out at the top of Swartberg with your bike for the exhilarating cycle down the switchbacks to the edge of the Great Karoo.

The high dunes make Wilderness one of the safest and most popular paragliding training areas in the country. Take a tandem flight among the instructees, their sails flapping like the wings of fledgling chicks as they attempt their first clumsy flights or watch the colourful canopies of the accomplished as they soar over the Map of Africa, a bizarre geological feature shaped exactly like the African continent. Contact Wings over Wilderness (tel: 044 877-0079) or Cloudbase Paragliding (tel: 044 877 1414).

Diving and snorkelling opportunities abound on the coast with its many bays and coves. Contact Garden Route Divers (tel: 082 771-5543) and if it's solitude you seek, contact the Wilderness Eco-Tourism Association (tel: 044 877 0045) to arrange a fishing permit.

KNYSNA

Knysna used to be a sleepy village with a disproportionate number of resident hippies, who have now either moved or cashed in on the tourism explosion. Its surroundings are awesome. The town rolls back from the shores of a huge lagoon into the indigenous forest behind. The lagoon is sheltered by the hills which stand between it and the sea. The Knysna Heads, two steep sandstone cliffs, guard the entrance to the lagoon. The sea is treacherous here and many boats have come to grief in the passage, one of the reasons why Knysna never really took off as a port.

Knysna has its own microclimate meaning the sun often shines when the surrounding coastline is fog- or rain-bound. The sheltered waters of the lagoon, a mosaic of marine blues, islands, beaches and salt marshes, are the major habitat of the Knysna sea horse and of the vast oyster beds, which are responsible for the town's only festival of note.

Before tourism, its main industries were timber and a little boat-building. Both timberyard and boatyard are still in business although on a much smaller scale. The vast and thriving forests east and north of the town are home to the last known and rarely seen forest elephant (until recently there were only three of them). Some conservationists want more elephants released into the forest but an acrimonious debate has blown up with some people claiming the newcomers would not be true forest elephants and thus not worthy of introduction. The recent attempts to introduce more animals have been disastrous (see *The Knysna Forests* below).

Tourist information
Knysna Tourism Tel: 044 382-5510

Accommodation
Knysna is well supplied with backpackers and freshly done-up B&Bs. Ask for a reduced rate in the low season (May–September).

The Caboose Gray St; tel: 044 382 5850. Double R139, single R99. B&B-style accommodation with overt train theme, although the staff don't know much about trains. Near the station, restaurants and centre of the village.
Knysna Backpackers 42 Queens St; tel/fax: 044 382 2554; email: knybpack@netactive.co.za. Double R110, dorm R45. The town's longest-lived backpacker, in an old house with wooden floors and a view of the lagoon.

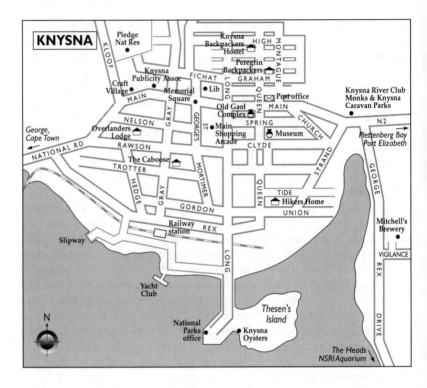

Overlanders Lodge 11 Nelson St; tel/fax: 044 382 5920; email: overlanders@ imaginet.co.za. Double R130, dorm R50, camping R40. Huge place with a jacked-up travel and information centre. For the budget conscious, there is free vegetarian food every night, and they also hand out a discount voucher for shops and restaurants in town.
Peregrin Backpackers Lodge 16 High St; tel/fax: 044 382 3747; email: peregrin@knysna.lia.net. Double R65 per person, dorm R50. Prices drop for each additional night you stay.
Hikers Home 17 Tide St; tel: 044 382 4632. Double R36 per person, dorm R28, camping R20 per person. Centrally located, groovy backpackers.

Eating and drinking
Lots of little restaurants and coffee shops dotted about town. There is a new waterfront style complex near the station with a few bars and restaurants and the usual spread of takeaways. Most seem to be aimed squarely at flush tourists and the place jumps in the summer – go before or after. As expected, there is plenty of fresh fish and at least a good view to look at while eating. Tapas, the best waterfront bar of the lot, sadly burned down a few years back.

Things to see and do
Adventure
Water-borne adventures include canoeing on the lagoon and up the Goukamma Rivers. The Knysna Heads and the Featherbed Nature Reserve

have great hiking and climbing (but you have to go with a tour). The best option is a canoeing, hiking and abseiling trip with SEAL Adventures (tel: 083 654 8755; email: seals@mweb.co.za).

The rocky coastline has nailed many ships over the centuries, so there's good wreck-diving for the suitably qualified. Snorkelling and diving on the reefs outside the Heads is excellent: enquire at the Adventure Centre (tel: 044 384 0831; email: robinwest@hotmail.com). The centre also offers creeking (kloofing up-river), windsurfing and surfing instruction, waterskiing and, at the other end of the adrenalin scale, a Township Trail.

The deep, cool Knysna forests – not eucalyptus plantations, but thousands of hectares of aged stinkwoods and yellowwoods, tree ferns, Knysna louries and legends – have trails for hikers, bikers and horses. Take a horse, from Southern Comfort (tel: 044 532 7885), mountain bike from Outeniqua Biking (tel: 044 532 7644; email: info@gardenroute.co.za) or hiking trail. The hiking is self-guided and on well-marked trails through the State forests; the Forestry Department (tel: 044 382 5466) issues excellent maps. Harkerville Backpackers (tel: 044 532 7777; email: bacpac@mweb.co.za) is a good base – they'll point you in the right direction and rent you a bike.

If you can't secure a place on the famous Otter trail (see page 160), the one-day Kranshoek and the overnight Harkerville trails give you a taste of what you've missed. And if you're there in mid summer check out Abseil Africa's 'Lost world' abseil route at Kranskoek (tel: 021 424 1580; email: abseil@iafrica.com).

For sedentary adventurers
The Knysna Oyster Festival, a quiet break from more pressing pursuits, takes place in early July.

BUFFELS BAY
The lagoon has had the effect of limiting development on the beach on the other side of the headland from Knysna, with the exception of Buffels Bay, a seaside dorpie at the west end of the beach. There is not a lot to do here except lie on the beach and its isolation is perfect because it means nothing will distract you from what might be the best beach time of your trip. If you can get to it, the Norman-style church at Belvidere, on the sea side of the lagoon, is worth visiting. There is a halt here, but once again tell the conductor. The beach at Brenton-on-Sea is an 8km stretch of beauty but tough to get to without a car.

GOUKAMMA NATURE RESERVE
This small coastal reserve between Knysna and Sedgefield has around 48km of footpaths and a 14km-long beach which is completely unspoiled. You can hire canoes to explore the waterways but I find the free trails much more rewarding.

Accommodation
Wild Side Backpackers Buffels Bay; tel: 044 383 0609 or 382 6266. Double R70, dorm R45–50. A lovely place in an airy, converted beachfront restaurant. The thundering surf is the underlying theme. There are dorms inside and excellent

doubles which open on to a central, sun-warmed courtyard at the back. They will pick you up in Knysna. There is a braai (R30) on the beach every evening.

Things to see and do

The trails lead past oyster beds on the beach, over fynbos covered dunes and around Groenvlei, a freshwater lake. Most of the trails are a couple of hours long. One of the striking things about it is how few people there are. Go midweek and you will have 2,230ha of nature reserve to yourself. Wildlife includes eland, bontebok and small antelope species, and the birdlife is prolific. If you are staying at Buffels Bay, the main part of the reserve is on the other side of the Goukamma River and reached by a rickety suspension bridge. Permits are issued free. The beach is not safe for swimming because of vicious rip currents, and hikers should carry plenty of drinking water as it gets hot out here.

THE KNYSNA FORESTS

The coastal plain was once almost entirely covered by indigenous forest, a rare sight in an otherwise arid land. To prosper, forests like this need plenty of rain, at least 750mm a year, which is provided in abundance here at the foot of the Outeniqua Mountains.

The forests, which contained magnificent hardwood trees (including white stinkwoods, Cape ash and majestic Outeniqua yellowwoods), were decimated by woodcutters. The loggers went for the big trees, some of them over 600 years old. They built logging roads, smashing young trees in the process. There was no control and no replenishment and when the government finally appointed a conservator in 1874, it was almost too late. In 1886, Comte de Vasselot de Regne, a French forester, was appointed by the Cape government to investigate the state of the forests and was shocked to discover that more than three-quarters of the indigenous forest had been seriously damaged by reckless tree-felling. He immediately stopped logging operations and divided what was left into sections, permitting felling only in some sections while other areas were given a chance to recover.

It has been a battle to preserve the natural forests ever since. Both state and private timber companies have huge tracts of plantation forest – all of it exotic pine and eucalyptus – and they have agitated constantly for more land to be made available for commercial plantations. Happily, many of the people living here are keenly environmentally aware, not least of because of tourism considerations, and have resisted pressure from the loggers. The tourism boom has helped too as the government realises that the country's natural attractions will ultimately earn much more foreign exchange than forestry ever will.

For the elephants, however, it was too late. The big herds had been shot out or driven away as humans encroached on their territory, and by the early 20th century, there were only a handful left. By the mid-1980s, just three animals were thought to survive, understandably making themselves very scarce in the impenetrable greenery. The last elephant to be regularly spotted by foresters and other locals was an old female, and a debate raged in conservation circles when the national conservation authorities decided to translocate a few surviving juveniles from a culling operation in the Kruger National Park to the Knysna area. The fact that the truck bringing the first few elephants was involved in a horrific smash, which resulted in all of them having to be put down, didn't deter anyone involved and more juveniles were sent to join the old female in the forests. The experiment failed. The newcomers came from the bushveld and were unused to the vegetation, and far preferred feeding in the farmlands beyond the forest, which didn't please the farmers at all. They were moved again, this time to the Addo Elephant Park near Port Elizabeth. The remaining cow has rarely been seen since. She is old now – at least 60 years – and is the last of a dynasty.

Things to see and do
There are a couple of hiking trails into the forests. Just follow the little elephant marker signs and you won't get lost. If you do blunder off the path, don't waste your time thrashing around in the undergrowth because you will more than likely go round in circles. If you can, follow a stream or look for mushrooms which, in this part of the world, grow on the south side of big trees.

Accommodation
Southern Comfort Horse Ranch Fisanthoek (near Plettenberg Bay); tel/fax: 044 532 7885. En suite double R120, double R100, dorm R35–40, camping R20. This large horse farm is set right in the Knysna forest with a view of the Outeniqua mountains behind. Naturally, horseriding in the forest is the main attractions. The farm is halfway between Knysna and Plettenberg Bay and 2km off the N2. You can hitch or ride – ask to be dropped at the Garden of Eden.

Harkerville Backpackers Halfway between Knysna and Plett on N2. Follow signs; tel: 044 532 7777; fax: 044 532 7881; email: bacpac@mweb.co.za; web: www.linx.co.za/bacpac. 2-bed tree house R45 per person, dorms R35, camping R25. Smart backpacker in a forest setting. The place is surrounded by trails which lead off into the trees. The two-day Harkerville trail starts nearby. Meals available.

PLETTENBERG BAY
For a place that used to be a one-boat whaling station, Plettenberg Bay has come a long way. It has one of the most beautiful outlooks in the world, set as it is on the western end of a gorgeous curving bay that the Portuguese took one look at and named Baia de Formosa (*beautiful*). The western end of the bay is dominated by the Robberg (Cape Seal), a long, rocky peninsula – a mountain actually – which reaches out into the sea. The Robberg has been designated a nature reserve, and has trails and secluded beaches. It should be a World Heritage Site but that might take some lobbying. I have walked along the top of the mountain and seen hammerhead sharks drifting in the clear, blue coastal sea. It is without doubt one of the most spectacular attractions on the coast. To the east, the view across Lookout Beach, the bay and the Keurbooms Lagoon to Formosa Peak is one of the finest in Africa.

I wish the same could be said for the town. Its beauty has also been its downfall as the town continues to explode up the hills and into the valleys where old milkwood trees grow. Sometime in the 1970s, Plettenberg Bay started becoming trendy. Big houses were built overlooking Robberg Beach. Driven by an insatiable lust for holiday property and status, the property market went wild and the town became 'Plett'. It heaves during the holidays, both in December–January and over the Easter break as Jo'burgers and Capetonians share sunblock on its three beaches. This is not the best time to visit if you're looking for peace. But if you have a touch of cabin fever from travelling alone for too long, well then…. Out of season it doesn't look like the same place, as Outeniqua rust – a kind of moisture-induced lethargy of the brain – begins to afflict the locals. This may be the best time to visit because winter days are often sunny and warm, and you'll have the beach more or less to yourself.

The swimming is safe, there's good walking on the beaches especially on the Robberg, and the height of the town above the sea makes it an excellent place to spot whales when they arrive in the bay between July and October to calve and nurse their young.

Tourist information

Plett Eco Adventure Centre Tel: 044 533 3732; email: info@pletbay. The agents for many of the activities and accommodation in the area.
Plettenberg Bay Tourism Tel: 044 533 4065; email: plett.tourism@pixie.co.za, They handle all the official tourism business.

Accommodation

There is plenty of choice in town. Some places are brand-new; others have weathered the fluctuations of the local tourist economy.

Weldon Kaya Afro Village 1km west of town on the N2; tel: 044 533 2437; fax: 044 533 4364; email: info@weldonkaya.co.za; web: www.weldonkaya.co.za. Detached double R150, dorm R45. Calling this place unique doesn't do this family-run operation full justice. Perched on a five-acre spread high on a hill overlooking the bay, Weldon Kaya has whacky accommodation based on huts built in vernacular style out of traditional materials like kob – hand pressed clay – and thatch. The attached restaurant serves fine, cheap meals and has become something of a meeting point for locals who come up to see the live entertainment that the owners regularly organise. They are also a key link to local adventure operators.
Nothando Backpackers Hostel 5 Wilder St; tel/fax: 044 533 0220; email: deios@global.co.za. Double R130, dorm R40. Centrally located backpacker, spread over two houses so there is room to express yourself. All meals can be provided and they offer various tours.

Accommodation nearby

Stanley Island Keurbooms River, 4 miles east of town on N2; tel/fax: 044 535 9442. Double R160, dorm from R50, camping R30. An island which a couple of crusty ex-air force pilots have turned this into a fab backpacker with the undeniable attraction of its own private airfield from which you can take a trip over the bay in an open cockpit glider. There is a beach and forest nearby and trips in canoes, hiking, whale and dolphin watching tours are available. Accommodation is in chalets and cheap meals are available.

Garden Route Backpackers 17km east of town on the N2, Hog Hollow turn-off; tel/fax: 044 534 8837; email: gardenroutebp@hotmail.com. Double R110, single from R70, dorm R45–55, camping R35. A well-kept secret that travellers who have stayed here rave about as one of the best places in the Garden Route. Set on 200ha of farmland, the backpacker has massive rooms, cottages, luxury log cabins and uncrowded dorms. There are trails wandering off the property, animals such as monkeys, baboons and bushbuck in the forest. And what a campsite…. Meals are available.

Eating, drinking and nightlife

As one would expect from a serious holiday town, Plett has a huge selection of bars, pubs, restaurants and fast-food places. For top-rate, cheap grub go to the **Rod and Reel** (tel: 044 533 4290). Weldon Kaya (tel: 044 533 2437) runs a famous restaurant called **Crackers Deli** with meals aimed at budget travellers. At Nyati Mampoer (tel: 044 535 9739) 10km outside Plett you can watch *mampoer* (moonshine) being made and then taste it. It bites – you have been warned.

Things to see and do

Competition from the sunseeking crowds means that winter is a better time to visit. Hike on Robberg and out to the island, both fine snorkelling spots, or amble down the shining beaches. The long trek along Robberg beach to the end of the cape and back is thirsty, calf-numbing work but highly recommended.

Diving International (tel: 044 533 0381) will advise on snorkelling visibility and conditions or take you out to scuba dive while Ocean Life Surf Shop (tel: 044 533 3253) can tell you where the hot surf spots are. Lookout and Hobie beaches are usually the best for waves.

Plett is famous for its marine mammals, and dolphin- and whale-watching trips are offered from boats, sea kayaks, gliders and even aloft on a parasail by Ocean Safaris (tel: 044 533 4963; email: oceansafaris@yahoo.com). Ocean Adventures (tel: 044 533 5033; email: oceanadv@global.co.za) specialise in eco-tours of the bay and surrounding areas and offer unusual options such as overnighting in fisherman's huts on the Robberg.

THE TSITSIKAMMA COAST

Raw, surf-pounded coast, real forest and deep-sunken river valleys. That's the Tsitsikamma, whose name is derived from the Khoikhoi word meaning 'running water'. It's a wilderness, pure and simple – too mountainous and tangled in real forest to be developed. South African author Andre Brink caught the spirit of the place in his book *An Instant in the Wind*, a story about a wealthy European woman who hides away on the coast with her Hottentot slave, who later becomes her lover. It is the kind of coast where people *could* hide from the world. Great waves pound the rocky shore and the natural forests hangs in a great impenetrable mass on the mountain slopes. The area falls into the **Tsitsikamma Coastal National Park**, 80km or so of coast and forested mountains lying between the two Groot rivers.

Accommodation
Storms River

Stormsriver Rainbow Lodge 72 Darnell St; tel/fax: 042 541 1530. Double R120–150, dorm R50. Comfortable backpacker with a calm vibe. The owners are full of friendly and free advice, and they will help out with transport to and from the starts of trails and so on.

Storms Hikers House Darnell St and Saffron St; tel/fax: 042 541 1757; email: rallus@mweb.co.za. Dorm R35, camping R20. Bare-bones hikers' accommodation but with some of the best views on the coast. Very peaceful.

The Tsitsikamma National Park Tel: 042 542 1607; fax: 042 541 1629 has plenty of accommodation to offer and the campsite at Storms River is excellently situated. You can stay at the parks board chalets and campsites, which crouch on the grassy lodges by the craggy coast and watch the whales from the Agulhas lookout on the Lourie trail or explore the snorkel and diving routes.

Nature's Valley

This little village is at the western end of the park and will be a welcome place to nurse a sore body fresh from the Otter Trail.

Hikers' Haven 411 St Patrick's Av; tel/fax: 044 531 6805; email: patbond@mweb.co.za. Double R170, loft room R49. Lovely home-based backpackers in a very pretty place. They offer free use of their canoes so you can go and have sundowners on the river – if you find a size ten left-foot takkie, please return it to the author.

Things to see and do

The Tsitsikamma is such a rugged place that the only way in is on foot so it is natural that its main attraction should be hiking. The legendary Otter Trail traverses its coast, the Tsitsikamma Trail its forests. You can dip into the latter if you haven't time for the whole trail – the first and last sections are easily accessible.

The Otter Trail

The 41km Otter Trail is the Holy Grail of South African hikes. It is rugged and beautiful, running from the mouth of the Storms River to Nature's Valley, along the coast with its tidal rock pools and sometimes climbing steeply into the thickly vegetated hills. Although the overall distance is short, each day involves some fairly tough hiking and a couple of rivers can be crossed only at low tide.

The trail is so popular that with only 12 people per day allowed at any of the overnight huts, there is an 18-month waiting list to get on it. However, some people have found that if you turn up at the trailhead on a daily basis, you might just benefit from someone else not arriving to take up their booking, or from a booked party with a place or two spare due to last-minute no-shows who might invite you along. It pays to be persistent and travel in a small group.

If there's no chance of getting on the trail, you can get an idea of what the Otter offers by hiking and boulder-hopping the first-day route from the Storm's River mouth to the waterfall. Equally scenic is the route of the last day's hike from the eastern end of the unspoilt beach at Nature's Valley up to the promontory. There are great views back over this shining coastal walk. Nature's Valley is relatively unknown so you can escape the crowds who populate the trails to the viewpoints and sheltered Salt River mouth.

Accommodation is in basically equipped hikers' huts. Each overnight stop has just two six-bed huts each. The trail costs R50 per person per day. For bookings contact South African National Parks (tel: 012 343 1991; email: reservations@parks-sa.co.za).

Tsitsikamma Trail

The Tsitsikamma Trail runs parallel to the Otter Trail but inland at the foot of the Tsitsikamma Mountains, starting at Nature's Valley and ending five days later at Storms River mouth. While it does not have the Otter's seascapes, it is nonetheless an appealing hike. The route runs over the higher part of the coastal plateau, traversing natural forest, a few plantations and Cape fynbos. Fast-running clear rivers tumble down the slopes, providing enough opportunities to cool off and fill waterbottles.

The hike is not strenuous. The longest day is 17km and you can also break this trail up into shorter sections. Accommodation is in fully equipped overnight huts. The trail costs R47 per person per day and it's a lot easier to get a booking on it than for the Otter. Phone Safcol Central Reservations (tel: 012 481 3615; email: ecotours@safcol.co.za).

Day hikes

Four free day hikes – the Loerie Trail (1km), Blue Duiker Trail (3.7km), Waterfall Trail (6km) and the Mouth Trail (1km) – will give you a taste of the Otter and Tsitsikamma Trails. Contact the Tsitsikamma National Park (tel: 042 542 1067) for information.

More adventure

For more strenuous hikes, the Formosa and Witels peaks beckon. Mountain bikers can pedal for hours. A full day's ride leads up Mangold's Road into the Safcol Forest (by the Boskor sawmill) past Bloubos, the Witches Cave with its San rock paintings and, on a more technical section, to the Heuningbos Hut. Utopia Backpackers (tel: 044 531 6683) will advise and ferry you to the local adventure sites.

The world's highest bungee jump, 216m off the Bloukrans road bridge, is expensive but for some hard to resist. For a free adrenalin rush, watch one of your friends do it. Contact Face Adrenalin (tel: 042 281 1458; email: extremes@iafrica.com). Afterwards you might want to drag your rubber legs next door to recover at the **Bloukrans Backpackers Lodge** (tel: 042 281 1450; email: juline@intekom.co.za). Double R120, dorm R45. This is just a little cabin at the edge of the forest.

More sedate is a visit to the excellent Fynboshoek cheese farm (tel: 042 750 3879) or the Fern Farm (tel: 042 750 3877).

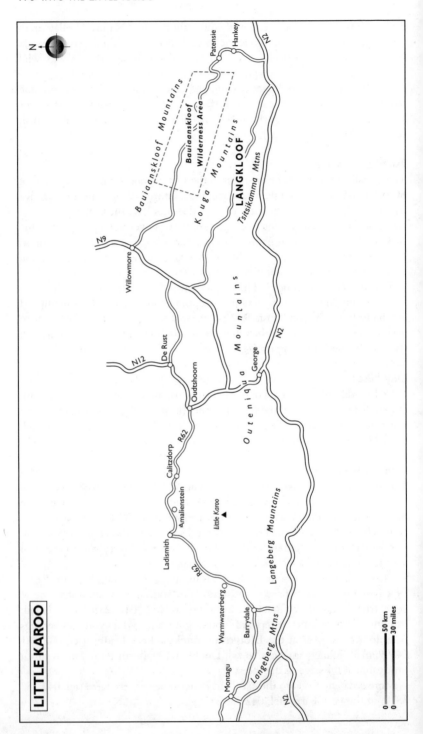

Into the Little Karoo

The Little Karoo is a semi-arid narrow plain lying between three mountain ranges – the Outeniquas and Langeberg to the south and the Swartberg in the north. It is about 280km long and at its widest point, stretches just 100km between the mountain ranges. Do not be put off by the words 'semi-arid' because it is a unique and beautiful valley and by far one of my favourite places in the country.

You arrive in the Little Karoo by one of seven passes over the mountains. It seems unbelievable that the lush Garden Route can be so nearby and yet so different to this landscape. Yet while little rain falls here, the fertile soil is irrigated by thousands of little streams that trickle off the mountains. The few major rivers that cross the valley have their sources in the Great Karoo, on the northern side of the Swartberg, and find their way into the Little Karoo through deep ravines. The journey into the valley is itself an experience as you climb up roads carved out of the red sandstone mountains and deep, narrow kloofs.

Of the varied wildlife that once lived here in abundance, including elephant, lion, leopard, eland, Cape mountain zebra and even buffalo, the ostrich – a desert bird which migrated from the north – is the animal most associated with the region. The valley is the perfect habitat for these flightless birds, able to survive without water for long periods and to exist on a diet of insects, lizards, vegetation and stones, the latter swallowed to grind up all the other stuff. The ostrich has also long been prized by humans for its meat, eggs, skin and black feathers which were once all the rage in European high society. Ostrich farming remains one of the regions big industries.

Before the hunters and farmers, the San were the first people to live here. The valley must have seemed a verdant pasture to people far more used to living in real deserts, and caves in the surrounding mountains are full of their paintings. As the settlement at Cape Town grew, so hunters and *trekboers* moved steadily eastwards in search of new land. The first Europeans found their way into the valley through a twisting defile through the Langeberg called Cogman's Kloof. Look at it from the south – all you can see is an impenetrable wall of sandstone. But the route was there, known only to the San.

It is difficult not to be moved by the beauty of the Little Karoo. When you breathe its crisp air and look at the sharply etched mountains in the desert light, you understand why people move here from literally greener pastures and never go back.

TOURIST INFORMATION

The region is being rediscovered, especially now that tourism is booming in South Africa, and there are some excellent marketing and tourism offices. The regional office is the Klein Karoo Regional Tourism organisation (tel: 044 272 2241; fax: 279 2667; email: kkdr@pixie.co.za). I also found the tourism office in Montagu (tel: 023 614 2471) particularly helpful.

GETTING THERE AND AWAY
Route

The best way to explore the region is on R62, the road which runs from Montagu in the west all the way to Oudtshoorn and on into the Langkloof. There is a growing spread of budget accommodation en route too. The R62 runs parallel to the Garden Route and could be combined with the latter in a circular journey. For my money, though, I preferred the solitude and beauty of the R62.

Public transport

This is sparse and a hire car is probably the best way of getting around.

Bus

Translux (tel: 021 449 3333) runs daily from Cape Town to Ashton, about 10km from Montagu.

Bicycle

Cyclists will enjoy the R62, a long but exceptionally quiet road which, apart from the steep Huisrivier Pass near Calitzdorp, has no major hills to conquer. Remember that distances between some towns are long and that the valley will positively bake in summer. If you're riding, take plenty of water.

GETTING AROUND
Montagu

If you are coming from the Cape Town direction, Montagu is the first town you'll hit. Although not technically in the Little Karoo proper – its vineyards and greener fields dispel any illusions of semi-desert – the town does sit at the historical entrance to the region.

I love Montagu. It is a gaggingly pretty town, embraced on three sides by craggy mountains. Iron-roofed houses, many of them Victorian, look on to wide, quiet streets and it is worth taking a stroll down Long Street to have a look at the old buildings. It is the kind of country town where you arrive and immediately find yourself wondering how much property is. Unfortunately, wealthy refugees from Johannesburg and weekenders from Cape Town have already had that idea and real estate prices are horrific. This influx does mean, however, that Montagu is on the ball and geared-up for travellers.

Tourist information

The tourism office (24 Bath Street) is phenomenally helpful. They even have a website: www.montagu.org.za.

Accommodation

Not surprisingly there are plenty of B&Bs here (how do they all survive?) and at least one excellent budget option.

De Bos Guest Farm Brown St; tel: 023 614 2532 or 082 921 8959. Garden flat R145; en suite room R110 for two people, R45 per person for three or more sharing. Fully equipped from R120 to R270 for six people. Backpackers' barn R35, camping R20 per person. This fabulous place on a farm at the edge of town just rambles and rambles. There are bungalows, a garden flat double, en-suite rooms for 1–3 people, a backpackers' barn and a small campsite which has its own bathrooms. Climbers have made this their base but there is enough room to ensure solitude. Breakfasts are provided on request. One of the best bargains in South Africa.

Eating and drinking

If you are hungry you have 17 restaurants and coffee shops to choose from which is staggering for such a small town.

Things to see and do

Apart from its renowned Muscadel wines and mineral springs, Montagu is known for its walking and rock climbing. Hiking trails twist off in multiple directions into the surrounding mountains and there is enough walking here to keep ramblers busy for weeks. Fine walks include the 17km Bloupunt hike and the 12km trek to Cogmanskloof. You can sleep over in the fully equipped huts near the start of the trails. Day hikers pay R5 per adult, R2.50 per child. Staying in the huts costs R40 per adult, R20 per child. Call 614 2471 to book.

A local pedal fanatic named Roy Brunings has developed and opened a couple of mountain bike trails which vary in length and difficulty from 'doddle' to notorious. He can guide you for a fee, but the trails are open to anyone who wants to go off on his/her own – just ask him for details and maps first. Since he maintains the trails, there is a nominal fee for using them: expect to pay R5–20 per person, depending on the trail. Contact Dusty Sprocket Trails (78 Bath Street; tel/fax: 023 614 1932 or 023 614 2471).

The town's other attraction is rock climbing. The crags west of the town have become the top sport climbing area in the Western Cape. Dozens of routes of various grades have been bolted and on warm, dry weekends climbers gather from all over the region (and the world) to do nothing but climb.

Barrydale

The R62 heads southeast from Montagu, skirting the northern flank of the Langeberg, and runs through lovely scenery. At Barrydale, it turns northeast and heads into the Little Karoo proper, leaving the vineyards behind. Barrydale has some old buildings and is worth wandering around but it feels like Montagu's slightly poorer relative.

Beyond Barrydale, the terrain becomes drier. You feel like you are heading into the unknown, beckoned by the purple Swartberg mountains in the distance. There are no towns or villages out here, so Ronnie's Sex Shop hits you like a speeding locust, right between the eyes. You can't miss it – it's a tiny, whitewashed, flat-roofed building alone in an otherwise dramatic desert landscape. Ronnie's isn't a sex shop at all – it's a roadside bar with a nice big fridge full of cold beer and cider. Ever since the owner painted 'Sex' between the 'Ronnie's' and 'Shop', he has been inundated with curious travellers. People as far away as Port Elizabeth have heard about the place. I should mention that the only reference to sex I could see was a pair of very skimpy red knickers hanging behind the bar.

They serve meals every day except Mondays and there is a small three-bed cottage at the bottom of the property; if you plan to stay, you had best phone Ronnie first (tel: 028 572 1153 or 572 1800).

If Ronnie's is full, there is always the hot springs resort 5km up the road on the slopes of Warmwaterberg (hot water mountain) which, despite an air of apparent seediness, is actually very nice. Accommodation is in a cavernous old building with the kind of long corridors that Jack Nicholson made famous in *The Shining*. Each room has its own bathroom across the corridor, with a huge, four-foot deep bath which is filled by hot, radioactive water straight off the mountain. Very therapeutic and you will appreciate it if you've been travelling by bike (or motorbike, as I had). There are paths leading up the mountain behind the spa and the views of the Little Karoo and the surrounding mountains make it worthwhile to stop here for a day or two of R&R. Stay at Warmwaterberg Spa (tel: 028 572 1609); R70 per person, full Karoo breakfast included.

Ladismith

The next town on the route is Ladismith, unremarkable except for its setting in the shadow of the Swartberg. The town is dominated by Toorkop (bewitched peak) which has two distinct summit pinnacles; early settlers believed a witch trying to cross the range at night was unable to cross the mountain and in a rage split the peak open with her wand. (It must have been an uphill struggle all the way too for the missionaries who came to minister to the Little Karoo's hardy settlers.)

It is a pretty town, known for its dried fruit, cheese and other dairy products. There are also ostrich farms, remnants of the great ostrich boom that raged through the Little Karoo at the beginning of the 20th century. When the market collapsed in 1914, it almost took Ladismith with it and it was years before the town recovered. Now tourism is the new boom and the locals are probably praying that it will be a lasting one.

Amalienstein and Zoar

Tourism has also taken over from religion in the two mission villages of Amalienstein and Zoar, 23km from Ladismith. The two villages sprang up out of the dust in the early 19th century and have grown into quite sizeable communities. A steady decline in agriculture in recent years meant rising poverty in the district but the locals have been proactive in preserving their heritage and luring travellers off the road. The Lutheran church has been restored in striking ochre colours and there is great accommodation in the form of a six-bed, self-catering establishment in Amalienstein: Aunt Carolina's Guest House, (tel: 028 561 1000); R90 per person, room only. Breakfast R20. Stay here – they could use the encouragement.

The road climbs away from the mission into the mountains via the Huisrivier Pass. If you are cycling, this is where you will curse the day you ever set foot in a bike shop. Or maybe you won't because it is a fantastic road. On the east side the road drops sharply into a long, wide plain so make the most of that screaming, high-speed descent.

Calitzdorp lies at the foot of the pass. This is South Africa's port wine capital, although thanks to petty and long-winded scufflings in corridors in faraway Brussels, they are not allowed to call it port any more. Somehow calling Calitzdorp the 'fortified sweet dessert wine capital' doesn't pack quite the same punch. A couple of hiking trails lead up to San paintings in the hills; ask for details at the information centre (tel: 044 213 3312). It is a nice, laid-back town but unless you are a fortified sweet dessert wine buff there's not a lot to detain you.

There is no real budget accommodation in town but if you are willing to make the trek (and I'm thinking of cyclists here), Red Stone Hills Holiday Farm (tel: 044 272 7121) has a couple of restored farm labourers' cottages, complete with wooden floors and open fireplaces and beautiful views of the river. Red Stone Hills is on the secondary road from Calitzdorp to De Hoop and not on the R62. From R200 for two people, R320 for four, R420 for six.

Oudtshoorn

This is the principal town of the Little Karoo, the place where the ostrich feathers came from back in the boom days. The first time I came here I hated it, but that had more to with a miserable eight-hour hitchhiking session from Beaufort West on a midsummer's day than anything else. The first thing many people tell you about Oudtshoorn is how hot it gets, which makes me wonder if that was why the army established its notorious Infantry School there. The heat in midsummer can be bludgeoning, often exceeding 40°C during the day and it feels as if the town is the forgotten dish at the bottom of a rock-wall oven. I am happy to say I quite like the town now and that it has a lot to offer the wandering traveller. There are a couple of ostrich farms open to the public, along with at least one of the ostrich 'palaces', plenty of fine old buildings, hiking and mountain biking, and the Cango Caves.

Tourist information
Klein Karoo Marketing Organisation Voortrekker St; tel: 044 272 2241; fax: 044 279 2667; email: kkdr@pixie.co.za.

Getting there and away
Train
The *Southern Cross* express (tel: 021 405 3871) runs weekly between Cape Town and Oudtshoorn, leaving Cape Town at 18.15 on Friday, arriving 09.14

on Saturday morning and departing Oudtshoorn at 17.40 on Sunday, arriving
Cape Town at 08.40 the following day. The train stops at George, Swellendam
and various other towns. Fare R250 (1st), R165 (2nd).

Bus
Translux buses (tel: 021 405 3333) run to Oudtshoorn daily. Intercape
Mainliner buses (tel: 021 386 4400) cover the Garden Route between Cape
Town and Port Elizabeth/East London.

Accommodation
Oudtshoorn Backpackers Paradise 148 Baron Von Rheede St; tel: 044 272 3436;
fax: 044 272 0877; email: jubilee@pixie.co.za. Double R140, dorm R35, camping R25.
Roomy place with the welcome rarity of en suite bathrooms for all rooms. They also
give you a free ostrich egg for breakfast, which is like getting your three daily meals in
one sitting. In an effort to make people stay longer, you get 30% off your third night
and your fourth night is free.
Oudtshoorn Backpackers Oasis 3 Church St; tel/fax: 044 279 1163; email:
backpackersoasis@yahoo.com. Double R106 and up, dorm R40, camping R25.
Home-based backpacker with a much-needed swimming pool. This is an adventure
centre with mountain biking, abseiling, rock climbing and caving on offer. Discounts
are available for local excursions. Your third night here is free, as is your pick-up from
George railway station.

Things to see and do
Museums
Most of the feather palaces are not open to the public except for **Town House**
(corner of High and Loop Streets, tel: 044 272 7306), built in 1909, which
retains its furnishings of the period. *Open daily 08.00–17.00. Admission is free.*

The **C P Nel Museum** (corner Voortrekker and Baron Von Rheede Streets,
tel: 044 272 7306) is a collection of artefacts related to Oudtshoorn (naturally
much of devoted to the ostrich industry) but also offers a fascinating study of life
in the Klein Karoo. *Open Mon–Sat 09.00–13.00 and 14.00–17.00. Admission is free.*

The Ostrich boom
Ostriches built Oudtshoorn. This odd-looking bird with its long neck and
backward knees was the focus of a frenetic industry that, at its peak, had
750,000 birds jammed into the Little Karoo and all of it driven by fashion.
When the first ostrich feathers reached London, they created a storm; every
society woman had to have feathers on her hats and dresses. In 1880, 74,000kg
of feathers worth R1.8 million were exported; by 1913, exports reached
almost 465,000kg worth more than R2 million. The feather barons were
making pots of money and they spent it on ostentatious palaces made of
sandstone and corrugated iron. At the industry's peak, ostrich feathers were
as important as gold, diamonds and wool to the export economy. The start of
World War I killed the boom instantly and fashion, as fickle as always, never
looked back at the ostrich feather. The Klein Karoo went bust and ostrich

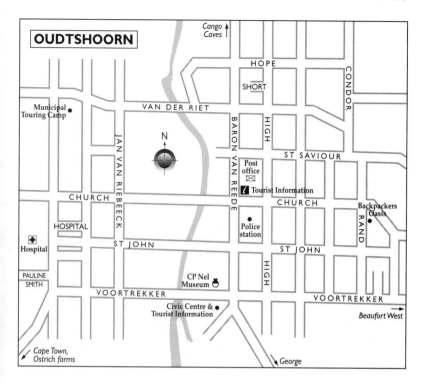

numbers plummeted. Only later did the big birds make a comeback when the government embarked on a marketing exercise to sell the feathers for dusters and the tender meat to the European market. There has been a revival of fortunes and there are now about 90,000 birds in the Little Karoo, producing about 120,000kg of feathers a year and a lot of *biltong*. But there will never be any more feather barons

There are two ostrich farms close to Oudtshoorn open to visitors. **Highgate** (10km from town on the Mossel Bay road; tel: 044 272 7115; email: hosf@mweb.co.za) offers the full ostrich experience, which includes riding the poor things. Backpackers get a discount. *Open daily 08.00–17.00. Admission R20.* **Safari** (tel: 044 272 7311; email: safariostrich@mweb.co.za) offers much the same experience. If you don't have transport, Safari might be the better option since it is on the edge of town. *Open daily 07.30–17.30. Admission R20.*

The Cango Caves

The caves must be South Africa's most famous tourist attraction. They are pretty spectacular, it has to be said. These limestone caverns stretch for several kilometres through chamber after chamber, absolutely packed with stalactites and stalagmites. Unfortunately (or fortunately), much of the system is closed to the public to preserve the formations; human breath and the passage of bodies does a lot of damage very quickly. A two-hour guided tour takes you through three of the chambers, with an 'adventure' option at the end which involves a lot of squeezing through very tight, small spaces. The formations are magnificent and the caves may be the biggest you will ever see. The downside is that you will be sharing the experience with a lot of tourists. The caves are 20 miles from town on the Prince Albert road. *Open daily 09.00–16.00. Admission R20.*

The Swartberg Pass

If you have a car then you must have a crack at the pass which is regarded as being one of the country's most dramatic. It was built between 1881 and 1888 by Thomas Bain, South Africa's ubiquitous 19th century road engineer and it is a true engineering achievement. The climb up the southern slope is dramatic enough, but it is the northern side – 10km of knuckle-whitening switchbacks – that takes the breath away. If you fear heights, go to the beach instead. At the foot of the pass, you are now in the Great Karoo, the immense scrub desert that stretches to the Orange River and beyond. Keep going until you reach Prince Albert, a typical Karoo town that has been saved from extinction following the arrival of city people escaping the rat race. Expect lots of art galleries and coffee shops but also lots of lovely old houses. There are a couple of B&Bs but no backpackers as yet. By taking the R407 from Prince Albert, you can return to Oudtshoorn via **Meiringspoort**, another incredible roadway but this time following a river through the Swartberg. The circular route taking in the Cango Caves and Prince Albert is an easy and interesting day trip.

Getting away

There are several ways out of Oudtshoorn. Two routes head back over the Outeniquas to George and the Garden Route. If you are heading this way, do your soul a favour by taking the old road over Montagu Pass – a track which follows the rail route over the mountain range. The pass is a fairly rough gravel track which, although passable in a normal car, is mainly kept open so that the railway maintenance crews have easy access to the railway.

A second way is to stick to the R62 which disappears briefly at Oudtshoorn; to pick it up again, take the N12 to De Rust, turn right on to the R341 and follow the signs to Uniondale. After going through Uniondale Poort, turn left on to the R62 at Avontuur. The road then swoops down into the Langkloof (Long Valley), gorgeous apple- and orange-farming country.

The third option is to take the thrilling gravel road south from Avontuur over Prince Alfred's Pass and wind down through the kloofs and forests to Knysna. The pass is yet another of Thomas Bain's masterpieces, a narrow road that claws its way over the Outeniquas, sometimes following the course of the Fuchs River or else clambering over the mountain on a throat-drying gradient. I have tackled the pass both by car and by motorbike. On my last trip heading south on the bike, I switched off the engine and coasted for 17km from the summit to the little settlement at De Vlug, about a third of the way down. From here, the road climbs up into the forests and then drops down into Knysna (there is also an alternative route down to Plettenberg Bay), often running through great sweeps of natural forest, huge yellowwood and stinkwood trees and ferns crowding in thickly to the side of the road. It would make a superb bicycle trip but try to get someone to give you a lift to the top.

About two miles below the summit, there is a B&B called Cloud Corner placed in the most incredible position on a saddle overlooking a deep, wild valley. I stopped to get information but there was no-one around. It may be worth asking the tourism offices in Knysna or Plettenberg Bay for details.

THE LANGKLOOF

The road down the Langkloof is particularly fine, hemmed in by mountains on both sides. To the south, the Tsitsikamma Mountains divide the Langkloof from the lushness of the Garden Route on the coastal strip, while the Kouga Mountains mark the northern boundary. Both ranges are exceptionally rugged and, other than the Kareedouw Pass at the southern end of the valley and a rugged jeep track over the northern range, there are no routes over the mountains. The only way into the kloof is where it opens up at either end, which gives the valley an isolated feel, despite the many fruit farms, packing houses, homesteads and villages that line it.

The journey along the valley is wonderful. The road is in excellent shape with very little traffic and it is a nice alternative to the N2 which runs along the coastal plain. If you are cycling, I recommend doing the valley from west to east as the gradient is almost entirely in your favour, making it a freewheel most of the way. The towns en route are quiet and pretty, earning their keep from apples and a bit of tourism on the side. Places worth stopping in are Haarlem, a few miles east of Avontuur, where there is a fine church built by the Berlin Missionary Society, Misgund for tea and *koeksisters*, and Joubertina, about halfway along the valley.

Tourist information
Langkloof Tourism Tel: 042 2273 1263; email: info@eastcape.net

Accommodation
Options are improving but as with all these pretty farming districts, there are more B&Bs than backpackers.

Louterwater Estate Louterwater; tel: 042 272 1724. R100 per cabin. Four hiking cabins sleeping four.
Die Kraaitjie Joubertina; tel: 042 273 1516. Fully equipped self-catering houses.
Fairview Misgund; tel: 042 275 1607. R125 per person, R20 for breakfast. House with three double en-suite rooms. Meals available.
Assegaaibos Hotel Assegaaibos; tel: 042 288 0700. R120 including full breakfast. Roomy hotel with lots of 1970s décor and appeal. Pub meals available.

Things to see and do
Activity-wise, there is not a lot to do except drink in the fantastic scenery. There are a few short day hikes and a bit of mountain biking. The San were

the first people to live in this fertile valley and there are plenty of their paintings to see in the caves and rock overhangs. Most the sites of the latter are on private land; ask at the tourism office where to find accessible rock art.

A narrow gauge railway, built nearly a hundred years ago, runs the length of the valley between Avontuur and the harbour at Port Elizabeth. The 285km two-foot gauge railway used to carry all the fruit down to the cooling sheds in PE but it has fallen on hard times as much of that traffic has been lost to road. The lower section of the line is still in use as far as Joubertina, hauling apples and oranges in season and logs the rest of the year while occasional special trains venture as far up as Misgund. The *Apple Express*, a steam-hauled passenger train runs, from Port Elizabeth to Thornhill a few times a month (see page 191).

THE BAVIAANSKLOOF WILDERNESS AREA

If there is one place I will return to over and over again, it is the Baviaanskloof (the ravine of baboons). This rugged wilderness seems to have slipped off South Africa's radar and yet people who live on its boundaries nearby speak about it with reverence and longing. The Fingo people call it *Mtunzini* – the place of shadows – because of its dark ravines and towering mountains.

The *kloof* is not a ravine so much as a deep, wide valley down which the Baviaanskloof River, a dry watercourse on its upper reaches for most of the year, winds its way to the sea. In the west its slopes are dry, reminiscent of the Great Karoo which lies on the other side of its northern mountains, but in the dark cool valleys to the east dew clings to ferns and yellowwoods, wild figs and white stinkwoods flourish in the damp soil, and *fynbos* grows thickly on the mountains. The area spans more than 100,000ha, but the local conservation department hopes to buy up a further 200,000ha which will make Baviaanskloof the country's third largest designated wilderness.

Game has been reintroduced to the central part of the wilderness and there are buffalo in the acacia thickets and large herds of kudu on the slopes as well as dozens of smaller antelope and predators. Plans to stock the park with rhino are on the backburner. You will of course, hear the constant bark of baboons and the endless chatter of birds as well .

At the western entrance to the valley, near Willowmore, the hills are covered with typical Karoo scrub but in the depths of the kloof itself, the vegetation is thick *bushveld* with huge sweeps of acacia trees, as well as peppercorn trees, wild figs and the unique Baviaanskloof cedars. It is a world of huge red cliffs, strange rock formations, ravines and hills. In the 215km between each end of the *kloof*, the twisting gravel road crosses three mountain passes, two of which are hairy propositions for the unwary.

Ancient rivers made the deep ravines leading off the main valley and even though the place feels dry and hot, hundreds of little streams trickle down the slopes. Near the eastern end of the kloof, the Kouga River weaves through the mountains from the south to join the Baviaans. A dam has been built here so there is always water at the east end of the valley.

The wilderness is open to anyone who wants to visit. At the time of writing, the R332, the road that runs the length of the *kloof* is a public carriageway, serving the farmers and small communities that exist there. The few people who live here work on the farms although even that is changing as farmers give up trying to wrest a living from the valley; over 150 years or so of often poorly managed agriculture has sucked the water out of the river and the water table has dropped significantly. Now it's the turn of the conservationists who believe that stopping farming will allow the subterranean aquifers a chance to recover. Make no mistake: it is a wild place; even when you stand on the hills and look into the valley, it feels utterly remote and untamed.

Getting there

A tough one if you don't have a car since there is basically no public transport through the *kloof*. However, you could catch a minibus taxi from Port Elizabeth to Patensie and hitch into the park from there: traffic is sparse but at least it will be heading in the right direction.

Accommodation

Aside from the camping option above, there are a couple of B&Bs in the area as well as chalets operated by the conservation department at Geelhoutbos.

Eastern Cape Nature Conservation Department (off R332) Tel: 042 283 0270. Six-bed chalets cost R160 for the first four people plus R30 for each additional person, 8-bed chalets cost R360 for the first six people plus R30 for each extra person.
Zandvlakte Farm Sandvlakte (on R332); tel/fax: 044 945 1002; email: sandvlak@global.co.za; web: www.home.global.co.za/~sandvlak/. R150 per person, self-catering cottage R80 per person per night. B&B with stunning views of mountains and traditional Afrikaner farm hospitality. They can arrange horseriding trails into the mountains.
Baviaanskloof Guesthouse Rust en Vrede Farm, near Sandvlakte; tel: 044 945 1160. R60 per person per night for 2 people; 4 people R45 per person and R30 for each additional person. Two self-catering cottages on farm. One cottage can sleep 6, the other 12. The farmer manages the 78km mountain bike/4X4 trail over the Baviaanskloof Mountains (R65 per vehicle, R5 per person, mountain bikes R20).

Things to see and do
Hiking

The park is divided into two wilderness areas – Guerna and Berg Plaatz – over which a network of footpaths has been established. The hiking is excellent and very safe. All the hikes are short, no more than a day, but you can tailor your route to spend a day or more in the wilderness. There are a couple of rough-and-ready overnight shelters. You will have to be completely self-sufficient with food, sleeping bag and a stove. There are plenty of water points but you would do well to carry an extra waterbottle as it can be fearsomely hot out here.

Mountain biking

There are two trails in the park as well as the rugged 'main' road itself. One of the trails is a privately owned 80km-long jeep track that crosses over the

Baviaanskloof Mountains into the Longkloof (see above) and should not be attempted without proper preparation. The other trail is run by Eastern Cape Nature Conservation and needs to be booked in advance.

Camping

One of the best things to do is to pitch a tent at one of the campsites and head off on day hikes. There are three campsites in the park, all situated on the banks of the Kouga River (after its confluence with the Baviaanskloof River). The excellent sites at Rooihoek and Doodsklip (only a few kilometres apart) are by far the best; the third site, Komdomo is situated at the park entrance and is a little too close to the road. Each campground is limited to no more than 30 people with five people on six sites and all the sites are situated away from each other. The sites are protected by a buffalo-proof fence, minimising a nocturnal encounter with these often cantankerous beasts. At the time of writing, park and camping fees were ridiculously low – R10 for an entry permit and R6 per person per night to camp. You need to be fully self-sufficient.

Fishing

The bass fishing in the dam is excellent I am told but you will have to supply your own gear.

Bookings and permits

Eastern Cape Nature Conservation Department, tel: 042 283 0270 or 041 373 8891.

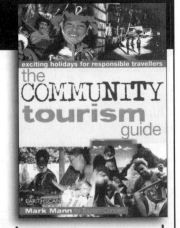

Settler Country and the Eastern Cape

The Eastern Cape stretches from Jeffrey's Bay in the west, along a wild, lush coast to the southern end of the Drakensberg in the east. It is country where aloes grow in thick clusters on rugged hillsides, and trout streams and cold mountain rivers tumble down valleys in rolling hill country that looks like Scotland. It is very different country with none of the Western Cape's fynbos or the dry scrub of the Karoo. It is also one of the most heavily populated parts of the country, traditional home of the Xhosa people and, in places like the Wild Coast, clusters of their huts dot the green hills.

The Wild Coast, north of East London, was the name given by sailors to the coast off which hundreds of ships have been lost. In truth, the whole region, which is known as the Transkei, is wild in parts in the same way that Colombia is wild. There are deep, secret valleys, many of them no-go areas where marijuana is grown by peasant farmers. With dozens of wide, sluggish rivers it is difficult country to develop and there are few roads, which makes getting around an interesting task.

There are two major towns – Port Elizabeth and East London, both harbour cities – and hundreds of *dorps* and villages, many of them built by the English settlers who began arriving in 1820. The place names are all English but you will know immediately that you are in the land of the Xhosa.

HISTORY

From Algoa Bay, where Port Elizabeth stands today, to the Great Fish River is a 300km-wide band of bush-covered hills, harsh land in the dry season, beautiful and lush in the wet. This was the land given by Britain to the 4,000 or so early British settlers, many of them veterans returning from the Napoleonic Wars, who were allocated farms in the frontier districts of the Cape. Between the Fish River, which was the frontier, and the Kei River was more fertile country in which nine bitter frontier wars would be fought between the black tribes and the British settlers and army.

This really was frontier country. There were wild animals to contend with and the Zuurveld (sour fields – you'd have thought the name would have been a warning) where most of the settlers were allocated farms proved unsuitable for agriculture: the first three wheat crops were destroyed by rust. There was also pressure from the black settlers, the Xhosas, moving southwards through

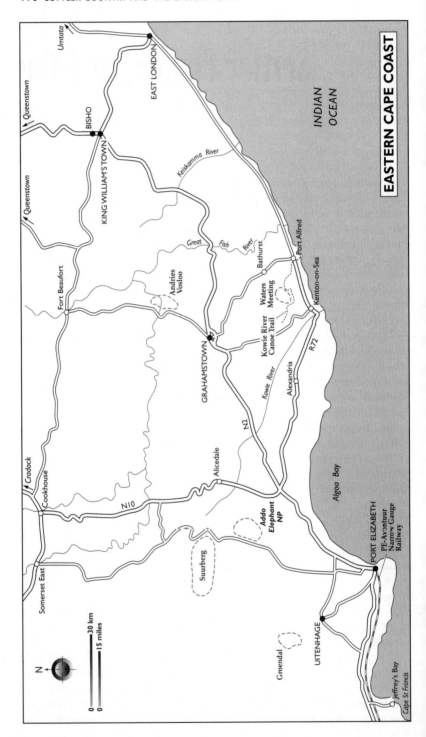

what was later known as the Transkei. There was a lot of bitter fighting and at one stage, the British had thousands of soldiers deployed on the frontier, struggling to protect the settlers from Xhosa raids.

There were few farmers among the settlers; most of them were from Britain's towns and cities and had little idea of how to work the land. Of the 1,004 men who had arrived in the Zuurveld in 1820, only 438 remained by 1823. After the first crops failed, many packed up and headed for Grahamstown, the settler city.

The area is uniquely English still, reflected in the names of such towns as Cradock, King William's Town, Bathurst, Beaufort, Jamestown, Cathcart and Alexandria.

Orientation

This guide covers the district from west to east, starting at Jeffrey's Bay and moving up into the Wild Coast but there is no best way of travelling through it. Some people prefer to start at the eastern end and work down the coast to finish up in the Garden Route. For me, the attraction of moving from west to east was the feeling of setting off into wild country, not something one often gets in modern South Africa.

GETTING THERE
Train

Port Elizabeth and East London are both served by daily trains to and from Johannesburg and there is a twice-weekly train between East London and Cape Town. The *Amatola* runs between Johannesburg to East London, and the *Algoa* serves Port Elizabeth. Both trains run daily in each direction, with sleeper accommodation in all classes and a full dining car service.

Leaving Johannesburg, the trains run via Kroonstad in the Free State province to Bloemfontein (see page 273). At Springfontein, 130km south, the line splits with the *Amatola* heading southeast through Queenstown to East London and the *Algoa* carrying on through the junction at Noupoort to Port Elizabeth. Both southbound trains depart in the early afternoon, allowing one the pleasure of seeing some of South Africa's ugliest (industrial) scenery, while the best part is done in darkness. On the northbound journey, however, the early departure is perfect, with both trains traversing dramatic scenery all afternoon.

There is no direct rail link from Garden Route to Port Elizabeth. The mountainous terrain and the many rivers which have cut deep canyons into the coastline would have made this a prohibitively expensive exercise. Only the narrow-gauge railhead at Avontuur comes close; Knysna, at the end of the branch line from George, is just 40 kilometres away, separated by the rugged Little Langkloof Mountains. If you coming from the Langkloof, you could try and beg a ride on of the regular freight trains running between Joubertina and Port Elizabeth – it's a country branch line and the attitude is much more relaxed.

For enquiries phone: 041 507 2662 (Port Elizabeth) or 043 700 4208 (East London).

Bus

Most budget travellers use the Baz Bus which runs daily along the coast, stopping in many of the towns en route and running through the Wild Coast/Transkei to Durban. Translux (tel: 041 507 1333) and Intercape Mainliner (tel: 041 586 0055) buses run between Cape Town, Port Elizabeth and East London, but only Translux buses go on to the Transkei and Durban in KwaZulu-Natal. The fare from Port Elizabeth to Durban is R200.

Cycling

The N2 – the main Cape Town–Durban national road – is a busy through route but it has the benefit of wide verges. The R102 from Jeffrey's Bay is a beautiful but winding road with plenty of hills. It also goes to Port Elizabeth via Uitenhage which is a bit of a long way round.

Hitchhiking

The N2 is busy enough for there to be plenty of options but its through-route status means that drivers are usually in too great a hurry to stop and pick up hitchhikers. Heading north, hikers have a choice of routes but the N10 to Middelburg is by far the busiest.

JEFFREY'S BAY

Jay Bay really should be part of the Garden Route but, according to the boundary makers, it is firmly a part of the Eastern Cape. It is a new town, proclaimed only in 1968, although it started out in 1849 as a trading store on shores of St Francis Bay. The town is unashamedly a holiday town and not a very pretty one at that as the usual foul facebrick architecture predominates.

The beach and swimming are excellent and if you are a surfer, you'll already have heard about Jay Bay. The fine right-hand break at Supertubes is world famous and the town is a stop on the world professional surf circuit because of it. In July, when the heavy swells roll up from the Southern Ocean, surfers arrive from all over the world, drawn by the promise of minute-long rides which is an eternity in surfing terms.

Not surprisingly, the town seems geared towards the surfing culture with surf shops, surf tours, surf dens, and the whole place has an exceptionally mellow vibe. The fact that the surf scene really only cooks in winter means that the town hums all year round and doesn't get all bleak and depressed out of season like many other holiday towns. This doesn't mean that only surfers will enjoy the place. The beach is nice, there are whales in the bay in spring and the area is great for cycling and walking in.

Accommodation

Aloe Afrika 10 Mimosa St; tel/fax: 042 296 2974 or 082 576 4259; email: aloe@agnet.co.za. Double R50. Aloe is a lovely wooden house high on the hill overlooking the bay. It is small and friendly and the owners will welcome you into their home. The main rooms are in two doubles overlooking the garden.

Derek is a great adventurer and will take you mountain biking, hiking or in a minibus taxi to the nearest township so you can have tea with his assistant Sempiwe's grandmother.

Surfpackers 9 Pepper St; tel: 042 293 2671; fax: 042 296 2840; email: navarresurf@hotmail.com. Double R120, dorm R40. Big, former holiday house two minutes from Supertubes and a magnet for a lot of surfers. The bar is full of surfing pictures, not to mention a couple of hoary, grizzled legends having a pint or two. The interesting people alone make this worth stopping in. Lots of room and enough space to hide yourself away in.

The Beach House Pepper St; tel: 042 293 2671; fax: 042 296 2840; email: navarresurf@hotmail.com. R150–200 depending on room. Lovely holiday home with predictably very nice view from the balcony. It's run by the owners of Surfpackers but aimed at travellers who don't mind spending a little bit extra. Two huge doubles, fully self-contained and beautifully finished.

Jeffrey's Bay Backpackers 12 Jeffrey St; tel: 042 293 1379; fax: 042 296 1763; email: backpac@netactive.co.za. Double R100, single R60, dorm R40. Clean place right on the beach and close to the village. Dolphin Beach, where everyone swims, is a couple minutes' walk away. There is a pool as well, which is a bonus in summer.

Island Vibe Backpackers 10 Dageraad St; tel: 042 293 1625; fax: 942 293 3469; email: ivibe@lantic.co.za. Double R140 per room, dorm R40, camping R25. I have not seen this place myself but travellers rave about it. It has plenty of space, the doubles have their own bathrooms and there are secluded decks where you can lie and listen to the sea.

CAPE ST FRANCIS

An exclusive holiday village south of Jeffrey's Bay with a fine beach and more good surfing. The place is unique among South African seaside towns for having a strict building code by which homeowners could only build cottages with thatched roofs, which has saved it from being an environmental disaster. Many of the houses are built overlooking a system of canals leading into the Kromme River which adds to its pleasant feel. It also has the smell of lots of money about it.

Accommodation

Seal Point Backpackers and Surf Lodge Da Gama Rd; tel: 042 298 0054; fax: 042 298 0184; email: seals@iafrica.com. Double R180, dorm R45, camping R25. A very different set-up with large self-catering doubles which sleep four. As accommodation for families on a budget, this one is tops. The owners can organise just about anything – bush trips or paddling in canoes on the Kromme River. Meals available.

Things to see and do

Apart from the obvious attractions of the sea, there are plenty of trails in the surrounding countryside. Just put on your boots and walk. The Cape St Francis Nature Reserve, which lies on the coast between the Cape and St Francis Bay is a good place for whale and dolphin spotting.

PORT ELIZABETH

Situated in the beautiful sweeping curve of Algoa Bay, Port Elizabeth is the country's fifth largest city. It is a one of the bigger and oldest ports although it has seen its importance slide somewhat in recent years. Bartolomeu Dias, the first European to land here, called it *Bahia de Lagoa* (Lagoon Bay). Then everyone forgot about it except for a couple of *trekboers* from the Cape who settled here. From 1799 until 1820, the lonely British outpost of Fort Frederick was the only settlement but the arrival of the British settlers changed everything. Cape governor Sir Rufane Donkin named the wind-blown settlement after his wife who had died of fever in India.

Given its position in relation to the Garden Route and Eastern Cape, it is likely that you will hit PE (as it is known everywhere) at some time in your travels. It is a jumping off point for various national parks including the Addo Elephant Park and the magical Baviaanskloof (see page 181). It is also served by two of the domestic airlines and hopefully these links will further inspire its revival.

Port Elizabeth is also playwright Athol Fugard's home town and naturally the city features in some of his works, most notably in *A Lesson from Aloes*, which captures the spirit and tension of the city in the late 1960s.

Locals call it the 'windy city' because of the notorious wind that can sometimes blow for weeks, driving people crazy. However, every time I've been there, winter or summer, I have had nothing but gorgeous, hot days. The fear of wind is certainly no reason to stay away.

It is, in parts, a lovely city with scores of Victorian buildings and some impressive monuments but its outlook has been trashed by a high-level freeway running between the city and the seafront. A little ironically, PE really boomed on the back of the motor industry but the decline in that sector (not helped by a less than buoyant economy) has hit the town quite hard. The city centre has battled with the same problems as other South African cities as businesses and shops flee to the safety of the suburbs, but it will be easier to reverse the trend here than in Johannesburg which can only be a good thing. At the time of writing, things were looking better than they had done for years and certainly tourism growth has had a positive effect.

Despite its problems, PE is a friendly place and its people are genuinely helpful. I had a traffic policeman apologise for stopping me but 'orders are orders, you know.' The presence of the University of Port Elizabeth means there is a good crowd of young people and a relatively vibrant nightlife too.

Tourist information

PE has a very helpful tourism information office (tel: 041 585 8884 or 582 1315; fax: 041 585 2564; email: pepa@iafrica.com; web: www.pecc.gov.za.

Getting around

PE is known as the 10-minute city because of its size. Of course it won't feel like the 10-minute city if you schlepp all the way to Humewood on foot with a heavy backpack. Take a taxi or better still, one of the municipal buses.

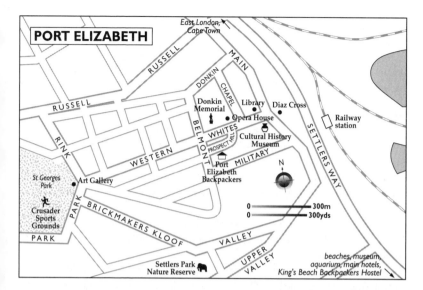

Accommodation

Port Elizabeth Backpackers 7 Prospect Hill, Central; tel: 041 586 0697; fax: 041 585 2032; email: pebakpak@global.co.za. Double/twin R130, dorm R45–50. A really central backpacker set in a 100-year-old building which is perfect for the city. They offer all kinds of tours to Addo and townships and since the owners are both travellers themselves, they somehow make the experience that much more special. You can hire bikes here which helps solve any transport hassles.

Jikeleza Lodge 44 Cuyler St, Central; tel: 041 586 3721; fax: 041 585 6686; email: winteam@hinet.co.za. Double R130, single R110, dorm from R45. Quiet backpackers' lodge with a large garden to hide in. It has been around for a while which is always a good sign.

Kings Beach Backpackers 41 Windermere Rd, Humewood; tel: 041 585 8113; fax: 041 585 1693; email: kingsbbp@agnet.co.za. Double R110, dorm R45, camping R30. As its name suggests, it's close to the beach and nightlife, and there is a good vibe out here. The Baz Bus stops here which means that a lot people don't move on. Tours on offer.

Lungile Backpackers 12 La Roche Drive, Humewood; tel: 041 582 2042; fax: 041 582 2083; email: lungile@netactive.co.za. Double R120, twin R100, dorm R35, camping R25. Voluminous establishment overlooking the bay and city. It's a smart place as backpackers go with a pool and neatly trimmed lawns. Lots of room but ask for the double cabin if you want your own space. Meals (and tours) available.

Other backpackers

Calabash Lodge and Tours 8 Dollery St, Central; tel: 041 585 6162; email: calabash@iafrica.com

Cape Recife Backpackers Marine Dr, Humewood; tel: 041 585 4004

Amakhaya Backpackers 3 Third Av, Walmer; tel: 041 581 6485; email: amakaya@global.co.za

Things to see and do

The main attractions are the beaches of which PE has about ten. The best, or at least the best-known, are Humewood Beach and Kings Beach. The water's warm and they are pretty well sheltered from whatever wind might be blowing, more or less.

Museums and buildings

The large **Port Elizabeth Museum** (Beachfront; tel: 041 586 1051) has loads of archaeological and anthropological exhibits and succeeds in blending cultural and natural history. The Snake Park and Tropical House are in the same complex; both show the species you can expect to find in the province. *Open daily 09.00–16.30. Admission R10 adult, child R5. Fee includes entrance to Oceanarium.*

Buildings worth having a look at include the **Campanile**, the unmistakable bell tower on the foreshore, and the main public library built in 1835. The 50m-high Campanile was built to commemorate the arrival of the settlers of 1820; there's a great view from the top but that's all. You can take a free 3 mile walking tour 'in the footsteps of the 1820 settlers', looking at various buildings and sites in the old Hill area of central Port Elizabeth. The guide book that tells you what you are looking at, however, costs R5, from the tourism office.

The Apple Express

This steam-hauled passenger train runs from PE to Thornhill a few times a month. The *Apple*, which has been called a national treasure, is constantly threatened with withdrawal and yet has been saved every time. Now operated by the Apple Express Society, rather than by Spoornet who own the line and everything else on it, the passenger train, which is invariably pulled by a chunky NG G16 Garratt steam engine, runs regularly from Humewood Road, PE's narrow gauge station, to Thornhill. The ride involves crossing the 80m-high bridge over the Van Stadens River gorge, the highest narrow gauge bridge in the world. The train stops short of the bridge so passengers who like scaring themselves can walk over the spindly iron structure and then take photos as the train eases over shortly afterwards. A *braai* is held at Thornhill. Contact the society for information and bookings (tel: 041 507 2333; fax: 041 507 3233 or 083 773 0065).

If you're there in September and feeling fit, you can race the train in the annual Great Train Race in September. The runners invariably win.

Addo

Addo is going to be one of Africa's great game parks. It is already famous for its healthy 200-strong elephant herd. The park was proclaimed in 1934 to protect the remaining 11 animals from being hunted – they had retreated into thick bush – and a fence was hastily erected around the area. But there are plenty of other mammals too (about 50 species in all) including buffalo and black rhino. Predators include leopard but no lion, as yet.

At the time of writing, the transformation of Addo into a super park was under way. This involves joining the park to the nearby Zuurberg reserve and also extending its boundaries southeast to the coastal strip which will incorporate a marine reserve. When this is done, Addo will cover about 400,000 hectares of striking biodiversity. There will be biking and pony trails, hiking paths and rafters and kayakers will be able to run the Great Fish River through the reserve.

Getting there and away
If you are driving, take the R335 from PE. While you do need a vehicle to go game viewing, the main camp is easily accessible to hitchhikers. From there you should be able to beg a lift from someone without any hassle. Note that a lot of the backpackers in PE run trips to the park; this may be less of a hassle but it will be more expensive.

Accommodation
The cheapest accommodation is at the main rest camp (tel: 042 233 0556). Chalets R300 for two people per night, breakfast included; rondawels R220 for two people, also with breakfast.

GRAHAMSTOWN
Grahamstown is the English capital of South Africa, ever since it became the garrison, sanctuary from Xhosa raiders and, for many who couldn't hack the life of an African farmer, the place to which they eventually scurried to set up general dealerships and bakeries for those who could. The original frontier town was founded in 1812 as a fort to garrison the troops sent to protect the settlers from marauding tribes pressing down from the east. A Colonel John Graham selected the site, an old burned-out farmhouse lying in the lee of some hills and near the headwaters of the Qoyi (Rushing) River. It was a struggling military town until the 1820 settlers arrived and turned the settlement into a trading and hunting centre. There were still large herds of wild animals moving through the frontier territory and the town thrived on the hunting trade. At one time, there were 174 registered ivory traders vying for the many tons of tusks passing through town every year.

The town has a distinctly English feel, reflected in the settlers' cottages and Victorian and Georgian buildings and churches, of which there are said to be 52. The most imposing building is the **cathedral of St Michael and St George** which was built bit by bit from 1828. The cathedral dominates the town as it divides the main street like a great island.

The focus of the town is Rhodes University, the country's third biggest English university after Cape Town and Wits and this naturally gives the town its vibrancy. Grahamstown is also home to a disproportionate number of schools – at least six of them – which adds to the liveliness. After days on the road moving from one little town to the next while researching this book, it was wonderful to arrive in a place where everything didn't close at five and there were still people on the streets after dark.

The town does get awfully quiet during school and university holidays although not in the July break when the annual **Grahamstown Arts Festival** takes place. The festival is diverse with plays ranging from Shakespeare to local improvisation theatre. Local (as in South African) bands play in the hotels and pubs, buskers add their own special carnage during the day.

The plays and shows are staged at venues all over town, including the 1820 Settlers Memorial which is a massive, and, it must be said, fearsomely ugly building on a hill overlooking the town. The festival is a good place to get to grips with South African culture but you need to plan in advance as accommodation gets scarce. Many of the students do not hang around for the festival and it is possible to rent a room in one of the university residences for about R95 per night, which is a relative bargain since people rent their houses out at extortionate rates around this time. Many students living in digs also let out their rooms to festival goers. To book, phone 046 603 8111.

Tourist information

Tourism office 63 High St; tel: 046 622 3241; email: mandy@tg.ru.ac.za

Getting there and away
Train

Grahamstown is served by a branch line which joins the main Port Elizabeth–Bloemfontein line at **Alicedale** and a weekdays-only return train connects with the *Algoa* passenger train here; departs Alicedale 08.00, arrives Grahamstown 09.50; departs Grahamstown 14.30, arrives Alicedale 16.00.

The connection is only good for passengers on the southbound *Algoa* who want to get to Grahamstown, or travellers wanting to catch the northbound *Algoa*. If you're heading to or from Port Elizabeth, then you're better off going by bus.

Bus

Greyhound (tel: 046 622 2235) operate services to PE and Johannesburg. Otherwise, there are **minibus taxis** to PE, Port Alfred and Kenton-on-Sea – these go from the railway station forecourt.

Accommodation

Old Gaol Backpackers Somerset St; tel: 046 636 1001; email: oldgaol@hotmail.com. Double R90 per room, dorm R35. This really is the old gaol and you do sleep in the cells which have been brightened slightly with the addition of two beds per cell and a carpet on the stone floor. The steel doors are low and heavy and the graffiti on the walls is the real thing. It is a unique place to stay but go with a friend. Lots of foreign students base themselves here so the living room/kitchen is always alive and vibrant.

Stone Crescent Hotel Tel/fax: 046 622 7326; email: stonecrescenthotel@yebo.co.za. Double R100, single R55, dorm R45. All rooms have bathrooms. This farm 8km outside Grahamstown (on the N2 towards PE) makes up for the distance from town in the quality of its service and its setting in the hills.

Eating and drinking

It's worth checking out the scene while you are in town. Being a student place, there are a lot of bars and fast-foody places. The **Rat and Parrot** on New Street, a general drinking pub, has the student vote. The **Monkey Puzzle**, in the botanical gardens (be careful in the gardens at night), is much more of a locals' hang-out. It has live bands on Sundays. The cheap food includes kudu steaks. You can also pay R15 and sit outside for a *potjie*. **The Vic,** a rough-edged bar in the Victoria Hotel, used to be one of the main student hang-outs, but it's become a little rough these days.

Things to do

The country's only *camera obscura* can be seen in the **Observatory Museum**, one of four parts of the **Albany Museum**, on Bathurst Street. The device projects a panoramic view of the town onto a screen in a darkened room. The first diamond from the Kimberley strike was valued here by Dr W Atherstone, sparking the rush for the diamond fields. (The diamond rush ended Grahamstown's rule as the colony's second city as the railways bypassed it and many of its citizens joined the rush to the north.)

The Albany's other parts are the **1820 Settlers Memorial Museum, Fort Selwyn** and the **National History Museum**. Grahamstown has South Africa's second coelacanth, caught, and stuffed in 1952. The coelacanth is a primitive fish and was thought to be have been extinct for millions of years until a trawler hauled one up in its nets off East London in the 1930s. Since then more have been found and there are real fears that the fish could *really* be threatened as bounty hunters, knowing that scientists will pay big money for them, go out of their way to catch them.

A local factory, **African Musical Instruments** (tel: 046 622 6252; email: ilat@giraffe.ru.ac.za) runs guided tours where you can see traditional instruments such as xylophones and thumb pianos being made.

Last time I was here there was a terrific old cinema on Somerset Street, called **His Majesty's**, which was the biggest and oldest cinema in the southern hemisphere but sadly, someone burned it down a few years ago. The ancient **Odeon** is also worth a look. The Odeon is a classic, cavernous place where the seats and sound haven't changed since it opened. Take blankets, a six-pack and pizza. Smoking is allowed in the gallery, which may be the reason the HM burned down in the first place.

THE SUNSHINE COAST

There has been amazingly little development on the coast between PE and East London and what towns and settlements do exist are generally quite pleasant. **Kenton-on-Sea** is a little seaside resort built in the hills and on a superb beach. Many of the houses are timber-framed cottages and they blend in with the landscape. There is not a lot to do in Kenton except swim, walk on the beach and maybe relax for a few days. Out of season it is a very quiet spot and you will feel like you have the place to yourself. Since it is a holiday town, all amenities, such as banks, restaurants and groceries, are to hand.

Accommodation

Bushman's Backpackers 49 Kenton Rd; tel/fax: 046 648 2545 or 046 648 1393; email: kellystours@imaginet.co.za. Double R110, single R45, dorm R40. Only one place for now so luckily it's a good one. The natural attractions (hiking, biking, walking on the beaches) could soak up plenty of your time. If it does, note that your fourth night is free.

PORT ALFRED

Port Alfred, which extends from the sea up the banks of the Kowie River, really was a port once and there was a thriving, but small, trade with Grahamstown and the interior. George Pauling, the railway contractor who later played a major part in much of the country's early railway construction, wanted to tap into the potential traffic from the new harbour at Port Alfred, extended the branch line from Grahamstown to the sea and formed the Kowie Railway Company.

The port, however, was a total loss, the estuary on which it was built silting up faster than it could be dredged, and the railway found itself without any traffic. The company stubbornly continued running trains until in 1911. A train derailed and fell off the high Blaaukrantz Bridge, killing 31 people. The resulting claims from what remains one of the country's worst train crashes bankrupted the company. The tracks are still in place but there have been no trains for years.

Accommodation

Port Alfred Backpackers 29 Sports Rd; tel: 046 624 4011; fax: 046 624 2397; email: backpackers@imaginet.co.za. Double R100, dorm R40, camping R20. A done-up and clean backpacker where the owner is also the manager which does wonders for a place.

Things to see and do

Port Alfred is a holiday town with a good beach and safe swimming. There are a couple of short, free hiking trails – ask for details at the **tourism office** (tel: 046 624 1235; fax: 046 624 4139). The wide and gentle Kowie River is worth exploring and you can do the real Huck Finn thing and paddle your own canoe on the three-day **Kowie Canoe Trail**. Phone the Riverside Caravan Park (tel: 046 624 2230) to book. The trail leads 23km upriver to a perfect horseshoe bend where there is an overnight hut with *basic* facilities. The horseshoe is a remarkable sight, although it is best seen from the viewpoint high above the valley (see Bathurst below) as the river doubles back on itself to a point where it almost joins up at the beginning of the loop. The lush, natural forest that grows on the land between the bends of the river is called the **Waters Meeting Nature Reserve**, which has an 13km meandering trail which can be tackled as part of the canoe trail. The trail has all the best ingredients for adventure – paddling up river in an open boat into a wilderness, sleeping by the river in a crude hut and listening to birds cackling and cawing in the forest. And it's cheap at R60 per person day including canoe hire.

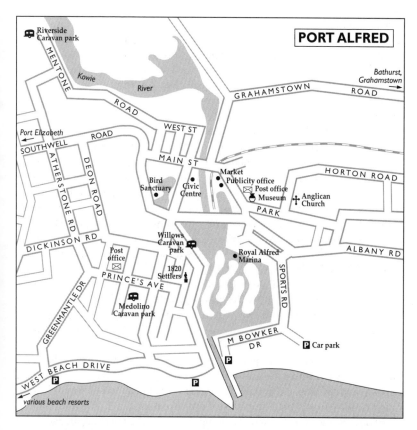

PORT ALFRED

(Map labels: Riverside Caravan park, Kowie River, Bathurst, Grahamstown ROAD, GRAHAMSTOWN ROAD, MENTONE ROAD, WEST ST, Port Elizabeth, SOUTHWELL ROAD, ATHERSTONE RD, DEON ROAD, MAIN ST, Bird Sanctuary, Civic Centre, Market, Publicity office, Post office, Museum, Anglican Church, HORTON ROAD, PARK, Willows Caravan park, Post office, DICKINSON RD, 1820 Settlers, PRINCE'S AVE, Royal Alfred Marina, SPORTS RD, ALBANY RD, GREENMANTLE DR, Medolino Caravan park, M BOWKER DR, Car park, WEST BEACH DRIVE, various beach resorts)

Tharfield Nature Reserve

This is 15km east of Port Alfred and has hiking and horse trails, both of which have sections along the beach. There are a couple of hiking options, from 1–3 day trails and there is a lovely treehouse in an old yellowwood tree overhanging a natural pool in a forest. The trails are run by 3 Sisters Treehouse Trails (tel: 046 675 1269; email: jan_webb@hotmail.com). You need to bring basic camping gear – sleeping bag, cup, plate and cutlery – as well as food but there are cooking utensils and fresh water at the treehouse. Overnight trails start at R50 per day which includes horseriding on the beach.

BATHURST

The quintessential settlers' town, a collection of very English country village houses and churches huddled in the downland countryside. The heat aside, it is a corner of England perfectly preserved in Africa. The Anglican and Wesleyan churches are both in original condition, the former being one of the oldest unaltered churches in South Africa. Both churches were used as places of refuge and for defence during the Frontier Wars of the 1800s when Xhosa warriors streamed out of the Transkei on cattle raids.

The hotel has the **oldest pub** in South Africa and it is the only truly English pub I have seen in the country. It's not called The English Pub (which is a warning to anyone looking for such a thing) but the Pig and Whistle which is slightly better. The pub serves real pub food (bangers and mash and a glass of cold lager for R22) and local beer. Sadly, though, there is little demand for warm ale here.

When you've had lunch, ask them to point you in the direction of the **Horseshoe Bend lookout**, about four miles down a dirt road from the hotel's front door. You look down into the valley from about 170m above the river and in the deep silence, you will hear the chatter of birds and creatures crashing through the thick natural forest below.

One of the town's simplest attractions is the most evocative. The **toposcope** on top of Ballies Beacon has a 360° view of the surrounding countryside and it is from here that the settler farms were surveyed. Brass plaques record the names of the leader of each settler party, the county they came from and the ship they sailed in.

EAST LONDON

This port on the Buffalo River has the charm of an English seaside town, without the inclement weather. Its economy tends to fluctuate wildly but the port is generally busy these days, while tourism prospects are looking better than they have done in years.

From as early as 1688, sea captains had commented on the river's suitability as a place to land supplies but a port was established only in April 1847 when Fort Glamorgan was built at the start of the Seventh Frontier War. The wars were tying up a lot of men and equipment, most of which had to be moved through rough country from Port Elizabeth or Port Alfred. However, like most ports at river mouths, the entrance kept silting up and, until the river was dredged, East London was a difficult place to land. Most ships would anchor at sea with passengers being lowered in wicker baskets and brought ashore by lighter.

East London's most famous idea is the *dolos*, a unique interlinking concrete construction block designed by Eric Merrifield, the port engineer, and which is now used in harbour construction and breakwaters all over the world. Named after the knuckle bone used by witchdoctors in divination, the shape of the dolos ensures that it gets entangled with other dolos blocks, forming an unbreakable barrier against the waves.

East London is a small place and it is not really a place travellers would bust a gut to get to. It is, however, a jumping-off point to the **Transkei** and **Wild Coast** as well as the lush hiking country in the **Hogsback**. The town is a transport hub with a daily train to and from Johannesburg and a twice-weekly train to Cape Town. There are also domestic flight connections to all the major centres.

Getting there
Train
The *Amatola Express* runs daily between Johannesburg and East London. It departs Johannesburg 12.45, arrives East London 08.30; departs East London 12.00, arrives Johannesburg 08.15. Fares 1st R240, 2nd R168

BALLIES BEACON

It must have been daunting for the settlers to look out from Colonel Jacob Cuyler's camp on top of the beacon and on all sides see nothing but wilderness stretching to the horizon. The view from the hill is of wild, untamed bush country, hazy mountains far away in the distance and the smoke of bushfires. Even on winter days the countryside bakes in the heat. Looking out at those hazy distant mountains must have worried them, especially those settlers who were not farmers, and there were more than a few of them: many of the brass plaques here say 'London', and many of those men would have been veterans of the Napoleonic wars come to make a fresh start in Africa.

Names like Bradshaw, Mandy, Cotter, Phillipps, from places such as Gloucestershire, Surrey, Nottingham and Pembrokeshire, are forever tied to the ships they came on. The Sephtons came to Salem from London; one of their descendents still farms today, not in the Eastern Cape but in Groot Marico in the far northwest. (It is worth noting that he is the best farmer in the area, someone who is actually making a living from agriculture. unlike many of his neighbours who believe farming is their birthright and yet they don't seem to do well at it.)

The settlers, no doubt homesick for the green fields of England, comforted themselves with familiar names. Their farms and settlements were called New Bristol, Green Hills, Collingham, Coombs, Trentham Park, New Essex, Lushington. But others, revealingly, were called Thorn Park and Botany Bay.

The plaques also record the area each party was sent to and its distance from the beacon. The furthest farm, Hildon, was 130km west of the beacon. To the east, however, the farms were all close to the beacon, the furthest no more than 20km away. Beyond that lay Xhosa country. The war veterans could not have known that they would be involved in battle after battle when the frontier wars began soon after their arrival. It was a struggle for land and cattle, in which the settlers eventually prevailed. A century and a half later, there are still echoes of those wars and some people believe that the issues have not been satisfactorily dealt with.

Bus

The Baz Bus stops here and also runs through the Transkei to Durban. Translux (tel: 043 700 1999) and Intercape Mainliner (tel: 043 722 2254) buses run between Cape Town, Port Elizabeth and East London but only Translux buses go on to the Transkei and Durban in KwaZulu-Natal.

Tourist information

Phone 043 722 6015. Not the most helpful bureau in the country – they don't give out phone numbers.

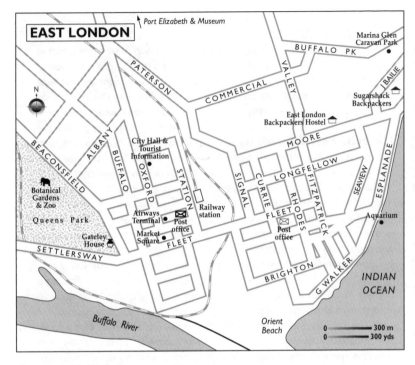

Accommodation

East London Backpackers 11 Quanza St, Quigney; tel/fax: 043 722 2748; email: kaybeach@iafrica.com. Doubles R100, en-suite double R130, dorm R40. Situated on the beachfront, which is where you really want to be.

Sugarshack Backpackers Eastern Beach Esplanade; tel/fax: (043) 722 8240; email: sugarsk@iafrica.com. Double R100, dorm R40, camping R30. Right on the beach. Call for free lift from station.

Things to see and do

East London does have great swimming beaches. Orient Beach is especially nice and there's great surfing at Nahoon. Orient is just one side of the harbour breakwater, close to the city centre, Nahoon is at the mouth of the Nahoon River. The reef break at Nahoon is prized by local surfers but there have been quite a few shark attacks at the spot – some of them fatal – in recent years. Sharks do not usually cause problems around East London. However the sea is warm and sharks do inhabit the coastal waters. There are fewer sharks than in the sea off KwaZulu-Natal but you should be aware nonetheless.

One of the city's best attractions is the **East London Museum** (Oxford Street; tel: 043 743 0686) on the north end of Oxford Street, whose exhibits include the world's only dodo egg and a coelacanth, a primitive fish with stumpy fins. The coelacanth was believed to have been extinct for about 80 million years until this one was caught by a fishing trawler in 1938. Others have since been found but this was the first and East London is proud of it. The museum also has terrific displays of Xhosa and Fingo culture.

East London is a reasonably mellow place during the day but it has a thriving nightlife (well, compared to Bloemfontein at any rate) in its many bars and few clubs. There are plenty of restaurants. Not to be outdone by the Mother City, East London has **Latimers,** its own waterfront development in the harbour, where much of the action happens.

THE WILD COAST AND TRANSKEI

The Transkei is South Africa's own Colombia. It is a huge piece of territory jammed between the Drakensberg mountains and a rugged, dangerous coast. It is a land of hills cut by deep river valleys and since 1600, the traditional home of the Xhosa people. Dozens of ships have wrecked on its lethal shoreline and the survivors called it the Wild Coast. Its history is colourful, bloody and turbulent. There were wars between Xhosa and the settlers, internecine killing, cattle raids and cattle massacres. It had 'independence' foisted on it by the Nationalist government, an act that probably did more damage than anything else in its history.

Despite all this, it is a magical place. White painted Xhosa huts dot green hillsides where boys look after the family cattle and goats. It is not uncommon to see women in traditional dress, wearing colourful headdresses and smoking long-stemmed *umbhekaphesheya* (tobacco pipes). Deep, brown rivers uncoil in the deeply incised valleys and flow into the sea in great muddy swathes. Old colonial towns bake in the heat while the country gets on with its life.

The San and Hottentots were the first people here and the caves are full of San art. By 1600, a group of the Xhosa people known as the Hlubi had begun migrating slowly into the area from the north, part of the great migration of people down the southeast coast of Africa. According to history, a group of the Hlubi, led by a woman called Xhosa, were the first to encounter the Hottentots, whose language with its clicks had an indelible effect on the Xhosa language. Modern Xhosa is peppered with clicks, certainly more so than Zulu or Sotho.

The migration continued as far as the Great Fish River and it was here that all the trouble started. European settlers had been trekking in the opposite direction, also looking for new lands. The arrival of the British settlers in the Eastern Cape in 1820 only raised tensions. By 1879, when Britain formally annexed the Transkei and its territories, British troops and settlers had fought nine frontier wars against the Xhosa.

On October 26 1976, the Transkei was granted independence from South Africa, the first of the independent homelands to be awarded such a status. The fact that not a single country in the world recognised these little sideshows as sovereign states was ignored. The legislature was based in Umtata, the capital, and all the trappings were provided – a government, an army, lavish buildings, even an airline. In effect the Transkei became a dumping ground for all the people the South African government decided were not its citizens. The land was ravaged by overgrazing and poor

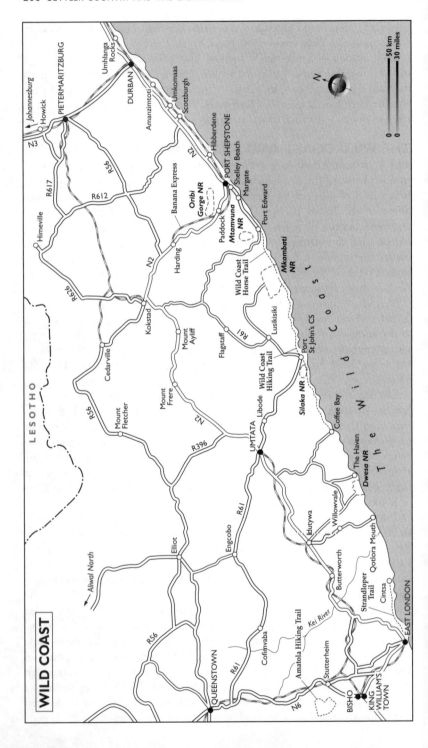

agriculture and the poverty-struck inhabitants were forced to become illegal emigrants to South Africa. It was a farce.

While the homeland naturally reverted to South Africa in 1994, it does have a self-contained feel about it. This is partly because it is the home of the Xhosa but also because it is a physically challenging place to travel in. The only major road, the N2, bisects it from east to west and to get down to the coast or up into foothills of the Drakensbergs means taking side roads off the main artery. In some places, as at the mouth of the Umtata River, to get to the other side of the river by road means half a day's drive via Umtata. Those deep river valleys mean the land is a place of footpaths. Everyone walks in the Transkei so it is somehow fitting that one of its main attractions is hiking. There are three trails worth looking into: the first two are footslogs along the beach, the last is a multi-day horse trail on the upper part of the coast (see page 191).

For the adventurous traveller, the Transkei is promising. The warm Mozambique current that flows down the coast ensures a sultry climate, and it is certainly more of a winter than a summer destination. Winter days are warm and clear, but summers are hot, sticky and violent.

Safety

Not long ago the Transkei was off limits to travellers because of the dodgy security situation there. The hiking trails along the coast were abandoned after hikers were attacked, and driving off the main routes was asking for serious trouble.

The situation has improved. A number of backpackers have opened and travellers are now flocking across the Great Kei River. However, it will pay to be vigilant. This is an economically depressed area and flaunting your relative prosperity, cameras slung around neck and that sort of thing, is asking for trouble. You should get advice from locals about where not to go. There are no-go areas in the region, especially in the marijuana growing areas where, I am told, even the police and army do not even set foot.

If you are hitchhiking, use common sense at all times – just because you are on holiday is no reason to become complacent about your personal safety.

Women travellers should also be wary of travelling alone in the Transkei – if you are solo, use the shuttles and Baz Bus to get around and make use of locals you know you can trust to take you places.

Do all your banking and personal administraton before going – banks do not exist in the smaller Transkei places.

Getting there and away

East London is the jumping-off point if you are coming from the south.

Bus

Translux (tel: 043 700 1999) and the Baz Bus both run through Umtata. To get to the coastal towns you will have to take minibus taxis or even better make use of the shuttles that various backpackers operate to and from Umtata.

Cintsa

The little town of Cintsa is at the edge of the Transkei. Spending time there feels like standing at the side of a swimming pool and plucking up the courage to dive in. Look across the river, though, and you will feel that urge to get going into the wildness on the other side.

There is a long beach on which you can walk forever, with scope for horseriding, surfing and general reserve-gathering before embarking on the big mission north, or recovering from the Kei if you're heading south.

Accommodation

You should set aside a couple of days for Cintsa, since it has what are arguably the best backpackers in South Africa.

Buccaneers Backpackers Cintsa West; tel: 043 734 3012; fax: 043 734 3749; email: cintsabp@iafrica.com. Doubles (en suite beach cottages) R110 per room, dorm R45, camping R30. Amazing backpacker complex high on a hill in Cintsa West with predictably fine view of the sea and lagoon. The cabins and bungalows spread out among the trees so that you hardly know they are there, and the overall feeling is one of space and privacy. There is a decent bar where you can get dinner and breakfast is served on the balcony of the owners' house. A lot of their activities are included in the price – sundowners on the beach and use of all the equipment like surfboards and canoes. Baz Bus stops here. Buccaneers also runs various trips into the Transkei and to look at local community projects such as the local school and township where you can actually meet the people and maybe have a game of footie with the school kids. It is a good way of putting something back into the community. The guides have lived here most of their lives and are passionate about the place.

Dwa-Dwa Backpackers Cintsa; tel: 043 734 3055; fax: 043 734 3312; email: arena@iafrica.com. Self-catering rondawel R140, dorm R50, camping R25. Another resort-style backpacker where you can stay in separate rondawels. Plenty of gear like canoes and surfboards on offer too. Baz Bus stops here.

Cintsa Backpackers Moonshine Bay, Cintsa; tel/fax: 043 734 3590; email: moonshine_sa@hotmail.com. Double R150, dorm R50, camping R30. Literally at the end of the road and overlooking the bay. Nice, fresh-looking place. They also run tours into the Transkei.

Things to see and do

Beach hiking

The Strandloper Trail (tel: 043 841 1046; email: meross@iafrica.com) is a classic five-day, 56km coastal trail, from the mouth of the Kei River to Gonubie, just outside East London. The trail follows the coast with a lot of walking on the beach and a bit of scrambling inland where cliffs rise up out of the sea. No more than 12 people can start the trail per day so you feel like you are hiking utterly alone (other than the 11 people with you, of course). Accommodation is in fully equipped huts along the way. The first and last sections of the trail – Kei Mouth to Double Mouth (15km) and Bosbokstrand to Gonubie (30km) – can be booked as weekend trails. It's moderately difficult but suitable for any reasonably fit hiker. The managers can organise transfers to and from East London. The trail costs R160 per person for the full five days.

Horseriding
Glendale Trekking Centre runs a horseriding outfit on the beach at Cintsa. It's a friendly family operation and the owners seem more intent on saving horses than making a quick buck: a lot of the horses are getting a second chance at life after being saved from abusive owners and nursed back to health. As if being kind to some love-crazy horses wasn't enough, riding out on these wide, empty beaches with the surf crashing around the horses' legs is pure tonic. Rides cost R100 for two hours. Book through Buccaneers Backpackers (see above).

Across the Kei
The Transkei really only starts when you cross the Great Kei River, which as South African writer T V Bulpin says, 'deserves its name, not only for the enormity of its valley, but for the fact that it has long been a divider in the affairs of man, providing a natural frontier between tribes and a memorable landmark for all travellers'.

You could spend a lifetime wandering down the Transkei's side roads and paths and still not see it all. But two places you should visit are **Coffee Bay** and **Port St Johns**.

The former is one of those little colonial settlements that never really prospered and probably no-one remembers how it was founded in the first place. The village apparently got its name when coffee beans from a wrecked ship were washed up on the beach. The locals at least had one basic commodity taken care of for a couple of years, but there is definitely no sign at all of any hyperactivity in today's Coffee Bay.

Its most famous landmark is 8km away at **Hole-in-the-Wall**, a massive offshore stack through which the sea has eroded a large, almost navigable, hole. When the sea gets up, it pounds through the hole like a cannon, which makes you wonder why anyone would try to swim through it, as too many people have tried to. In terms of pure spectacle though, it's worth walking 16km to see.

Accommodation
The Coffee Shack Coffee Bay Beach; tel: 047 575 2048; email: coffeeshack@wildcoast.com. Double R55 per person, dorm R45. There are also double rondawels on the other side of the stream, R120–140. Daily shuttle to/from Umtata.

Hiking the Wild Coast
Coffee Bay was also one of the overnight stops on the **Wild Coast hiking trail** which ran the length of the Transkei in four sections. At the time of writing, the trail was supposed to be open but no-one could tell me what the situation actually was. Many of the original huts have collapsed and they were

supposed to be rebuilt. Ask at any of the backpackers or at the Buccaneers Adventure Centre for an update.

Of the four sections, the most scenic are the first two stages, from the Mtamvuna River to Port St Johns and then from Port St Johns to Coffee Bay. 'Most' is a relative term because the whole coast is spectacular. It is rugged stuff; you walk on the shore as much as possible but where the land drops straight into the sea, you have to detour far inland. There are numerous river and estuary crossings which are potentially lethal. You should move as far as you can upstream and cross only on an incoming tide. Do not wear your backpack but strap it to a lilo and propel this in front of you instead.

Even if the trail is not officially open, you might consider hiring a guide – certainly someone who can speak the language and understand the customs – and doing it off your own bat. You must get up-to-date information about your route first and make sure there is no security risk. There was a nasty incident a few years ago when some hikers shot at and killed some youths who were stealing from their campsite at night. Parts of the coast are lawless and there are people who will resent you walking through their marijuana fields. If nothing else, see *The Beach* before you travel. It's a shockingly bad film, but it does raise some valid points about how we should behave in other people's countries.

You will be walking or camping on other people's traditional land and it is important to get permission from all the headmen on your route. You might be invited to stay in villages en route, under the protection of the headman and it could be an opportunity to experience another culture close up. There are also a few resort hotels on the coast and even if you don't stay in them, you should be able to get permission to camp in their grounds. It is very much a self-guided adventure, with all the risks and rewards that entails. If you do decide to go, tread with respect and humility – that attitude will get you a long way.

Port St Johns

PSJ has a spectacular setting on the estuary of the Umzimvubu River. It was named after the Portuguese merchantman *São João* which ran ashore close by in 1552. This incident apparently failed to be a strong enough warning to the traders who *did* establish a port here in the 19th century. PSJ flourished briefly as a trading centre but it was not popular among ship captains given the number of ships that wrecked trying to get into the estuary.

Now it is a sleepy backwater kind of town where people arrive and sometimes never leave – they just become part of the scene. The annual, and secret, marijuana growers' competition is judged 'somewhere nearby' and this may account for a lot of people not going home to their jobs and mortgages. The beach, like most Transkei beaches, is somewhere you could spend a lot of your life and the great Big Voodoo River has a strangely hypnotic power. PSJ is reviving as a holiday spot and there are a couple of backpackers, plenty of B&Bs and even a tourism office (tel: 047 544 1206).

There are two parts to PSJ – the centre, and Second Beach, about 5km down the coast. Not much in Second Beach so if you want cheap groceries, stock up in town.

Accommodation

A nice choice of places for budget travellers. All the backpackers offer shuttles to and from the Baz Bus stop in Umtata.

Port St Johns Backpackers First Beach; tel: 047 564 1517; email: psjbackpackers@wildcoast.com. . Double R110 per room, single R80, dorm R40, camping R30. Set on the hill overlooking the Big Voodoo. Good view
Ikaya le Intlabati Second Beach; tel/fax: 047 564 1266. Double R100–140, single R50. An upbeat, upscale backpacker that will appeal to travellers who want a bit of peace and luxury. It's right on the beach but has its own garden. No dorms, only cottages.
Amampondo Beach Backpackers Second Beach; tel: 082 630 7905; email: mashia@hotmail.com. Double R110, triple R55 per person, dorm R45, camping R25. Popular backpacker in a large house. Travellers rate their tours to visit *sangomas* (traditional healers) who will guide you around their village.

Things to see and do

The town is one of the few places where you can have a pretty genuine dose of real South African life. There is a *sangoma* (traditional healers) village where you can watch the practitioners at work: one of the *sangomas* will show you around. You can also stay with a local family, eat their food, sleep in their hut and experience life in the Transkei the way most of its people do (see Amampondo Beach Backpackers above).

Go rafting on the Big Voodoo. This may strain the budget a little but I have to say, just do it. The Umzimvubu is a great, lost river. It is probably South Africa's third largest river but it remains little-known because of its remoteness. It winds through the Transkei's back country down a valley where you see almost no-one. They are there, of course, watching from the hills. If you do not trespass, you will pass freely. The only sure way of running the river is to go with Umzimvoodoo (tel: 011 477 1149; email: umvoodoo@mweb.co.za) who operate out of PSJ. They run three-day trips in season (October to April) when the summer rains fill the river to a decent level.

Wild Coast Horse Trail

This community-run trail is one of the best African adventures, running for 4–6 days along some of the most spectacular and inaccessible scenery of the Wild Coast. Trailists are met at the Wild Coast Casino and escorted along the beach to the Mzamba River where the horses await. The guides are characters – Jabu, a *sangoma*, arrives adorned with the colourful garb, beads and bangles that are the trade-mark of his status; Wonderful, the river and hiking guide, lives by his name.

There are two overnight stops in simple tented camps on the banks of the Kwanyana and Mtentu rivers. The stops are long enough to allow you to explore the inland on foot or by canoe or wander amongst game in the Mkambathi Nature Reserve. With permission, you will be welcomed by local communities to watch ceremonies and spontaneous gatherings; don't miss out on the local beer. Contact Amadiba Adventures (tel: 031 205 5180; email: cropeddy@iafrica.com).

THE EASTERN CAPE INTERIOR

The accepted wisdom of touring South Africa is to journey along its coast because it is generally easier, cooler and there is more to see. But there are some wonderful places in the interior that will reward the adventurous traveller.

Tourist information

Stutterheim Tourist Office Tel: 0436 32322.

Getting there and away

Train

The *Amatola Express* stops in Stutterheim on its daily journey between East London and Johannesburg and, more to the point, gets there in daylight which gives hikers enough time to get to the start of either of the Amatola trails. The **train journey from East London to Johannesburg** is one of my best journeys as much of the most exciting terrain is traversed in daylight. The railway starts climbing as it leaves East London station and keeps climbing until it reaches the flat plains of the Free State, 500km away. It makes two mountain crossings – the Amatola and Stormberg ranges – on its march to the *highveld*. Before the 'new' line was opened in 1949, 'the Eastern Main Line 'draped itself like spaghetti over the ridges of the Winterberg and Stormberg ranges in order to gain height without excessive expenditure on earthworks' say the writers of *The Great Steam Trek*. The route of the new line is no less dramatic as the railway twists and turns through the mountains, plunging into tunnels and clawing its way up steep hillsides. Northbound trains cap the day with a climb up the Stormberg by the Bushmanshoek Pass at sunset. As rail journeys go, this is one of the best.

Safety

The region is one of the country's most populous but unemployment is high. Do not be an obvious tourist and do not draw attention to yourself. Hitching is probably not a good idea in this area and take care if you're travelling by minibus taxi. Stay out of townships unless you're with a local and someone you *know* you can trust.

Things to see and do

The Hogsback

The Hogsback is a well-watered mountain range with dozens of walking trails running through its thick forests. Where much of the surrounding country is plains and aloe-encrusted hills, the Hogsback is high country where mists swirl among the stands of pine.

The Xhosa called the place *Qabimbola* (red clay on the face) for the clay pits where they used to get the clay to cover their faces and it was one of their strongholds. A lot of bloody fighting took place here during the Eighth Frontier War and that this association with past violence may account for the spookiness of the mists in the forests. Or there is the fairy theory, which says that enchantment is spread by fairies living in the forests. To be honest, I find more people believe the latter story.

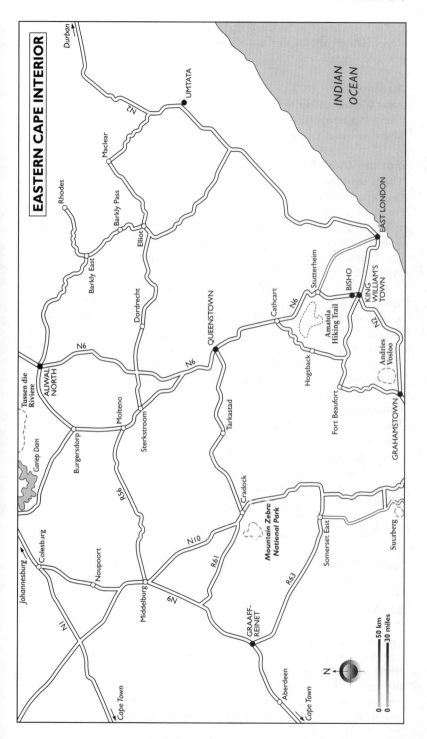

There are lovely walks across the range to waterfalls and viewpoints off the ridges. These 'piggy walks' are all day hikes. Walking aside, there isn't much else to do except relax.

Accommodation
Away With the Fairies Hogsback; tel: 045 962 1031; fax: 045 722 8240. Double R120, dorm R45, camping R25. Backpacker in a relaxed home at the edge of the forests. Walking optional. A shuttle bus runs from Sugarshack Backpacker in East London.

Into the Amatolas
The Amatola Mountains rise up out of the coastal plain and give rise to some excellent hiking country. Two trails stand out – the two-day Kologha Trail and the legendary Amatola Trail.

The **Kologha trail**, which winds through indigenous forest and skirts the placid, trout-laden Gubu Dam, starts at the Isidenge Forest Station; you'll need to arrange a lift or catch a minibus taxi here from town. You need to book by phoning Mr Roswell; tel: 043 683 2474.

The 105km **Amatola Trail** is a one-way trail looping over the Amatola Mountains and through dense forests. The trail ends in the Hogsback, an area of heavily-wooded hills with a village straight out of rural England. There are walks and rivers to fish in. This trail is a harder to get to as it starts at the Pirie Forest Station, about 25km south of Stutterheim. You can try to organise transport through the tourist office in town (tel: 0436 32702). There should be plenty of minibuses on this route. Bookings can be made through Rob on 043 683 2474.

Queenstown
A settler town founded in 1847, this prosperous town is noted for being built around a hexagonal centre, the idea being that this gave the defenders a clear field of fire down all the streets. As it was, Queenstown was never actually attacked by anyone and the hexagon is now a garden.

The town's **Frontier Museum**, stocked with 1820 Settler artefacts, is worth a look, as is the **Municipal Art Gallery**. The fishing in the dams around the town is supposed to be excellent. Otherwise, not a whole lot going on. The country east of the town, however, is beautiful especially as one approaches the foothills of the Cape Drakensbergs. Here, little country towns like Rhodes and Barkly East get by on agriculture and trout fishing in the clear mountain rivers. It is difficult country to explore without your own vehicle.

Sterkstroom
At the foot of the Stormberg Mountains, Sterkstroom is one of the stops on the *Amatola Express* route and is little more than a railway junction. But it does have a nature reserve (tel: 04592 8 for information), where you can amble freely and lose yourself in the magnificent scenery of the surrounding mountains. The reserve, which is about 2km outside town, has a basic campsite and a couple of chalets. Northbound trains arrive at 17.45, southbound at 02.40. Worth doing as a break on the run to Johannesburg.

KwaZulu-Natal 11

KwaZulu-Natal can be split up into three very different regions, and each with its own feel. Zululand, to the north, is not a defined geographical region in the legislative sense but rolls over the fecund tropical country between the Tugela River in the south up to Swaziland and the Mozambique border in the north. Durban and the Natal South Coast is prime holiday country where thousands of Gautengers migrate for the summer holidays and take up all the hotel rooms and space on the beaches. The interior is the rolling farmland of the Natal Midlands and acacia veld on the hills and valleys of southern Natal, dominated by the immense Drakensberg mountain range that runs southwest through the country in a jagged spine.

Each region offers a very different experience. The beautiful game parks are mostly in Zululand and the region is rich in Zulu history and culture. The Drakensberg region is an adventure kingdom, a place to go hiking in the country's highest mountains. The Natal Midlands which sprawl out from the foothills of the 'Berg is downland farm country, and Durban, a port and the country's third city, is a holiday town with a subtropical climate, fine beaches and surfing, with good transport links to the rest of the country. Durban makes a good base to explore the Drakensberg and is the logical jumping off point for the game parks. If you do only one thing in the province, you should go to the game parks – they are magnificent. The south coast has developed as a local holiday destination and sadly its towns have lost their seaside charm as over-development has trashed the skyline.

HISTORY

The history of the province is vibrant and very bloody, with four major conflicts having spread across it since the beginning of the 19th century. Given its importance, it was perhaps inevitable that various factions in South Africa's history should take part in the long and bitter struggle for control of the province. Firstly, it is invariably excellent farm country, lush and well watered, great for cattle and crops and the rivers run year-round. There was no fear of having to eke out a living here.

As always, the rock art at countless sites proves that the San were the first people here. It was excellent hunting country for them, as nowhere else in the country were there as many wild animals as there were here. By 1600,

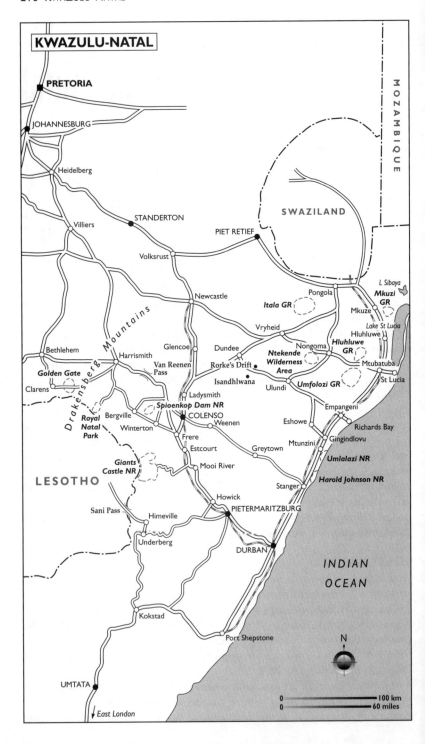

KWAZULU-NATAL

MOZAMBIQUE

■ PRETORIA

JOHANNESBURG

Heidelberg

SWAZILAND

Villiers

STANDERTON

PIET RETIEF

Volksrust

L Sibaya

Newcastle

Pongola

Itala GR

Mkuzi GR

Mkuze

Vryheid

Lake St Lucia

Drakensberg Mountains

Glencoe

Dundee

Hluhluwe

Bethlehem

Harrismith

Van Reenen Pass

Rorke's Drift

Nongoma

Hluhluwe GR

Ntekende Wilderness Area

Mtubatuba

Golden Gate

Isandhlwana

Ulundi

Umfolozi GR

St Lucia

Clarens

Ladysmith

Empangeni

Royal Natal Park

Spioenkop Dam NR

Bergville

COLENSO

Weenen

Eshowe

Richards Bay

Winterton

Frere

Gingindlovu

Estcourt

Greytown

Mtunzini

Giants Castle NR

Mooi River

Umlalazi NR

LESOTHO

Stanger

Harold Johnson NR

Howick

Sani Pass

Himeville

PIETERMARITZBURG

Underberg

DURBAN

INDIAN OCEAN

Kokstad

Port Shepstone

N

UMTATA

0   100 km

0   60 miles

↓ East London

however, the San were under pressure from the great migration of people from the north. Among the migrants was a clan called the Nguni who would develop into the Zulu nation.

Between 1800 and 1830, there was great upheaval in the region as a series of catastrophic events known as the *Mfecane*, which in Zulu means 'the crushing' or 'forced migration', took place. A drought coupled with pressure to find new grazing lands resulted in three decades of bloody fighting between rival clans. At this point, the Zulu were a tiny tribe who would probably have been swamped by stronger tribes if it had not been for the fact that one of its sons, Shaka, became the paramount chief after an epic period of intrigue, plotting, assassination and bloodletting. Shaka, the illegitimate son of Senzangakhona, had earned the respect and trust of his mentor, the paramount chief, Dingiswayo. Shaka was fearless and a masterful tactician and it was on Dingiswayo's wishes that he succeeded Senzangakhona when the latter died in 1816.

Shaka very quickly set about training up a new army and developing tactics that became the scourge of other tribes. He called up all the able-bodied men, told them to forget about marriage and formed them into *impis* (regiments). He abolished the long throwing spear and introduced a short stabbing assegaai which meant that the warriors had to close quarters with the enemy and deal with them in hand-to-hand combat. His most revolutionary tactic was an attacking formation known as the bull and horns in which the 'head', made up of a strong regiment or two, would attack the enemy's centre head-on while two 'horns' would manoeuvre around the flanks of the enemy and attack from behind in a pincer movement. He revolutionised warfare, leaving a trail of devastated opponents in his wake. By 1818, 30 chiefs had submitted to him and within seven years the entire region between the Tugela and Pongola Rivers was under his control. In 1827 the Zulus went on the rampage, possibly sparked by the death of Shaka's mother, Nandi. Whole clans were annihilated and Mzilikazi and his people, the Matabele, were driven from Zululand, barely stopping until they reached Zimbabwe. In 1828, Shaka was murdered by his half-brother, Dingane, who continued by subjugating every clan in the region as far as the *highveld*.

The first Voortrekkers and their wagons rolled into Zululand in 1836, also looking for new land. Dingane lured trek leader Piet Retief to his royal enclosure to celebrate a land pact and then put him and his followers to death. The *impis* fell on the Boer encampments and killed all the women, children and camp followers they found. The Boer reaction was quick and ruthless. Nearly a year later, on December 16 1838, Andries Pretorius lured the Zulu army to a carefully chosen killing ground on a bend in a river. Protected by a laager of wagons and employing two lightweight cannons, the Boers killed around 5,000 Zulus that day and the river ran red with blood. The battle of Blood River became a national holiday – the Day of the Vow, so called because the Boers had promised God that they would keep the day holy if they prevailed.

Dingane fled and his brother Mpande took over. Mpande signed a deal with

Pretorius and Natal was declared a Boer Republic with its capital in Pietermaritzburg. This of course, did not suit the British who by now had established a trading post at Port Natal, where Durban stands today. The British sent troops from the East Cape frontier and annexed Natal. The Boers packed up their wagons and retreated back over the Drakensbergs to the Transvaal and Orange Free State republics.

The British and Zulu kept an uneasy truce until 1879 when, propelled by the interests of the Empire, Britain invaded Zululand, an event that was to cost both sides dearly. At the end of that war, Zululand was divided up into Native Reserves which formed the basis of the independent homeland of KwaZulu that was created by Pretoria in the 1970s. Mangosouthu Buthelezi, KwaZulu's chief minister, ruled a fragmented territory and dominated the Zulu monarchy.

During the 1980s, KwaZulu again became a killing ground as the ANC and the Inkatha Freedom Party battled for dominance of the province. As always the politics hid murkier goings on and all sorts of ancient rivalries erupted. For years, lasting up until the mid-1990s, a low-key civil war waged in the rural areas. There are still areas of rural KwaZulu-Natal that are no-go areas.

DURBAN

Durban is the third city and the busiest port in South Africa. It is an industrial and holiday town, built around a superbly sheltered bay and mile after mile (four, in fact) of exquisite beachfront. Its outstanding feature is its position around the vast sweep of the bay, protected by a low wooded headland called the Bluff. People, including many of its own tourism officials, like to compare Durban with Miami. It does look a lot like Miami; it even has a Golden Mile of highrise hotels on the beachfront, but with fewer Art Deco buildings, and the sea is warm. That's where the similarities end.

Durban was the traditional playground for 'vaalies', a derogatory name for someone from the former Transvaal province (now carved up into four smaller provinces). The Easter, July and Christmas holidays would see what looked like the entire Transvaal descend on the city's beautiful golden coast, jam its roads and fill its hotels, for which the locals both hated them and loved them. Durban still is a holiday town although it's definitely a lot shabbier these days. The town council tries hard to promote the place and vaalies still flock down in the holiday season but the whole occasion seems a lot more muted.

On the plus side, it is a vibrant African city now, and you can physically see it emerging as an African trading city. The markets are full of traders from the rural areas and from Mozambique. The Mozambique–Durban trade route is so popular that the only cross-border train that Spoornet has not axed is the twice-weekly through train between Mozambique and Durban.

The city is the centre of the country's Indian community, most of whom are descendants of indentured labourers brought over from India in the 19th century. When their contracts were up, they were given the choice of returning to India or staying on to farm here. Most stayed. It's really the only place in South Africa where you can get a genuine curry on the street (although this will be hotly debated) in the form of a *bunny chow*, a half-loaf of bread with mutton, chicken, beef or veg curry inside. The Indian influence is everywhere in the city, from the colourful shops in Grey Street, a little south of the central business district, to the temples and flashes of colour, smells of spicy cooking. The Indian influence is most strongly experienced in the district bordered by Grey Street and Russell Street in the west part of town. Here you will find spice shops, tailors, general stores selling anything, hawkers with their pavement vegetable stands and informal barber shops spring up under colourful plastic tarpaulins. In Russell Street, Zulu women, herbalists, sell roots to be used to make *muti*, traditional medicine.

The city's better hotels line the beachfront, almost from the channel where the bay opens into the sea, right up to Blue Lagoon. The area around the channel is the less salubrious end of Point Road, full of massage parlours, escort agencies and dodgy bars, all doing brisk business with visiting sailors. This will also be the site of Durban's Waterfront development and one wonders if the hookers will be allowed to stay on. The business district straddles two one-way roads, Smith Street and West Street, which both end just short of the Marine Parade on the seafront. To the south, the Victoria Embankment curves round the bay in a luscious sweep, fronted by luxury apartment blocks, the Durban Club, shipping offices and the two yacht clubs.

Northwards, Durban continues to sprawl up the coast, across the Umgeni River, to the resort town of Umhlanga Rocks, and inland to the Berea Heights, a range of hills which overlook the bay and coastline. Behind the city to the north and south are the huge townships of KwaMashu and Umlazi. The former adjoins the Valley of a Thousand Hills, spectacular hill country dotted with thousands of huts perched on every available surface. The best views are from Botha's Hill, a village on the southern edge of the valley.

Practical details
When to go
Durban is best in the winter when the days are mild and the water is still warm enough to swim in. The city's subtropical climate means hot, wet and humid summers and the heat can be overpowering especially since it doesn't let up at night. It is the kind of place that demands a fan in summer. Add to this the crowds of holidaymakers over December–January and you have a potentially explosive situation. The sea, warmed by the Mozambique Current, is always pleasant for swimming.

Telephone
The area code is 031.

Tourist information
Durban has an organised tourism information centre at Tourist Junction (160 Pine Street; tel: 031 304 4934). Look for the old restored station building. Open Mon–Fri 08.00–17.00, weekends 09.00–14.00.

Getting there and away
Airport transfer
All the domestic airlines and some international carriers fly directly to Durban.

Buses run between Durban International Airport and the City Air Terminal, corner Smith Street and Aliwal Street. The fare is around R40 one way. The Airport Shuttle Bus (tel: 031 469 0309) is a 24-hour service from the terminal to anywhere in Durban. Fares start at R70 for 1–2 people and then R10 for every additional person. There are also meter taxis outside the terminal building – expect to pay around R100. The airport is 15km south of the city centre.

Bus
Durban probably has one of the best municipal bus services using smaller buses known as Mynahs. Look for the picture of the mynah bird, get on and tell the driver where you're going. Mynahs are frequent and reliable although, like everywhere else in this country, the bus service vanishes at night.

Commuter trains
Metrorail (tel: 031 361 8123) operates an extensive commuter train service out of the city but few of the trains are likely to be of any use to travellers. One exception is the train to Park Rynie, a South Coast resort town 50km south of Durban. Single fares are R15 in 1st, R10 in 3rd.

Minibus taxis
Minibuses run everywhere and the system can be quite confusing. Their main routes are between the city and the townships. The safety issues raised in Chapter 3 naturally apply here too.

Car hire
Tempest Car Hire (tel: 031 368 5231), one of the cheapest national car hire firms, have a branch at the airport. Expect to pay R120 per day including insurance, plus R0.77 per kilometre. They do have special deals for seven days or more.

Getting around
Most attractions in the city centre are within walking distance of each other.

Safety
Durban's population has grown rapidly, especially since the 1994 elections. As the country's population continues to shift from the countryside to the cities, the army of urbanites is growing. One inevitable effect of this has been increased crime, some of it targeted at tourists who are easy pickings.

Basic rules
• Don't wander aimlessly on the beachfront at night, especially on the beach itself where there are no lights. Most of the muggings and stabbings seem to happen in this part of the city. Wherever you are in the city, walk with

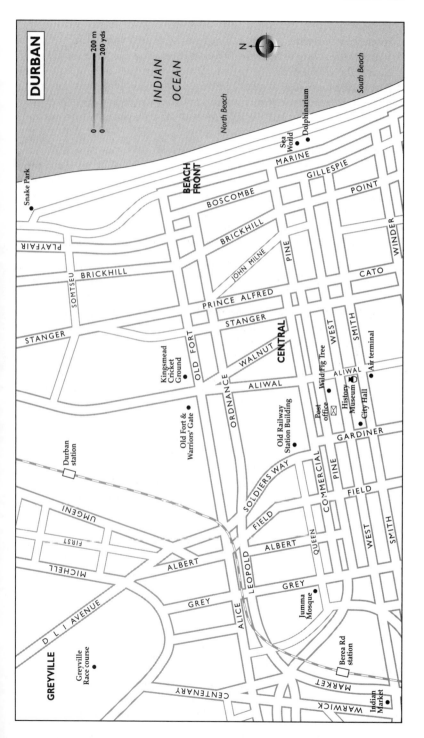

DURBAN

0 200 m
0 200 yds

N

INDIAN OCEAN

North Beach

South Beach

Snake Park

BEACH FRONT

PLAYFAIR

SOMTSEU

BRICKHILL

STANGER

BOSCOMBE

BRICKHILL

JOHN MILNE

MARINE

Sea World

Dolphinarium

GILLESPIE

POINT

WINDER

PINE

PRINCE ALFRED

STANGER

CENTRAL

CATO

Kingsmead Cricket Ground

OLD FORT

WALNUT

ALIWAL

WEST

SMITH

Wild Fig Tree

Air terminal

Old Fort & Warriors' Gate

ORDNANCE

Post office

History Museum

City Hall

ALIWAL

GARDINER

Durban station

Old Railway Station Building

SOLDIERS WAY

COMMERCIAL

PINE

FIELD

QUEEN

WEST

SMITH

FIELD

ALBERT

UMGENI

FIRST

MICHELL

ALBERT

LEOPOLD

GREY

Jumma Mosque

GREY

D L I AVENUE

ALICE

Berea Rd station

Greyville Race course

GREYVILLE

CENTENARY

WARWICK

MARKET

Indian Market

purpose and try not to be a tourist – this includes not openly wearing a moneybelt or having a camera slung casually around your neck.
- Lone women should avoid the Point Road area and everyone should be careful there after dark.
- The nearby townships, Umlazi and KwaMashu, are not the most welcoming places. If you must see them, go with a friend or someone you can trust who knows the area, can speak the language and will keep you out of trouble.

Accommodation

Like the rest of the country, Durban's backpacker scene has boomed and there are now plenty of places to choose from. Most of the better ones tend to be in big old houses on the ridge in Berea or Morningside but if you want to be central, check out the places in town as well. Morningside's Florida Road is where a lot of the nightlife happens these days and it is a safer area to walk around in at night than, say, the beachfront.

Mully's Mom's 15 Nimmo Rd, Morningside; tel: 031 312 8976. Double/single R65 per person. A friendly and clean place whose calmness older travellers will appreciate. Mully's is close to town and the beaches.

Tekweni 169 Ninth Av, Morningside; tel: 031 303 1433; fax: 031 303 4369; email: tekwenihostel@global.co.za; www.tekweniecotours.co.za. Double R120, en suite double R160, dorm R50. A huge place that sprawls over three houses, at least one of which is always quiet. There is a pool which will be much appreciated on Durban's summer days. Tekweni also has its own tour company/community project offering trips to Valley of 1,000 Hills as well as the 'Berg and game reserves.

Brown Sugar 6 Kinnord Place, 607 Essenwood Rd, Essenwood; tel: tollfree 0800 004 951 or 031 209 8528. Double R100, en suite double R140, dorm R40, camping R25. Breakfast included. Big old Last Outpost colonial house with loads of space. Great view of the sea as well. Obligatory pool, free shuttles to the beaches and an on-site tour company. Meals are available.

Smith's Cottage 5 Mount Argus Rd, Umgeni Heights; tel/fax: 031 564 6313; email: keithws@hotmail.com; web: www.smithscottage.8m.com. Double R100, dorm from R40. Smaller place away from the chaos of the city. They have tropical garden and a pool. The owners are adventure and travel pros.

Traveller's International Lodge 743 Currie Rd, Morningside; tel/fax: 031 303 1064; email: travellers-lodge@saol.com. Double R140 per room, dorm R50. One of Durban's survivors which can only be a good thing. There is a travel company on the premises as well.

Eating and drinking
Drinking

To find out what's going on in Durban, have a look at the listings pages in the *Daily News* and the *Natal Mercury*, the city's two daily newspapers. Durban's recreation used to be limited to the beachfront where there were scads of bars, restaurants and clubs but too many muggings have turned the place into a wasteland at night. There are still a couple of restaurants and bars, aimed mainly at the holiday crowd, of which **Joe Kools** (137 Lower Marine Parade) is one of the better ones.

For a somewhat more earthy experience, try the **Victoria Bar** in Point Road which attracts all sorts of locals. Two other restaurant-bars, also in or near Point Road, but daytime only, are **Thirsty's**, Point Road waterfront and **Charlie's Croft**, 18 Boatman's Road.

Much of the nightlife has moved up to Morningside's Florida Road and you can wander around here quite safely. In the city itself, and back on Point Road – one of the best options is **330**, a nightclub at 330 Point Road with a heaving dance floor.

Durban is currently regarded as the fountain of South African music with the 'Durban sound' becoming a genre of its own. Certainly some of the bands coming out of Durban have a sparkle that others lack. This could be due to those warm winters which means an appreciative audience throughout the year. This means a lot of places have live music which always adds a new dimension to an evening out.

For theatre, try the **Playhouse Complex** in Smith Street which contains five theatre venues where there's always something going on.

Eating
The cheapest and best food is usually found in the city's Indian restaurants which, given Durban's sizeable Indian population, makes sense. In take-away cafés in the Indian district you will be able to buy cheap *bunny chow*, a loaf of bread sliced in half, the middle scooped out and mutton, chicken, beef or veg curry poured into the crust. Notable *bunny chow* purveyors are **Patel Vegetarian Refreshment** (202 Grey Street; tel: 031 306 1774) and **Angaans** (86 Queen Street, tel: 031 307 1366), where all kinds of traditional and cheap Indian food is available. For a more formal dining experience try the **Pakistani Restaurant** (92 West Street), one of the best restaurants in town. And it's cheap.

Things to see and do
Durban definitely has an English seaside town feel about it too. Think Hastings and you won't be disappointed. The **Marine Parade**, formerly a road, is now a largely pedestrianised area with long stretches of parking near the main beaches. The idea was to get rid of the traffic but the cars are still there in their thousands. The Marine Parade is the last refuge of the remaining rickshas, once a vibrant, human-powered transport fleet industry numbering almost a thousand carriages, highly decorated by their Zulu drivers with beadwork, streamers and paint. Now, less than 20 are left, pulling tourists around the Golden Mile and somehow there is an odd feeling about using them. On the other hand, these guys need the money so....

Beaches
The beaches are the best part of the whole beachfront experience. The water temperature averages around 20°C. Starting at **South Beach** at the end, the sand runs in an unbroken line for about 3km up to **North Beach** and the **Bay**

of Plenty. Beyond this the coast is undeveloped and used mainly by fishermen. All the main beaches have lifeguards and are protected by shark nets.

A few piers reach out into the sea, and these are mostly used by fishermen and surfers looking for an easy way out to the backline. When the surf is good, the piers are great vantage points to watch the action. North Beach is a legendary surf spot and site of an annual international surf contest which takes place in July. Even if you're not interested in the surfing, it's worth going to watch the antics of the beautiful people.

In summer, of course, the beaches heave with people. There are more beaches at **Umhlanga Rocks**, a resort town a few miles north of city. **Anstey's** and **Brighton Beach** are less crowded options on the other (south) side of the Bluff.

Indian district

The Indian district around Grey Street and Russell Street is worth walking around, if only to see the fusion – or not – of different cultures. The **Jumah Mosque** on Queen Street is the biggest mosque in the southern hemisphere and is an interesting mix of colonial and Islamic features. You can go on a guided tour but it may be easier to ask someone to show you around.

The nearby **Madressa Arcade** is a tight alley full of traders where you can buy anything you didn't know you needed, or wanted. In Victoria Street, you can throw yourself into the bedlam of the fish and meat market – a strong stomach will help – and look for wood and stone carvings and beadwork in the adjoining hall. This is an African market, something you are unlikely to see anywhere else in the country.

Parks

For a bit of peace, head for the calm **Botanical Gardens** opposite the Greyville Racecourse in Lower Berea or the stretch of pristine mangrove swamp at the **Beachwood Mangroves Nature Reserve** just north of Durban. *Admission to the gardens is free.*

The **Umgeni Bird Park** (tel: 031 579 4600), on the north side of the Umgeni River, is one of the world's finest bird sanctuaries, with about 300 exotic and indigenous species enjoying Durban's excellent weather. The noise made by hundreds of birds in the three huge walk-in aviaries is deafening. *Open daily 09.30–16.30. Admission R20.*

The **Natal Sharks Board** (tel: 031 561 1001), which looks after the shark nets off Durban's beaches, offers tours of its facility. You can watch them dissect a shark and find out how shark nets work. The unit sends boats out every day to check the nets and recover any sharks that have been caught in them. It is fascinating stuff especially if you have any lingering fear of these creatures. *Open Tue, Wed and Thu at 09.00 and 14.00. Admission R20.*

Museums

Durban has a rash of museums and cultural sites. An added bonus is that most of them are free.

Durban Natural Science Museum (City Hall, Smith Street; tel: 031 311 2245 or 311 2247) is an excellent introduction to South African wildlife. *Open Mon–Sat 08.30–16.00. Admission free.*

Local History Museum (Smith Street and Aliwal Street; tel: 031 311 1111) has artefacts from Durban's recent colonial past. *Open Mon–Sat 08.30–16.00, Sun 11.00–16.00. Admission free.*

Durban Art Gallery (City Hall, Smith Street and Aliwal Street; tel: 031 311 2264) exhibits work of mainly local artists although some international work is represented. *Open Mon–Sat 08.30–16.00, Sun 11.00–16.00. Admission free.*

The Natal Museum of Military History (Old Fort Road; tel: 031 332 5305) has an extensive collection of military gear and uniforms, including a couple of old tanks and aircraft. It's the kind of place that somehow seems fitting given the province's history. *Open daily 09.00–17.00. Admission R10.*

NORTH FROM DURBAN

There are three main routes out of the city: north to Zululand and the game parks and the coastal reserves of Maputaland, west to the Drakensbergs, battlefields and the *highveld*, or south along the coast towards the Transkei.

Getting there and away

Bus

The region is served by a whole gamut of minibus taxi services and local bus companies. Buses run from the new Durban Station, NMR Avenue. Greyhound (tel: 031 309 7830) and Translux (tel: 031 361 8333) also operate long-distance bus services from here.

Train

You can go by train west to the *highveld* and north into Zululand proper. The *Trans Oranje Express* runs weekly between Durban and Cape Town, leaving Durban on Wednesdays at 17.30, arriving Cape Town on Fridays at 06.05, and departing Cape Town on Mondays at 18.50, arriving in Durban on Wednesdays at 07.15. The *Trans Lubombo Express* between Durban and Maputo in Mozambique leaves on Tuesdays and Fridays at 19.35, arriving Maputo at 18.15 the next day, and departs Maputo on Fridays and Mondays at 09.30, arriving in Durban at 07.35. The train runs via the game reserves in northern Natal and also passes through Swaziland.

The daily *Trans-Natal Express* between Johannesburg and Durban is one of the best-patronised trains in the country, offering a quick overnight service between the two cities. It is of some use to travellers heading to the Drakensbergs or to the Zulu War and Anglo–Boer War battlefields as it stops at Pietermaritzburg, Estcourt (both jumping-off towns for the Drakensbergs) and Ladysmith which is in the heart of battlefield country. Unfortunately, it is an overnight train which means that sightseeing is limited and also that you arrive at many stations at awful hours of the night. If you are going to the battlefields, a hire car would be a much better option.

Leaving Durban, the train runs briefly south before swinging into the hills surrounding the city, twisting through tunnels, over bridges and scarily sharp curves in the haul up the escarpment, through Pietermaritzburg and then up into the rich farmland of the Natal Midlands, home of Jersey cows, fine schools and a good dose of colonial fervour. In summer, you'll have a bit of light in the first part of the journey; in winter, though, it's dark before the train leaves.

PIETERMARITZBURG
The old capital of Natal, Pietermaritzburg still retains a definite last outpost feel. Many people wish it still was – you'll recognise them by their bumper stickers with the little Union Jack and the words 'Natal – the Last Outpost'. Some people rave about 'Maritzburg, or 'PMB', preferring its slow pace and quiet streets to life in the bigger cities; others cannot wait to leave.

One city guide says it has 'the vigour and strength of Africa in tandem with the elegance and architectural refinement of the British Empire'. Whatever. The city is embraced by wooded hills. It was founded in the valley by Voortrekkers who laid out its neat grid of streets in 1838. The Zulus called the valley *Umgungundhlovu*, the place of the elephants; the Voortrekkers instead chose to name it after two of their leaders, Gert Maritz and Piet Retief.

The British took over in 1843 and turned the town into a garrison. The occupation resulted in some exquisite architecture, including its ornate town hall built in 1900, wide avenues and streets of Victorian houses. Many of the buildings have been listed by the Historical Monuments Council, including the beautiful Victorian railway station which has been well-preserved despite the constant rail traffic. All this adds colour to its distinctly unhurried pace.

Practical details
Tourist information
Tourist office Commercial Rd/Longmarket St, next to the City Hall; tel: 033 345 1348.

When to go
PMB is 725m above sea level and, although it has none of Durban's humidity, summer days can get punishingly hot. I have been here when the temperature hit 41°C. Winters are cool but not icy and even in the Drakensberg winter days are usually clear, fine and surprisingly hot.

Getting there and away
Train
The *Trans Natal Express* passes through Pietermaritzburg twice a day, southbound at 05.45 and northbound at 20.40.

Bus

Greyhound (tel: 031 309 7830) and Translux (tel: 031 361 8333) buses run through PMB on their way to and from Johannesburg. The Cheetah Coach (tel: 033 342 4444) runs twice a day each way between Durban and PMB. The one way fare is R35.

Minibus taxis

The cheapest way of getting from Durban to PMB. You should pay no more than R15 one way. The easiest place to find a taxi is outside the railway station.

Hitchhiking

The main Durban–Johannesburg N3 national road just skirts the town. If you are coming from Durban, the best place to pick up a ride is at the tollgate outside Durban. Try and get a lift going all the way as hitching elsewhere on this road is a nightmare.

Accommodation

Sunduzi Backpackers 140 Berg St; tel: (033) 394 0072; fax: 033 395 6536. R25 dorm, R15 for camping. Owners will organise trips to the Drakensberg mountains.
Ngena Backpacker's Lodge 293 Burger St; tel/fax: 033 345 6237; email: victoria1@cybertrade.co.za. Double R140, en suite double R150, dorm R50. Spotless place that seems to be aimed at the upper end of the backpacker market (any place that provides linen and towels is already one rung higher than the rest). It is situated right in the middle of town so everything is close by.

Things to see and do

The University of Natal has a campus here (the other campus is in Durban) and the place can get quite vibrant during term time. During vacations though, man, does it get quiet. Unlike Grahamstown in the Eastern Cape, the town doesn't revolve around the university, which may be a good or bad thing, depending on your point of view. Apart from its heritage, the city is also known for the **Duzi Canoe Marathon**, an annual canoe-and-running marathon which involves three days of paddling and running with your boat from 'Maritzburg to Durban. On June 16, though, it really gets going as thousands of otherwise sane, but fit, people run the **Comrades Marathon** between Pietermaritzburg and Durban, 90km of pure self-torture.

The best way to see the city is to go on one of the self-guided walking trails. It's not a big place and you don't want to be sitting in a car here in summer as temperatures in the high thirties are common. Buildings worth seeing include the classic Victorian edifice of the **City Hall**, the old **Parliament Buildings**, and the **Church of the Vow** (Longmarket Street; tel: 033 394 6834), which was built by the Voortrekkers in 1841 to commemorate their victory over the Zulus at the Battle of Blood River in 1838. The church is now the **Voortrekker Museum**. *Open Mon–Fri 09.00–16.00, Sat 08.00–12.00. Admission R5.*

Another good museum is the **Natal Museum** (Loop Street; tel: 033 345 1404), which has a collection of natural history, ethnology, Bushman paintings

MOHANDAS GHANDI

In 1893, a young Mohandas Ghandi, newly arrived from India to settle a lawsuit in the Transvaal, was kicked off a train at Pietermaritzburg after being denied entry into a first class railway carriage. It was his first experience of racial discrimination and it alerted him to the plight of Natal's Indians, but Ghandi wasn't particularly interested in politics until that moment.

The Indians in Natal, having been released from their contracts as indentured labourers on the sugar plantations, had almost no rights as citizens and Ghandi's reputation as a highly influential lobbyist and leader grew.

During the Anglo-Boer War, he served as a stretcher bearer and was at the bloody battle of Spioenkop, sparking his convictions as a pacifist. He set up an ashram near Durban in 1904, while his political career took off as a member of the Natal Indian Congress.

He was arrested in 1913 after leading a march of working class Indians from Newcastle and over the Transvaal, setting off a strike of Indian workers in the south. There was a tremendous uproar in India and he was released, returning home to India almost immediately. By then they were calling him a great soul, a Mahatma.

and its own section on Mohandas Ghandi who, as a young lawyer, practised in here. **Macrorie House** (Loop Street and Pine Street; tel: 033 394 2161) is a typical colonial house and monument to early settler life. *Open Tue–Thu 09.00–13.00, Sun 11.00–16.00.* There's even a museum for the Comrades Marathon, at **Comrades Marathon House**. If you're thinking of doing the marathon, look at the scale model of the course first and check out those gradients. Then decide.

THE NATAL MIDLANDS AND ESHAYAMOYA COUNTRY

There is no place quite like the Natal Midlands, a belt of green pastures and steep hills and little towns and villages with red-brick houses and slate roofs. The fields are full of black-and-white dairy cows and Aberdeen Angus cattle. It could be England and many of the people who live here are of recent English descent. The towns and farms reflect a strong English character and they trade on it. You can go trout fishing and drop into little roadside restaurants for tea and scones. It's the Cotswolds in Africa, which is probably not what you came to Africa to see in the first place.

There is a route through the area called the Midlands Meander that ambles through these little villages and stops at the craft shops. It includes the private schools like Hilton College and Michaelhouse, themselves echoes of England. While the route is all very nice, I have to say I prefer the wilder side of the country. The Zulus call it Eshayamoya country – steep hills crowding deep river valleys, with the Drakensberg Mountains looming over all of it.

Accommodation

Glen Arum Farm Nottingham Road; tel/fax: 033 234 4425. R100 per person. The hills above Balgowan hide this excellent farm where you can gather your wits before heading off into the Eshayamoya Country. Glen Arum has two fully equipped self-catering cottages; one sleeps five and the smaller (and nicer) one sleeps two. Bring supplies because it's a long way to the nearest grocery store. There is a pool and a tennis court and you can walk anywhere on the rambling farm.

Things to see and do

On your way to the Drakensbergs, however, there are some things worth taking a detour to see. The first is the **Howick Falls** where the uMgeni River drops over a 90m precipice, the second highest and one of the loveliest waterfalls in southern Africa. Downstream, the **uMgeni Nature Reserve** has hiking trails on the slopes along the river and there is a fair amount of game in the reserve.

One of the best ways to experience a waterfall is to abseil down beside it, and the abseil at Howick is one of only two in the country (the other is at the Elands River waterfall at Waterval Boven, Mpumalanga). The **Howick abseil**, run by adventure company Over the Top (tel: 083 527 7097) is also one of the country's highest at over 107m and probably the only abseil that ends in a boat in the plunge pool at the base. Over the Top also run wildlife and birding safaris, guided hikes in the Drakensbergs, whitewater rafting, horseriding, deep sea and surf fishing, and mountain biking. They have unique township tours, photographic safaris, and African art tours where you learn to paint African wildlife in the bush.

THE NATAL DRAKENSBERG

The Drakensberg Mountains present a magnificent rock wall of peaks and pinnacles running 200km from north to south at an average height of 3,300m above sea level, and 1,650m above the surrounding country. The tall peaks are the sources of almost all the east-flowing rivers in the province and there are few places in the range where you cannot see or hear some river rushing down the slopes.

The range actually starts further north in Mpumulanga, forming the great divide between the low lying country to the east and the great high plateau that is the central part of the country, but here it becomes a colossal range, full of foreboding. To the Voortrekkers it looked like the back of a sleeping dragon (*draken*). The Voortrekkers became intimately acquainted with the range, crossing it at least twice. They took the wheels off their wagons and lowered them down the slopes like sleds, only to be faced with the same slog back over the mountains when the British annexed Natal.

The Zulus called the mountains *uKhalamba* (the barrier of spears), an apt name as this rock fortress kept people out of the high country and protected what is today the kingdom of Lesotho. It is lonely, rugged country and a hiker's dream. You can walk for days and not see anyone, the range having literally hundreds of different paths and trails. You can hike for a day up a steep river valley or traverse the whole, an epic trek that takes about two weeks to complete.

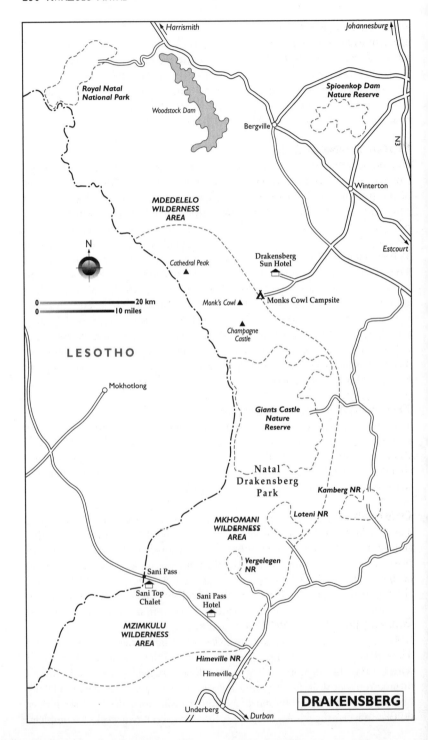

DRAKENSBERG

The range is also rich in San rock art, especially in the Giant's Castle area. The San lived here until late in the 19th century; the mountains harboured a lot of game and with the caves to provide shelter and a constant supply of water, it must have been close to paradise. However, San raids on British settlements resulted in harsh retaliation from the settlers and by the end of the century the San had gone. Their incredible paintings remain, however, and are a fine reward for those who trek up the steep slopes.

Practical details
Tourist information
The KwaZulu-Natal tourism office (tel: 031 304 4934) has a good, free map of the province which shows the basic location of the Drakensberg parks and camps. More detailed maps of each area are available at all the park offices.

When to go
The best time to visit the 'Berg are in spring (September–October) and autumn (March–April), but any time is spectacular. In summer the mountains are green and the rivers are swollen from the summer rains. However, that same summer rain usually comes in the form of violent afternoon thunderstorms which can make hiking miserable, not to mention dangerous if you are caught out in high and exposed country. Winter days are often also magical with crisp and clear air. However, winter means snow and if you hike at this time, you must be prepared with proper high altitude trekking kit. That means a proper four-seasons sleeping bag, sturdy, waterproof hiking boots and a tent designed to cope with snow, blizzards, high winds and rain. Temperatures often drop way below zero at night. You should always sign the mountain register (there is one at the start of all the major trails) and state when you expect to be back. If something happens, the rangers will know about it and also where they should come looking. Remember to sign out when you come back.

Orientation
The Natal Drakensberg region is normally divided into the Northern, Central and Southern Drakensberg. The northern section includes the Royal Natal National Park, easily the most striking part of the range. The central 'Berg encompasses the Giant's Castle Game Reserve while the southern 'Berg, although less spectacular, has some of the best and least crowded hikes.

Getting there and away
Car
The northern and central sections are reached by heading west off the N3 national road between Howick and Harrismith. A network of roads, mostly dirt, runs along the foot of the mountains from Royal Natal National Park to Himeville in the south. If you have a car, it is worth taking the time to do this drive.

Train

You can take the *Trans Natal Express* train to Mooi River or Estcourt but if you are coming from Durban, the timings are inconvenient since you arrive late at night.

Bus

Some of the backpackers in Durban and Pietermaritzburg run shuttles to the 'Berg. Sani Pass Carriers (tel: 033 701 1017) run buses from Durban, Pietermaritzburg and Kokstad to Sani Pass in the southern 'Berg. A one-way ticket costs R120, or R220 return. Buses run daily to Pietermaritzburg and on Mondays, Wednesdays and Fridays to Durban. Booking is essential.

Hitching

The 'Berg should be quite easy to reach, but you may have to be patient. From a safety point of view it is probably one of the safer regions to hitchhike in (of course, there are never any guarantees).

Accommodation

Every possible taste is catered for, from luxury hotels to bare-bones campsites. Budget travellers have a wide choice with the national parks offering the best value for money. A basic campsite should cost around R30 per person, chalets are around R90–120 for a two-bed chalet, R120–160 for a four bed chalet. There is often a community levy of about R5 per person, and this money is spent on upliftment in the local communities.

Some of the trails have mountain huts (R50 per person) or caves (R30 per person), both of which need to be booked before setting off. Otherwise take a tent – there are almost no restrictions on where you can camp on top of the 'Berg but obviously common sense prevails. Camp away from precipices, for example, and always out of the wind if possible.

Things to see and do

There is too much information on local trails to cram into a general guide. What follows is a mix of trails. Some are well-known, accessible routes, others not so famous and hence less trafficked.

Northern Drakensberg
Royal Natal National Park

This park comprises the northern and finest part of the range, where the mountains form a massive amphitheatre 8km across, flanked by the Eastern Buttress (3,400m), and the Sentinel (3,500m). The Tugela River hurls itself over the edge of the rock wall in a series of falls 900m high and tumbles down a wooded gorge before emerging in the open valleys below. The precipices of the Amphitheatre are broken by rock pinnacles and huge gullies. Above them the land slopes up to the watershed at Mont-aux-Sources, 3,500m above sea level.

The park boasts dozens of trails of varying length and difficulty. On arrival you are given a map of the park and a brief outline of the trails but the office does sell an excellent guidebook to the park. There is plenty of game, including a healthy population of Cape clawless otters which you might be lucky enough to see.

Mont-aux-Sources

This is one of the best-loved hikes in the 'Berg. Apart from the spectacle of KwaZulu-Natal, thousands of feet below, rolling away to the ocean, it is a view that you can have without the relentless, body-busting slog that characterises so many Drakensberg walks. The mountain is named for the two rivers that begin their journey to the sea from its high slopes. By a strange fluke, the rivers are the country's biggest – the westward flowing Orange River and the east-flowing Tugela. Their headwaters are also just a few kilometres apart.

From the edge of the rock wall you look into the Amphitheatre and across at the Western and Eastern Buttresses. The Amphitheatre seems to sweep round in a great arc, enclosing all the country below it. Vultures and buzzards soar on the thermals above the plateau, emphasising the dizziness you will feel in the rarified high-mountain air.

A number of paths cross the plateau to different outlooks over the valley far below. Be careful though when the wind is blowing, or in the mist, as some hikers have blundered over the edge and into folklore.

You can camp just about anywhere you like on the plateau although there are a couple of caves to sleep in as well. The best sites are near the head of the Tugela waterfall where the view is unbelievable. You must be self-sufficient and completely prepared for unexpected changes in the weather – snow in mid-summer is quite common. In an emergency, ask for help at the nearby guard hut.

Getting there

The easiest way up there is to drive around the back of the Drakensberg back into the Free State and head up the north side to the Sentinel Car Park where you sign in. It may seem like cheating but the slog up from the base of the Amphitheatre brings you almost exactly to the Sentinel car park, after which the route to the top is the same.

Follow the path around the Sentinel to the chain ladders (literally iron rungs linked by chains bolted securely into the rock) and climb to the top. The ladders can be quite a hairy proposition when the wind is blowing but there is an alternative route to the top through the Gully, about half a mile before the ladders. Note that the Gully is steep and involves a bit of scrambling. Take extreme care, especially if the rock is wet from rain or mist.

Accommodation

Mahai and Rugged Glen Campsite Tel: 036 438 6303. Camping R20 per person plus R5 community levy.
Tendele Hutted Camp Tel: 036 438 6411 (information), 033 845 1062 (reservations). Upper camp: 2–6 bed chalets R195 per person; Lower camp 2–4 bed chalets R180 per person. Various self-catering lodges and cottages, sleeping between 2

and 8 people. More expensive than most but it is excellent accommodation, and comes fully equipped with towels and linen.

Central Drakensberg
Giant's Castle Game Reserve

Giant's Castle reserve is a huge park which embraces rolling grasslands as well as the high peaks of the central Drakensberg – including its 3,250m namesake Giant's Castle – within its 34,000ha range. It is one of the best places to see game in the region with black wildebeest, red hartebeest, mountain reedbuck and the majestic eland among its antelope species.

The abundance of game in earlier times also attracted the San to the area and the caves and rock galleries are covered with their rock art, much of it depictions of hunting. There are an estimated 50 caves containing more than 5,000 paintings in this reserve alone. There are guided tours (R10 per person) of the galleries every hour from 09.00 to 15.00.

Hiking opportunities include the long, satisfying haul up Giant's Castle and in the valleys around Injasuti, 33km north of Giant's Castle. The latter area has some excellent trails, especially that from the main camp up to Centenary Huts, and the circular route via Grindstone Caves. From Centenary Hut, which perches on the spur that separates Injasuti from Giant's Castle, you can see the central 'Berg in all its towering glory, from Cathkin Peak in the north to Giant's Castle in the south.

Getting there

Access to Giant's Castle and Injasuti is off the N3 at the Mooi River tollgate or the Estcourt off-ramp about 20 miles further on. Follow the signs to the Central Drakensberg and Cathedral Peak

Accommodation

Giant's Castle Tel: 0363 353 3718 Chalets for R210 per double and a mountain hut which costs R48 per person. There is a R10 community levy payable on entrance to the reserve.

Injasuti Tel: 036 431 7848. Cabins for hiking groups (R90 per person but with a minimum charge of R270), chalets (R110 per person in the low season, R120 high season and a minimum charge of R220–360 depending on season) and a campsite (R28 per person low season, R32 high season). There are also three tented self-catering doubles for R56 per person. The mountain hut has been stolen but you can overnight in caves (R16 per person). Always take a tent up the mountain in case you get caught outside. There is a R10 community levy and a R10 gate fee. You must book in advance.

Mount Lebanon Backpackers Mount Lebanon Park; tel/fax: 033 263 2214. Doubles R60 per person, dorm rooms R50. Situated at the foot of Mount Lebanon, near Giant's Castle, on 500 acres of its own land with trails, a bit of trout fishing and caves with San paintings. They will pick up in Mooi River (R30).

Drakensberg International Backpackers Lodge 21 Highmoor Rd, Kamberg; tel: 033 263 7241. Double from R100, dorm R45, camping R35. Set right at the edge of

Giant's Castle reserve and close to the start of all trails, rock art sites. They offer a pick-up from the Wimpy in Mooi River as well as a shuttle to PMB or Durban (R120).

Inkosana Lodge Tel: 036 468 1202; email: inkosana@futurenet.co.za. Double R160, en-suite room R220, dorm R60, camping R30. An alternative to the park accommodation. The lodge is in Winterton, about 42km from the Cathkin Peak and Monks Cowl area, but the owner is a 'Berg *fundi* (South African slang for expert) and can advise on the best trails to do, where to go and, basically, how to get the best of your visit. It is a good place to chill for a while. Meals are provided and they do a free pick-up from the Baz Bus stop in Mooi River.

Things to see and so
The northern part of the Central Drakensberg has plenty of hiking and camping opportunities on the slopes of Drakensberg giants such as **Champagne Castle**, **Cathedral Peak** and **Cathkin Peak**. In the Monk's Cowl area, the hike up Sterkhorn to the right of Cathkin Peak is highly recommended, especially the squeeze up a tight chimney at the top which brings you out on to a peak no more than 3m in diameter. The slog up Gray's Pass to the top of Champagne Castle is another beautiful hike, offering views of the northern 'Berg. There is a cave up there that you can use as a base (but book it before leaving.)

Booking and permits for both hikes must be arranged through the Drakensberg Conservation Services office, tel: 036 468 1103. Permits cost around R16 per person. There are no chalets, only campsites (R27 per person).

The Southern Drakensberg
The Southern 'Berg often gets forgotten, which is a pity because it has some of the best scenery. The foothills are rolling farmland leading up to the slopes of Garden Castle, the southernmost reserve in the greater Natal Drakensberg Pass.

Rhino Castle
Of all the mountains that deserve to be climbed in the 'Berg, the 3,000m Rhino Castle is probably the easiest and certainly one of the most rewarding. It is a stiff nine-hour walk from the park office but the trail follows the Mlambonja River for most of the hike which means a ready supply of drinking water as well as many mountain pools to cool off in. The crux is a three-hour slog up Mashai Pass but once you are on the summit plateau, it is a 30-minute stroll to the summit beacon. And the view of course is outstanding.

Accommodation
You can overnight in Pillar Cave, about two hours from the start but there are other caves (R16 per person) and hikers' huts (R43 per person) in the reserve. You also need to buy a permit (R16). For bookings and permits contact the KwaZulu-Natal Conservation Services, tel: 033 701 1823.

Sani Pass

The little towns of Underberg and Himeville are useful bases for exploring the region. Himeville is a pretty town at the foot of Sani Pass which is one of the best and most thrilling ways to travel into Lesotho. Sani Pass is an ancient route that was first used by the San to cross the mountains. It has long been an egalitarian trade route between the mountain kingdom of Lesotho and Natal, used equally by legitimate transport companies as by gun runners, dope smugglers and cattle rustlers. It is an exceptionally rugged road, terrifyingly steep in places and not for nervous drivers. The final ascent to the summit at Sani Top is via a series of switchbacks on a sheer mountainside.

Getting there and away

The 23km road has been 'refurbished', which is at best a relative term, and normal two-wheel drive vehicles are supposed to be able to negotiate it. If you are thinking of trying it in a hire car, you had better check the fine print in your hire contract first. Until recently, the officials at the South African border post, five miles below the summit, used to refuse entry to two-wheel drive cars.

A popular option is to leave your car at the border post, clear immigration, and then hike to the top. Brave – and I mean very brave – mountain bikers can slog to the summit in about two hours if all goes well (the altitude gain is about 885m in 8km). The reward, though, is infinite, if a little hairy, as the descent is rapid and frantic and not for inexperienced bikers.

You clear Lesotho immigration at the top after which the Sani Top Chalet with its cold beer (or hot breakfast if it's winter) is an excellent place to spend a few hours. You can carry on in to Lesotho on this road and quite a few travellers use the pass as their entry point into the mountain kingdom of Lesotho. You do not need a visa for Lesotho if staying less than 30 days but you will need a multiple entry visa if you want to get back into South Africa.

Accommodation

Sani Lodge Underberg; tel: 033 702 0330; fax: 033 702 1401; email: suchet@futurenet.co.za. Rondawel R120, double R110, dorm R40, camping R25. The lodge, six miles from Underberg on the Sani Pass road, makes a great base camp to explore from. They offer various tours up the pass and to see San paintings. All meals provided on request. A few local tour operators run trips up the pass in modified sightseeing vehicles.

Sani Top Chalet Sani Pass; tel: 033 702 1158. Double R180 per person B&B, backpackers self-catering, dorm R50. Perched on the very edge of the 'Berg (in Lesotho) and looking down 3,280m into the valley below, this ranks as one of my favourite cheap places to stay. It is rustic and the surroundings are wild. In winter, when the snow is piling up outside, you can look at the view though the picture window while putting your feet up next to a log fire. Their breakfasts are also cheap and legendary. Superb.

INTO LESOTHO

This tiny mountain country, entirely surrounded by South Africa, is the home of the Basotho people who have adapted to a difficult life among these high mountains. It was a British protectorate until 1966, when it was granted full independence.

It is definitely off the beaten track and a challenging place to travel in, mostly because of the nature of the countryside. The experience is likely to be rewarding, however. You will more than likely have the place to yourself (along with the Basotho, of course), but be prepared to travel slowly. More details are given in *Chapter 15*.

SOUTH FROM DURBAN

The coastline north and south of Durban are known, unsurprisingly, as the north and south coasts respectively. The south coast is a popular holiday destination and as a result it has been developed for most of its length. The little seaside towns have become holiday resorts with malls, highways and timeshare complexes.

The beaches are nice and the sea is warm. There are some good surf spots and for hikers, the Oribi Nature Reserve near Port Shepstone is wonderful. The region is a good jumping off point for the Wild Coast and Eastern Cape so it would make sense to start the journey southwards from one of the nicer resorts such as Port Edward.

Getting there and away
Train
A railway line runs south, mostly along the sea front, to Port Shepstone, 110km away. Metrorail (tel: 031 361 7609) used to run a commuter train service all the way but trains now run only as far as Park Rynie, a resort town 50km from Durban. Single fares are R10 in 1st, R5 in 3rd.

Bus
The Baz Bus (tel: 021 439 2323) runs along the coast daily each way on its way to and from the Eastern Cape. Minibus taxis run from Durban station, stopping at all towns en route. The fare is around R20–30. The Margate Mini Coach (tel: 039 312 1406) runs from Durban to Margate, one of the nicer, but bigger, towns on the coast.

Hitching
The N2 runs the length of the coast but it is a fast road and difficult to hike on. You might have better luck on the old coastal road which, unlike the N2, goes through all the seaside towns.

Accommodation
The Spot North Beach, Ambleside Rd, Umtentweni; tel: 039 695 1318; fax: 039 695 0439; e-mail: surfsa@worldonline.co.za. Double R100, dorm R45, camping R30. Right on the beach and perfect for going to sleep to the sound of thundering surf.

The Mantis and Moon Backpackers Station Rd, Umzumbe; tel: 039 684 6256. Double R110 per room, dorm R40, camping R30. Umzumbe is one of the smaller towns with a fine stretch of beach. Tours are on offer and they will teach you how to surf. Or not. Breakfast included. On the Baz Bus route.

Things to see and do
Oribi Gorge
Up the road from Port Shepstone is Oribi Gorge, a proclaimed nature reserve. The gorge is 25km long, 5km wide and 400m deep. The 1,809ha reserve is made up largely of sandstone cliffs and forests hiding bushbuck, and vervet and samango monkeys, the occasional leopard and masses of birds. The park is controlled by the KwaZulu-Natal Conservation Services (tel: 0331 845 1000) who also manage run the hutted camp in the reserve.

The Alfred County Railway
Natal once boasted four narrow gauge (two-foot) railways, mostly built in the early part of the century to serve isolated farming communities and connect to the nearest important railheads. Alan Paton's description in *Cry The Beloved Country* of waiting for the train on the Donnybrook line captures perfectly the essence of these little railways. Only one of them, operated by a private company called the Alfred County Railway, is still open. The line runs from Port Shepstone inland to Harding through dramatic territory, draped like a necklace over the hills. When the railway first opened locals called it the 'Mae West Line' because of its many curves.

While most of the traffic is timber from Harding, the ACR operates the steam-hauled *Banana Express* from Port Shepstone to Izotsha, little more than hour inland. At the moment the service is running once a week, leaving Port Shepstone at 11.00 and returning at 12.30. Fares are R36 in 1st and R24 in tourist class. Children aged 3–12 travel at half fare. On Saturdays, there is a six-hour round trip to Paddock, R80 (R40 for children). The journeys are evocative of Natal and Paton's descriptions of it as the train rattles through cane fields and around hillsides dotted with white-painted Zulu huts and puffs up the steep grade to Izotsha. Go now before another chunk of Natal history is obliterated. Contact the ACR, tel: 039 682 4821.

Into Zululand

The name 'Zululand' still has a powerful ring to it. It is a beautiful, vibrant and often strange place. One gets the feeling sometimes that there are eyes watching you from the green hills, and maybe it's true. A lot of turmoil has shaped this province and there are bound to be echoes of it.

Maputaland in the northeast contains large game parks, including the massive coastal park at Lake St Lucia, now a World Heritage Site, and the Big Five reserves at Umfolozi and Hluhluwe. The latter two offer some of the best and most affordable chance to see lion, leopard, elephant, rhino and buffalo as well as many other species of 'plains game'.

The eastern part of the province embraces the various Zulu and Anglo–Boer War battlefields, the often disturbing and chilling places where so much of this country's history was shaped.

THE BATTLEFIELDS ROUTE

The centenary of the Anglo–Boer war has been celebrated by many of the towns around which the conflict took place. As it is, much of this turbulent part of South Africa's history is well-preserved and documented and it resonates throughout the region. If you like battlefields then this is the place to visit them. All the Anglo–Zulu war battlefields are also nearby.

Since the vital, then newly built railway lines were the focus of so much of the Anglo–Boer war activity, many of the battlefields are on the line of the railway which also makes getting to them without a car eminently possible. The railway linking the coast and the Reef was completed in October 1895, spurred by the discovery of gold on the Witwatersrand a few years earlier. The railway naturally became the centre of much fighting.

History

After murdering his brother Shaka in 1828 and taking his place, Dingane tried to establish trading relations with the British who by now had a small settlement at Port Natal. The British were wary but left the Zulu alone at first. However, when Cetshwayo, Dingane's successor, began building up the Zulu regiments, the colonists at Port Natal started getting nervous. The causes of the Zulu War are a mess of intrigue, fear and politicking, but what is clear is

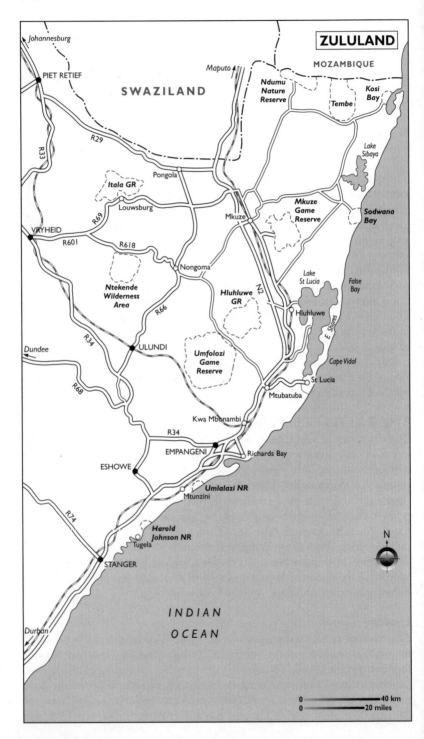

that a warlike king who had many of the same personality traits as the revered chief Shaka, was a threat to British aspirations in Zululand and Natal..

On December 11 1878, the British issued an ultimatum to Cetshwayo demanding that the Zulus abandon the traditional military structure and allow missionaries into the region. The Zulus rejected this, as the British government seemed certain they would, and in January 1879, a British column under the command of Lord Chelmsford crossed the Tugela River into Zululand. Chelmsford camped in the shadow of a sphinx-shaped mountain called Isandlwana where he divided his forces into two columns. Leaving half in the unprotected camp, he took the rest of his army off on a futile search for the elusive Zulus *impis* (regiments) he suspected must be nearby. On January 22 1879, with Chelmsford still blundering around Zululand, a horseman out on patrol from the camp at Isandlwana looked over the edge of a deep ravine and found the Zulu army – 25,000 strong – camped in utter silence. The response was immediate. Even as the patrol galloped frantically back to raise the alarm, the *impis* were pouring over the edge of the ravine and running down the flat plateau towards the camp. The officers had barely enough time to get the Welsh guardsmen into defensive formations before the Zulus fell upon the camp in a fury. In less than two hours it was all over – 1,300 soldiers had been killed and the survivors were stampeding away from the camp in a mob back in the direction of Natal, pursued and picked-off by the Zulus as they ran.

The survivors fled across the Buffalo River, some heading for the mission station at Rorke's Drift where a detachment of engineers and Welsh regulars was based. Defences were hastily put together before a Zulu regiment, reportedly 4,000-strong, attacked the mission after dark. The story goes that the 100 defenders repulsed wave after wave of Zulu attacks, until the *impis* retired to the hills at dawn; However, some historians doubt the official and accepted version of events. That the mission was held is fact but whether there were more than a few un-coordinated rushes by a group of over-excited young warriors is open to question. Certainly, after the appalling carnage of Isandlwana, the British commanders in Natal needed a morale-boosting, chest-thumping victory and the 'stand' at Rorke's Drift might have been tailored to achieve it. Eleven Victoria Crosses were handed out after this engagement, which cheered the disillusioned army up a little and they went back to chasing the Zulus. Four months later, on July 4 1879, the Zulu kingdom was crushed at the battle of Ulundi, Cetshwayo's capital. The *impis* fell upon the British with supreme courage but the solid square of redcoats did not waver and poured volley after volley of rifle fire into the Zulu ranks.

Tourist information
KwaZulu-Natal Tourism Board Dundee, tel: 0341 22121, fax: 23856

Accommodation
Dundee is the most convenient town from which to explore the Zulu War battlefields. There are scads of B&Bs and prices vary. **Gunners Rest** (55 Pongola Crescent, Dundee, tel: 034 212 4560, fax 034 212 4562, or 082 690

7812) offers accommodation in an en suite double. R120 per person including breakfast.

Things to see and do

The battlefields are fascinating to visit bu spooky – Isandlwana, on an overcast day, seems to vibrate with ominous feeling. Pat Rundgren of Gunner's Rest Battlefields Tours (tel: 034 212 4560, fax 034 212 4562 or 082 690 7812) runs one of the cheapest and most entertaining tours of the battlefields. He sits you down on the top of **Isandlwana** mountain and describes the battle in vivid detail. Later in the day you visit the mission at **Rorke's Drift** where the old buildings have been preserved more or less as they were in 1879. Rows of white stones mark the defensive lines which were made of biscuit boxes and rocks. Tours cost R110 per person if you use your own vehicle, about R200 if Pat takes you in his Kombi.

LADYSMITH

Ladysmith was a strategic town along the railway to the north and by besieging it and cutting the line, the Boers almost brought the British Empire in Africa to its knees. The town was cut off for 118 days before being relieved. On November 15 1899, an armoured train was dispatched from Pietermaritzburg and headed up the line towards Colenso, a few miles south of Ladysmith. Young war correspondent Winston Churchill, who had just arrived in the country to report for the *London Morning Post*, was among the personnel on the train. Churchill, a graduate of Sandhurst, had seen active service Cuba, India and the Sudan, and he was aware of how good at soldiering the Boers were, commenting that 'the individual Boer, mounted, in suitable country, is worth four or five regular soldiers'.

The armoured train was ambushed just outside Colenso and derailed as the crew started reversing frantically back towards Estcourt, 33km behind. Churchill was taken prisoner and interned in Pretoria. He made a few attempts to escape, finally succeeding on his third attempt. It was impossible for him to make his way through Boer lines to rejoin the British forces in the south so he headed east for the neutral territory of Portuguese East Africa. In doing so, he made sterling use of Kruger's railway to Delagoa Bay, clinging to the underside of a freight wagon and evading the Boers who were by now very interested in finding him. Shortly afterwards, he was back in Natal, ready to join another attempt by the British forces to relieve Ladysmith. When he was first captured, Boer general Joubert said of Churchill that he was nothing more than 'a bit of a newspaperman'.

Tourism information

The Tourism Information Office (tel: 036 637 2992) has a self-guide brochure.

Getting there and away
Bus and car

Ladysmith is bypassed by the new N3 deviation but Greyhound (tel: 031 309 7830) and Translux (tel: 031 361 8333) buses pass through here.

Train
The *Trans Natal* stops in Ladysmith on its daily journey, northbound at 00.20 and southbound at 01.56. The *Trans Oranje* express between Durban and Cape Town also passes through Ladysmith once a week in each direction, eastbound (from Cape Town) at 01.01 on Tuesdays, westbound at 23.12 on Wednesdays.

Things to see and do
If you can cope with the necessary early morning arrival or departure, Ladysmith is worth spending a day in. Attractions include the excellent **Siege Museum** which houses artefacts, uniforms, photographs and documents from the siege. The Anglo–Boer War Centenary has stirred up plenty of fresh interest in the conflict and many of the museums have revamped their exhibits and arranged special events to coincide with key dates.

The **Emnambithi Cultural Centre**, 25 Keate Street, has a fresh perspective on some of the other forces that shaped South African culture and history. The centre houses the Ladysmith Black Mambazo Hall which has an outstanding display on this superb Zulu vocal group who were made famous by Paul Simon who recorded and toured with them in the 1980s. *Both museums are open from 09.00–16.00 on weekdays, 09.00–13.00 on Saturday.*

The **Soofi Mosque**, built in 1969 and now a national monument, is regarded as one of the most beautiful Mosques in the southern hemisphere. The Mosque obeys the decrees of Muslim canon law as it stands on the site of the original Mosque built by Hazrah Soofi Saheb. *Open from 13.00–14.00 and 17.00–21.00.*

One of the town's little quirks is its unique collection of electrical sub-stations, built in 14 different styles ranging from Cape Dutch to Art Deco.

The town is surrounded by a few major battlefields, including **Spioenkop** and **Colenso**. The battle for the hill at Spioenkop, which was of little strategic value, was one of the most futile of the war – over 2,000 men were killed, often in bitter hand-to-hand fighting, before the British retired. The other site at Colenso, or Tugela Heights, was the scene of the biggest battle ever to take place in the southern hemisphere, until any battle of the Falklands War. The town is full of both registered and unofficial tour guides who can take you around. Ask at the information office.

The nearby **Spioenkop Dam Nature Reserve** would make a good base to explore the area and has a pleasant campsite and chalets at the edge of the dam. Chalets must be booked through the KwaZulu-Natal Conservation Services (tel: 033 701 1823). There is a basic bush camp with huts on the other side of the dam but this must be booked at the main office in the reserve.

WEENEN AND DARKEST AFRICA
This little town whose name means 'weeping' in Dutch has experienced plenty of the trauma and bloodshed of South African history right on its doorstep. Weenen was founded in 1838 and was named in memory of the massacres carried out in Boer encampments in the area by Zulus after Piet Retief and his men had been clubbed to death in Dingane's royal enclosure.

The Voortrekkers were not the only people whose blood was spilt in great amounts. During the 1980s, this region was the centre of vicious internecine fighting between rival Zulu clans, especially in the Tugela Ferry area. As always it was dismissed as another manifestation of the feud between the African National Congress and the conservative Inkatha Freedom Party but in fact it was much more complicated than that. *My Traitor's Heart*, Rian Malan's excellent and moving biography of the country, is partly set in the Weenen area and I think the author comes closer to unravelling the problem than anyone else.

Getting there
Car
This is the easiest way – Darkest Africa (see below) is 25km from Weenen on the Tugela Ferry road.

Train
The *Trans Natal Express* (daily between Johannesburg–Durban) stops at Estcourt, 38km from Weenen; take a minibus taxi from there to Weenen. Unfortunately the train arrives at an unsavoury hour from either direction so you should arrange to overnight in Estcourt. If you ask very nicely – and pay for his petrol – Piet Opperman will pick you up in Weenen.

Things to see and do
The town spreads over a hot, fertile valley and is interesting as a typical Zululand farming town. There is plenty of game including eland and kudu which get along peacefully in the nearby **Weenen Biosphere**. However, the most compelling reason to come here is to camp at **Darkest Africa** along the banks of the Bushman's River.

The Bushman's rises in the foothills of the Drakensbergs but at Weenen it leaves the farmlands of Natal and plunges into wild country of Zululand: thick, rugged hills covered in indigenous *bushveld* and aloes. At one point, the river thunders over a waterfall and runs into a deep valley. With sheer red cliffs rising straight out of the water on one side and a small acacia-covered plain on the other, this is one of the remotest and best campsites in Africa. Darkest Africa (tel: 036 354 1806) was the creation of local farmer, Piet Opperman, who hacked a small access road out of the mountainside (at times there is a 100m drop from the side of the road straight into the river) and made a campsite under the acacias. There is hot water from wood-fired donkey boilers and a well-hidden mess tent with a gas-operated stove and fridge. R30 per person per night.

You can walk on the trail up to the waterfall or just lie about under the trees. Swimming in the river right in front of the camp is reasonably safe, but if it's flowing fast, stay ashore as there are some mean rapids immediately below the camp. Kayakers and rafters have about 2km of superb whitewater to play in – the take out is on the right bank where the terrain opens up. Don't go below this point as there is a low-level bridge downstream, a nasty obstacle to run in to. The Bushman's joins the Tugela River about a mile downstream from the bridge.

MAPUTALAND
David Larsen

Like nowhere else in South Africa, Maputaland has the untamed quality of a frontier territory, undiscovered by most, yet virtually unmatched in its natural beauty. Of all the regions of the country it is the one that most retains the quality of raw Africa, hippo paths crisscrossing the landscape between mud-hutted villages, qualities which continue to give it its magical allure.

Those who know it have often kept it a secret, for here in Maputaland, Cinderella's golden slipper, is South Africa's first natural World Heritage Site, the Greater St Lucia Wetland Park, which dominates the south of the region.

Maputaland is in the far northeastern corner of South Africa, pressed up against Swaziland and Mozambique in the north. Its coastal plains are bounded in the east by the Indian Ocean and in the west by the spine of the Ubombo or Lubombo mountain range. Just inland of the coast a series of wetlands and estuaries are the remnants of a time when the sea stretched far inland. The 38,000ha Lake St Lucia is the largest of these, and the largest estuarine system in Africa.

On the seaward side of the lakes are some of the largest vegetated dunes in the world which preserve the rare dune forest. Further inland, in the north of the region, another rare vegetation type, sand forest, covers much of Tembe Elephant Park and Ndumo Game Reserve, and in the south, the Hluhluwe–Umfolozi Park hosts prime examples of *bushveld* and *thornveld*. These diverse habitats are home to perhaps the richest variety of bird life in South Africa, as well as the full complement of game, from the 'Big Five' including the endangered black rhino, which was rescued from extinction through the efforts of staff at Umfolozi Game Reserve, to the shy red duiker, a miniature antelope which is on the Red Data Species list of endangered wildlife.

Safety
In venturing into Maputaland, be aware that many of the areas you will visit are the territory of dangerous animals. If you have little experience of African wildlife, find out from local people what to watch out for. Around lakes, for instance, do not stand closer than three metres to the water's edge. A crocodile can remain hidden under water for up to two hours and, if given the opportunity, will take prey close to the bank. Maputaland is also a malaria area, and precautions should be taken in this regard.

Bookings
Most of the conservation areas in Maputaland are managed by the KwaZulu-Natal Nature Conservation Service (NCS). Entrance to the majority of Maputaland's reserves costs R35 per vehicle and R10 per person. Most of the reasonably priced accommodation within the game reserves and parks is run by the NCS. While campsites are booked at the office in each area, all other accommodation is booked through the Reservations Officer (KwaZulu-Natal Nature Conservation Service, PO Box 13069, Cascades Pietermaritzburg, 3202, tel: 033 845 1000/2, fax: 033 845 1001, web: www.rhino.org.za).

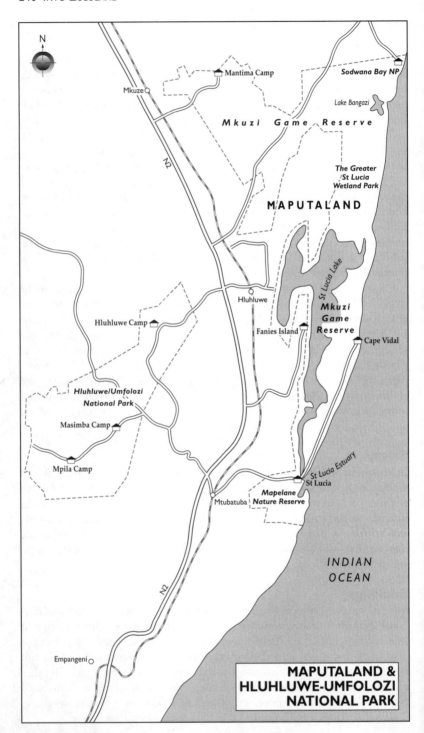

**MAPUTALAND &
HLUHLUWE-UMFOLOZI
NATIONAL PARK**

THE GREATER ST LUCIA WETLAND PARK

The Greater St Lucia Wetland Park, with the tourist town of St Lucia, is the gateway to the region. With over 300 bird species, it is not surprising the Greater St Lucia Wetland Park was one of the first in South Africa to be proclaimed a wetland of international importance under the Ramsar Convention. In addition to wetlands there are several other diverse habitats in the park including grasslands, forests, mangroves, vegetated dunes, and the intertidal ecosystem on the coast. In recognition of this rich diversity, the park was proclaimed a World Heritage Site in December 1999.

Of the 260,000ha park, 38,000ha is the expanse of lake, islands and estuary known as Lake St Lucia. Surrounding the lake itself, the Park is made up of several proclaimed conservation areas in their own right. It stretches from the mouth of the Umfolozi river at Maphelana in the south and, moving north, includes the Western Shores and Eastern Shores of St Lucia Game and Marine Reserves, False Bay Park, Cape Vidal, Sodwana Bay, Mkhuze Game Reserve, and the Maputaland Marine Reserve.

There is something for everyone in the Park from deep sea fishing trips, angling, snorkelling, scuba diving, boating, game viewing, birding, hiking and mountain biking trails.

Maphelana
Getting there and away
Reached from the N2 south of Mtubatuba, Maphelana, on the south side of the Umfolozi river mouth, is a surf and ski-boat fishing destination, but there is also safe swimming at low tide, and a short self-guided trail.

Accommodation
Contact NCS booking office listed above; 5-bed log cabins: R100–390. Camp sites: R38–120; tel: 035 590 1407, fax: 035 590 1039.

Eastern Shores
St Lucia Town and Estuary
Getting there and away
The Eastern Shores region is accessed via the town of St Lucia. Turn off the N2 at Mtubatuba and follow the signs to St Lucia.

Things to see and do
From the town, boat tours on the lake are an excellent opportunity for seeing hippo and water birds. Boat trips on the NCS-managed *Santa Lucia*, leave at 08.30, 10.30 and 14.30 and sunset cruises go out on Friday and Saturday evenings for R51 per person (tel: 035-590 1340). There are also several privately run boat operations and a large number of tour guides based in the town.

On the outskirts of the town, the **Crocodile Centre** (tel: 035 590 1387) is the only research centre for crocodiles in the country that's worth a visit. Along with crocodiles, there are a number of other reptiles on show including many of South Africa's most poisonous snakes. *Open daily 07.30 –17.00.*

During the summer months, November to March, the pristine coastline of the park comes alive with rare loggerhead and leatherback turtles returning to their original nesting sites to lay their eggs on the beach. Night trips can be organised to see the turtles for R300 per person. Another night activity in the park worth doing is a chameleon tour where you are guaranteed to see chameleon and probably a host of other nocturnal animals at R105 per person. For both tours contact Shaka Barker Tours (tel/fax: 035 590 1162).

Accommodation

There are three caravan and camping areas at **Sugarloaf**, **Iphiva** and **Eden Park**. Reservations: tel: 035 590 1340; fax: 035 590 1343.

African Tale Adventures and Backpackers 3 Main Rd (between St Lucia and Mtubatuba); tel: 035 550 4300; fax: 035 550 4469; email: africantale@hotmail.com; web: www.africantale.co.za. Double R110, dorm R40, camping R25. Classic place with doubles in traditional Zulu beehive huts.

Cape Vidal

Cape Vidal is famous for its angling and snorkelling as well as short self-guided trails through the dune forest on the highest vegetated dunes in the world.

Accommodation

There are campsites in dune forest near the beach which can be booked (tel: 035 590 9012; fax: 035 590 9007).

Things to see and do

The Eastern Shores host numerous self-guided trails, animal and bird hides ranging in duration from a few minutes to the five-day, 65 km **Emoyeni Trail**. Starting and finishing at the Mission Rocks office, the latter is probably the only trail in the country where one can walk self-guided through Big Four country, watching carefully for elephant, leopard, buffalo and black rhino, to say nothing of crocodile and perhaps the most dangerous of all, hippo. Winter is the ideal time to do this hike as you miss the heat, rain and malaria. This is a trail for the serious backpacker. You need to carry your own tent, provisions and gas cooker as no fires are allowed. The cost is negligible at R25 per person per day.

For the less adventurous the **Mziki Trail** enables you to explore some of the same area in three one-day routes and stay at a central trail hut – an old World War II radar hut on Mount Tabor. R35 per person per day. Both trails can be booked by calling the Mission Rocks office (tel: 035 590 9002).

The **St Lucia Wilderness Trail** has its base camp at Lake Bhangazi South. Guided by a ranger the trail is the only access visitors have into the Tewati Wilderness area North of Cape Vidal. The five-day trail can include canoeing on Lake St Lucia and costs R1,300 per person all inclusive. Book through the NCS booking office listed above.

Western Shores

Charter's Creek, Fani's Island, and False Bay Park, are all accessed off the N2 further North of Mtubatuba, the latter through the town of Hluhluwe. All are destinations for bird-watching, and fishing. Short self-guided trails serve the bird-watchers. Fani's Island has boats for hire and Charter's Creek offers guided boat tours. Mountain biking is also popular in these areas.

Accommodation

Charter's Creek: Contact NCS booking office listed above; tel: 035 550 9000; fax: 035 590 1191. 4-bed rest huts: R60–210. Campsites: R25–70.

Fani's Island: Contact NCS booking office listed above; tel: 035 550 9035 fax: 035 550 9051. 2-bed rest huts: R60–105. Campsites: R25–70.

False Bay Park: Book by phoning 035 562 0425. 4-bed rustic huts: R75–150; campsites R20–70.

Mkuze Game Reserve

In the northwest corner of The Greater St Lucia Wetland Park is the 40,000ha Mkuze Game Reserve, proclaimed a protected area since 1912. It is accessed off the N2 at the town of Mkuze along 16km dirt road through a gap in the Ubombo Mountains.

Mkuze is known for its hides that are excellent for game viewing, especially in the dry months (June–August). There is another opportunity to get out of your car at the spectacular **Fig Forest**, where guides will interpret the wonders of the park to you.

Accommodation

3-bed rest huts: Contact NCS booking office listed above; tel: 035 573 0002/3, fax: 035 573 0031. R85–220; campsites: R25–35.

Sodwana Bay

Access to this northeastern corner of the Park is only for 4x4 vehicles via the towns of Hluhluwe and Mbazwane. Sodwana Bay is a diving destination from where numerous dive charterers operate, while Ozabeni further South, is a birder's paradise.

Accommodation

Contact NCS booking office listed above; tel: 035 571 0011. 5-bed log cabins: R100–250; campsites: R60–100 at Gwalagwala and Ozabeni.

Hluhluwe–Umfolozi Park

On the southwestern border of Maputaland, on the other side of the N2 highway from the Greater St Lucia Wetland Park lies the Hluhluwe–Umfolozi Park. At 96,000ha this is one of the largest game parks in South Africa. The Park includes both Hluhluwe and Umfolozi, two of Africa's oldest game reserves, both founded in 1895, and the linking Corridor Reserve proclaimed in 1989.

The park provides Maputaland's Big Five experience. Prides of lion imported from Kruger National Park after a lone male migrated to the area from Mozambique mid-19th century. Cheetah and the endangered wild dog also reside in the park. Part of Umfolozi's proud heritage is that its efforts saw the black rhino brought back from near extinction.

Vehicle trails wind through much of the park and there are also hides and three self-guided foot trails. Guided day walks are conducted from Mpila and Hilltop camps and guided night drives can also be booked.

From mid-March to mid-December you can follow a four-day wilderness trail into the heart of the Umfolozi wilderness area (R1,200 per person inclusive). There are also shorter weekend wilderness trails during the same season (R650 per person per night).

Accommodation

There are no camping facilities in the park, but there is affordable self-catering hutted accommodation at Masinda, Mpila and Hilltop camps. There is also rustic accommodation at Sontuli, Nselweni and Mndindini bush camps: R130–200. Contact NCS booking office listed above.

Pongola Nature Reserve

With the best tiger fishing in the country, the Pongola Nature Reserve on the banks of the Pongolapoort dam is primarily a fishing resort, although the reserve is also home to game.

Accommodation

There are caravan and camping facilities in the Pongolapoort Nature Reserve(NCS); contact NCS booking office listed above.

Ndumo Game Reserve

Ndumo Game Reserve lies on KwaZulu-Natal–Mozambique border. It covers 10,117ha of land including a large number of pans which play host to a wide range of aquatic birds. Ndumo is famous as a birding destination being the southernmost limit of many tropical birds. It boasts the largest recorded bird list per hectare in the country with a total of 421 species.

Accommodation

Contact NCS booking office listed above; tel: 035 591 0004, fax: 035 591 1042. 2-bed rest huts: R100–130; campsites: R30–50.

Tembe Elephant Park

Tembe Elephant Park was established to protect a subspecies of elephant which used to migrate back and forth across the Mozambican border and came under threat from poaching. Still shy of humans the elephants are magnificent but elusive, and you will be lucky to spot them in the magnificent sand forest. Tembe is one of the wildest and most undeveloped of all South Africa's parks. The Park was closed to visitors until recently and is only accessible by 4x4.

There is no budget accommodation in the Park but guided game drives can be booked for R150–200 per person. Tel: 031 202 9090.

COASTAL FOREST RESERVE
Kosi Bay

Kosi Bay is a complex of four lake systems and an estuary which opens out into the sea. The area falls within the Kosi Bay Nature Reserve which in turn is part of the larger Coastal Forest Reserve. Kosi Bay Nature Reserve includes some of the largest remaining tracts of swamp and dune forest, coastal grassland and the biggest stand of naturally occurring raphia palms, which attract the rare Palmnut vulture, in South Africa. The area also includes mangrove swamps and rare wildlife such as the Tongaland red squirrel which occurs nowhere else.

Accommodation
Contact NCS booking office listed above; can be booked on tel/fax: 035 592 0236. 2-bed lodge: R150–225; campsites: R45–180.

Things to see and do
In the lake system ancient methods of fish-trapping are still used by local people. A 12km walk with a guide or a trip in a 4x4 will enable you to see them at work. Walking though the reserve without a guide, however, is not permitted. Perhaps the best way to experience the area is on the **Kosi Bay Hike** which leads around the lake system. The four-day hiking trail with a ranger costs R250 per person. The trails camps are equipped with tents and mattresses but hikers must provide their own food. To book, call 035 592 0236.

Mabibi
Further south from Kosi there are a number of pristine beaches which form part of Coastal Forest Reserve and can only be accessed by 4x4. Budget accommodation is only at Mabibi.

Accommodation
Campsites: R25–100; tel/fax: 035 592 0142.

Lake Sibaya
Lake Sibaya is the largest fresh water lake in southern Africa with a surface area of 77km^2 and an average depth of 13m. The lake used to be open to the sea. As a result of the closure of the estuary, the lake hosts several endemic fish species. Baya camp has a small pool and 3km walking trail with two hides for bird watching.

Accommodation
Contact NCS booking office listed above. 2-bed rest huts: R85–127.50.

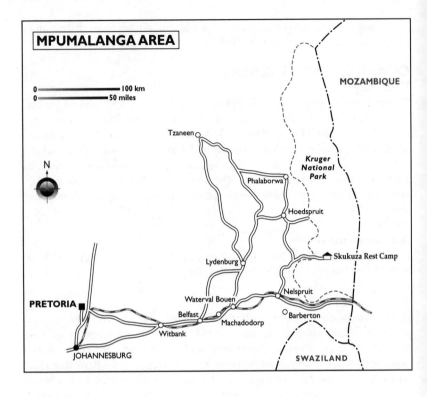

MPUMALANGA AREA

0 ▬▬▬▬▬ 100 km
0 ▬▬▬▬▬ 50 miles

N

MOZAMBIQUE

Tzaneen

Kruger National Park

Phalaborwa

Hoedspruit

Skukuza Rest Camp

Lydenburg

Waterval Bouen

PRETORIA

Nelspruit

Belfast

Barberton

Witbank

Machadodorp

JOHANNESBURG

SWAZILAND

Mpumalanga

As provinces go, Mpumalanga is one of the biggest. It spreads out over the northeast of the country, reaching from the outskirts of Johannesburg, spilling over the Escarpment that runs roughly north to south like a spine down the east of the country, and sprawling up to the Mozambique border. Mpumalanga is a region of two very different and contrasting landscapes. From Gauteng to the edge of the Escarpment, is *highveld* country: open grassland where cattle graze or huge fields of maize and sunflowers fill the horizon. Near Johannesburg, there are more thermal power stations than maize fields, fuelled by the vast reserves of coal around the *highveld* towns of Witbank and Middelburg. It is no paradise around here – these are industrial towns and the faster you can get past them, the better it will be for your spirit (and lungs).

The Escarpment region is hilly and covered in pine and eucalyptus forests (some say the biggest in the world) to a point where the land just drops away over a steep mountain range into the bushveld. At the foot of these mountains is the *lowveld*, hot bush country with some forests but mostly indigenous bush – mopani and acacia woodland, lots of hills and granite outcrops – big game country.

If you look at a map, you will see that the territory along the whole eastern border of the country, from Zimbabwe almost as far as Swaziland is occupied by a huge game reserve. This is the Kruger National Park and one of many compelling reasons to come here. In its physical size and animal numbers and variety, Kruger is the country's premier game park. And as a national park it is affordable for budget travellers.

The Escarpment offers a different experience. It is cooler country, often misty and with above average rainfall. It is the source of many rivers and the area is full of waterfalls and rushing mountain streams. The forested slopes of the Transvaal Drakensbergs are marked with dozens of hiking and mountain biking trails, there are old mining towns to wander about in, campsites at the edge of the earth and rivers and pools to swim in.

HISTORY

The region was originally home to a couple of smaller tribes such as the Pedi and Venda people who had peeled off from the great southward migration. Later, during the *Mfecane*, scattered groups of Swazi, Ndebele and Shangaan people drifted into the area, trying to get as far away as possible from the upheavals in Zululand and the *highveld*. The Ndebele, led by Mzilikazi (the great road, on account of the swathe he carved across the territory) inflicted a reign of terror themselves, conquering local tribes, taking the young men and women and killing everyone else. Mzilikazi, always living in fear that the Zulu king Shaka would keep chasing after him, moved on to settle in present day Zimbabwe.

Until the first parties of Voortrekkers arrived in the area in 1838, the only Europeans here were ivory hunters and the odd missionary. The Portuguese had established settlements in Mozambique as early as the 16th century but had done little exploration in the area except for a few abortive expeditions to find gold and more successful forays to capture slaves.

In 1838, trek leader Louis Trichardt trundled through the northern parts of the province on his way to Delagoa Bay, now Maputo, the capital of Mozambique. Later, after the Boer Republics of the Transvaal and Orange Free State were established, the Boers wanted little to do with the British-ruled colonies in the Cape and Natal and opened up a trade route to Delagoa Bay instead. Eventually, under Transvaal president Paul Kruger's inspiration, a railway was built from Delagoa Bay to Pretoria; by the time it was completed though, gold had been discovered in the Transvaal and life for the Boers was to change forever.

In 1874, there was a gold strike near Sabie and diggers from all over the world rushed to the Transvaal. Mining camps sprang up in the hills around Sabie and Pilgrim's Rest and the trade route flourished. It was not a rich strike, however, and prospectors battled to make their claims pay. When the news of the big strike on the Witwatersrand reached Pilgrim's Rest, there was a rout as the diggers stampeded for the *highveld*.

Some miners stayed on and the reef was worked until 1971 when Transvaal Gold Mining Estates, the principal miner, decided to call it a day. The region's mining history is very visible. There are old mine workings in the hills and the detritus of mining such as rusty cocopans and rock crushers, and the little mining towns of Barberton and Pilgrim's Rest still have a rough-edged feel about them.

Now the region's key money-earners are green gold – timber – and citrus fruit, mainly oranges. Tourism is booming, too, with people drawn by the province's abundant wildlife.

Orientation

You have to be well east of Witbank, an industrial and coal mining town, before the countryside starts looking pleasant. The area around Belfast and Machedodorp is one of the country's premier trout-fishing region and the landscape is very English –rolling green hills, cut with icy cold trout streams and dams. It is mostly a weekend retreat for affluent Jo'burgers and, while there are plenty of cute B&Bs and smart trout lodges, they are certainly not budget places.

When to go

The *lowveld* is hot and humid in summer and mild and dry in winter. Temperatures on summer days can easily top 40°C, although afternoon thunderstorms, which are common at this time of year, do have the welcome effect of breaking the heat. This is a malaria area and the risk of contracting it is significantly higher in summer.

Winter is generally a better time for game viewing as the animals tend to gather near waterholes and the *bushveld* is generally less thick. In summer, the rains mean plentiful water and it can be difficult to see animals as the countryside turns green and lush.

Summers on the Escarpment are also hot although average temperatures are much lower than in the *lowveld*. The region is part of the summer rainfall area and it can sometimes rain for days. Winters are cool and up on the high country and winter nights around Belfast – and days for that matter – can be bitterly cold with temperatures dropping below freezing.

GETTING THERE AND AWAY
Train
The *Komati* passenger train runs daily in each direction between Johannesburg, Nelspruit and the border town of Komatipoort. It's an overnight train with the standard sleeper accommodation and a catering car for light meals. The train takes about 12 hours to cover the 530km from Johannesburg to the border. Fares: R121 in 1st, R85 in 2nd, R48 in Economy.

On Fridays only there is a train from Pretoria to Hoedspruit, departing at 18.45 and arriving at 08.06 the next day, returning on Sunday at 14.17 and arriving in Pretoria at an unfriendly 03.17. Take the *Komati*.

If you are heading towards the northern part of the Kruger Park, the weekdays-only train from Kaapmuiden (38km east of Nelspruit) to Hoedspruit might be of some use. This train connects with the daily *Komati* leaving at 05.11 and arriving in Hoedspruit at 08.34, and returning from Hoedspruit at 15.34, arriving at Kaapmuiden at 19.08, just in time for the westbound *Komati*. The connection is quite tight so late running could mean an overnight wait at Kaapmuiden which I cannot recommend. .

Bus
The Baz Bus (tel: 021 439 2323), runs daily via Sabie to Nelspruit and then on to Swaziland. Translux (tel: 011 774 3333) and Greyhound (tel: 011 333 3671) also run coaches daily to Nelspruit.

Panthera Azul (tel: 011 337 7438) have a daily coach service via Nelspruit to Maputo in Mozambique. Any bus line called 'Blue Panther' has *got* to be worth using.

Car
The N4 toll route is the main road from Pretoria to Nelspruit and the *lowveld*. The N12 heads east out of Johannesburg to join the N4 at Witbank. There is prettier and quieter road leading off from Belfast and over the Escarpment via Long Tom Pass.

Hitchhiking
The N4 has the most traffic but drivers tend to tear along this road. You may

have better luck heading to Sabie from Belfast on the R540 but there is a lot less traffic on this country road. I have had mixed success on the roads from Nelspruit to Sabie and Graskop, once hiking for hours without a ride and another time getting a string of lifts one after the other.

GETTING AROUND

Having your own transport will help, especially if you plan to visit the Kruger National Park. The best place to hire it will be in Nelspruit although cheap car hire is a bit thin on the ground here. All the major agencies have offices here: Avis (tel: 013 741 1087), Budget (tel: 013 741 3871), Imperial (tel: 013 741 3210).

DOWN TO THE ESCARPMENT
Waterval Boven

I once called Waterval Boven an 'uninviting railway town at the lip of the escarpment', a servicing point for steam locomotives needing replenishment after the long slog up from the *lowveld* but which had since fallen on hard times. I am happy to eat my words. Although the town's days as an important railway town are history, it has been given a nice shot in the arm by tourism and adventure travel.

Getting there

'Boven is about 2km off the main N4 and buses drop passengers at the turn-off into town. Many people come on the daily train – the eastbound Komati arrives at 01.30, the westbound at 23.00. The backpackers is a mere 200m up the road from the station and they'll wait up if they are expecting you.

Accommodation

The Climbers Inn 3rd Av; tel: 013 257 0363; fax: 013 257 0299; email: gusberg@rocrope.co.za. Double/family room R140 per room, dorm R35 (R60 with dinner), camping R25. Lovely old stone house in the middle of the village, managed by friendly people. The house is famous around the world climbing circuit but it is more than a climbers' den. They can help out with tours and non-rock adventures but if you want to learn to climb, Gustav is one of the most reassuring instructors you could hope for. Alex, who is French and knows a thing or two about cooking, will cook meals on request. Mountain Club members get a discount.

Elandskrans Holiday Resort Elandskrans (5km out of town); tel: 013 257 0175. Camping R12.50 per person. Basic 1970s-era holiday resort which has had a bit of a revamp. The campsites are excellent as they look out over the Elands River valley and more importantly, for climbers at any rate, over the climbing area.

You can also camp for free near the crags but get advice from Gustav at the climber's hostel as he can tell you where the best places are.

Eating and drinking

With all the climbers and other adventurers coming to town, there has been a 200% increase in the number of decent restaurants and pubs. The **Whistle** and **Trout** (tel: 013 257 0698) serves good, reasonably priced meals while the **Shamrock Arms** (tel: 013 257 0888), the closest thing to an Irish pub the country has, takes care of the drinking side of things.

For more information, contact the Info Bar, tel: 013 257 0444.

Things to see and do
Waterval Boven's position at the edge of the Escarpment has been its saviour. It has an impressive **waterfall** (Waterval Boven means 'above the waterfall', and there is a town at the foot of the Escarpment called, naturally, Waterval Onder). The deep *kloofs* and valleys around the town have become the country's most popular sport climbing area with dozen of bolted routes. On weekends climbers flock to the town and set up camp above the crags or in town at the newly established climbers and backpackers' hostel.

But it is more than just a climber's place. There is mountain biking in the surrounding hills, fly-fishing in the Elands River and a superb two-day hiking trail that loops down the Escarpment. The trail is a lesson in Escarpment geography – it's steep and rocky. Luckily you hike downhill.

More sedentary but no less impressive adventure involves watching the Elands River plunge over the lip of a 60m-high cliff into the valley below; when the river levels have been boosted by summer rain on the *highveld*, the waterfall truly is thunderous. Doing an abseil (R95) off the crag alongside it adds an extra dimension to the waterfall experience. Ask at the Climbers' Inn for details.

A steam train, the **Oosterlyn Express** (tel: 013 257 0512), runs down the escarpment to Waterval Onder and back on most Sundays. The depot has a couple of steam locomotives which are cared for by a dedicated bunch of railwaymen. The train also serves as transport for the hikers who have completed the two-day Elandskrans trail (tel: 013 257 0175).

Sabie
Sabie is a forestry town on the edge of the escarpment, nestling at the foot of Mount Anderson, the highest mountain in Mpumalanga. Its main attractions are the hiking and mountain bike trails into the surrounding hills and a couple of stunning waterfalls. The Sabie River is a lovely stream and good for swimming near the waterfalls (below).

Accommodation
Sabie Backpackers Lodge 185 Main Rd; tel: 013 764 2118; email: ghoeks@iafrica.com. Double R100, dorm R40, camping R25. There is also a tree house for R50 per person. At last... a backpacker in Sabie! Clean and quiet. Trips down the Sabie River, horse riding, abseiling and hiking can be arranged.
Merry Pebbles Resort (off the gravel road to Ceylon Forestry Station); tel (013) 764 2266. Camping R40 per person. Merry Pebbles is a fine camping ground but only go there out of school holidays. Once you've moved away from the caravan parking area and its power supply, you can pitch your tent in a little clump of trees at the edge of the bubbling Sabie River. There are spotless toilets and showers and an endless supply of free firewood, courtesy of the sawmill outside town.

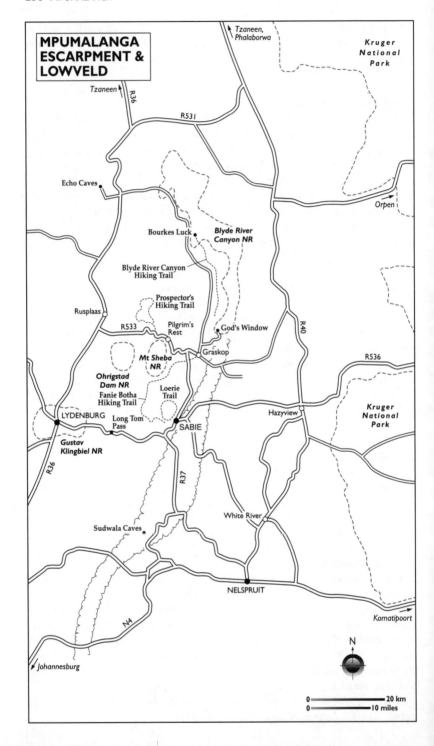

MPUMALANGA ESCARPMENT & LOWVELD

Tzaneen, Phalaborwa

Kruger National Park

Tzaneen

R36

R531

Echo Caves

Orpen

Bourkes Luck

Blyde River Canyon NR

Blyde River Canyon Hiking Trail

Prospector's Hiking Trail

Rusplaas

R533

Pilgrim's Rest

God's Window

R40

Graskop

R536

Mt Sheba NR

Ohrigstad Dam NR

Loerie Trail

Fanie Botha Hiking Trail

LYDENBURG

Long Tom Pass

SABIE

Hazyview

Kruger National Park

Gustav Klingbiel NR

R36

R37

White River

Sudwala Caves

NELSPRUIT

Komatipoort

N4

Johannesburg

N

0   20 km
0   10 miles

Things to see and do

The four-day **Fanie Botha Trail** (tel: 013 759 5432) leads up the flanks of Mount Anderson and then traverses the range through forests and along mountain streams as far as Graskop. It costs R30 per person per day. Shorter loops are possible. Overnight huts have bunks, mattresses and cooking utensils.

The 14km circular **Loerie Trail** starts at the Ceylon Forest Station, 5km from Sabie town, and heads back above the river towards town before swinging up into the trees. It traverses a lot of pine plantation but also covers a section of natural forest, passes a few waterfalls and then home. You can start the walk from the Castle Rock caravan park at the bottom of the road heading out of Sabie to Graskop. The Loerie Trail is free.

This is amazing cycling country; plenty of quiet logging roads and jeep tracks and some dedicated mountain bike trails, including a 24km 'yellow' route which starts at Castle Rock caravan park and heads into the hills. There is also a 13km technical (red) route but it is poorly marked and peters out. The tar roads in the area are generally quiet and the road from Sabie to Graskop and then over the pass to Pilgrim's Rest would make a nice two-day tour. The ride up **Long Tom** Pass on the main Sabie–Lydenburg road is worth doing but only if you are impervious to pain. Of course, the long, screaming blast down, is just reward for your efforts.

There are some lovely **waterfalls** in the Sabie area. Some of them, such as the Bridal Veil and Elina Falls, are on the 17km Loerie day trail. The Lone Creek Falls and Horsehoe Falls are a few kilometres outside town on the gravel road past the sawmill and Ceylon Forestry Station. You could walk to them but it would be much easier to cycle or drive.

Graskop

Graskop perches on the edge of the Escarpment, literally looking across the *lowveld* all the way to Mozambique. There isn't a lot to divert one here but it is a jumping off/end point for a couple of trails.

Getting there

Minibus taxis leave from outside Nelspruit railway station and head north. Try and get a taxi going all the way to Sabie rather than just Hazyview. If you can't, get off at Hazyview and get another taxi up to Sabie. It might take some time. Do not, under any circumstances, go to Bushbuckridge, the sprawling settlement east of Hazyview – it is not particularly safe area.

If you are driving yourself, Sabie is at the end of the R537 from Nelspruit. You can also take the R37 and turn right for Sabie when you hit the Long Tom Pass.

There is a railway line that winds its way up from Nelspruit, through the forests, to Sabie and Graskop. Sadly, its passenger trains are history. Right now, however, you're on your own.

Accommodation

Panorama Rest Camp (just outside Graskop on the Hazyview Rd); tel: 013 767 1091. Prices range from R130–300 for a whole chalet. A standard holiday resort with 2–6 bed chalets with a gorgeous view of the *lowveld*.

Things to see and do

Ten kilometres away is **God's Window**, a lookout right on the edge of the Escarpment, set in a stand of natural forest which clings precariously to the cliff. The view is stupendous and on clear, still days you can hear the chatter of birds in the forest far below. God's Window is about 10km Graskop on a circular drive that turns off the R532 Graskop–Bourke's Luck road. The lovely **Berlin** and **Lisbon waterfalls** are nearby (follow the signs of the R532).

The town is also the near the start of the 32km 2–3 day **Blyde River Canyon hiking trail** (tel: 013 759 5432), which rambles north along the Escarpment, down the valley of the Treur River and into the head of the canyon itself. The trail is a good way of experiencing the wild moorland and spooky rock formations in the area. Accommodation is in fully equipped hiking huts, most of them near mountain streams or waterfalls, which are always welcome at the end of a hot day. It is a year-round trail but winter nights will be icy (but dry) and summer days will be sweltering with misty mornings and thunderstorms in the afternoon. It is a one-way trail so you will probably have to hitch back to the start or arrange a pick-up before setting off. The trail costs R30 per person per day and R15 for children under 16.

Pilgrim's Rest

This preserved mining town is about 15km west on the R533 over the hills from Graskop. Founded during the 1874 gold rush, the town became a centre for the hunters, prospectors and adventurers who were wandering around the region. Gold mining stopped in the 1970s but the town is preserved as a national monument.

The quiet main street is fronted with buildings made of wood and sheets of corrugated iron, the standard construction materials in all these gold rush towns and when the jacaranda trees bloom in late spring, Pilgrim's really is a pretty place. It is worth stopping here but I can't help feeling that it's a little too preserved – too many shops selling things to tourists and not enough real living going on. The most genuine place is the bar in the old **Royal Hotel** (itself a wonderful specimen of mining town architecture) which attracts the same rough and sometimes unsavoury characters that made Pilgrim's the subject of sermons everywhere in its mining days.

Accommodation

The nicest places to stay are in the restored miner's cottages above the town. The furniture is original and ancient and the huge claw-footed iron baths a real treat. R150 per night; tel: 013 768 1211 for bookings.

Things to see and do

The **Prospector's Hiking Trail** starts at a forestry station just across the Blyde River and loops into the forested hills overlooking the town. The route takes you past a couple of abandoned mine workings, which are more interesting than they sound, but on the whole this is not the most exciting trail I've done; the nearby Fanie Botha trail is much prettier and there are more places to swim.

Bourke's Luck

This would be a totally unremarkable town if it weren't for its **potholes** (thankfully not in the road this time), a sequence of deep holes that have been scoured out of the rock by the action of water and grit at the confluence of the Treur and Blyde Rivers.

Things to see and do

At Bourke's Luck the Blyde River rushes down the steep, deep **Blyde River Canyon** into Swadini Dam which pools around the base of high mountains. The overall spectacle of the canyon is best seen from the lookout point of the R532 at the Three Rondawels, a distinctive outcrop that looks like three round huts. The canyon opens up far below in greens, blues and red sandstone.

A more impressive way of experiencing the canyon is to run its upper reaches on a rafting trip. The one runnable section is 8km of almost continuous whitewater and has been voted one of South Africa's most exciting stretches of river. You will need to go with an experienced rafting company of which a couple operate in the area. Hardy Ventures (tel: 013 751 1693) offer a two-day trip down the canyon for around R790 which includes transport and meals, and Spectra Ventures (tel: 013 741 4293) offer trips on the Blyde as well as the tamer Sabie and Olifants Rivers. The Otters Den campsite (tel: 015 795 5250) at the foot of the canyon is one of Africa's best-sited places.

THE LOWVELD AND BIG GAME COUNTRY

The term *lowveld* should refer to the whole country east of the Escarpment but it's usually accepted that it encompasses the subtropical part of the province, from the Limpopo River in the north to the Swaziland border in the south.

It is hot and humid in the summer (although not nearly as humid as Durban) and temperatures in the high 30s are a daily occurrence. Fortunately, the summer heat blasts are often cooled by afternoon thunderstorms when the rainy season starts in November and continues through February. Winter is a far better time to visit when the days are warm and dry, but it can get icy at night, especially in the bushveld.

Nelspruit

A hot little town and provincial capital of Mpumalanga province, situated in the centre of the country's orange-growing region. If you like orange orchards then you will love Nelspruit, or its surroundings anyway. But otherwise there's not a lot to do here. Some locals have taken to relieving the intense boredom by having a buddy drive their pick-up trucks at high speed through underground parking garages while they lie on the cab roof and watch the concrete whizz past just centimetres from their faces. So it isn't really a place to dally and I wouldn't waste holiday time looking for action here. The Kruger Park is less than an hour away and there is beautiful forest and waterfall country around Sabie and Graskop.

There are people who believe that Nelspruit, which is surrounded by the country's finest game parks and something of a tourist transit centre as a result, will become the country's second city. It *is* a good jumping off point to get to Kruger National Park and other game parks in the region and the town does have all the usual amenities – a good tourist office, car hire companies and latterly a couple of backpackers.

Tourist information
Nelspruit Tourism Tel: (013) 755 1988; fax: 013 755 1350.

Accommodation
Most backpackers offer tours to Kruger Park and some have hiking, mountain biking, sightseeing and rafting trips as well. Check out their Kruger Park offerings, especially if you don't have a car, as it might be an easier way to get in to the reserve.

Old Vic 12 Impala St; tel: 013 744 0993. Double R100 per room, single R50. Quiet, home-based backpacker with a pool (probably the first thing you'll need if you're here in mid-summer.

Nelspruit Backpackers 9 Andries Pretorius St; tel: 013 741 2237; fax: 013 755 2311; email: nelback@hotmail.com. Double R120, dorm R45.

Funky Monkeys 102 Van Wijk St; tel/fax: 013 744 0534; email: funkymonkey@yebo.co.za. Double R110, dorm R45, camping R25.

Kruger Park Backpackers 7 Apiesdoring St, West Acres; tel/fax: 013 737 7224; email: krugback@mweb.co.za. During the week you pay R795 which gets you two nights at the backpacker and two days/one night all inclusive in the park. The weekend deal is R995 and gives you three days/two nights in the park. If you don't have a car, this is a reasonably cheap way of getting into Kruger without the hassles that go with trying to hitchhike in, as they specialise in trips to there.

Things to see and do
Trips and wilderness trails
With Kruger Park nearby, it's no surprise that the town has plenty of operators offering tours of it. Some of the trips including one of two nights on a wilderness trail which is one of the best ways to see wildlife. Tracking animals in their environment is as pure as the bush experience gets. Most of the trails offer at least two nights camping out in the bush, which is also wonderful. You can lie in your sleeping bag and listen to the squeals, grunts and snortings of the *bushveld* at night. Jackals yip, hyenas laugh maniacally and lions moan, a chilling sound if it's close.

By overseas standards, most of the tours are well-priced but they still distort daily budgets. If you've cooked enough of your own meals, you may feel justified in splashing out here. Ask questions and ensure that they are clear about what is on offer. Then decide if it's worth it.

Operators
Trans Frontiers Walking Trails Tel: 015 793 3816
Livingstone Trails Tel: 011 867 2586 or 011 867 5978; email: livtrail@uskonet.com
Wild Adventure Tel: 013 737 7224; email: krugback@mweb.co.za; web: www.argo-navis.com/krugerpark

Hoedspruit

Other than its proximity to Kruger, there is not a lot to say about Hoedspruit. Its main reason for existence is the air force base which is home to a Mirage fighter squadron.

Klaserie

The nearby town of Klaserie has an excellent backpacker which would be a fine base for exploring the park. The Backpack Safari Lodge (tel: 015 793 3816; email: nyani@nix.co.za) is about 50km from Orpen Gate into the central part of Kruger. The owners run tours into the park as well as rafting trips on the Blyde River and tours of a traditional village. En suite double R150, dorm R50.

KRUGER NATIONAL PARK

'Kruger', as it is colloquially known, is a South African institution, unmatched in its diversity of animal life and geography. It is a massive park, two million hectares of wilderness more than 330km long and 200km wide, reaching from the Limpopo River and the Zimbabwe border in the north down to the Crocodile River in the south. As such, it covers more than 90% of South Africa's border with Mozambique. The park covers 14 different ecozones and supports 174 species of mammal, 500 species of bird, 114 reptile species, 49 species of fish and 39 species of amphibian.

The greatest concentration of animals is in the central and southern part of the reserve but the north, although often dismissed as monotonous mopani forest, has large herds of elephant and species such as the roan antelope, not often seen elsewhere. Large herds of elephant are often seen in the area around the rest camps at Letaba and Olifants (well, of course), and there are cheetah and lion as well.

The park has become one of the country's national heritage sites. It is easily accessible, with 2,624km of tarred and gravel roads, and you can drive in for a day or stay over in one of the 26 rest camps and lodges. Accommodation varies from relatively luxurious chalets to basic self-catering rondawels and there are also plenty of campsites. Some of the camps are mini cities complete with restaurants, garages and supermarkets; while some people hate this aspect, its tarred roads and mass-transit appeal strongly to others. Yet nowhere in southern Africa does game viewing in this variety come as cheaply as it does here. There are many private game reserves, most of which abut Kruger, and most of which charge well over R1,000 per person per night.

Getting there and away

Naturally, walking is not allowed outside the rest camps, unless it's with a ranger on an official walking trail (see *Getting around* on page 258).

Hitchhiking

Some travellers do the brave thing and hitch to the entrance of the park. Some of the rest camps – Skukuza, Orpen and Crocodile Bridge – are at, or close to, the park boundary and it is fairly easy to get a lift to them. Once there you could ask around to see if anyone is keen to take you along with them on their daily game drives. Offering to contribute towards petrol would help oil the wheels here.

Car hire
The easiest way would be to hire a car for a day or two. Although this might stretch the budget a little, it is worth saving yourself the hassle of hitching to the park and then trying to bum rides with other visitors.

Tours
Another way of getting into the park is to go on one of the tours run by the various backpackers in Nelspruit. There are various options, lasting from one to three days and some offer walking trails and night drives. Weigh up the pros and cons before deciding – you might see more (and pay more) with an organised group, or you might not. At least with your own vehicle you are completely independent of time and other people.

Train
The nearest stations to Kruger are Malelane, and Komatipoort where the daily Komati passenger train calls daily each way.

Malelane
Little station near the main southern entrance to Kruger. There's not much here other than a restaurant in train carriages. The *Komati* does stop here and it might be an option if you're heading for Kruger. Remember the transport hassles start *inside* Kruger.

Komatipoort
A quiet town on the banks of the Crocodile River, just 10km from Kruger and terminus for the Komati. It is more of a border town than anything else and, unless you are heading for Mozambique or Crocodile Bridge in the southeast section of Kruger, there isn't much point in going there.

Getting around
There are seven guided wilderness trails which cost around R800–1,000 per person. You are based in a bush camp and go out on day walks with an armed ranger. This is less of a trail and more of an exciting ecology lesson, learning about the bush and ecosystems. You will not get too close to the animals, yet the sightings you have will be magnificent, even heartstopping sometimes. All trails must be booked in advance through South African National Parks (tel: 012 343 1991; fax: 012 343 0905; email: reservations@parks-sa.co.za).

You can get to Kruger's front doorstep by train. Be warned, however, that you cannot just walk through the gates of the park: at some stage, unless you're doing a walking trail, you're going to have to get inside a vehicle. Hire cars are available at Skukuza, the largest camp in Kruger, and at Phalaborwa which is near Hoedspruit. You might try bumming a lift at the park gates, especially since entry is charged per person. However, once in the park, you can only

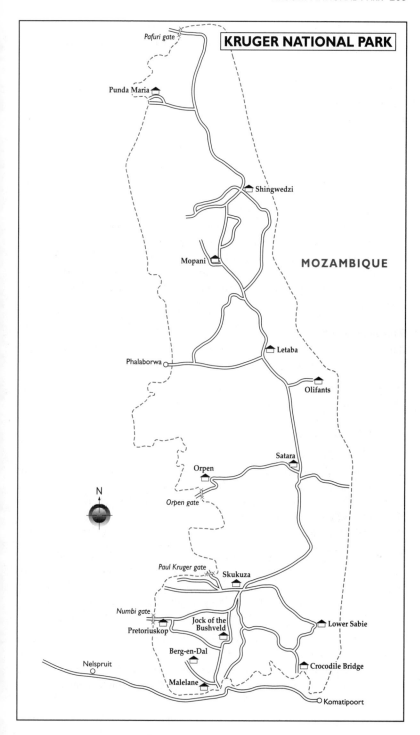

Pafuri gate

KRUGER NATIONAL PARK

Punda Maria

Shingwedzi

Mopani

MOZAMBIQUE

Phalaborwa

Letaba

Olifants

Satara

Orpen

Orpen gate

N

Paul Kruger gate

Skukuza

Numbi gate

Pretoriuskop

Jock of the
Bushveld

Lower Sabie

Berg-en-Dal

Nelspruit

Crocodile Bridge

Malelane

Komatipoort

hitch at the rest camps, and it's likely to be a frustrating experience. Cycling is not allowed mainly because you'd be such an easy target for a passing carnivore or irascible buffalo.

Accommodation
Where to stay
All the lodging is run by the state conservation department and is consequently a lot cheaper than the cheapest of the private reserves. All rooms have fridges and air conditioning and most have en suite bathrooms and kitchenettes. All units have a braai area outside. An en suite rondawel will cost R250–350 per night, depending on size and position. Campsites start at around R50 per tent site.

Warning
All overnight visitors have to stay in one of the camps and it is imperative that you reach your intended camp before the gates close, usually around sunset. Never leave your vehicle unless at a place where you are clearly permitted to. This is raw Africa: you are in the territory of many animals with whom interaction is usually painful for the human. Kruger, and the surrounding *lowveld*, is a malaria area so take precautions.

The rest camps
The rest camps alone would fill an entire book. What follows is a broad selection, starting in the south and working northwards.

Berg-en-Dal One of the nicer camps set among trees and bushes and blending well with the landscape. The area around the camp is good for spotting wild dog and white rhino and has a healthy population of leopard. Accommodation is in fully equipped three-bed chalets and cottages sleeping six in two bedrooms.

Lower Sabie A smaller camp which means it feels like you are in the bush. The surrounding country is grassland with marula trees and numerous waterholes. Game includes white rhino, elephant, lion, cheetah and large herds of buffalo. Accommodation is in five-bed cottages and huts with 1–5 beds. Some huts are not well equipped.

Skukuza This is the park's headquarters and is a veritable town complete with banks, supermarkets, an airport and car hire agencies and it certainly does not feel like wild Africa. Its advantages are its proximity to Nelspruit and the fact that you can more or less get anything you need here. But move on quickly – this is not why you came to the bush.

Satara The second biggest camp in the park but it has more personality than Skukuza. It is certainly more spread out. The area around the camp is excellent grazing and you will see plenty of antelope including eland, waterbuck, and possibly a rare sable, as well as giraffe and zebra. Lots of antelope means plenty of predators, especially lion. Accommodation is in cottages and 2–3 bed rondawels. Most of the latter are not well equipped.

Olifants This is a wonderful camp, set among old trees and perched on a hill overlooking the valley of the Olifants River far below. It is the only place I have seen a leopard in the wild, spotted from a lookout over the valley. Accommodation is 2–3 bed rondawels, some with kitchens.

Letaba A pleasant camp overlooking the Letaba River in the centre of the park. This is great elephant country. Accommodation is in cottages and 2–4 bed rondawels but not all of them have kitchens or bathrooms.

Mopani Situated towards the less travelled north of the park, this camp is the newest and one of the best-placed. The nearby dam is an animal magnet so it's definitely a spot where you can sit and watch the animals come to you. Accommodation is in large, fully equipped cottages.

Shingwedzi People who know about it love this camp for its rugged design and its remoteness. The game viewing is excellent, especially in the area of the camp itself. Accommodation is in two types of cottage, some thatched and others brick-and-tile. Ask for a cottage with kitchen and bathroom as some of the units do not have these vital things.

Bush camps There are a couple of lovely bush camps spread out through the park. These places are a lot less crowded and the facilities more basic (you will have to cook for yourself). Accommodation is mostly in 4-bed huts that tend to more expensive than the chalets and rondawels at the large rest camps, starting at R550 per night and rising sharply. If there are four of you, it might be worth looking into. For more details, ask at one of the larger rest camps or contact South African National Parks (tel: 012 343 1991 or fax: 012 343 0905).

Eating

The bigger camps all have restaurants where the food ranges from good to institutional, none of it very cheap. You will save a lot more money by cooking for yourself; just remember to stock up with supplies at a supermarket outside the park since those inside really only have basic stuff. While most of the accommodation is self-catering, not all the rondawels, for example, have kitchenettes and even those that do might not have cooking utensils. Find out when you book and take the necessary gear with you if you have to.

MOVING ON TO MOZAMBIQUE

The journey east is exciting as you feel like you are heading into Africa proper with every kilometre the train puts between you and Johannesburg. The transition from relative calm of South Africa to the vibrant chaos of Mozambique is somewhat shocking (see *Chapter 17*).

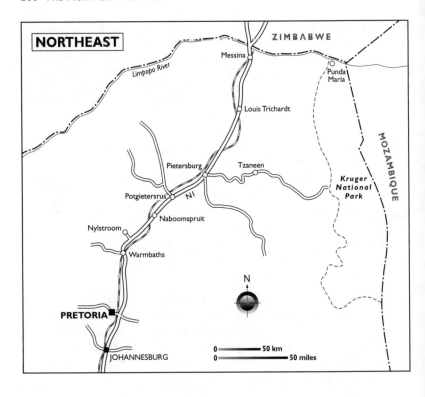

The Northern Province

The Great North is often overlooked by travellers. This might have something to do with South Africans' attitude towards it themselves, dismissing the province as a bit of a conservative backwater where repeated droughts have baked the soil as hard as concrete and wrecked the prospects for tourism. All of which shows what a little bit of bad and biased television reporting can do.

It is, in parts, spectacular country; flat, *highveld* plains broken by immense mountain ranges that give rise to magical places such as the Wolkberg and the deep, lush forests of Magoebaskloof, and a harsh land of red soil, covered with thorn trees. The Soutpansberg, a thickly forested mountain range which runs east–west, divides the *highveld* from the *lowveld*. The range is the traditional home of the Venda people, a small tribe descended from the Rozvi people in Zimbabwe. North of the Soutpansberg is *bushveld* country – mopani trees and baobabs stretching to the horizon.

This part of the country probably has one of the greatest proliferations of provincial and private game parks and nature reserves of anywhere in Africa, mostly carrying only soft-skinned game – antelope, giraffe, small predators – but there are some heavyweight Big Five parks as well. There are hiking trails in the mountains and wilderness trails in many of the nature reserves. The Wolkberg is a designated wilderness area where you can wander and camp at will among mountains and forests that the Venda say are enchanted.

HISTORY

Excavation in a chain of limestone caverns called the Makpansgat near Potgietersrus has shown that humans were living in the region well before the Early Stone Age. Then came the San whose legacy is the rock art that colours the walls of caves and overhangs throughout the region. From them too comes the story of the unmistakable baobabs, the 'upside-down tree', according to legend uprooted and cast back to earth by angry gods. After the San came the Venda, an offshoot of the Rozvi tribe, who wandered south across the Limpopo sometime in the 12th century and found a cool, fertile plateau in the Soutpansberg. They called the mountains Venda, a pleasant place, and settled there.

In the 16th century, a princess from the Karanga tribe in Zimbabwe fled from her enemies and settled in the huge cycad forests in the southeast. She and her descendents were said to possess rain magic which frightened off attackers during the great conflicts in the 19th century. Modjadji, the Rain Queen, a title which is still given today, and her people were left in peace. Today when the rain falls in the province, people still give thanks to Modjadji (see page 257).

In the southeast, the Pedi established their homeland in the mountainous country to the east and prospered under the wise leadership of a chief named Sukhukhune. When Mzilikkazi, 'The Great Road', came storming in from the south on his destructive path to Zimbabwe, the Pedi were one of the few tribes who escaped more or less intact.

The first advance parties of Voortrekkers reached the Soutpansberg in 1836. They were not to go much further north but instead turned east, hoping to find a route to the sea. The first party under Johannes van Rensburg were massacred in the bush. The second party, led by Louis Trichardt tentatively explored the lands to the north and then in 1837 set off east for Delagoa Bay. When they reached the *lowveld*, the trekkers died off one by one as they struggled through the hot, malarial territory. There were no survivors.

In 1847, another trekker leader, Hendrik Potgieter, arrived in the area and founded Zoutpansbergdorp, a trading post where farmers, hunters and missionaries crossed paths. The town became an ivory trading centre, but constant fighting and brawling made it an ungovernable place. In 1867, the Europeans abandoned the town and it was sacked and destroyed by the Venda. The tribe remained in control of the territory until as late as 1898 when the Transvaal Republic regained control. Then came the war that changed everything, although there was relatively little action in this part of the country.

Orientation
The region extends about 450km north from Pretoria to the Limpopo River, to the Botswana border in the west and the Kruger National Park in the east. The area includes the northern half of the Kruger National Park (see page 242).

When to go
The *highveld* areas experience the common South African summer and winter pattern: dry in the winter with mild days and icy nights and very hot in the summer with frequent afternoon thunderstorms. The *lowveld* area, north of the Soutpansberg and down near the Kruger Park, is mild in winter and fearsomely hot and humid in summer. The Magoebaskloof area is generally cool and often misty. The Soutpansberg and Wolkberg areas enjoy the usual mountain weather, mostly when you don't need it – thunderstorms in summer, very cold at altitude in winter and hot and wet the rest of the time.

GETTING THERE AND AWAY
The main N1 national road heads straight out of Pretoria and hardly kinks until it reaches the Zimbabwe border. It is regarded as one of the most dangerous roads in the country because of the high volume of traffic, much it unsafe minibuses being driven at ridiculous speed with too many people on board. If you are driving, take care – in some places, the road is no more than two lanes wide with a gravel shoulder.

Train

Two trains run daily in each direction between Johannesburg, via Pretoria, to the copper mining town of Messina, 17km short of the Zimbabwe border: the *Bosvelder* (bushvelder) and the *Doily*, both overnight trains. The latter is aimed at traders heading from and to Zimbabwe.

The *Bosvelder* overnight, all-class sleeper: **Northbound** Departs Johannesburg at 18.50; arrives Pretoria 20.09; arrives Messina 10.16. **Southbound** Departs Messina 14.45; arrives Pretoria 03.59; arrives Johannesburg 05.30.
The *Doily* **Northbound** Departs Johannesburg 18.07; arrives Pretoria 19.17; arrives Messina 09.26. **Southbound** Departs Messina 17.00; arrives Pretoria 07.02; arrives Johannesburg 08.45.

There is little to choose between either train except perhaps the timings. The *Doily* runs later in both directions which is a bonus in winter. The southbound *Bosvelder* runs through a landscape of bushveld and baobab trees in the late afternoon before tacking the dramatic pass through the Soutpansberg.

The southbound *Doily* is a colourful train, carrying traders from Zimbabwe and further north who generally have with them a staggering array of curios and goods to sell in South Africa. At the end of the month, matrons with heavy carrier bags of doilies (decorative lace mats) virtually commandeer the train at Beit Bridge, heading for the flea-markets of Johannesburg. There are Zambians with malachite chess sets and Zairoise with carved hardwood masks. Sellers will roam the train, trying to flog their goods. Some of the stuff is beautiful, some ugly beyond belief. Of the two trains, the *Doily* is much more of a genuine African rail experience. It's an overnight service with 2nd and Economy class accommodation only and a catering car which serves light take-away meals.

Bus

Translux (tel: 011 774 3333) runs buses daily between Pietersburg and Johannesburg. Other bus companies on the route are North Link Tours (tel: 015 291 1867) and North Star City Bus (tel: 083 250 4921).

Minibus

Minibus taxis also run between Johannesburg, Pretoria, and Messina; if you use them, choose your bus with care and do not be bullied by the touts.

WARMBATHS

The first town of any size after Pretoria, Warmbaths is named after the hot springs which have made the town famous. The spa is reckoned to be the best in the world after the one in Baden Baden but I've heard other spa resorts make this claim too. Funny how none of them claim to be *better* than Baden-Baden, though.

Things to see and do

Next to the spa is the **Warmbaths Nature Reserve** (tel: (014) 736-2200) which has guided walks and game drives, horse-trails.

The town is also close to **Mabalingwe Game Reserve** (tel: 014 736 9000), a Big Five park with budget accommodation for backpackers. It's not the biggest game park you'll ever visit but for ease of access it is hard to beat.

Game drives (R55), night drives (R50) and guided trails (R35) are offered. The reserve is 50km from town on the R516 to Thabazimbi. For R50 (return), they will pick you up from the petrol station at the Warmbaths turnoff on the N1.

Accommodation
4-bed wooden cabins (R45 per person) set among trees.

PIETERSBURG
The provincial capital is a fairly large but mellow city. It earned its city status in 1992 – before then it was just a big town and it's debatable whether anyone noticed. There are not many diversions here but it is a useful centre for banking, car hire and doing the general admin that comes with travel.

Tourist information
This is handled by the Pietersburg Marketing Company (tel: 015 290 2009).

Getting there and away
Car hire
The cheapest place to get a car is Tempest (tel: 0800 031666). The major agencies also have offices here and they often have weekend or three-day specials.

Things to see and do
One place worth visiting is **the Bakoni Malapa Northern Sotho Open-air Museum**, 8km from town on the road to Chuniespoort. The museum shows the both the traditional and modern lifestyle of the Bakoni people, an offshoot of the northern Sotho.

While you're here, you should also see the **Hugh Exton Photographic Museum** (tel: 015 290 2010), which displays a history of the town based around the 23,000 glass negatives taken by photographer Exton during the first 50 years of the town's history. As an example of an ongoing photo essay, it is unsurpassed.

The **Pietersburg Museum** (tel: 015 290 2182) depicts the history of the city and its surroundings back to the Stone Age. The building itself is wonderful, all steep tin roof, cool verandas and a gorgeous clock tower.

The **Art Museum** (tel: 015 290 2177) is regarded as the finest art collection outside of the major metropolitan centres.

INTO THE GREAT, WIDE OPEN
The prime attraction of the region are the game parks and the wildernesses and hiking trails. There are plenty of the former scattered about the province, although most of them are near to one or other of the small towns that dot the N1 and railway corridor.

There are too many reserves to describe in full. Most of the smaller nature reserves are well stocked with antelope, zebra, wildebeest, giraffe and smaller mammals. Others may have resident rhino and even buffalo, elephant, lion and leopard. The following is a list of some of the reserves closest to the line of rail.

Getting there could be a problem late at night. Your best option is to call in advance and have someone meet you at the station. Alternatively, hire a car in Pietersburg and spend a few days touring the region.

Lapalala Wilderness

Lapalala (tel: 011 453 7645; fax: 011 453 7649) is famous around the world for running nature awareness programmes for children from all over the planet. If you want to learn about the *bushveld*, this is the place to do it.

The reserve is situated in the Waterberg Mountains, west of Potgietersrus. Game includes black and white rhino and 'plains game' – zebra and various species of antelope. There are trails led by experienced guides.

Getting there and away

Getting there without a car will require some patience. The reserve is about 32km west along the R520 from Naboomspruit. Hitching is possible but expect to spend time with your thumb in the air.

Accommodation

There are ten fully equipped self-catering camps which can sleep 2–10 people. Prices start at R92 per person in an eight-bed hut, rising to R108 per person in a two-bed hut; at Kolobe Camp, rates start at R165 per person per night. Staying at the fully catered Rhino Camp costs R475 per person per night and includes game drives. You can get a cheaper rate if you go during the week.

Ben Lavin Nature Reserve

Ben Lavin (tel: 015 516-4534) is a beautiful reserve 12km east of Louis Trichardt. Game includes giraffe, zebra, warthog and wildebeest. Black-backed jackals howl at night to make for a truly soulful bush experience. You can walk freely around the reserve on a network of hiking paths. I have a soft spot for this place as it's come a long way against tough odds.

The reserve was also the pioneering centre responsible for reintroducing the red-billed oxpecker to the region. Oxpeckers, those birds you see clinging fiercely to the flanks of big animals, are vital to the well-being of many mammals, including rhino, buffalo, various antelope and common, or pasture, cattle, since they clean the animals of disease-bearing ticks. But the birds had been wiped out in most of South Africa's farmland because farmers were dipping their cattle in poisonous dips, the birds were still eating the ticks and being poisoned. A local farmer who was part of the Ben Lavin management committee spent years trying to get local farmers to change their dips, with some success. The birds were reintroduced in the late 1980s and have thrived since.

Getting there and away

Even without your own transport, the reserve is fairly easy to get to. Daily trains all stop in Louis Trichardt from where you can hitch, catch a minibus taxi from outside the station, cycle or, of you are feeling strong, walk.

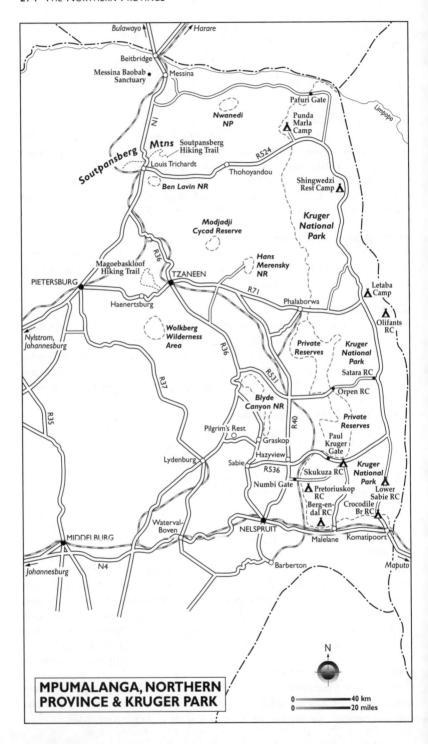

MPUMALANGA, NORTHERN
PROVINCE & KRUGER PARK

Accommodation

There are fully equipped self-catering 3-bed cottages for R230 per cottage. Meals are available but the joy of this place is in eating your own food under the night sky.

Other parks and reserves

Potgietersrus Nature Reserve and Game Breeding Centre Tel: 0154 491-4314. Divided by the railway line, the breeding centre boasts exotic mammals like Madagascan lemurs and Asian hog deer as well as indigenous animals such as rhino, sable and herds of antelope. There is a 3km walking trail.

Nylsvley Nature Reserve Tel: 014 743-1074. The province's biggest reserve, Nylsvley, is 20km south of Naboomspruit. Its main attraction is its prolific birdlife, drawn by the 4,000ha of wetland.

Percy Fyfe Nature Reserve Tel: 012 346-3550/1/2. This famous reserve, 35km north of Potgietersrus, has walking and mountain biking trails. Difficult to get to without transport, though.

Pietersburg Game Reserve Tel: 0152 295-2011. Large game reserve just south of the town, boasting 21 species of game including white rhino, eland, springbok (the national animal and one facing difficult times) and the amazing gemsbok (oryx). Walking trails.

Messina Nature Reserve Tel: 01553 3235. Famous for its baobab trees, around 12,000 of which grow in the reserve. The Bushmen believe these trees grow upside down, having been thrown down in anger from heaven. Game includes sable antelope and giraffe. Walking trails may be arranged.

THE WOLKBERG WILDERNESS AREA

Rider Haggard is said to have looked down into the ghost-filled mists of a valley in the Wolkbergs and been inspired to write *She*. The deeply incised river valleys and sculpted ridges of the Wolkberg wilderness also had the same effect on John Buchan, creator of *Prester John*. There must be something about the place – I was inspired enough to include it in this travel guide, but not to suggest for a second that this book is a literary masterpiece.

True mountain wildernesses are rare in this part of the country so the Wolkberg part of the northern Drakensbergs is a welcome change to the monotony of the *highveld*. The rugged terrain has defied development and settlement which cannot be said for the much of the rest of the province. The Wolkberg is no place for softies. Its rugged tracks and paths are often barely visible especially in summer when the grass is thick and luscious, and the various rivers, swollen with summer rain, complicate route finding even more.

Tourist information

The wilderness area is managed by the Forestry Department (tel: 015 276 1303).

Getting there and away

The nearest town is Haenertsburg on the R71 between Pietersburg and Tzaneen and there are plenty of minibus taxis between the two towns if you do not have your own wheels. Hitching to the wilderness area is a double edged sword – the road from Haenertsburg doesn't go anywhere else and traffic is scarce.

Things to see and do

It is a tremendously rewarding place. You may pitch your tent anywhere – always obeying the tenets of minimum impact camping – but there are some favourite spots such as by the **Three Waterfalls** which is one hour's hike from Serala Forest Station, and anywhere in the Lost Forest. Buy your permits (R25 per person) at the forest station before setting off (tel: 015 276 1303). There is a basic campsite at the forest station which is really there to help hikers who arrive late at night but you could set up camp there and do day hikes into the wilderness.

MAGOEBASKLOOF
Tzaneen

This busy little town basks in a valley surrounded by forest-covered hills. It is a pretty enough town, surviving on forestry and agriculture but there is not a lot to do on a Saturday night, and most out-of-towners come for the hiking.

Accommodation

When you've done the nearby trails or spent time getting lost in the Wolkbergs, it's nice to rest up for a day in the area and nurse those pleasantly aching calves rather than rushing off elsewhere. Luckily, Tzaneen now has two backpackers to choose from.

Satvik Backpackers Satvik Farm, George's Valley; tel: 015 307 3920; email: satvik@pixie.co.za. Cottage R250, double R140, dorm R45, camping R20. Cottages on the edge of a big farm dam. Meals available but ask early. They are 2km from Tzaneen on the R71 to Pietersburg.

Arbor Park Lodge 30 Geelhout St, Arbor Park; tel: 015 307 1831; email: arborpark@mweb.co.za. Double R295 including breakfast, dorm R50. Jacked-up and clean backpackers out in the suburbs (which in this place is not that far). They offer all kinds of day trips including hiking and canoeing.

Things to see and do

The nearby **Dokolewa** and **Grootbosch trails** meander through plantations and natural forests in the hills above Tzaneen. The Dokolewa is arguably the nicer of the two and it also has proper hiking huts as opposed to the simple lean-to shelters of the other. The route takes you through some of the biggest remaining tracts of indigenous forest left in the country, down into misty valleys and along cool forest streams. Vines hang in ropes from tall trees and the vegetation is lush and thick.

On misty days you might find yourself looking over your shoulder as you wander down the quiet paths of the dense **Magoebaskloof Forest**, named

MODJADJI, THE RAIN QUEEN

In the 16th century, a refugee princess from the Karanga tribe in Zimbabwe found shelter in the deep valley of the Molotutse, forming the nucleus of the Lobedu people and marking the beginning of the rule of Modjadji, the Rain Queen. The princess brought with her the rain-making magic of her family and she used its power to keep her enemies far away from the sanctuary she and her followers had chosen.

Rain is the most important thing in a dry world like this. Much of the land is barely arable and relentless droughts have stalked the land all through South Africa's history. The princess's powers were widely known, even as far away as Swaziland to the southeast, and she and her descendents used them to great effect: no-one dared make trouble with Modjadji in case she withheld the life-giving rain.

This fear resulted in the isolation of the Lobedu people, something which successive queens wisely made little effort to dispel. When the terrifying upheaval – the Mfecane or 'forced migration' – was taking place among the tribes of southern Africa, the Lobedu were left alone while elsewhere whole tribes were subjugated or wiped out.

Modjadji's secrets have never been revealed: when rain falls in the province, people still give thanks to her.

Down in the very beautiful Mooketsi Valley, there is a small museum dedicated to Modjadji. The museum itself is set next to an immense cycad reserve, the world's largest concentration of a single species of these strange plants. The cycads in the reserve, the tallest in Africa with stems up to 10m high, have enjoyed the protection of the Rain Queens of the Lobedu for hundreds of years.

after the chief of the Tlou, a Sotho clan. In 1894, the Transvaal Republic government sent a punitive commando to pit down the restive tribes in the area. Makgoba and his people fled to the sanctuary of the forests, chased by an 6,500-strong army made up mostly of Swazi warriors fighting for the Pretoria regime (not the last time something like this would happen). Two Tlou women were caught; one was killed and the other tortured, and Makgoba was flushed from his hiding place. He accepted the Swazi challenge of a single combat contest with the Swazi leader and lost, and his severed head was taken to the commando leader in support of the Swazis' bounty claim.

The forests were left alone for a long time after that bloody episode until much of the land was bought for commercial forestry. Much of the forest (although not enough) has been preserved. To the lasting gratitude of hikers everywhere, the Dokolewa trail has been rerouted to traverse less pine plantation and more forest, a welcome sign that the forestry department is taking its stewardship seriously.

The Dokolewa trail costs R47 per person per day. Huts are fully equipped and there are cold showers for the brave. The trail is managed by Safcol (tel: 012 481 3615; email: ecotours@safcol.co.za).

VENDA

Venda once had the farce of 'independence' thrust on it by the Pretoria government back in the 1980s and it still shows the scars of the experiment. Much of the land has been trashed by goats and unviable farming and yet the region retains a feeling of pure Africa about it. This is reflected in the villages that dot the slopes of the Soutpansbergs, rock art sites and the mysterious spiritual sites of Lake Funduduzi and Lwamondo Kop, giant cycads and the deep gorge on the Mutale River.

Things to see and do

The dominant feature of the area are the Soutpansberg (Salt Pan) Mountains, named for a large salt lake at the western end of the range. The range runs east to west and is the barrier between the *highveld* and *lowveld*. The **Soutpansberg Trail**, an 80km, 5-day hiking trail traverses the range, twisting along through natural forest and bushveld. It is regarded as one of the country's toughest, although shorter options are available. Its attractions are the forests which hide a prolific number of birds species and vervet monkeys, as well as the very African landscape – you can look out over valleys at Venda villages hiding in the mountain mists.

The trail starts at Hanglip Forestry station just outside Louis Trichardt and runs directly east, which raises the only problem – getting back. You should be able to hitch or even get a minibus taxi but check with the rangers at the forest station to see if they can't 'arrange' something for you. Shorter options are possible. The trail costs R30 per person per day. It is popular so you need to book through Safcol central reservations (tel: 012 418 3615; email: ecotours@safcol.co.za).

ON TO ZIMBABWE

Messina

This is a copper mining town which has found a new lease of life now that the borders between Zimbabwe and South Africa have opened up fully. It is not quite at the border and it has escaped much of the fluidity that pervades border towns the world over. Unfortunately, that doesn't mean there's a lot to do here – it's really just a place to change money and stock up on a few travel essentials before heading over the border.

There are plenty of minibus taxis from town to the border which makes hitching difficult because every one of them will stop and try and pick you up. The fare is a mere R10 between the border post and town. Once you've cleared South African immigration and customs, you cross the Limpopo River on an impressive bridge and enter the somnambulance of Zimbabwean customs. From here there are plenty of buses and taxis north to Bulawayo and Harare. One legendary company to look out for is Shu Shine Bus Services who charge Z$100 (about R15) per person to take you in relative comfort to Bulawayo from the border. You could also get to Rutenga and catch daily train to Bulawayo although late timings might make this a somewhat unattractive journey for some travellers.

The Free State

A reputation for being nothing more than thousands of hectares of maize has somewhat sullied the Free State's chances of making it as a tourist destination. It is mostly flat but its eastern boundary, along the Lesotho border, is in the foothills of the Maluti Mountains, with dramatic sandstone outcrops, caves with San rock art and some good hiking. The eastern Free State provides the easiest access to Lesotho (see page 284).

The province could also witness the next big boom in tourism for under these sandstone cliffs lurk *sangomas* (traditional healers), horseriders, fishermen, hippies, dinosaur hunters, B&B owners, farmers who talk tourism rather than maize and even a couple of guys who are planning to

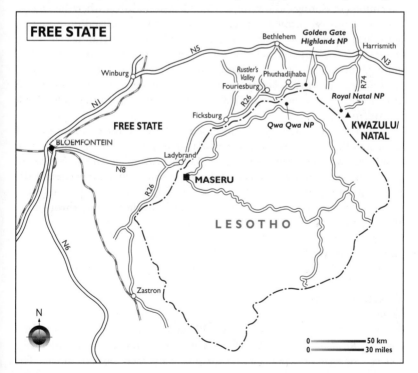

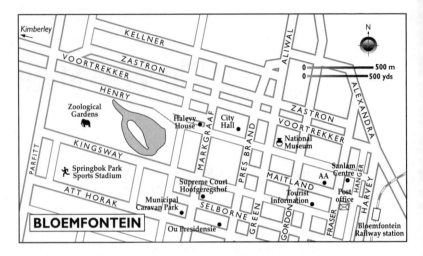

reopen the railway that runs down the foot of the Malutis. As long as ecotourism is expected to boost the South African economy, the people here will be hatching clever tourism plans.

BLOEMFONTEIN

Both the provincial capital as well as the country's judicial capital, Bloemfontein (spring of flowers) was founded around 1854 when the Orange Free State was proclaimed a republic. Then it was just a handful of houses, apparently named in memory of 'Bloem', a local farmer's favourite cow which jumped a fence and got eaten by a lion. There are no lions here any more, although the zoo has 'liger', a cross between a lion and a tiger.

Hobbit creator J R R Tolkien was born here in 1892, and jaded locals will tell you there can be no better place than Bloemfontein to nurture a fertile, or bizarre, imagination.

Bloemfontein is literally in the middle of the country, quite hot and quite mellow. Its natural beauty lies in its tree-lined streets and the bulk of Naval Hill which dominates the town. For the Afrikaners, it's an important city, a cultural, historical and soulful place. In the 19th century, it was the heart and soul of the Orange Free State Republic and its occupation by the British in the middle of the Anglo–Boer War sent shockwaves through the Boer nation.

Tourist information

For tourist information, tel: 051 405 8489.

Getting there

Train

Four passenger trains pass through Bloemfontein – the daily *Algoa* and *Amatola*, the *Diamond Express*, which starts its journey here, and the *Trans Oranje* so it's easy to spend a day or three here and then move on at will. The

Diamond Express runs daily to Kimberley, giving you a connection to the *Trans Karoo* if you want to head for Cape Town.

Bus
Bloemfontein is bypassed by the main N1 national road and Translux, Greyhound and Intercape buses stop here. Phone the Cape Town or Johannesburg bureaux for ticketing and timetable information.

Accommodation
Taffy's Backpackers 18 Louis Botha St; tel: 051 31 4533. Double R40 per person, dorm R30, camping R25. Bikes for hire so you can get around this very flat town at will. The fifth night is free.

Things to see and do
Buildings worth seeing include the **Old Residency** (where the republic's presidents used to live) on President Brand Street, the **Old Raadsaal** (government assembly) with its thatched roof and dung floors, the Greek/Renaissance inspired **Fourth Raadsaal** and the Herbert Baker-built **Anglican Cathedral** on St George's Street.

There is an **Anglo–Boer War Museum** on Monument Road, near the fairly sobering **National Women's Memorial** which commemorates the 27,000 Boer women and children who died in concentration camps during the war. The 40m-high sandstone obelisk towers over statues of two women, one holding a dying baby, the other looking out over the plains of the Free State. The ashes of British activist Emily Hobhouse, who alerted the outside world to the existence of the camps, are buried at the foot of the monument.

IN THE FOOTHILLS OF THE MALUTIS
The eastern Free State with its beautiful sandstone landscapes is the most compelling reason to come here. Breaking up the flat monotony of the maize fields are isolated flat-topped mountains and strangely sculpted balancing rocks and lazy rivers with willow trees lining their banks. There are caves in the mountains where the walls are covered in cave art, sometimes defaced with Xhosa graffiti, dating back to the 17th century. (Does that qualify as an attraction?). The hills and caves gave shelter to the Sotho people during the Mfecane (the great crushing), when the expansion of the Zulu empire sent ripples throughout the country. With the fields burned and the granaries looted, some clans turned to cannibalism, and no-one was safe. The time is brilliantly captured in Dr Peter Becker's *Hill of Destiny*, the story of the rise of Moshesh, the legendary leader of the Sotho people.

Golden Gate National Park
This is one of the country's oldest parks, proclaimed in 1963 to conserve around 5,000ha of sandstone country. Antelope species have thrived and hikers will see plenty of eland, springbok, red hartebeest, blesbok, zebra and wildebeest.

The park is also a sanctuary for the rare bearded vulture, the lammergeyer, which breeds on the cliffs. Lammergeyer – loosely translated, the name means lamb-getter because of the bird's predilection for sheep – were almost extinct when the park was proclaimed. Another rare bird that occurs in the park is the bald ibis, along with jackal buzzards, black eagles and blue cranes, which, when they were still South Africa's national bird, were stamped on to every five cent piece.

Things to see and do

The 2-day **Rhebok trail** traverses the park, allowing you to get up into the high country. Accommodation is in a basic hiker's hut.

There is budget accommodation in the form of 2-room bungalows with double and single beds and camping is permitted at Glen Reenen rest camp. The main Brandwag camp is quite large and a bit soulless. For bookings, tel: 058 256 1471; fax: 058 256 1475 or contact the main national parks office in Pretoria (tel: 012 343 1991; email: reservations@parks.co.za).

QWA-QWA NATIONAL PARK

The 22,000ha Qwa-Qwa park shares a boundary with Golden Gate but offers an altogether different experience. The scenery is similar – all sandstone outcrops and densely wooded valleys where white stinkwood, yellowwood and wild olive trees grow – but the park has the added attraction of a Basotho Cultural Village which depicts the history and culture of the South Sotho people. How much you enjoy it depends on how you feel about living museums. It is a good insight into Sotho life and the *ngaka* (traditional healer) will explain the uses of various herbs and plants.

Things to see and do

The **Avondrus trail** is a 2-day, 2-night circular trail with an overnight in a simple hut and there is also a 2-day horse trail in the park. Horseback is a good vantage point for game spotting – you sit up high and the game doesn't seem to take much notice. Accommodation is in a basic overnight hut. No riding experience is necessary Some living museums are tacky but not this one. The trail costs R140 per person. For QwaQwa bookings and information contact Free State Eco-Tourism, tel: 058 713 4415 or 721 0300; fax: 058 713 4342 or 721 0304.

RUSTLERS VALLEY

It's difficult to come up with a decent description of this place but 'Free State eco-village' comes closest. It lies in the shelter of a deep, quiet valley, a place so secluded that cattle thieves used to hide their trophies there. The cattle rustling has stopped and the valley is now basically a new-age community where a bunch of very dedicated people are looking for alternatives to modern living, and making them work. For years, Rustlers has also been the site of an annual music festival – always over the Easter weekend – which has earned it a loyal following of the global trance community as well as assorted other travellers and backpackers.

The valley is recovering from a massive fire that destroyed many of the buildings but what has emerged is a calm retreat with a much mellower attitude than it had in the past.

Accommodation is in little cottages, costing upwards of R60 per person per day, including breakfast. Self-catering is cheaper and are welcome to camp, or sleep out in the open or do whatever pleases you, as long as no attitude is involved. For information, tel: 051 923 939 or email: wemad@rustlers.co.za.

There are drumming workshops, sweat lodges every full moon, sound therapy courses and Ayahuasca workshops, as well as world music festivals on the summer solstice and spring and autumn equinoxes. There is a two-day hiking trail which circles the entire valley with an overnight stop in a cave.

ZASTRON

The real reason for going to Zastron, an otherwise unremarkable town which nestles down in the far southeast corner of Free State province, is to see its exquisite Bushman paintings. The caves in the surrounding sandstone hills were natural galleries and strongholds for the Bushmen. The Hoffman Cave is one of the best galleries, containing a perfectly preserved 4.5m long and 1.5m wide frieze depicting Bushmen hunting eland, the large, magnificent antelope which figures in so much of their work.

The Zastron train runs on the last weekend of the month, leaving Johannesburg on Friday night and returning on Sunday. Accommodation in Zastron is limited to the municipal campsite.

BETHLEHEM

Bethlehem was founded in 1864 and is a nice Free State town with willow trees lining the banks of the Jordaan River (named by Voortrekkers as their 'River

THE ZASTRON TRAIN

The Zastron train from Johannesburg is one of the those little railway weirdnessses. It is a train which reflects a sadder side of South African life, aimed at workers in Johannesburg travelling to visit their families down in the northeastern Cape and southern Lesotho once a month. The migrant labour system is one of apartheid's echoes. Black people were banished to their so-called 'homelands', often pieces of wasted, dry earth which they had never seen in their lives, most of which had been granted 'independence' by Pretoria and having a puppet 'government' in power.

Meanwhile, cheap labour was still needed in South Africa's mines and factories, most of which were in the rich Pretoria–Johannesburg–Vereeniging triangle, and so the migrant labour classes were created. Workers could get temporary residence in Johannesburg but their families had to stay behind in the homelands. At month end, pay day, special trains would be laid on to take workers back to their families. The Zastron train is a reminder of this.

Jordan') and wide, quiet streets. Life barely ticks over here and there's not a lot to do. It is a good place to explore the eastern part of the Free State. The scenery – sandstone outcrops and buttresses – is dramatic and the area's caves are covered in Bushman paintings. It's easily one of the most beautiful parts of the country, especially in the green of mid-summer. It gets very cold in winter, though.

Tourist information
Tourist office Tel: 058 303 5732

Things to see and do
The buildings made from sandstone are lovely; they include the **Magistrate's Office** on Louw St and the **Nederlands Gereformeerde Moederkerk** around which the town was built.

Bethlehem's main attraction is the **Sandstone Steam Railroad**, a private operation which is hoping to take over the Bethlehem–Bloemfontein railway line and begin running passenger and freight trains. Progress has been slow as the state railway operator bickers over the fine print. Hopefully by the time you read this, the Sandstone will be properly in business, not least of all because the region needs regular passenger trains (tel: 011 805 3237; web: www.sandstonerail.co.za).

HARRISMITH
Harrismith, at the foothills of the northern part of the Drakensbergs, is better known as a halfway point on the main road between Johannesburg and Durban. Named after the colourful Cape governor Sir Harry Smith, it is a pleasant but unexciting town. It last boomed during the Kimberley diamond rush in the early 1870s, becoming a staging point on the transport route. Now its coffers are partly filled by the hordes of motorists who pass through during school holidays on their way to the coast and back.

Things to see and do
Most of the town's attractions centre around the flat-topped mountain which dominates it. The **Harrismith Wildflower Gardens**, containing about 1,000 species of plants found in the Drakensbergs, are at the foot of the mountain, about 5km out of town. The nearby **Mount Everest Game Reserve** covers about 1,000ha of mountainside, stocking, among other species, a couple of rhino. Horses or 4x4 vehicles are available for hire. A number of bolted sport climbing routes have been opened on the Everest's impressive cliffs.

HEADING INTO LESOTHO
Lesotho is an off-the-beaten track destination. The overriding features of this tiny country, home of the Basotho people, are hills and mountains. A British protectorate until 1966, when it was granted full independence, Lesotho has had a bit of a rough time of late. An army-backed coup in 1998 resulted in an invasion by the South African army, just like they used to do in the bad old

days when chasing ANC guerrillas, except this time the South Africans ran into unexpectedly stiff resistance. All is now quiet on the eastern front, and Lesotho needs tourist revenues more than ever before.

The country earns most of its foreign exchange by selling water to South Africa and supplying cheap labour to its gold mines. But, as in the rest of the region, tourism has the greatest potential for job creation.

Tourist information

You do not need a visa for Lesotho if staying less than 30 days but you will need a multiple entry visa to get back into South Africa.

Pony trekking

The country's finest attraction is pony trekking. Riding tough-spirited Basotho ponies, you can head into the soaring Maluti Mountains, ambling from village to village where the locals are eager to welcome you as a guest.

Journeying by horse is undoubtedly the best way to see the country – there are few villages or fences and fewer roads – and the high plateau sits on top of the world creating an incredible feeling of space. Up, here the few villages compete for a foothold on the slopes with tiny vegetable gardens and cacti clinging to the ledges.

The small, fearless Basotho pony is known for its sure-footedness and endurance, essential qualities as you will see. No riding experience is necessary – the pony takes care of business while you gorge yourself on peaks, shimmering rivers and deep canyons. You can get some decent fly-fishing in as well. Get off and walk when you get a sore backside, which will happen, make no mistake, and let the scruffy, smiling kids escort you.

Accommodation is in spotlessly clean huts, built for the trailists and equipped with an extraordinarily full range of kitchen utensils. Schedules are flexible so you can dawdle as long as you wish to. The community-run treks are organised by Malealea Lodge (tel: 051 447 3200; email: malealea@mweb.co.za; web: www.malealea.co.

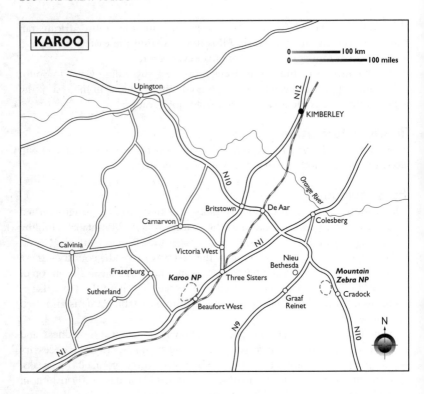

The Great Karoo

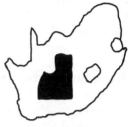

Years and years I've trekked across it,
Ridden back and fore,
Till the silence and the glamour
Ruled me to the core;
No man ever knew it better,
None could love it more.

Percival Gibbon

The Karoo, the great thirstland, is my favourite part of the whole country. To some people, it is a featureless landscape to be crossed as fast as possible on the long drive from the *highveld* to the Cape. For me, it is a magical place where the late afternoon sun turns the land into shadows in the valleys and hollows and wide, clear horizons that become sharply etched in fiery sunsets. Its appeal is heightened by its rich fossil finds which show that the Karoo was once covered by lakes and swamps and was a haven for all kinds of creatures before the water dried up.

The Karoo is a vast and moody semi-desert, a land of wide, sunbaked wastes broken by sills of ancient rock and distinctive conical koppies. It is genuine big sky country, blanketed with Karoo grass and scrubby bush and dotted with tough sheep. In summer, the midday heat is bludgeoning and yet nights are sharp and cold, and well below freezing in winter.

The San name for the place means 'great thirst' and the scarcity of surface water frightened off most people; the only people who came this way were hunters and missionaries, and eventually the Voortrekkers and their great oxwagon trains. But it is not completely arid – the dry river beds fill briefly with water in the short rainy season and the water sinks into the ground. The invention of the windpump quite literally altered the landscape forever. The underground water was tapped by drillers and the plaintive creaking of windpumps sucking water up from deep boreholes is one of few sounds that disturbs the immense silence of this place.

With water supplies tentatively secured, settlements began springing up all over the Karoo. Most were farming towns, little oases of Victorian houses with tin roofs and cool verandas looking on to wide, tree-lined streets, surviving off the largesse of sheep farming. But travellers came here too, drawn by the clear, crisp air and its magnificent loneliness. It captivated writers and artists, many of whom arrived and stayed. Olive Schreiner, author of *Story of an African Farm*, never left: she is buried in a tomb on a high mountain overlooking the vast spaces. The little town of Prince Albert has been revived as artists snapped up the cheap Victorian houses and turned the place into a colony. The same is happening at Nieu Bethesda, an exquisite village at the eastern edge of the Karoo, as people give up their rat race lives in the cities and buy an acre or two of desert peace.

Orientation

The Karoo is a huge dry space, stretching from the edge of the *highveld* grasslands and savannas, south and west almost to the sea and is contained only by the high mountain ranges that divide the fertile coastal plain from the hot, dry interior. The N1 national road and the main Cape Town–Johannesburg railway line bisect it along a southwest–northeast axis.

Travelling in the Great Karoo

There are dozens of cute and pleasant dorpies all over the Karoo but I have limited the scope of this guide to a couple of places, namely Kimberley, which is the logical jumping off point, Colesberg, Nieu Bethesda, Graaff Reinet, Cradock and Beaufort West, based on the attractions in or near the towns. The whole region is worth a guide on its own.

When to go

Avoiding rain is not really a problem as the Karoo averages 360 days of sunshine a year. Summers are violently hot although nights are much cooler, while winter days are usually mild but with bitter nights.

GETTING THERE AND AWAY

The region is huge and you really need your own wheels to explore it properly. However, there are trains and buses on the main arterial routes and a bicycle exploration of some of the backroads would be a marvellous way of travelling.

Train
Train information
Cape Town Tel: 021 449 3871; Johannesburg Tel: 011 773 2944

A good number of passenger trains cross the Karoo (mostly at night, which is a pity) and with careful planning you could get to most of the areas described in this chapter relatively easily. The timetables take up whole pages, so only arrival times in key Karoo towns are given.

Trans Karoo Overnight sleeper express between Pretoria, Johannesburg with Cape Town, running via Kimberley. This is the only train which covers the complete distance between the *highveld* and Cape Town. Southbound: arrives Kimberley 20.30; arrives Beaufort West 04.23. Northbound: arrives Beaufort West 18.05; arrives Kimberley 01.53.

Diamond Express Overnight service linking Pretoria and Johannesburg with Bloemfontein, via Kimberley. Runs daily except Saturdays. Southbound 06.00. Northbound: arrives Kimberley 19.50.

Trans Oranje Weekly service between Durban and Cape Town, via Kimberley. Takes two nights/one day. Westbound: arrives Kimberley 12.37; arrives Beaufort West 20.37. Eastbound: arrives Beaufort West 03.31; arrives Kimberley 11.13.

Algoa Express Daily overnight service between Port Elizabeth and Johannesburg, running via Cradock and Colesberg. Southbound: arrives Colesberg 01.32; arrives Cradock 04.43. Northbound: arrives Cradock 19.01; arrives Colesberg 22.29.

East London–Cape Town A twice-weekly overnight service which runs via De Aar. It's one of few trains that stops in Beaufort West at a decent hour. Westbound: arrives Colesberg 00.46; arrives De Aar 03.40; arrives Beaufort West 07.44. Eastbound: arrives Beaufort West 19.09; arrives De Aar 22.59; arrives Colesberg 02.45.

The Taxi Daily service between Mafikeng and Kimberley. All classes. Southbound: departs Mafikeng 07.00; arrives Kimberley 16.00. Northbound: departs Kimberley 06.57; arrives Mafikeng 16.26.

Johannesburg–Kimberley via Mafikeng Weekly overnight service, leaving Johannesburg on Friday, returning on Sunday. Southbound: departs Johannesburg 19.00 (Friday); arrives Mafikeng 01.02; arrives Kimberley 10.02. Northbound: departs Kimberley 15.30 (Sunday); arrives Mafikeng 22.49; arrives Johannesburg 05.28.

Fares

Johannesburg–Kimberley 1st R135, 2nd R110; Cape Town–Beaufort West 1st R135, 2nd R110; Port Elizabeth–Cradock 1st R135, 2nd R110; Port Elizabeth–Colesberg 1st R135, 2nd R110.

Bus

Translux (tel: 021 405 3333), Intercape Mainliner (tel: 021 386 4400) and Greyhound (tel: 021 418 4312) all operate buses on the main N1; Intercape also operates a service via Upington in the Northern Cape.

Cycling

The quiet roads are an absolute blessing for cyclists and you could crank along for days without worrying about what's coming up behind you. Combining bike and train travel is a good way of unlocking the Karoo's secrets.

Hitchhiking

Traffic dwindles considerably once you head away from the main N1 or N12 arteries. The backroads of the Karoo are some of the loneliest roads in the world. Either someone will give you a ride out of sheer pity or you will spend days slowly dying of thirst. I have had mixed experiences here – once I had to walk back to the town I had left two hours earlier because no-one would stop, another time I waited for six hours in one spot but when I walked back to the junction, I got a ride within a minute. Take a full waterbottle, a hat and a book.

Motorcycle

I researched this part of the book on the back of a 20-year-old off-road motorbike. It didn't matter that it had an all-out top speed of 80km/h (along with some pretty impressive vibrations) because the Karoo is perfect motorcycling country – wide, empty roads, no rain and a landscape you can lose yourself in, all of which encourages sedate biking.

An Englishman named Ted Simon described it best in his book about his four-year circumnavigation on a Triumph Tiger.

> For me fifty miles an hour (80km/h) is a perfect speed, the golden mean between dawdling and drumming vibration. At this excellent rate I can spin and tumble along all day in comfort, and see where I'm going. There are now some five hundred miles between me and Cape Town. By nightfall I should be well within a day's ride. I fly past Strydenburg and Britstown feeling like Pegasus on wheels. In the early afternoon some clouds mount a few scattered fortresses in the sky but I am able to ride under them before they can release their leaden charges. Now the heat is building up and the road is steaming. The sun drilling through the haze begins to poach my eyes in a hard diffuse light, and I stop for a few minutes to lean forward on the handle bars and doze, cocooned in still, warm air and the song of the black, long-tailed Sacabula birds perched like crotchets on the telegraph wires.

Jupiter's Travels

KIMBERLEY

Kimberley is South Africa's diamond capital, a small clump of high-rise buildings dwarfed by the big landscape around them. Kimberley is sometimes laughed off as a one horse-town (usually by South Africans unfortunate enough to be living in Johannesburg) but it is a pleasant place with a rich history, growing rapidly since the first diamonds were found here in 1868, and large scale diamond mining still takes place. The town remains the headquarters of global diamond mining conglomerate De Beers.

Kimberley is a placid town, with almost none of the security risks of the larger cities.

History

In 1871 diamond deposits were found on Colesberg Kopje, a little hill on a farm owned by the De Beers brothers, sparking off an insane diamond rush.

Prospectors and fortune seekers poured in from all over the world and a year after the first strike, there were 50,000 diggers feverishly working claims. Colesberg Kopje was levelled and then became a massive hole in the ground as the miners dug deep into the diamond-bearing kimberlite pipes. (When mining stopped in August 1914, 28 million tonnes of ground and the equivalent of three tonnes of diamonds had been removed from the hole which was (800m) deep with a perimeter of almost 2km.) Fortunes were being made and lost every day as digging continued. The strike didn't peter out and a town was built in its dust. In 1873, the town was named Kimberley in honour after the Earl of Kimberley, British Secretary of State for the Colonies.

The town boomed. A tramway was built – a section of it is still in use today – and electric street lighting, the country's first, was installed. Diggers who got lucky bathed in soda water and literally burned their money lighting cigars.

It was in this chaos that Cecil John Rhodes, financier and empire builder, began his career. As the diggers went deeper so the mining became more dangerous and costly, and the only solution was to amalgamate claims. Rhodes and fellow entrepreneur Barney Barnarto made the most of this opportunity and began buying up claims. In 1888, Rhodes' De Beers Mine and Banarto's Kimberley Mine were merged. Barnarto pocketed a cheque for more than £5 million while Rhodes and the De Beers company went on to rule the diamond world. Rhodes used his staggering earnings to finance his empire-building dreams on the Witwatersrand when the gold strike there set off another rush in 1886 and also in Zimbabwe where his British South Africa Company effectively occupied and controlled the whole country. Rhodes also financed the construction of 600km of railway from Kimberley through Bechuanaland to Rhodesia.

The rise of Kimberley spurred the construction of the railway from the Cape and the first train arrived in 1885. When gold was discovered in the Transvaal Republic, the line was extended across the *highveld* to Johannesburg. Kimberley's importance as a railway junction was assured and when the Anglo–Boer War broke out in 1899, the Boer forces rode hard for Kimberley and the other strategically important rail junctions. The town and its population of diggers, diamond kings and whores was besieged by Boer forces for 124 days from October 14 until February 15 1900. Rhodes was in Kimberley for the entire siege and Boer gunners tried repeatedly to demolish his lodgings at the Sanatorium Hotel. The attempts by British forces to relieve Kimberley account for some of the town's saddest history.

Under the command of Lord Methuen, the British forces skirmished slowly up the railway line, tentatively testing the Boer strength. On November 28, 1899, the British were severely mauled in a Boer trap at Modder River, 33km south of Kimberley, when they ran into more than 2,000 Boer riflemen hidden in trenches dug into the river banks. Two weeks later it happened again, this time at Magersfontein. It would be two months before Lord Methuen resumed his attempts to relieve Kimberley.

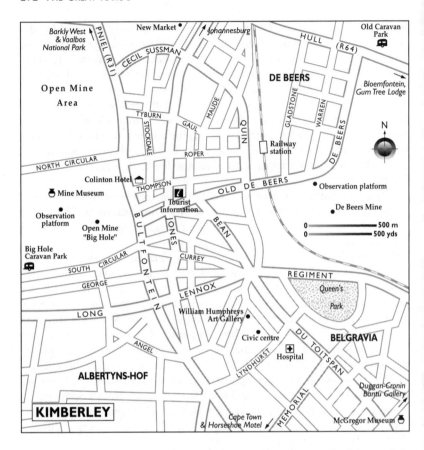

Naturally, the centenary of the Anglo–Boer War has resulted in a mini-tourist boom for Kimberley and if you are interested in this sort of thing the various battlefields, monuments and museums are worth visiting especially the exceptional museum on the hill overlooking Magersfontein.

Tourist information

Tel: 053 833 1434, fax 053 831 2937, email: tourism@northerncape.org.za; web: www.northerncape.org.za.

Accommodation

Kimberley has not yet made it on to the backpacker circuit but the B&B industry has boomed especially since the Anglo–Boer War centenary reawakened interest in the town.

Forwardene Kay's B&B 18 Rhodes Av; tel: 053 861 2484. Double rooms R140–200. This place has lasted a couple of years, always a good sign in the fickle B&B industry.
Enid's Inn 44 Memorial Rd; tel: 053 833 1969; fax: 053 832 6320; email: enid@kimberley.co.za. Doubles R120–250.

Carrington Lodge 60 Carrington Rd; tel: 053 831 6448; fax: 053 833 5012; email: spanhc@kingsley.co.za. Doubles R150–200. Breakfast included.

Things to see and do
Museums
Some of Kimberley's diamond town flavour remains. The original open cast mine, the **Big Hole**, has been turned into a tourist attraction (well at least as attractive as an 800m-deep hole can be). It is an impressive sight, though, and shows what desperate, greedy people can do with just picks and shovels.

The **Kimberley Mine Museum** (Tucker Street; tel: 053 833 1557) is a restored mining village at the edge of the hole, complete with corrugated iron buildings and includes all kinds of relics including 48 original mine houses, Barney Barnarto's boxing academy and the De Beers private railway coach. The museum is served by a vintage electric tram which runs from the City Hall and past a few historical buildings. *Open daily 08.00–18.00. Admission R10.*

The **Africana Library** (Chapel Street) contains documents and photographs detailing the history of the northern Cape, including missionary Robert Moffat's translation of the bible into seTswana. *Open Mon–Fri 08.45–12.45, 13.30–16.30, Sat 09.00–13.00. Admission free.*

The **Alexander McGregor Memorial Museum** (Chapel Street; tel: 053 842 0099) is a natural history exhibit, concerned mostly with animals, birds, insects and geology of the region. *Open Mon–Sat 09.00–17.00, Sun 14.00–17.00. Admission free.*

There is also a **Railway Museum** (tel: 053 838 2376) at the station on south end of the main platform. Outside is a massive 225-tonne class 25NC steam locomotive, representative of the engines which worked the main line south to De Aar until the end of the steam era in 1992. *Open Mon–Fri 10.00–16.00. Admission free.*

Other attractions
More steam locomotives lie awaiting their fate outside the engine shed at Beaconsfield, but some are occasionally steamed for special trains. If you want to see them, phone 053 838 3131.

Historic buildings around the town include the **City Hall**, the **De Beers head office** on Stockdale Street, the **Dutch Reformed Church** on Hertzog Square, and the **Kimberley Club**, Du Toitspan Road. The latter's members included Cecil John Rhodes and Barney Barnarto.

Two houses of note are those belonging to Robert Sobukwe and Sol Plaatjie, men who had a dramatic impact on the course of black nationalism in South Africa. Plaatjie, who was a founding member of the African National Congress and its first secretary-general, started his career as a war correspondent during the Anglo–Boer War. His house is in **Kimberley's Civic Centre**.

Robert Sobukwe, the founder and first member of the Pan Africanist Congress, spent his later years practising law in Kimberley while under a banning order. Dismayed with the ANC's passive stance, he broke away in

1958 and rallied great support for large-scale anti pass-law protests in 1960. Sobukwe was arrested after police killed 69 anti pass-law demonstrators at Sharpeville in 1960 and he was sent to Robben Island. After serving nine years, he was released to live under house arrest in the township of Galeshewe.

MAGERSFONTEIN

> Of the awful sights and privation I won't speak, only I must say that
> we had no water for 32 hours and dozens died through want,
> wounded of course. I got through with my helmet knocked off, two
> bullets through my kilt and one through my spats.

> Lance-Corporal W Wicks, Black Watch Regiment

Along with Isandlwana in KwaZulu-Natal, Magersfontein is one of the most evocative but chilling and saddest battlefields in the country. The site is a wide, flat plain dominated at its northern reaches by a range of rocky hills. This striking place was the site of one of the bloodiest engagements of the whole war, a battle that was to have its echoes in the foul trench slaughter in France, 15 years later.

Under pressure from Lord Methuen's column which was advancing slowly up the railway line from the Orange River to relieve Kimberley, the Boers retreated northwards after a week in which three battles were fought. One of their commanders, General Koos de la Rey, masterminded the next defensive line – the low hills at Magersfontein. Having witnessed the stunning success of the defensive trench line at Modder River, de la Rey decided to repeat the experiment. Breaking the military tradition of always occupying the high ground, he had his men dig a line of trenches running east to west slightly forward of the hills. White painted stones were dropped in the veld a few hundred feet in front of the trench line so the Boer riflemen would be able to determine the range of the advancing British troops, even at night.

By December 9 1899 both sides had been reinforced and Methuen decided to attack Magersfontein. The Highland Brigade was chosen to lead the dawn assault on the main hill after a night approach march, while the Mounted Brigade would work around the Boer left flank. The Guards Brigade would be held in reserve.

The British believed the Boers were dug in in top of the hills which they proceeded to paste with a lengthy artillery barrage on the afternoon of December 10. The bombardment did nothing but alert the Boers that the attack was imminent.

Shortly after midnight on December 11, the 3,400 men of the Highland Brigade, marched off into the cold, rainswept night. The darkness and rain made navigation difficult and to keep the Brigade together, men in the front ranks were roped together. At 03.45, the Brigade found itself closer to the hills and further west than expected and hurried orders were given to extend into attack formation. At that instant, at a range of 400m, the Boers opened fire, causing carnage in the packed ranks of the Highlanders.

Some of the Highlanders charged the Boer line, others desperately sought cover on the exposed ground. Major-General A G Wauchope, the much-loved and respected commander of the brigade, was killed almost immediately and the leaderless troops began to blunder about in confusion. Some of the Brigade reached the foot of the hills and began climbing. Then the British artillery, not knowing that Highlanders were on the slopes began pounding the hills once more. Caught between sustained Boer rifle fire and bursting shells, the Highlanders were driven off.

For the rest of the night and morning of the first day, isolated groups tried to break through the Boer line without success and a mid-morning reinforcement of Gordon Highlanders also failed. The Highlanders were pinned down, lying out in the open, while the Guards Brigade's advance was checked by General Cronje. The Boers sniped at anything that moved on the plain before them and the Brigade lay there on the veld, baking in the sun, listening to wounded men screaming for water.

At midday, a Boer force attacked the Highlanders' right flank and drove them back. By late afternoon there was no firing and both sides spent the next night where they lay on the field. The next day General Cronje allowed a short truce so that the British could collect their dead and wounded and at midday Methuen pulled back from Magersfontein.

It had been a terrible day. The official British figures listed 948 men killed, wounded or taken prisoner. Boer losses were 87 killed, 168 wounded and 21 captured. It was the only the second time that trenches had been used in modern day open warfare (the first was at Modder River ten days earlier), a lesson that was not lost on the British and one that would be repeated with staggering futility on the Western Front 14 years later.

Things to see and do

The battlefield is dotted with memorials to the combatants of both sides and, tucked away on top of Magersfontein Hill, is an excellent **museum** displaying uniforms, equipment, documents and photographs. The site is now a **nature reserve** and there are a couple of self-guided trails. *Open Mon–Sat 08.30–16.00. Admission R5.*

HEADING SOUTH

The N12 national road heads south from Kimberley over the Orange River and into the Karoo proper. It closely follows the railway line until Belmont, passing Anglo–Boer War battlefield sites at Modder River, Graspan and Belmont. At many of the river crossings there are fortified stone blockhouses, erected by the British to house troops charged with protecting the bridges from Boer commando attacks.

The Kimberley tourism office (Bultfontein Street and Lyndhurst Street; tel: 053 832 7298) has free maps and guides to the various battlefields and museums on the N12 Battlefields Route.

The towns en route are mostly nondescript farming towns although there are fine examples of Karoo architecture in Britstown and Victoria West. Both towns are more notable for being the places where you turn off the N12 to head west to Calvinia, an infinitely nicer place at the western edge of the

Karoo. Britstown, is also the junction for the N10 national road to Upington and Namibia and east to De Aar.

De Aar

De Aar is the quintessential railway town, the premier railway junction where the Cape Main Line meets the lines from Namibia and Port Elizabeth. It is the kind of place you arrive in and want to leave immediately – nowhere else in the country is there a town which reflects the railways' general decline as painfully as De Aar does. It used to be the junction for the passenger train service to Namibia but unfortunately that service no longer runs although protracted negotiations were in progress at the time of writing to change this. Many of the passenger trains described at the beginning of the chapter pass through De Aar. If you are planning to head west under your own power towards Calvinia or north to Upington and the Kalahari, this is your stop.

De Aar once had a fine steam locomotive depot which drew tourists from all over the world, and was a place which was revered by enthusiasts. Apart from the occasional working special, steam has now gone and the depot is in ruins. De Aar's other claim to fame is being the central ammunition and ordnance storage depot for the South African Defence Force. A place to dally only if life in very small towns intrigues you.

CALVINIA

This prosperous little town is at the edge of the Karoo in a region known as the Hantam. The town, which was named after religious reformer John Calvin, lies at the foot of the Hantam Mountains. It is a wool processing centre but don't let that put you off. Calvinia is one of the nicest towns in the Karoo with some lovely restored houses.

Getting there

If you don't have your own car, you're looking at a fairly tough hitchhiking session. Since Cape Town is only four hours away to the southwest, there is much more traffic in that direction than eastwards across the Big Empty. Take a hat and plenty of water.

The roads to Calvinia traverse some of the Karoo's starkest and emptiest country and the distances between towns are huge: Victoria West to Calvinia is about 400km. If you didn't feel insignificant before, you will now. The sense of isolation is intoxicating: huge sweeps of empty country; places where sheep flock to lonely windpumps at sunset. The few towns, which look almost overwhelmed by the vastness, are enticing oases where tin roofed houses huddle under the trees. It is magnificent country, especially at sunrise and sunset.

Accommodation

Hantamhuis, Dorpshuis, Tuishuis 44 Hoop St; tel/fax: 027 341 2201. R95–140. Three restored Victorian houses. These are B&Bs but all meals are available on request.

Things to see and do

People come here for the outdoors, both night and day. Stargazers love the clear Karoo nights and Calvinia enjoys about 80% starlight (it's no coincidence that the country's main observatory is situated just down the road – in Karoo terms – in Sutherland). In spring, the desert comes alive as **wildflowers bloom** in a brief but vivid show and locals are only too eager to direct you to the best spots. The flat-topped **Hantams mountain** that defines the town has some excellent hiking trails including a six-hour trek that traverses the summit plateau.

If you are fortunate enough to be around at the end of August, just before flower season you may be a witness to the **Calvinia Meat Festival** which is basically a weekend of barbecuing, meat tasting, recipe-swapping, beer drinking and the local version of dancing to country and western. Drum majorettes march in the streets and local lovelies enter the local beauty pageant contest in hope of winning the Miss Meat Festival title, which for all sorts of reasons could be a somewhat disturbing trophy to have on the mantelpiece.

BEAUFORT WEST

Beaufort West owes its fragile prosperity to the N1 national road and railway which pass right though the centre. A plan to build a bypass was angrily vetoed by the town's residents who fear Beaufort would become a ghost town if it lost its road traffic.

Despite the trucks and cars passing through at all hours, it's a very quiet place with some of the finest Karoo architecture I have yet seen. The town is definitely worth taking a stroll around but overall it scores low on the excitement scale. It is, however, the jumping off point for the Karoo National Park, the entrance to which is a few miles south of town off the N1.

Getting there

Train

The *Trans Karoo* and *Trans Oranje* expresses and the nameless twice-weekly train between East London and Cape Town pass through at night.

Bus

Both Greyhound and Translux buses drop-off here. Call the Cape Town or Johannesburg offices for information.

Hitchhiking

The N1 is a busy stretch of road, especially during school holidays. Getting out of town might be easier than getting in, though. All traffic has to slow right down to go through the centre and there are a couple of traffic lights where you can try your luck. There are also a number of petrol stations where at least you have the advantage of being able to check out your ride before getting in the car.

Accommodation

Donkin House Donkin Rd (at the north end of the main road through the town). Double rooms R200, singles R150. There are no dorms but you could negotiate a good price for a three-bed room. Boarding house turned budget overnight stop which has endured for at least two decades.

Things to see and do
Karoo National Park

The park encompasses 20,000ha of Karoo wilderness over which herds of black wildebeest, springbok, mountain zebra, red hartebeest and gemsbok (oryx) roam freely. The park land was reclaimed from sheep farming and many of the antelope species have been reintroduced with great success, creating a model for similar exercises elsewhere.

The three-day **Springbok trail** starts at the main rest camp and climbs into the Nuweveld mountains. No more than 12 people (and no fewer than 2) may be on the trail at any time which means you are more than likely to have it to yourself. The trail costs R30 per person per day; accommodation is in equipped hiking huts. At the time of writing (August 2000) the trail was closed for re-routing but should be open again in 2001. It only operates in the cooler months between March and October.

There are two free nature walks, one of 12km and the other about 1km, a 4x4 trail which can be done with a parks vehicle and guide, and a short Karoo Braille fossil trail depicting the geology and palaeontology of the region.

Accommodation

There are two rest camps. The main camp has six- and three-bed Cape Dutch style en suite cottages and bungalows, and there is also a restaurant. Mountain View Camp is a basic self-catering camp with accommodation for just 25 people. For bookings, contact the South African National Parks Office (tel: 012 343 1991; fax: 012 343 0995; email: reservations@parks-sa.co.za).

LAINGSBURG

Like Beaufort West, this quiet place really owes its existence to sheep and goat farming. The town is more famous for being mostly obliterated in 1981 when a wall of mud and rock smashed through the sleeping town after heavy rains in the Karoo saw the Buffels River burst its banks. The water level lapped the tops of the arches of the graceful railway bridge south of the town.

MATJIESFONTEIN

This little siding on the Cape Main Line is the site of the Lord Milner Hotel, a cluster of restored Victorian houses, a red London bus (the real thing) and the beginnings of an impromptu railway museum. The hotel itself is a real budget breaker but I have to urge you to spend a night here.

Matjiesfontein (fountain of mat rushes) was a vital watering point for steam locomotives heading to and from the arid Karoo. The village was founded by a Scot named James Logan, who carved a farm out of the surrounding country and gradually developed the little hamlet, earning his income from a spring on

TOUWS RIVER

A railway marshalling yard at the top of the pass through the Hex River mountains. The yard was the site of a large steam locomotive graveyard – called a 'strategic reserve' – where hundreds of steam locomotives rusted away their last years. The idea was to store steam locomotives at selected locations in the Karoo as they would be well preserved in the dry desert air. If there was ever a repeat of the 1973 oil crisis, the railways would have had a massive supply of coal-burning engines apparently needing only minor attention before being put back into service. In reality, these reserves were just dumps and by the late 1980s most of the locomotives in them had been scrapped and turned into spoons.

the farm. Logan found that the dry crisp air of the Karoo helped cure him of a chronic chest ailment and he decided to develop Matjiesfontein as an international health resort. Olive Schreiner, the writer, spent much time here and raved about the purity of the air.

Since all trains stopped at Matjiesfontein, the canny Scot opened a dining room on the station platform to feed the hungry passengers – there were no dining cars on the trains in the early years. When the Anglo–Boer War broke out, the hamlet was used as a field hospital and a staging post for troop trains heading north. Major-General A G Wauchope, commander of the Highland Brigade who was killed at the battle of Magersfontein, is buried in a little cemetery near the hotel. There are also persistent sightings of a ghost, apparently a wounded soldier, who stands on the main road. When drivers slow down, thinking there's been an accident, the soldier disappears.

The Lord Milner Hotel, named for the then supreme commander of the British forces, has become an institution following a full restoration in the 1970s. It is a rambling Victorian building, set in well-tended gardens with shade trees and a cool covered courtyard with splashing fountains.

It's a good place to break the journey in either direction, especially if you're looking for a dose of Victorian desert culture. The hotel is quite pricey but there is the cheaper Losieshuis (boarding house) a little further down the street. The restaurant on the station platform has long since gone but the trains still stop here, although not for very long.

Getting there and away

A popular way of getting to Matjiesfontein is to take the *Trans Karoo* train from Cape Town, spend a night or two there and then catch the down train back.

Accommodation

Lord Milner Hotel Tel 023 551 3011. Doubles R190 per person B&B, singles R130 B&B. The attached Losiehuis is a cheaper option with doubles at R130, bed only, and singles for R170. Breakfast is R30.

COLESBERG AND THE UPPER KAROO

Heading southeast from Kimberley brings you over the Orange River to Colesberg, a popular overnighting place on the main Johannesburg–Cape Town road, and possibly the last place on earth that doesn't have email, which is a nice surprise. It is an easy town to flash through since the national road just barrels right past. A pretty town surrounded by rocky hills and flanked by a tall mountain called Coleskop, there is more to Colesberg than it seems. For starters there are 54 B&Bs competing for visitors. This means that there are good reasons not to rush through, which the kind woman who runs the museum assures me is true.

Coleskop used to be called Toverberg (magic mountain) which is a better name since, while you can see it from 50km away, it never seems to get any closer as you approach. The town started out as a lonely mission station in 1814 and was officially founded in 1830. Now a sheep farming centre, it has enjoyed a fairly quiet history although there was a bit of excitement during the early stages of the Anglo–Boer War.

Tourist information

The tourism office is on Murray Street (tel: 051 753 0678, fax: 051 753 0574).

Getting there and away

Train

For some unfathomable reason, Colesberg's station is a couple of miles out of town which is a bit of a hassle since the two passenger trains that call here do so late at night or early in the morning (see *Train information*, page 269). If you are coming by train, arrange accommodation in advance and have your hosts pick you up at the station.

Bus

Greyhound and Translux buses stop at the garages on each side of town. Once again, book accommodation ahead and have your hosts meet you.

Accommodation

The Gordon's Cottage 4 Stockenstroom Square; tel: 051 753 0390 or 051 753 0678. R65 per person per night for two people but the more people staying, the lower the price; you'll pay R40 per night if you and your mates fill the house. This fully restored Karoo cottage is one of the most gorgeous places I have been to: a real hideaway below the koppie. The house sleeps up to five people with another tiny 2-bed cottage at the back. There is a plunge pool which will be welcome on a summer's day. There is a fully equipped kitchen.

Colesberg Backpacker 39 Kerk St; tel: 051 753 0582; fax: 051 0642. Double R60, dorm R45, camping R25. Lovely backpacker in an old house on the main street. There is a lovely garden out back where you can cut the road dust with a couple of cold beers and listen to the asthmatic windpump sucking up water for the splash pool.

Eating and drinking

As well as a B&B boom there has been a mini-restaurant boom as well with at least seven places serving competitively priced meals. Mercifully, the town has escaped the attention of the fast food chains and the local restaurants serve good Karoo food like roast lamb – a local specialty, naturally – as well as some of the best pizza I have eaten. One word of warning – the English Pub is anything but English but it is worth dropping by to see what the locals are arguing about.

Things to see and do

There was, in fact, some chaotic fighting around Coleskop and if it weren't for the fact that carnage was taking place on an even more horrific scale on the Tugela River and around Kimberley on exactly the same days, this part of the town's past would be much more notable. As it is, it hardly gets a mention in the history books. Local historian Belinda Gordon is trying to raise awareness of this and she leads unique walking tours around the British and Boer encampments and to the battlefield at Suffolk Hill. Using letters written by soldiers, she recounts the events around the battle for Coleskop and its aftermath. For bookings tel: 051 753 0678.

The **Colesberg Kemper Museum**, housed in a beautiful building dating from 1862, covers local history in the form of photographs, documents and artefacts of pioneer lifestyles, as well as a collection of 19th-century toys. There is also an exhibition on the **Karretjie Mense** (little car people), a scattered group of semi-nomadic people who travelled around the Karoo on donkey carts. The Karretjie Mense subsisted on seasonal farm work such as sheep shearing, drifting from place to place. They speak a unique form of Afrikaans and are regarded as an independent people. Not many are left now, possibly as a result of declining fortunes in sheep farming.

The town is full of old Karoo houses which you invariably look at and wonder how to buy. There are guided walking tours but you can just wander around on your own and salivate over the gorgeous houses. There are also paths in the koppies leading up to San rock art sites.

Colesberg is within spitting distance of the large **Gariep** and **Vanderkloof dams**, both of which are on the Orange River. The former has a well-developed holiday resort with chalets and campsites and easily reached, even if you are hitching, but it's a bit of crowded experience over school holidays and weekends. The **Vanderkloof dam** is more remote and wilder as a result.

The 9,000ha **Doornkloof Nature Reserve** (tel: 051 753 1315) on its southeast bank has a couple of short trails and an overnight hut. Mammals in the reserve include kudu, mountain reedbuck, brown hyena, bat-eared fox and aardwolf.

Heading south

The road south from Colesberg divides at the edge of town, with the N1 turning off right to Cape Town and the N9 carrying on towards Port Elizabeth. There are not many diversions en route: Noupoort is a railway junction and

Middelburg *used* to be a railway junction. After Middelburg, the road climbs up the Lootsberg mountain pass and then drops into the most incredible Karoo plain on the other side and heads towards Graaff Reinet. The mountains to the west hide Nieu Bethesda, one of the country's gems.

NIEU BETHESDA
It would be difficult to find a little town as perfect and in such a lovely setting as Nieu Bethesda. The village sprawls over a valley floor at the end of a 25km gravel road from the nearest tar, encircled by hills and mountains, including the steep-sided Compassberg which, at 2,502m, is the second-highest mountain in the whole region.

The village is the place that progress drove past on the other side of the mountains. The wide streets are untarred and the Karoo houses are built on huge plots. It is quiet and calm and on Sundays the only thing moving might be Eisbein (see below).

Accommodation
The Owl House Backpackers Martin St; tel: 049n841 1642; fax: 049 841 1657; email: owlhouse@global.co.za; web: welcome.to/owlhouse. Double R110–120, dorm R45, camping R20. A classic Nieu Bethesda farmhouse with a rambling garden out back, a wood stove to keep chilly winter nights at bay, a resident cat named Leftover and Eisbein, a friendly dog of small brain. Katrin will make you feel totally at home. There is a double/triple garden cottage.

There are a couple of B&Bs in the village with prices for doubles ranging from R120–160 per night per person sharing. Prices often come down out of season. Recommended are House No 1 (round the corner from the backpackers) and Beaumont Cottage. It's a friendly place and everyone passes on business to everyone else.

Eating and drinking
The Old Waenhuis on Martin Street is the only place to eat and drink at night but a couple of coffee shops are open during the day. There is a small shop selling basic foodstuffs.

Things to see and do
The **Owl House**, the town's main tourist attraction, is one thing that puts Nieu Bethesda on the map. Belonging to reclusive artist Helen Martins, the Owl House draws travellers from all over the world who come to what is regarded as the finest example of Outsider Art. Withdrawing from the world, Martins made it her work to surround herself with light and colour. The house is full of red or green glass lit by the strong Karoo light and rows of jars are packed with ground glass, meticulously graded according to size and colour. The Camel Yard outside is full of cement and glass structures and figures, many of them life size. The theme of her work is mostly religious – with the help of a dedicated assistant, she turned her vivid dreams into cement

reality and there are churches, owls, a camel train of wise men heading east, pyramids and mermaids. It is a strange mix of western and eastern religion and an often disquieting look into the soul of a lonely person. *Open daily 09.00–16.00. Admission R8.*

The other attractions of the area are fine hiking trails, including a tough day hike up to the summit of **Compassberg**. It's worth checking out the **Sneeuberg hiking trails** which traverse a couple of the farms in the area, offering hikes lasting from 2–10 days. You overnight in rough huts or at farmhouse B&Bs. For bookings contact the Graaff Reinet publicity association (tel: 049 892 4248).

Ganora, a farm 8km out of Nieu Bethesda, has some excellent examples of San rock art as well as a couple of walking trails. The owners can also organise all sort of excursions such as horse riding, mountain biking and visits to fossil sites on surrounding farms. For bookings, tel: 049 841 1302; email: ganora@xsinet.co.za; web: www.freeyellow.com/members8/ganora-tours/index.html.

GRAAFF REINET

Graaff Reinet, punted by the local tourism authorities as the Gem of the Karoo, is one of the oldest towns in the country, founded in 1786 in an effort to police the troubled eastern frontier, and many of its oldest buildings have survived. Architecturally, the centre is wonderful and there are a couple of good museums. The imposing Dutch Reformed Church dominates the town from a central square, and many of the older buildings such as the town hall and war memorial, face the church.

The town is thriving, helped by generous input from the Rupert Foundation. Anton Rupert, creator of a multi-million rand tobacco and liquor empire, is the town's leading son and, although he lives near Cape Town, he has channelled huge sums of money into his home town. Based on the credo that the receiver must raise half the money, he has set up a trust which, for example, allowed residents to restore the facades of their homes. Rupert is on record as saying people don't appreciate anything that's free, which is why the Hester Rupert Art Museum charges a whopping 50 cent admission.

It is an interesting town to walk around: around 200 of the houses are national monuments and many of the civic buildings are open to the public or have become museums.

Tourist information

The town is keen on boosting its tourism potential and there is an efficient tourism information office at the corner of Church Street and Somerset Street; tel: 049 892 4248.

Getting there and away

There are no longer any trains to Graaff Reinet so your only option is by bus or to hitchhike. Two roads lead south from the town: the N9 to Willowmore and ultimately to the Garden Route, and the R75 to Port Elizabeth. For hitching purposes, both are reasonably busy.

Accommodation

A town like this is bound to be overrun with B&Bs and if you are prepared to do a little exploring you will find some sweet places. Rates here tend to be slightly lower than B&Bs down on, say, the Garden Route – expect to pay R90–150. Try and bargain out of season. There are a couple of self-catering places as well with rates ranging from R65 to R170 for a double. The tourism centre (tel: 049 892 4248)has a full list of prices and addresses.

Wiggill-In 17 Queen St; tel: 049 891 0929. Cottage R250 per night, or R70 per person sharing. B&B R85. A self-catering cottage on the north side of the town but close to everything (it's a small town). The whole cottage sleeps five in one double room and one three-bed room.

Eating and drinking

Graaff Reinet is proud to have 35 pubs which is a huge number for such a small place. One that serves reasonably priced food is the Number 8 Bar and Grill (8 Church Street; tel: 049 892 4464) which is housed in a shuttered Karoo house and is adorned inside with Springbok rugby memorabilia. Coffee shops and tea rooms perch on just about every street corner.

Things to see and do

The **Hester Rupert Art Museum** (Church Street; tel: 049 8922121; fax: 049 892 4319) houses an interesting collection of works donated by a huge spread of South African artists, dating mostly from the 1960s. There are some fantastic works here but, if nothing else, many of the paintings seem to anticipate the beginning of a difficult time in the country's history. *Open Mon–Fri 10.00–12.00 and 15.00–17.00, Sat–Sun 10.00–12.00. Admission 50 cents.*

The **Old Library Museum** (Church Street; tel: 049 892 4248) is an uneasy mix of incredible fossils in one hall, and a collection of wedding dresses in the other. Both are fascinating exhibits. The fossils have mostly been found in the area and the exhibition describes a scene of swamp and lakes where plant-eating mammals roamed. The fossils, which are around 230 million years old, were collected by Alex Bremner who spent 18 years digging around the district. *Open Mon–Fri 09.00–12.00, 14.00–17.00, Sat–Sun 09.00–12.00. Admission free.*

The **Valley of Desolation** is a geological phenomenon, a cleft in the rocky plateau of the mountain that looms over Graaff Reinet. The rocks and cliffs have been eroded away and the valley falls sharply in a jumble of contorted rock sculptures and weathered cliffs into the vast plain of the Great Karoo. If you're hiking, you look down into the valley and you'll wonder where you left your brain. The Cape Crag trail is a two-hour hike along the edge of the valley and there is also the two-day Drie Koppe (Three Heads) trail with an overnight in a hiking hut. For bookings phone the tourism association (tel: 049 892 4248).

The **Mountain Zebra National Park** is a lovely place which hardly seems to get a visit these days, cursed as it is by its location far off the beaten tourist trail. Yet for those who are willing to make the trek, the park offers an experience you will be hard-pushed to repeat elsewhere.

The area was proclaimed a park in 1937 to protect the last of a herd of Cape mountain zebra, the smallest of the species, and the conservation department has succeeded. Other species of antelope including wildebeest, springbok, klipspringer and bontebok, also live in the reserve. The terrain is classic Karoo country with wide plains and a landscape of conical koppies and odd-shaped hillocks and wild olive, kiepersol and white stinkwood trees everywhere.

What is nice about this place is that you are free to walk anywhere in the park. There is a three-day trail but most people opt for day hikes out of the camp, either to lookout points or to see Bushman paintings in the hills.

The park is about 25km from Cradock, on the R61. Having your own car would be the easiest way but the daily Algoa express between PE and Johannesburg stops briefly in Cradock, northbound at 19.05, southbound at 04.50. These are not the worst of times especially in summer. Cycling and hitching from Cradock should be easy – if doing the latter, make sure your lift is turning on to the R61 and not carrying on up the N10.

The rest camp (tel: 048 8812427) has 20 self-catering four-bed chalets (R270 for the first two people including breakfast, plus R66 per additional adult excluding breakfast) and the same number of campsites (R44 for the first two adults plus R11 per additional person). You can also stay in the Doornhoek Farmhoue which costs R475 for the first four people, including breakfast, and R66 for each additional adult.

CRADOCK

This is a pretty town which has so far managed to prevent the decay that has afflicted so many other country towns in the region. Amongst other historical buildings is Olive Schreiner House, former home of the famous writer (her best-known work, *Story of an African Farm*, is essential reading for anyone visiting this part of the world). The house is a fine example of Karoo architecture. Not surprisingly, the local library houses all Schreiner's works.

Accommodation
The municipal campsite (tel: 048 881 3443) is the cheapest place to stay but there are about ten B&Bs and guesthouses. Recommended is the Victoria Manor (tel: 048 881 1650) which is very good value, especially if you tuck into the huge dinner they serve. For general information about where to stay, contact the tourism office (tel: 048 881 2383).

Things to see and do
Cradock was also a stronghold for the anti-apartheid movement and the **Lingelihle cemetery** (tel: 048 881 1952) is a tribute to heroes of the struggle. While you are visiting graveyards, the trek up Buffelskop Mountain to **Olive Schreiner's tomb** is worth the 3-hour toil: at the top, you look out over Cradock, the Fish River and the Karoo and you will understand why she chose this as her last resting place.

306

Cross-Border Excursions

At some point on your travels you are likely to run up against one of South Africa's other borders. Since you've come all this way, it makes sense to explore a little bit further. You have a wide range of options here, since South Africa shares a border with Namibia, Botswana, Zimbabwe, Mozambique, Swaziland and Lesotho.

All these countries deserve more than just a short excursion, especially since the things worth doing and seeing there generally demand some kind of commitment. Since Mozambique, Swaziland and Lesotho are accessible enough for quick a foray or two, this chapter looks briefly at Swaziland and Mozambique (Lesotho is covered in *Chapter 15*).

INTO SWAZILAND

This tiny country, bordered on three sides by South Africa and to the east by Mozambique, is a country of mountains and high plateaux. A member of the Commonwealth, the country is governed by a strong hereditary monarch.

The climate is pleasant and temperate. Its ecological zones range from rainforest and mountainous highveld in the west to open savanna in the east. Temperatures rise and rainfall declines as the land falls off towards the east. The rugged Lebombo Mountains form the country's border with Mozambique. Its western border with South Africa is formed by the Mlembe Mountains. High rainfall – at least 1000mm a year – and the rivers which flow the range make the slopes of the Mlembe range beautifully green and cool.

History

Swaziland was settled in about 1750 by members of the Nguni people who were making their way southwards along the coastal belt. One group settled in the valley of the uSuthu River, the country's main watercourse, while others continued to move south into Zululand, only to run into the Zulus. Calling themselves Swazis after one of their chiefs, the clan thrived in the valley in spite of regular raids by the Zulu. The current Dlamini monarchy stretches back to the mid-18th century.

The first large-scale influx of Europeans followed the discovery of gold in the Piggs Peak area in the 1890s. The strike in what turned out to be a scanty gold-bearing reef, was short-lived. Meanwhile, the area had come under the control of the Zuid Afrikaansche Republiek and later the British after the Anglo–Boer War. Limited self-government was granted to King Sobhuza ll in 1964 and independence followed in 1968. There has been internal pressure to reform the monarchy and move towards multi-party democracy. Constitutional reform in 1993 introduced direct elections to the house of assembly in 1993.

It is one of the friendliest countries I have ever travelled in, the kind of place where the policemen at roadblocks stop you because they want to chat about your holiday. People wave hello from the roadside and smile at you in the streets. It is just an easygoing place. I like it.

Orientation
Swaziland is a tiny, landlocked country near the east coast of southern Africa, sharing a border with South Africa on three sides and Mozambique on the fourth. The capital is Mbabane.

Tourist information
Visas
Most visitors do not require a visa although exceptions include Austrian, French, German and Swiss citizens. Visas, however, are available free at the borders or the airport.

Money
The unit of currency is the *lilangeni* (plural *emalangeni*). It is tied to the South African rand, which is accepted more or less everywhere in the country. The cost of living is similar to South Africa. Barclays Bank has branches in all the major towns. Hours: Mon–Fri 08.30–14.30; Sat 08.30–11.00.

Telephone
The country code is 268. Add the prefix 09 if you are dialling from South Africa.

Getting there and away
Bus
The Baz Bus (tel: 021 439 2323; fax: 021 439 2343; email: info@bazbus.com; web: www.bazbus.com) runs between Durban and Johannesburg via Swaziland a couple of times per week.

Train
The *Trans Lubombo* passenger train runs twice-weekly in each direction between Durban and Maputo, leaving Durban on Tuesdays and Thursdays, and from Maputo on Thursdays and Sundays. The train passes through the eastern part of the country, close to the major game parks. Phone Durban train enquiries, tel: 031 361 7621.

Accommodation

Sondzela Backpackers Mlilwane Wildlife Sanctuary; tel: +268 528 3117 or 528 3871; fax: +268 528 3924; email: parksHQ@biggame.co.sz. Double R140, dorm R40, camping R35. Lovely ranch house at the edge of the Mlilwane reserve, set in a huge garden and with a lovely view across the valley to the mountains. There is also a pool. The staff can help you organise all your activities.

Myxo's Place – Woza Nawe Tel/fax: +268 50 58 363; email: mzn136@postcafe.co.sz. Double R120, dorm R40, camping R25. A Swazi family have opened their own home to travellers. This is the real thing. Be respectful because it's a great place. 5km from Manzini on Siteki Big Bend Rd. Look for the Big Surprise bottle store and turn right.

Things to see and do

Swaziland has become something of an adventure kingdom thanks to some devoted locals who run rafting, biking trips, horseriding trails and game viewing tours. There is great hiking in the forest-covered hills near the capital and superb rafting/kayaking on the Great Usuthu River. The country is probably best known for its well-run game parks and its growing popularity among budget travellers is reflected in the fact that three backpackers have opened up.

Game reserves

Possibly the finest attraction in the country, Swaziland's game parks are extremely good value compared to similar operations elsewhere in southern Africa.

The railway line runs close to four of the country's six game reserves – in fact, it divides the two biggest – but as with the parks to the south, the train does not as yet stop at the most convenient stations. You will have to get off at Mpaka and cover the remaining 40km on local transport (bus or minibus). You cannot get off at the Mozambique/Swaziland border as the railway crosses at a different place to the road.

Further north are the two national parks, Hlane Royal National Park, formerly a royal hunting ground, and Mlawula Nature Reserve.

Hlane, to which lion and elephant have recently been re-introduced, offers guided walking trails or self-guided game drives, for which you need your own vehicle of course. Accommodation is in self-catering lodges and cottages, or you can camp.

Mlawula, which is set in 16,500ha of bush, offers walking trails into the Lebombo Mountains. Accommodation is limited to one thatched cottage which sleeps six people in two bedrooms but it's a bargain at R180 per night (for the whole house) over the weekend, R130 per night during the week. There is also a tented camp – which has only one two-person, walk-in tent at the moment, at R60 per night. You can bring your own tent, too.

The reserves are run by Big Game Parks (tel: +268 404 4541; email: parksHQ@biggame.co.sz).

Mlilwane Nature Reserve, just outside Mbabane, is a smaller park with only soft skinned game – zebra, impala, wildebeest and the like. Some hippo live in a waterhole in front of the restaurant at the main rest camp. One of the reserve's main attractions is being able to ride around on a mountain bike or on horseback, both unique ways to go game viewing. Accommodation is in chalets, bungalows or traditional beehive huts – prices start at R65 per person, campsites are R35. Tel: +268 602 0261 for bookings.

Warning
Malaria is rampant in the *lowveld* (where the main reserves are situated) so be fastidious in using repellent, take malaria prophylactics and sleep under a mosquito net.

Hiking
Malalotja Nature Reserve, a few miles northwest of Mababane, is crisscrossed with walking trails. It is a rugged country of deep forests, gorges, potholes and pools that have been carved out of the rock by the Malalotja River. Wildlife includes zebra, wildebeest, oribi, jackal, serval and leopard. You probably won't see the Big Five predators but you will see everything else.

Accommodation is in furnished 6-bed log cabins or a 3-bed A-frame hut. Overnight camps are situated near potable water but have no other facilities so you need to bring your own gear, including a hiking stove. For bookings, tel: +268 434 3060 or 416 1151. (Swaziland's phone company, even more so than South Africa's, is guilty of repeatedly changing the country's telephone numbers. If none of these numbers work, call Swazi Trails on +268 416 2180 and ask if they can help.)

Rafting
The Usuthu River in the rainy season, running through a landscape of green bushveld and impressive rock-studded hills, is a fine stretch of water to paddle. Swazi Trails (tel: +268 416 2180; email: tours@swazitrails.co.sz) runs one-day rafting trips down the best parts most of the year round. You don't need any previous experience – you paddle stable, inflatable boats called crocodiles and the trips are led by qualified and experienced river guides. A full day costs R320 per person, including lunch and transport.

Swazi Trails also offers biking trips (R95 for two hours), caving (R180) and can help organise overnight horse trails to a remote camp on the higher reaches of the Usuthu River.

INTO MOZAMBIQUE
Maputo
The train crosses the border at Siweni and runs down to the little Mozambican town of Goba. The line has recently been refurbished, having been partially destroyed by rebels during the civil war. The going is still slow, however. The wrecks of derailed and blown-up trains still litter the bush, silent reminders of decades of terror. The countryside is still quite unpopulated, most people having fled to the towns during the war; many have not returned. Around Boane, the vegetation becomes more lush and tropical as the railway levels out

on Mozambique's coastal plateau. The slow roll into Maputo is through waving grass and reeds of the plain, and hundreds of cheering, screaming children run out of their trackside shambas, excited, as children are everywhere in Africa, by the miraculous passage of the train. Enjoy.

Getting there

There are plenty of buses to Nelspruit but only Translux and Panthera Azul carry on to Mozambique. The most hassle-free and safest way to get there is by train. The *Komati Express* no longer runs all the way through to Maputo but stops in Komatipoort at 06.00. Here passengers disembark and wait for the Mozambique Railways train to run up from the other side of the border and then return to Maputo. South African customs and immigration is handled at a lineside halt just before the great electrified fence that was built to keep Mozambique's huddled masses on one side but which fails to do so.

You then cross the fence into Ressano Garcia, a dirty, run-down border town where you clear customs on the station platform. When everyone is ready – and there is no telling when that will be – the train sets off for Maputo, running down the valley of the Crocodile River and then cropping down through a belt of hot, dry country before reaching the wide floodplain that surrounds Maputo. For the last 33km or so, the train wades through long, green grass and rattles past lineside villages where knots of shrieking, dancing children sing songs and throw gravel and generally get totally overexcited. Arrival in Maputo is normally around 12.00 although it is supposed to be earlier. But this is a very different place where time keeping is almost regarded as a waste of energy.

Accommodation

Maputo goes through phases of being unfashionably expensive, normally straight after a crisis like the run-up to the 1994 elections and more recently the floods that washed the southern part of the country into the sea. The problem is partly caused by foreign agencies paying their staff well, and in dollars, which distorts the local economy. What this means is that hotel accommodation in Maputo is not cheap and that which is cheap is often uninhabitable. There are, however, some notable exceptions.

Costa do Sol Costa do Sol, 8 miles from town. There are a couple of huge rooms upstairs in the same building as the superb restaurant and a few bungalows out back. A great place to stay with lovely views of the sea. The only hassle is that it is far from town if you don't have wheels. The upside is that the food is so good downstairs, you might not want to go to town.

Pensão Alegre 1374 Av 24 de Julho. Double Mt 300,000 (R130), room for married couple Mt250,000 (R108), single Mt200 000 (R86). The 'married' room has a double bed, the doubles have two single beds. Clean, roomy pension in decent location, close to the more chic part of town and its nice restaurants and bars.

Fatima's 1317 Av Mao Tse Tung; tel: +258 421 425. Dorm R50. Aimed at backpackers; the owner knows Mozambique and how to travel around it.

Hotel Central Rua de Mesquita. Double R100. Old hotel in classic colonial building with upstairs verandah. Clean rooms and a thriving bar downstairs. About 250m from the railway station.

Things to see and do

Maputo has a couple of really nice buildings and interesting museums and it is worth taking a long stroll around. Buildings you should not miss include the **Cathedral**, the **Museu de Geologica** (Av 24 de Julho), housed in the old synagogue, the **prefabricated iron house** designed by Monsieur Eiffel (next to the Tundumo Botanical Gardens), and the **railway station** whose shocking green paint job has actually started to fade quite nicely.

The **Museum of the Revolution** (Av de 24 Julho) is the fascinating, if biased, story of Mozambique's recent past, covering the period from the start of the struggle overthrow the Portuguese back in the 1960s.

The **Mercado Municipal** (Av de 25 Septembro) is an excellent introduction to the true chaos of African markets. The produce is fresh, sometimes disturbingly so. Be brave, have a good nosey around and watch your wallet.

Lourenco Marques: a Mozambique story

The hot and sweaty myth of Portugal in Africa. South Africans of a certain generation get all misty eyed when they talk about 'LM' and its prawns or sitting at the Costa do Sol's wide, cool veranda, looking at the sea and eating *peri-peri* chicken and chips and white, floury bread, all washed down with icy Laurentina beer. They remember wide avenidas of red acacia and jacaranda trees, mosaics on the pavements and red-tiled villas under the trees. Most of all, they remember the smell – the bay, the tropical heat rising from the city, infused with the sea and the permanent infusion of hot *peri-peri* sauce , like the bass line in a salsa tune.

I first went to Lourenço Marques (now Maupto) in 1973, when I was young and interested in only a few things – colonial architecture wasn't one of them. My enduring memory is walking with my dad down the Avenida de Marginal, the wide boulevard that runs almost the whole length of the city's seafront, lined with palm trees and benches where you could sit, feet up on the balustrade, and watch the ships sail slowly into the bay – right there, not 3m away (things really are exaggerated when you're little). Something about that road with the sea lapping the wall that dropped straight from the pavement into the bay, stayed with me. Later, walking down the street to our hotel, looking into the lit shop windows, we saw a bookshop with Tintin in Portuguese. *O Segredo do Licorne – The Secret of the Unicorn*. The idea of Tintin in another language was tremendously exciting and I promptly forgot about everything else, which was OK because the prawns and Laurentina were wasted on a seven year old anyway.

Then there was a war and no one came to LM anymore. The avenidas became potholed and the pavements cracked and subsided. The garbage wasn't collected, the power was off half the day and the Russians took all the prawns.

Every time I heard the word Mozambique, I thought of the Marginal and Tintin in Portuguese, and ached to go back.

In 1993 I hitchhiked into Mozambique with a friend to watch my back. LM, now renamed Maputo, was trashed. The streets were ruined and the mosaic pavements were lost under mountains of rotting, stinking filth. Deserted villas mocked the street with empty doors and windows and crumbling masonry. The avenidas were full of Russian trucks, some of them running, but many lying broken and wheelless on the central islands that run down the bigger avenues like Avenida se 24 Julho. The city was a big festering refugee centre, jammed with people who had fled the war in the countryside. Our hotel was a four-floor dump with a communal toilet that worked only when someone bothered to schlep a bucket of water up the stairs, which was seldom. Old LM, it seemed, was history. 'Let's get the hell out of here,' I urged.

But on the second day we went down to the Marginal and I was stunned. The palms were still there although some had suffered direct hits from wayward IFA trucks, and even the balustrade was mostly intact; a few pillars were missing here and there. Somehow it had survived the war, socialism and post-colonialism. There were other signs of life too – little restaurants where they sold Impala beer (the nearest thing to Laurentina) in big brown, unlabelled bottles with sediment at the bottom. 'If this doesn't make us violently ill, we'll survive Mozambique,' we agreed. There was the Club Mini Golfe, a putting course by day, and seriously wicked salsa and disco by night. Everyone wanted to believe that everything was going to be alright, from the waiter in the Snack Bar Rossio carefully opening our beers at the table (as is custom here, to prove it's not been tampered with) to the sweaty, flirting disco queens down at the Mini Golfe, shaking their booty to wailing trumpets.

Today's Maputo is a thriving African city, make no mistake. For starters, it could use a jolly good clean-up. But the remarkable thing is what a fantastic blend of culture this mix of Portugal and Africa is. It is the little things like the bread – Mozambicans are master breadmakers. You do not eat bread like this anywhere else in the world, except, well, Portugal. The red acacias and jacaranda trees still shade the avenidas, the beautiful cathedral gleams white and the massive colonial railway station, which is without a doubt my favourite building in Africa, has been spruced up. You now have a choice of two bars at the station where you can sit and drink *cerveja naçional* (national beer) and admire the brass cupola dome designed by Monsieur Eiffel (of Eiffel Tower fame) himself.

Plenty has changed here since 1993. The processions of gleaming 4x4s are the final proof that socialism is at its most undiluted, problematic, and the armed guards in darkened doorways have gone as have the hulks of trashed vehicles. Still, I was a little apprehensive; it seemed so brash all of a sudden. Would Snack Bar Rossio have survived this? But somehow, the LM myth survives. There's a Bicafé sign on every corner, pavement cafés full of people drinking espressos and … whoah! Laurentina! The beer with the yellow label. It will cost you about R6. There's money, specifically dollars, flowing into Maputo like water but, even though this is a dollar economy, the metical is worth 2,300 to the rand, which gives you a good feeling for once.

I took a stroll down Avenida de 24 Julho. It was dark already and the office workers were going home. But the streets were alive with people walking, talking, selling stuff at candlelit stalls, buses roaring off down the street, the conductors hanging from the gangway shouting out their destination – 'Matola, Matola … Maa-tooo-laaaah.' Down on the road to Costa do Sol, fish vendors crowded into the road holding up barracuda still dripping saltwater. In a little church in a quiet side street, a woman painted bright murals.

Costa do Sol was the logical place for dinner (Rossio would have to wait). Even the 1952 Union Castle guide for Southern Africa mentions the Costa do Sol – it's *that* old. It has been run by the same family for 40 years, a stubborn family who stuck it out through the guerra, even though the South Africans didn't visit anymore. The fish comes straight off the boats that pull up on the beach right at their front door in the afternoons. When we arrived, the place was humming, full enough for us to stand on the wide veranda and wonder – without laughing – whether we would get a table. The fish was predictably outstanding. It felt like I had come home.

Dawn brought a calm, spring day with dhows drifting across the flatness of the bay. Another day's fishing for the Costa, no doubt. There were joggers on the quiet streets and a diplomat walking his Maltese poodle down embassy row. 'Bom dia,' people said, making it sound like 'We are happy to have you, please enjoy this city.…' I went to the Mercado Municipal and watched the chaos of trading – vegetables, oranges and fish straight out of the bay. I walked a long way to check out all the old places: PeriPeri, the Café Continental and Café Djambu where old men still play chess sometimes and drink espresso. I found a bookshop selling Tintin in Portuguese. At Snack Bar Rossio, the waiter opened my beer at the table. A block down the road, some old boys were taking a break and dancing while a young guitarist belted out a number on an old acoustic.

Maputo is marinated in Mediterranean sensibility – enjoy your life, especially your food and drink and music, because no-one ever said on his gravestone 'I wish I had spent more time at the office'. The city is as mulatto as many of its people, a bit confused and chaotic in places, relaxed in others. You should go.

Appendix 1

GLOSSARY

Ag, shame!
(pronounced ugh shayme)
What a pity or How cute; can be used to gurgle at a puppy or express horror over a plane crash without any discernible change in tone or inflection

Armed response
24-hour armed security services, employed largely by nervous Johannesburgers

Bakkie
pick-up truck or ute (utility vehicle), ubiquitous transport. Can also mean a small dish or polystyrene cup

Biltong
dried, salted meat, usually cut up into strips; a national delicacy

Bladdy, blerrie
bloody (expletive)

Bliksem
to thrash soundly

Boerewors
farmers' sausage, the key ingredient to any successful *braai* (qv)

Bra
township slang for friend or brother

Braai
barbecue

Broekies lace
the ornate ironwork found on balconies and verandas of Victorian buildings

Bru
brother; term of endearment, mostly between male friends – or surfers – but women are sometimes called *bru* too. From the Afrikaans *broer*, brother

Bunny chow
half-loaf of bread with the inside scooped out and the crust filled with curry; a Durban speciality

Cabbie, tjorrie
(chawree)
car; often denotes souped-up special like a Ford Capri with a freeflow exhaust, mag wheels and fur on the dashboard.

Café
a corner shop where you can buy life's necessities – newspapers, cigarettes, chocolate, bread and slap chips (qv); nothing like a café in the European sense.

Check
to look at.

China
mate, friend (taken from the Cockney except that it is invariably pronounced 'Char-nuh').

Cordon sanitaire
the clear strip of land that separates a township from the main part of the town in just about every platteland *dorpie*; a relic of apartheid

Dagga, zol	marijuana
Donder	thunder, to hit (also see bliksem)
Donkey boiler	a wood-fired hot water system; in its crudest form it involves making a fire under a 44-gallon drum
Dorpie	little town or village (Afrikaans)
Furry dice, *nodding dogs*	accoutrements normally seen in hanging from the rear-view mirror of cabbies (qv)
Heita!	'hi' in township slang
Hey?	the inevitable interrogative at the end of a sentence; does not always require a response
Highveld	the high plateau in the centre of the country, lying west of the Drakensberg Mountains and east and north of the desert regions of the Karoo and Kalahari
Howzit!	hi, hello.
Impi	Zulu regiment of infantry
Izzit?	really?
Jol	party
Jozi, eGoli, Joeys, *Jo'burg*	Johannesburg
Just now	soon (or recently); maddeningly for some, it can mean 'at any time in the next few hours' and not actually 'now'; foreign travellers hate this expression
Kingklip	sweet-tasting, deepwater fish; similar to cod
Kloof	gorge, canyon (Afrikaans)
Kloofing	canyoning; a popular sport, *kloofing* involves following the course of a river down a mountain, moving slowly through the gorge, jumping into pools or abseiling where jumping is impossible, and plenty of swimming
Koeksuster	sweet, gooey, treacly pastry in the form of a plait; traditional Afrikaner comfort food
Kreef	crayfish or rock lobster; similar to a Maine lobster but without claws
Laarnie	a classy person or place
Lekker	very nice (pronounced 'laquer' by Afrikaners); the ubiquitous expression of approval
Location	township
Lowveld	the hot, low-lying region between the east coast and the Drakensberg Mountains, specifically the Mpumalanga region around the Kruger National Park
Mampoer, witblitz *(white lightning)*	moonshine brewed from just about anything that will ferment; peaches, raisins and plums are popular bases; it is wicked stuff, deserving respect
Melktert	milk tart; sweet pudding with cinnamon sprinkled on top; you either love it or hate it

Mlungu	white person; from Zulu, its literal meaning is the 'foamy scum from the sea' which has an uncomfortable resonance for anyone of settler stock
Muti	traditional medicine; its practitioners share the same status as university trained medics and homeopaths
Nooit	never
Now-now	immediately, sort-of; sooner than 'just now' at any rate
Oke	guy, man
Pap, mielie meal	stiff maize porridge; best with a sauce made of onions and tomatoes
Platteland	the countryside and all its *dorpies* (qv); literally, the flat lands, which kind of denotes the *highveld* (qv), but in fact includes anywhere away from the main towns.
Potviekos	stews cooked slowly in a cast iron, three-legged pot, over an open fire
Putco bus	generic term for a rural bus; Putco in fact is a ubiquitous bus company which has dominated the rural and urban bus transport scene for decades
Robot	traffic light
Rondawel	round hut usually with a thatched roof, based on traditional African designs; normally found in state-run parks and reserves
Rooibos	herbal tea made from a wild-growing bush that grows in the Cedarberg and a few other mountain areas in the Western Cape
Sangomas	traditional healers
Shebeen	township bar or speakeasy
Skebenga	bad person (see also *tsotsi*)
Skeem (pronounced skim)	to think
Skelm	crook; often a term of endearment as in 'you little skelm'
Skyf	joint; see *dagga*
Slap chips	hot chips in greasproof papers bags and normally doused in salt and vinegar; sold in all good corner shops everywhere
Stimela	train; a word that evolved in the Zulu language, dating back to the time of the first steam trains.
Stoep	veranda
Trek	to journey (from the Afrikaans for 'pull').
Tsotsi	township slang for bad person or criminal; corruption of 'zoot suit' from the 1940s and 50s when jazz, gangs, big American cars and sharp dressing were all the rage in Sophiatown, Jo'burg's mixed suburb
Tune (pronounced chune)	to tell, talk back

Vetkoek	sweet bun-like bread cooked in oil and used to mop up the *potjiekos*, or filled with savoury fillings
Vlei	a shallow lake or swamp
Voetsek	an impolite way of telling someone, or some dog, to go away
Voller, volksie	Volkswagen Beetle, a legendary and much loved car in South Africa
Windpump	wind driven water pump, seen all over the country, especially in the drier parts; a somewhat endangered species as the *platteland* (qv) is electrified and farmers install submersible pumps in their wells
Zola Budd, Mary Decker	minibus taxis named after the two 1,500m athletes (the former of South African birth) who clashed so spectacularly at the 1984 Los Angeles Olympics; the names refer to different Japanese marques, the 'Zola' being faster than the 'Decker'

Appendix 2

FURTHER READING

The story of South Africa has spawned a vast amount of literature. The country has been an endless source of copy, stories and legends for writers. Naturally, given the country's recent history, much of the local writing, both fiction and non-fiction, is devoted to the tortured history of the land under apartheid. Since the 1994 elections, much of this work has become dated and irrelevant except for its historical perspective. As South Africa moves on, its novelists have turned to other subjects but racial prejudice and its evil effects are still dominant themes in South African fiction. You could spend a lifetime immersed in writing about South Africa and not even scratch the surface. The following list of classics and seminal works contains some of my own favourites.

Non-fiction
South Africa's tumultuous years

Working chronologically, the first book worth mentioning is Trevor Huddlestone's *Naught for your Comfort*, the Anglican bishop's first-hand account of life and death in Sophiatown – Johannesburg's vibrant multiracial suburb which was razed in the 1950s.

Nelson Mandela's *Long Walk to Freedom* is an upbeat account of the idealism and history of South Africa's most respected man, and looks at the long road ahead.

One of the books that has outlived the elections is Rian Malan's *My Traitor's Heart*, an honest and searing look at the underlying causes of the country's problems, many of which remain as pressing as they were before 1994.

Greg Marinovich and Joao Silva's *The Bang-Bang Club* is the disturbing but gripping story of South Africa's four top news photographers, nicknamed the Bang-Bang Paparazzi, who covered the excoriating violence in South Africa's townships from the early 1980s until after the 1994 election.

For an insight into the difficult years between 1986 and the 1994 elections, journalist Shaun Johnson's *Strange Days Indeed*, a collection of newspaper columns from that time, cannot be beaten.

South Africa by Graham Leach, the BBC's southern Africa radio correspondent in 1976, 1977 and 1983, is an excellent frontline account of the politics of South Africa in those years.

History

History of South Africa by L Thompson and *South Africa: A Modern History* are the best general accounts of the country. *The Mind of South Africa*, written by Alistair Sparks, a former newspaper editor, an examination of the psyche and mindset of the country's different cultural groups is fascinating reading. More specialised histories include D Morris's *The Washing of the Spears*, a detailed account of the rise and fall of the Zulu nation and the British campaign in Zululand in 1879, Thomas Pakenham's *The Boer War*, still the definitive work on that conflict, *The Scramble for Africa* (also by Pakenham) which examines the European rush to acquire colonies in Africa, and Dr Peter Becker's *Path of Blood* and *Hill of Destiny*, two outstanding books on the rise of the Ndebele warlord Mzilikazi and the Sotho leader Moshesh. *Commando* by Deneys Reitz is one man's personal journal of nearly four years of fighting from horseback during the Anglo–Boer War.

Travel and adventure

There are fewer books than one might expect on South African travel. Travel writer Lawrence Green's evocative books are worth hunting down even if they are dated and his descriptions of South Africa span centuries while his own personal observations of life on the subcontinent are splendid. Look for *Tavern of the Seas*, *A Decent Fellow Doesn't Work*, *Where Men Still Dream* and *The Coast of Diamonds*. T V Bulpin is famous for his detailed histories of exploration and adventuring in the South African interior; *Lost Trails of the Transvaal*, *The Ivory Trail* and *The Hunter is Death* are noteworthy. Olive Schreiner's *Story of an African Farm* is the classic story of growing up in the South African countryside. The novel *Circles in a Forest* by Dalene Mathee is the story of a hard life in the Knysna forests at the turn of the century when this area was still a wild frontier.

Lost World of the Kalahari by Laurens van der Post is the strange but very readable story of the author's expedition into the Kalahari Desert in search of the San (Bushmen). It is a mix of fact and fiction and full of the same kind mysticism that surrounds the San.

Fiction

Alan Paton, Nadine Gordimer, André Brink, J M Coetzee and Athol Fugard are a just a handful of the South African writers whose excellent works have travelled overseas. Paton's 1948 classic *Cry the Beloved Country*, the story of a black father who travels to Johannesburg to save his son from execution for murder, was one of the first protest books and set the standard against which all the others are measured, and often found wanting.

July's People and *Six Feet of the Country* are both by Nadine Gordimer, winner of the 1991 Nobel Prize for Literature, and a prolific writer of novels and short stories. The former is the story of a black domestic servant who hides his white employers after South Africa plunges into civil war. André Brink has written a number of novels about the South African condition, many of them disturbing insights into the workings of the police state. *A Dry White Season*, one of his best-known, is about a man's investigation into the death while in police dentention of his black friend. *An Instant in the Wind*, is an evocative story set in the 18th century about a wealthy European woman hiding on the coast with her Hottentot slave who becomes her lover. Others of his to look out for are *Rumours of Rain* and *A Chain of Voices*.

Other notable writers include playwright Zakes Mda (*We Shall Sing for the Fatherland*) and J M Coetzee, winner of the Booker Prize, who wrote landmark works such as *Waiting for the Barbarians*, *The Life and Times of Michael K*, and *Disgrace*. Playwright Athol Fugard's works include *A Lesson from Aloes*, a play about the lives of a white bus driver and his wife who is coming apart at the seams and *The Road to Mecca*, based on the life of Helen Martin, the reclusive artist who lived in Nieu Bethesda.

Not all South African fiction is obsessed with apartheid. Marguerite Poland's *Iron Love*, about life in a Grahamstown boys' boarding school just before World War I, is a comment on institutions, puberty and unfulfilment. Sir Percy Fitzpatrick's *Jock of the Bushveld* is a lovely story of the life of a tough Staffordshire bull terrier in the Eastern Transvaal gold rush mining camps and *bushveld* in the late 19th century. Herman Charles Bosman is known for his wonderful and evocative short stories set in the South Africa of the 1920s. Collections of his work include *Cold Stone Jug*, an ironic look at his time in prison.

Health

Bugs, Bites & Bowels – the Cadogan Guide to Helathy Travel by Dr Jane Wilson-Howarth contains everything you need to know about staying healthy while travelling. Howarth also co-authored, with Dr Matthew Ellis, *Your Child's Health Abroad – A Manual for Travelling Parents*, published by Bradt Travel Guides.

Travel guides

For further coverage of neighbouring countries I recommend the range of Bradt Travel Guides: *Mozambique, Malawi, Tanzania,* and *East and Southern Africa: The Backpackers Manual* by Philip Briggs; *Zambia* and *Namibia* by Chris McIntyre. Also *Zimbabwe: the Rough Guide* by Barabara McCrea and Tony Pinchuk.

Finding books

South Africa is blessed with plenty of good bookshops and especially with secondhand dealers in the major centres. New books are generally, but not always, the same price as they are overseas, although local titles are very cheap. The Central News Agency, always recognisable by its giant red CNA lettering, sells books, magazines, music and stationery, and has branches in just about every reasonably sized town in the country although choice is limited in the smaller places. Exclusive Books (tel: 011 789 555), the local version of Waterstones or Barnes & Noble, has branches in various shopping malls throughout the country.

Some of the books mentioned above are no longer in print but can be found quite easily and cheaply in the country's secondhand bookshops, of which Cape Town and Johannesburg have plenty. In Cape Town, you should stroll down Long Street which has at least five or six secondhand dealers in the space of a few hundred metres. In Johannesburg, Books Galore (tel: 011 726 6502) has a couple of branches selling new and used books; its Tyrone Avenue, Parkview, branch has all Lawrence Green's books, for example, many of them first editions. Bookdealers of Bryanston (tel: 011 706 8774) has a couple of branches dotted around the northern suburbs, while Bohemsky's Books (tel: 011 646 9058) is an excellent shop owned by a dedicated book-loving couple and one of the city's longest-lived bookshops.

Finding South African books overseas is much more tricky. However, try the online book dealers such as www.amazon.com or www.barnesandnoble.com who have, or can find, just about any book in print. These sites also have links to secondhand online dealers and even a book search engine to which various dealers are linked.

Websites

There are a couple of good websites where you can do background research on the country and the region, and do a bit of trip planning too. Travel oriented sites worth surfing are www.africaguide.com, www.africandream.com and www.wtgonline.com, a travel advice site.

For African stories and news, try www.africa.com, www.iol.co.za, www.mg.co.za/mg and www.africanews.org – the last two are daily news sites belonging to local newspapers while africanews carries press stories from papers across the continent.

Index

Page references in bold indicate major entries;
those in italics indicate maps.
Abbreviations: NP = National Park